# SPICE & WOLF

## Lawrence
A merchant traveling with Holo. Heading north in search of Holo's homeland.

## Holo
Lawrence's traveling companion, a beautiful girl. Her true form is that of the wolf-god of the harvest.

## Elsa
A girl in the employ of the priest of the Church in Tereo. In love with Evan.

## Evan
A young miller. Entranced by the world outside his village—including merchants.

## Bishop Van
The bishop of St. Rio's Church in the town of Enberch. Conspiring with the town to control Tereo.

# Introduction

Seeking clues to lead them to Holo's homeland, Lawrence and Holo journey northward. Having heard that the church priest in Tereo knows the whereabouts of a monk who specializes in pagan gods, the two head for the rural village. There, however, they're greeted at the church by a stern girl named Elsa...

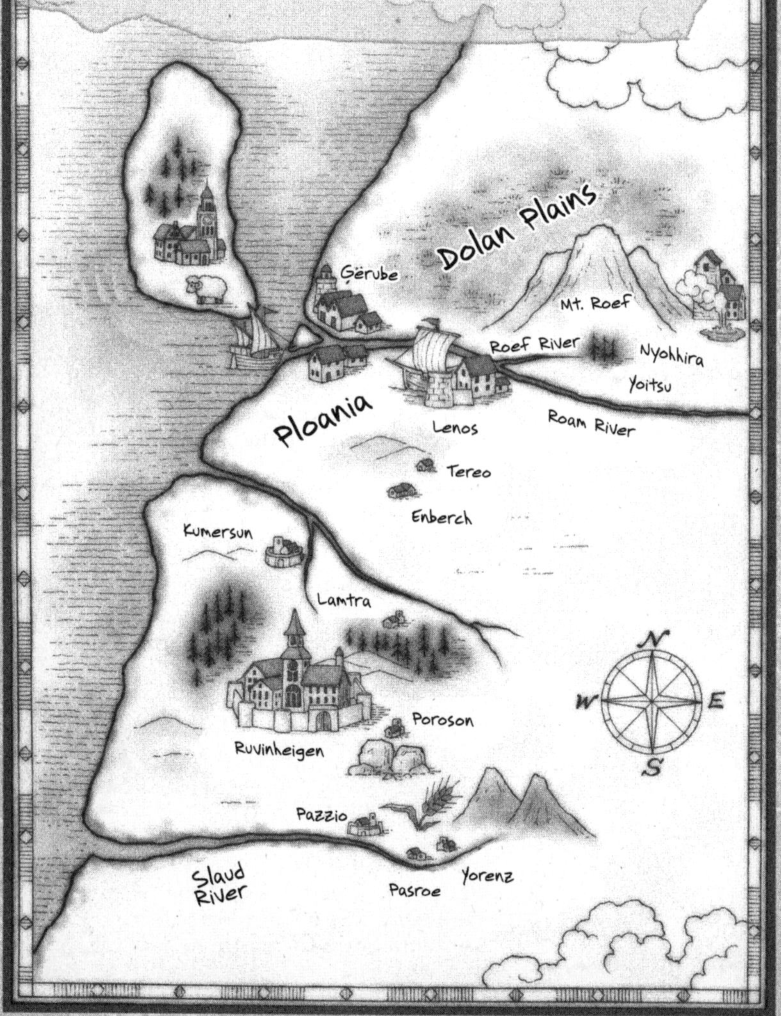

Dolan Plains
Gërube
Mt. Roef
Roef River
Nyohhira
Yoitsu
Ploania
Lenos
Roam River
Tereo
Enberch
Kumersun
Lamtra
N
W
E
S
Poroson
Ruvinheigen
Pazzio
Slaud River
Pasroe
Yorenz


Map illustration: Hidetada Idemitsu

# SPICE & WOLF
# CONTENTS

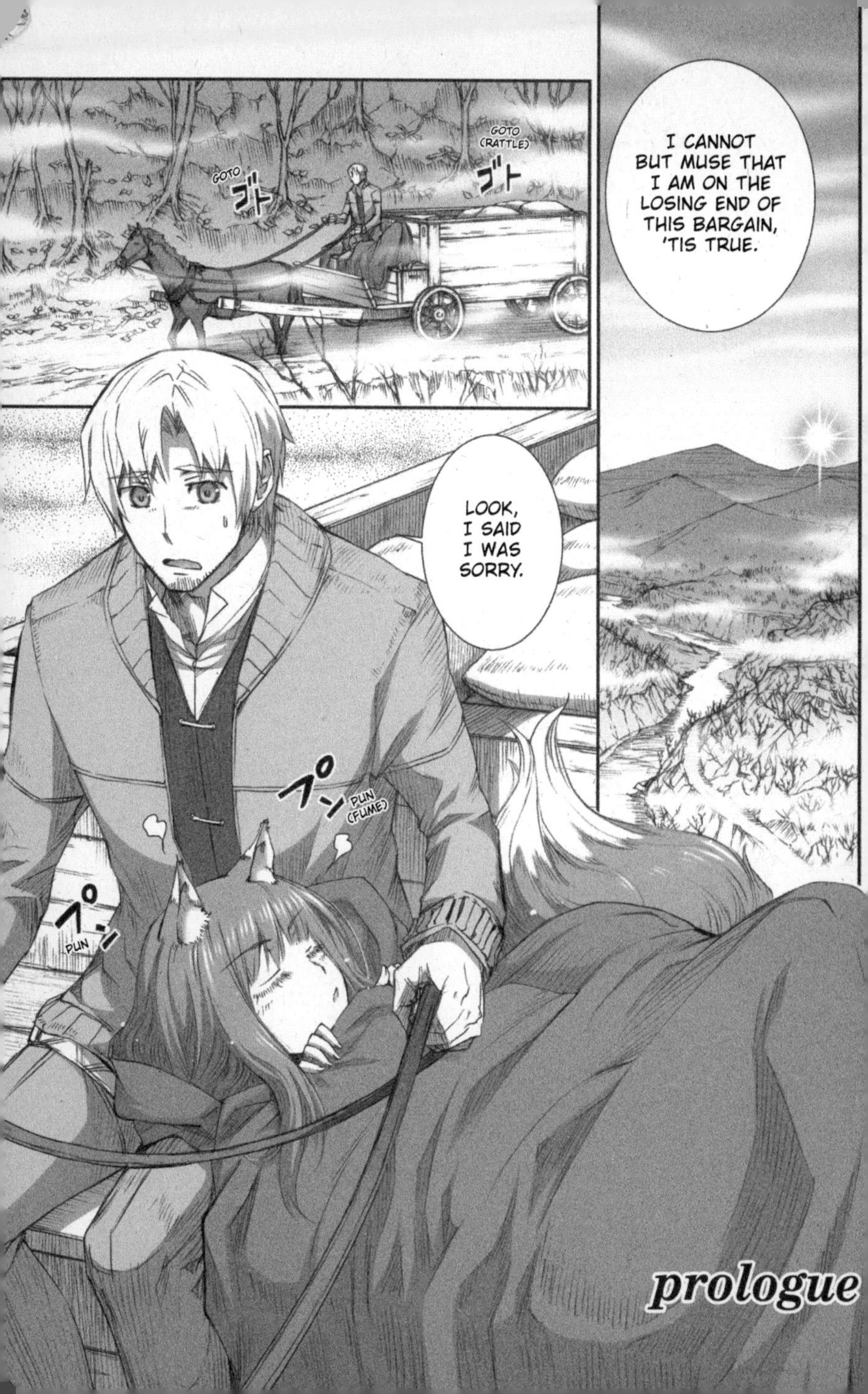
I CANNOT BUT MUSE THAT I AM ON THE LOSING END OF THIS BARGAIN, 'TIS TRUE.
ゴト
GOTO (RATTLE)
ゴト
GOTO
LOOK, I SAID I WAS SORRY.
プン
PUN (FUME)
プン
PUN
prologue

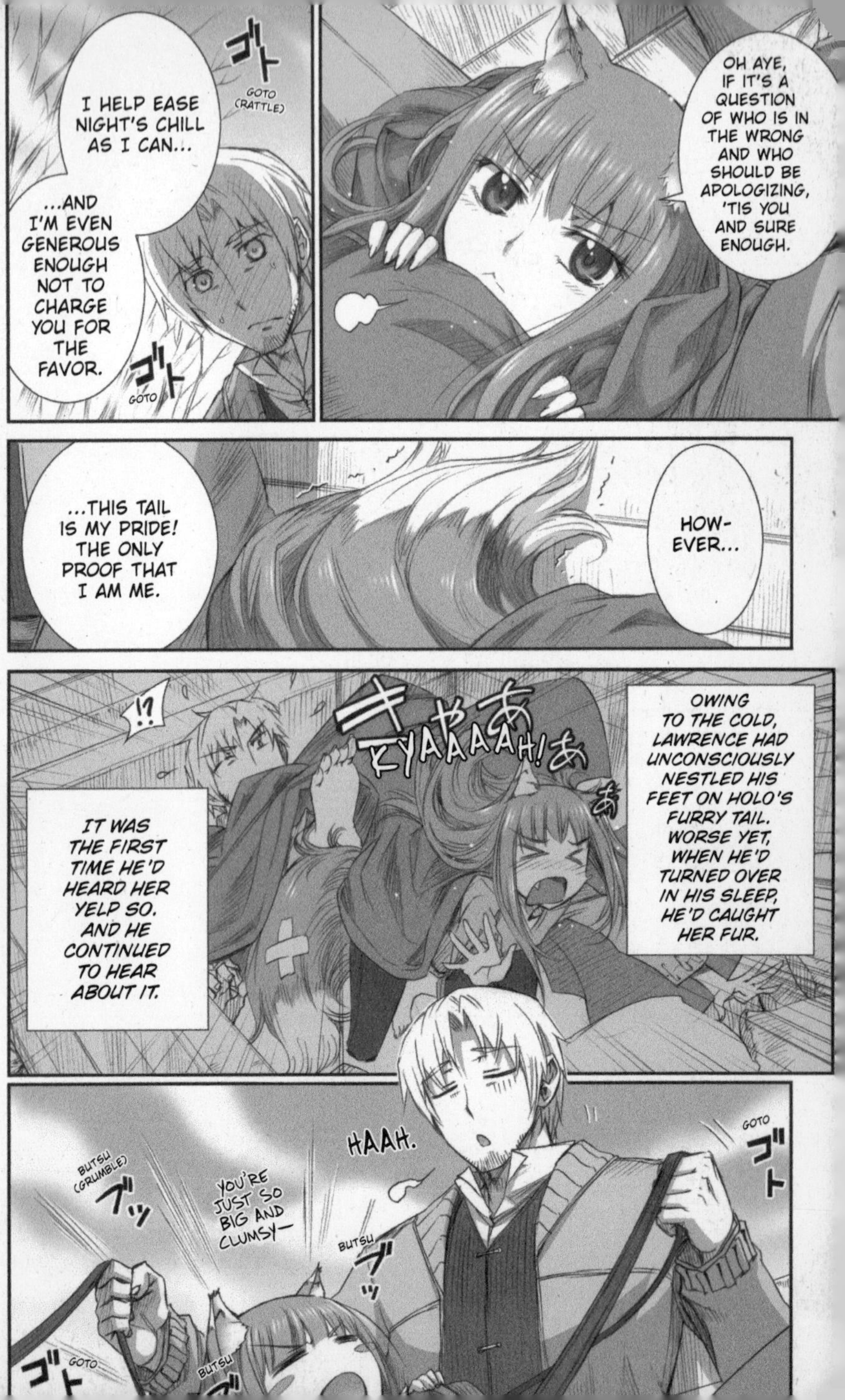

OH AYE, IF IT'S A QUESTION OF WHO IS IN THE WRONG AND WHO SHOULD BE APOLOGIZING, 'TIS YOU AND SURE ENOUGH.
I HELP EASE NIGHT'S CHILL AS I CAN...
GOTO (RATTLE)
...AND I'M EVEN GENEROUS ENOUGH NOT TO CHARGE YOU FOR THE FAVOR.
GOTO
HOW-EVER...
...THIS TAIL IS MY PRIDE! THE ONLY PROOF THAT I AM ME.
OWING TO THE COLD, LAWRENCE HAD UNCONSCIOUSLY NESTLED HIS FEET ON HOLO'S FURRY TAIL. WORSE YET, WHEN HE'D TURNED OVER IN HIS SLEEP, HE'D CAUGHT HER FUR.
KYAAAAH!
!?
IT WAS THE FIRST TIME HE'D HEARD HER YELP SO. AND HE CONTINUED TO HEAR ABOUT IT.
GOTO
HAAH.
YOU'RE JUST SO BIG AND CLUMSY—
BUTSU (GRUMBLE)
BUTSU
GOTO
BUTSU

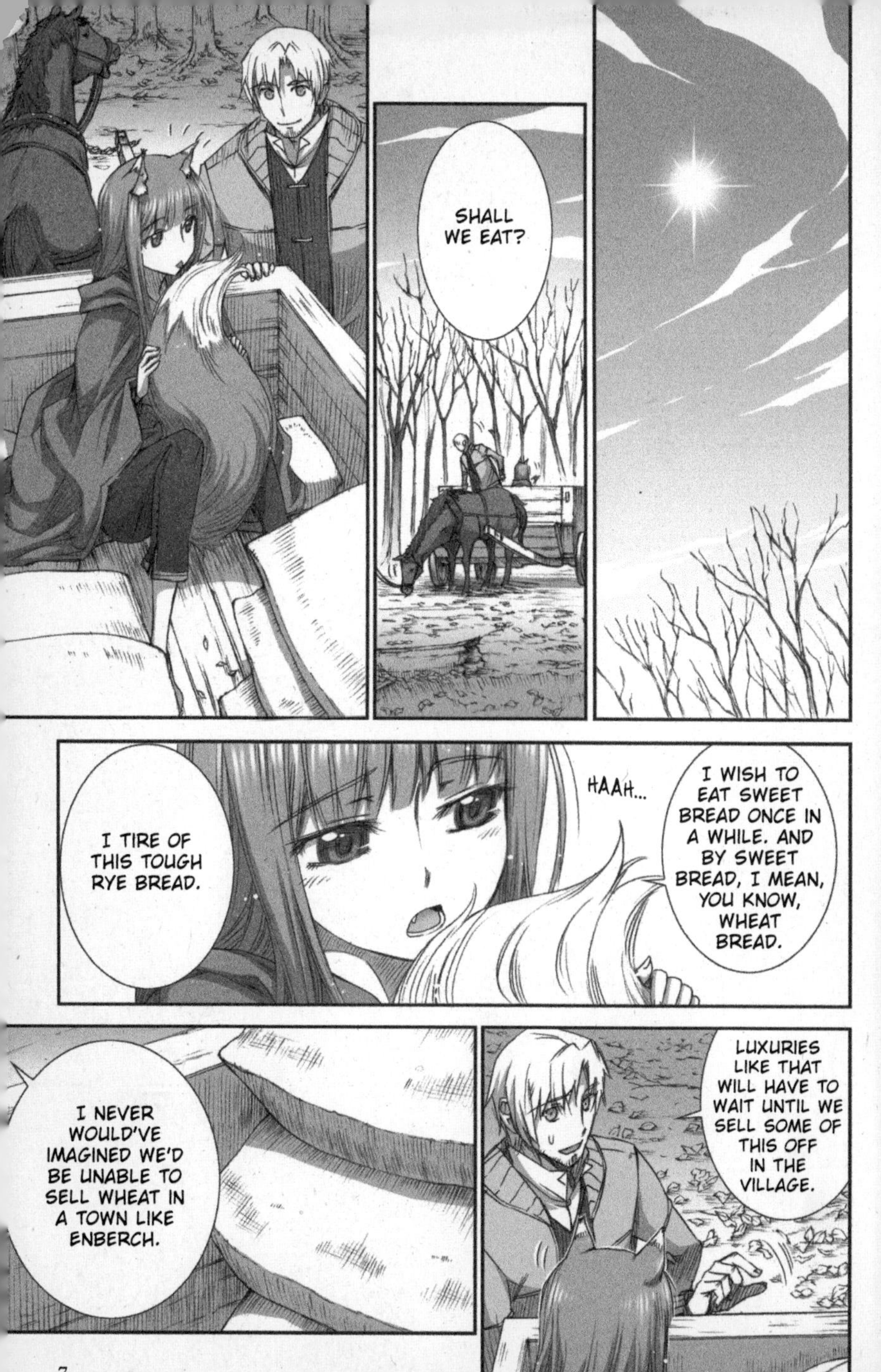
SHALL WE EAT?
HAAH...
I WISH TO EAT SWEET BREAD ONCE IN A WHILE. AND BY SWEET BREAD, I MEAN, YOU KNOW, WHEAT BREAD.
I TIRE OF THIS TOUGH RYE BREAD.
LUXURIES LIKE THAT WILL HAVE TO WAIT UNTIL WE SELL SOME OF THIS OFF IN THE VILLAGE.
I NEVER WOULD'VE IMAGINED WE'D BE UNABLE TO SELL WHEAT IN A TOWN LIKE ENBERCH.

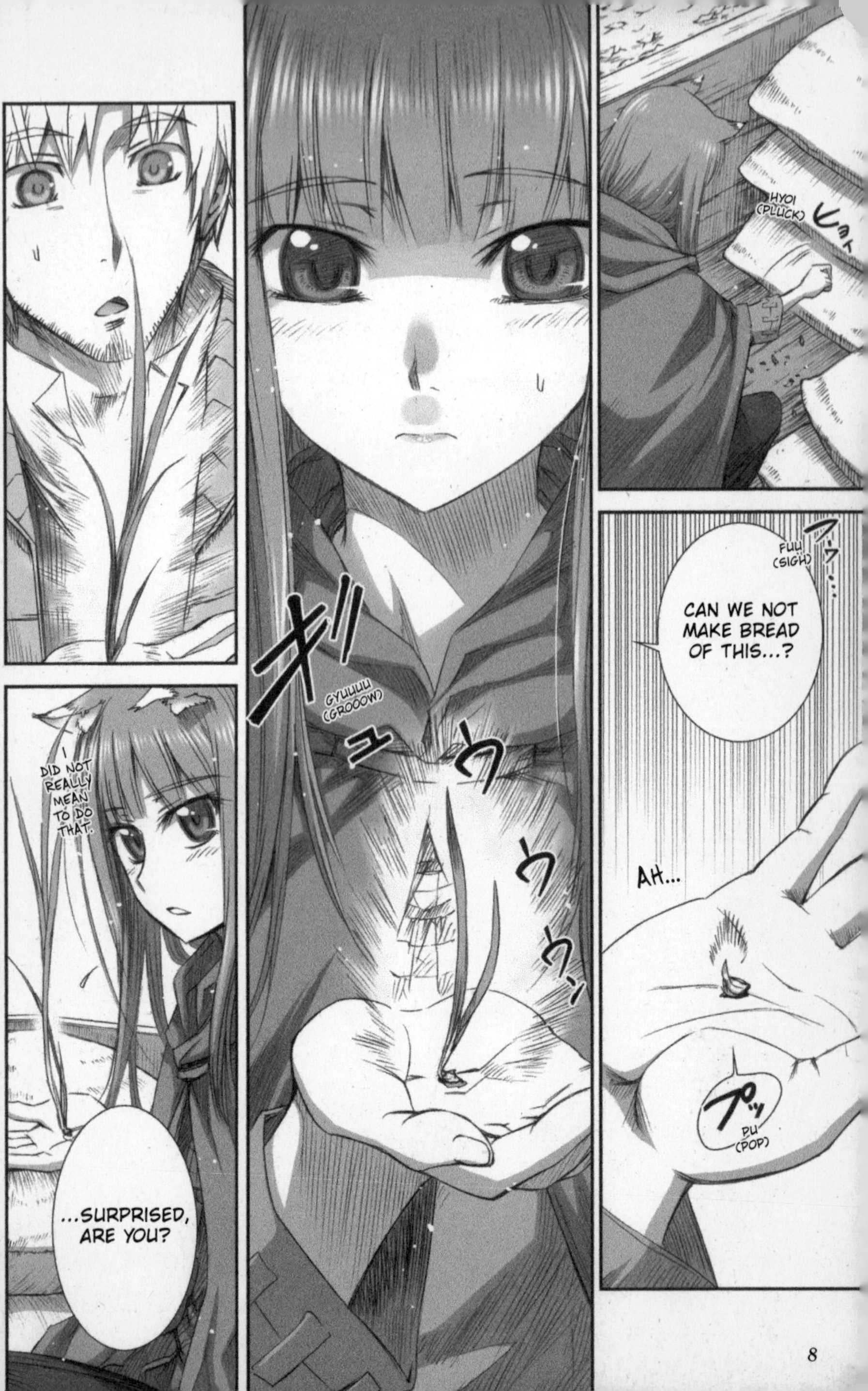
HYOI (PLUCK)
FUU (SIGH)
CAN WE NOT MAKE BREAD OF THIS...?
AH...
PU (POP)
GYUUUU (GROOOW)
I DID NOT REALLY MEAN TO DO THAT.
...SURPRISED, ARE YOU?

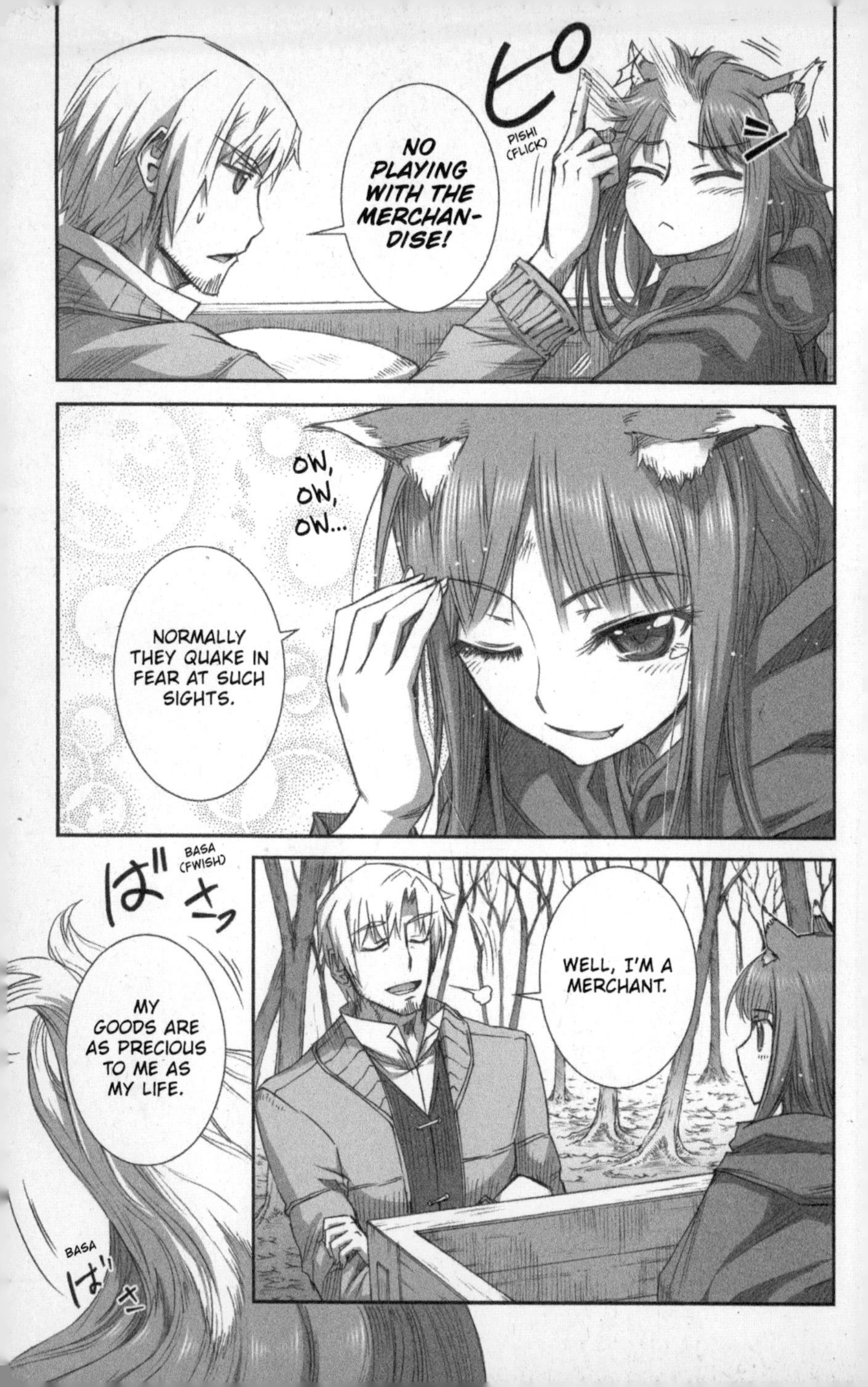
ぴ
PISHI (FLICK)
NO PLAYING WITH THE MERCHAN-DISE!
OW, OW, OW...
NORMALLY THEY QUAKE IN FEAR AT SUCH SIGHTS.
ばさっ
BASA (FWISH)
WELL, I'M A MERCHANT.
MY GOODS ARE AS PRECIOUS TO ME AS MY LIFE.
BASA
ばさ

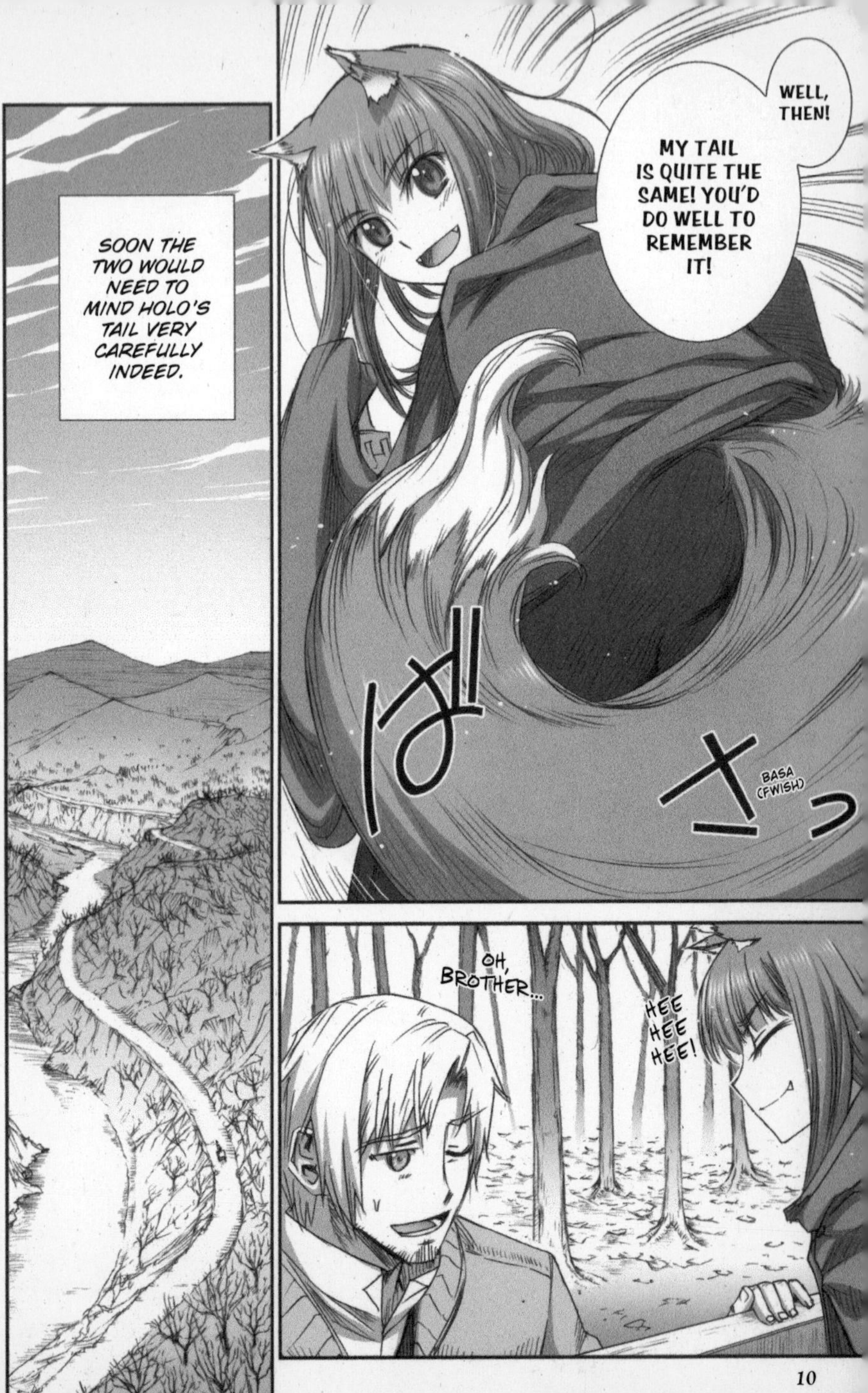
WELL, THEN!
MY TAIL IS QUITE THE SAME! YOU'D DO WELL TO REMEMBER IT!
ばさっ
BASA (FWISH)
HEE HEE HEE!
OH, BROTHER...
SOON THE TWO WOULD NEED TO MIND HOLO'S TAIL VERY CAREFULLY INDEED.

SPICE & WOLF

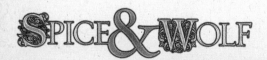

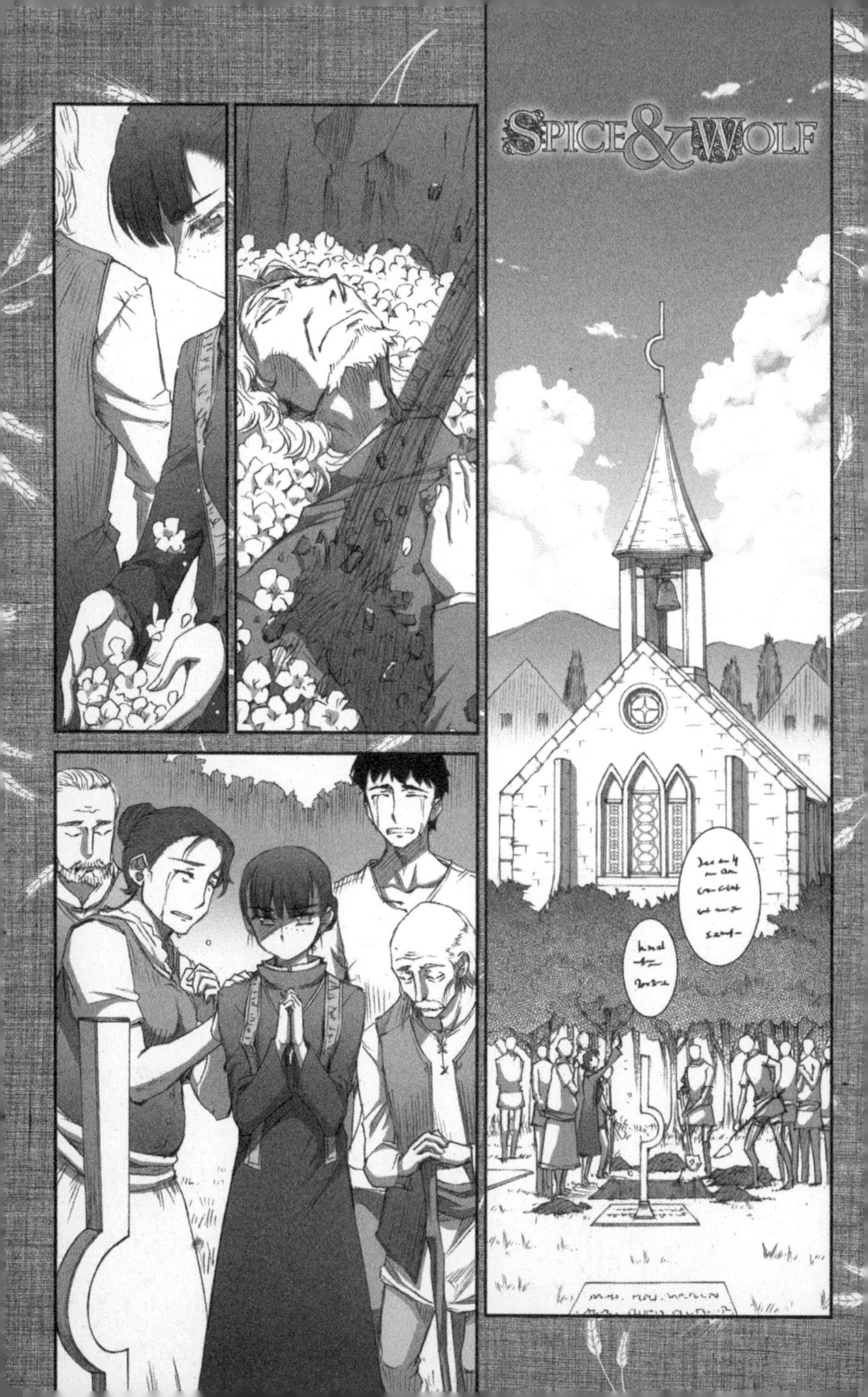
SPICE & WOLF

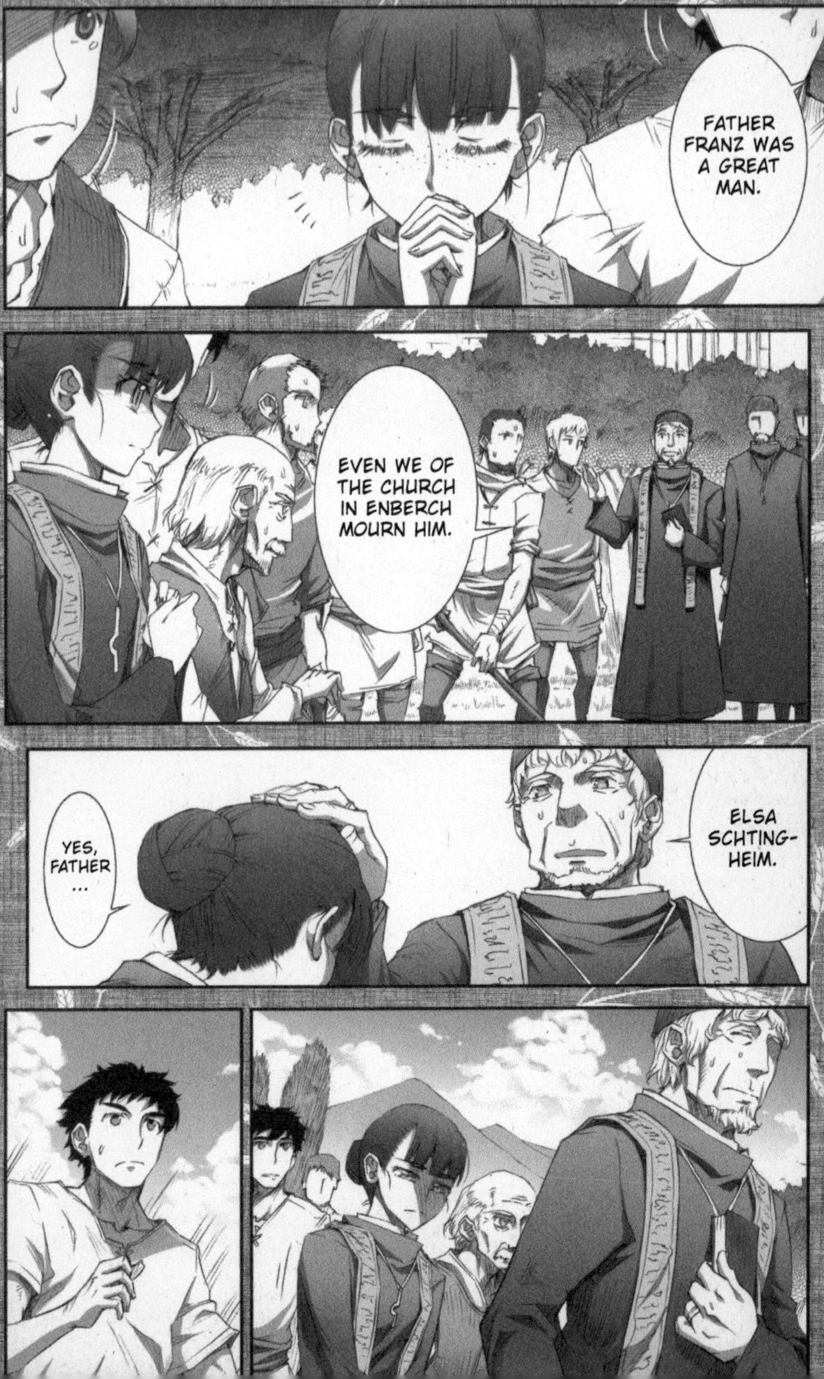
FATHER FRANZ WAS A GREAT MAN.
EVEN WE OF THE CHURCH IN ENBERCH MOURN HIM.
ELSA SCHTING-HEIM.
YES, FATHER ...

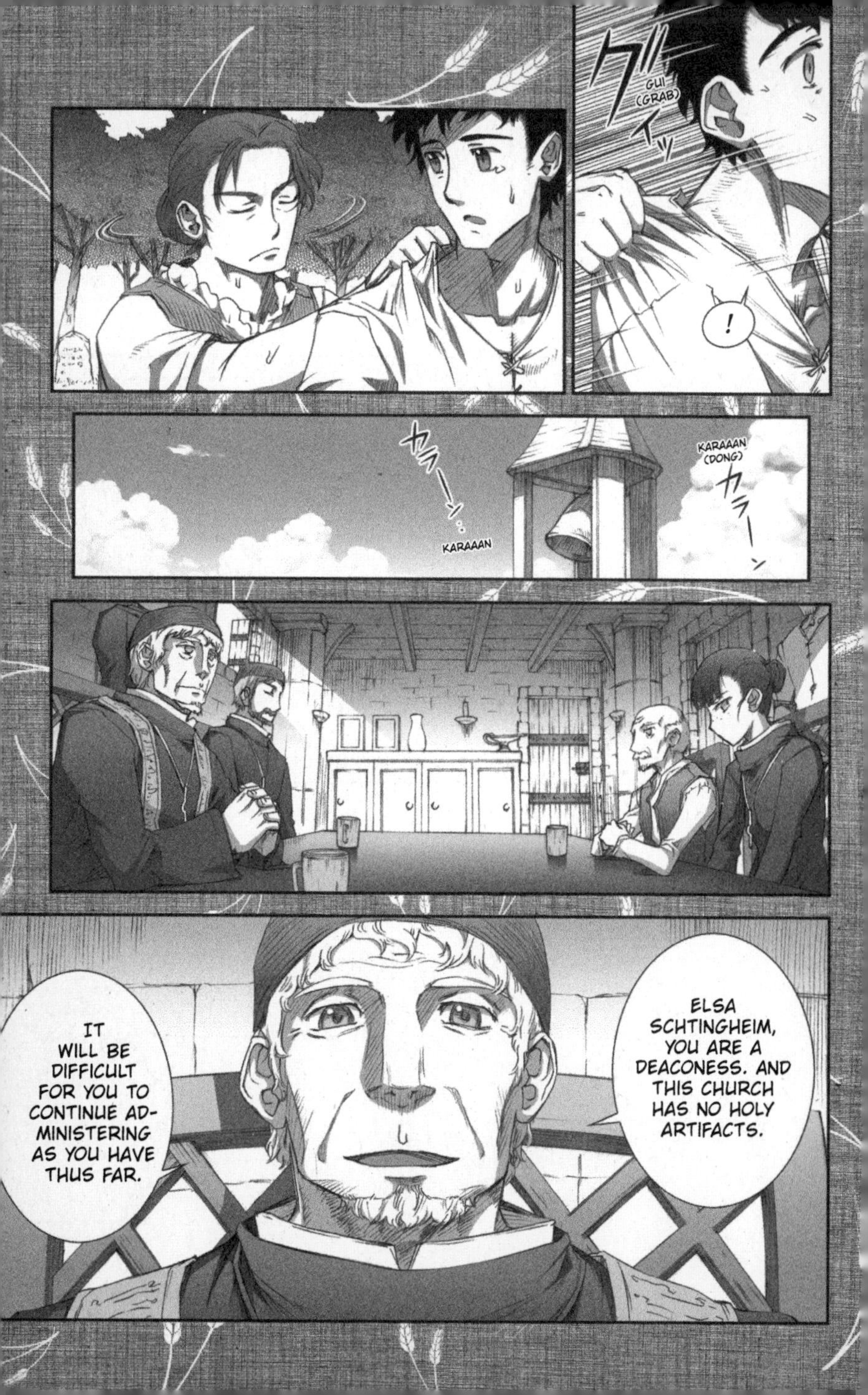
GUI (GRAB)
!
KARAAAN (DONG)
KARAAAN
ELSA SCHTINGHEIM, YOU ARE A DEACONESS. AND THIS CHURCH HAS NO HOLY ARTIFACTS.
IT WILL BE DIFFICULT FOR YOU TO CONTINUE AD-MINISTERING AS YOU HAVE THUS FAR.

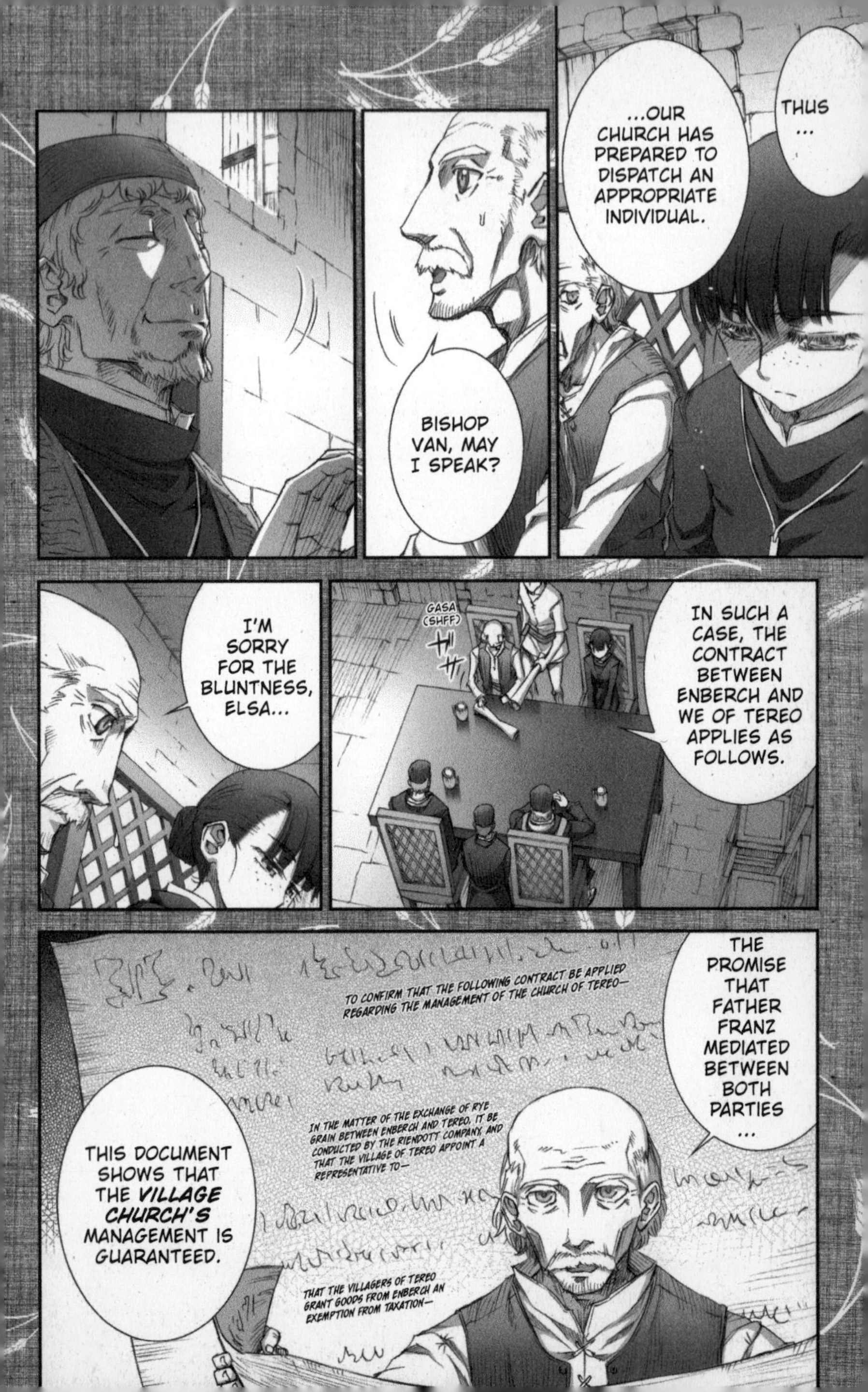
THUS ...
...OUR CHURCH HAS PREPARED TO DISPATCH AN APPROPRIATE INDIVIDUAL.
BISHOP VAN, MAY I SPEAK?
IN SUCH A CASE, THE CONTRACT BETWEEN ENBERCH AND WE OF TEREO APPLIES AS FOLLOWS.
GASA (SHFF)
I'M SORRY FOR THE BLUNTNESS, ELSA...
THE PROMISE THAT FATHER FRANZ MEDIATED BETWEEN BOTH PARTIES ...
TO CONFIRM THAT THE FOLLOWING CONTRACT BE APPLIED REGARDING THE MANAGEMENT OF THE CHURCH OF TEREO—
IN THE MATTER OF THE EXCHANGE OF RYE GRAIN BETWEEN ENBERCH AND TEREO, IT BE CONDUCTED BY THE RIENDOTT COMPANY, AND THAT THE VILLAGE OF TEREO APPOINT A REPRESENTATIVE TO—
THAT THE VILLAGERS OF TEREO GRANT GOODS FROM ENBERCH AN EXEMPTION FROM TAXATION—
THIS DOCUMENT SHOWS THAT THE VILLAGE CHURCH'S MANAGEMENT IS GUARANTEED.

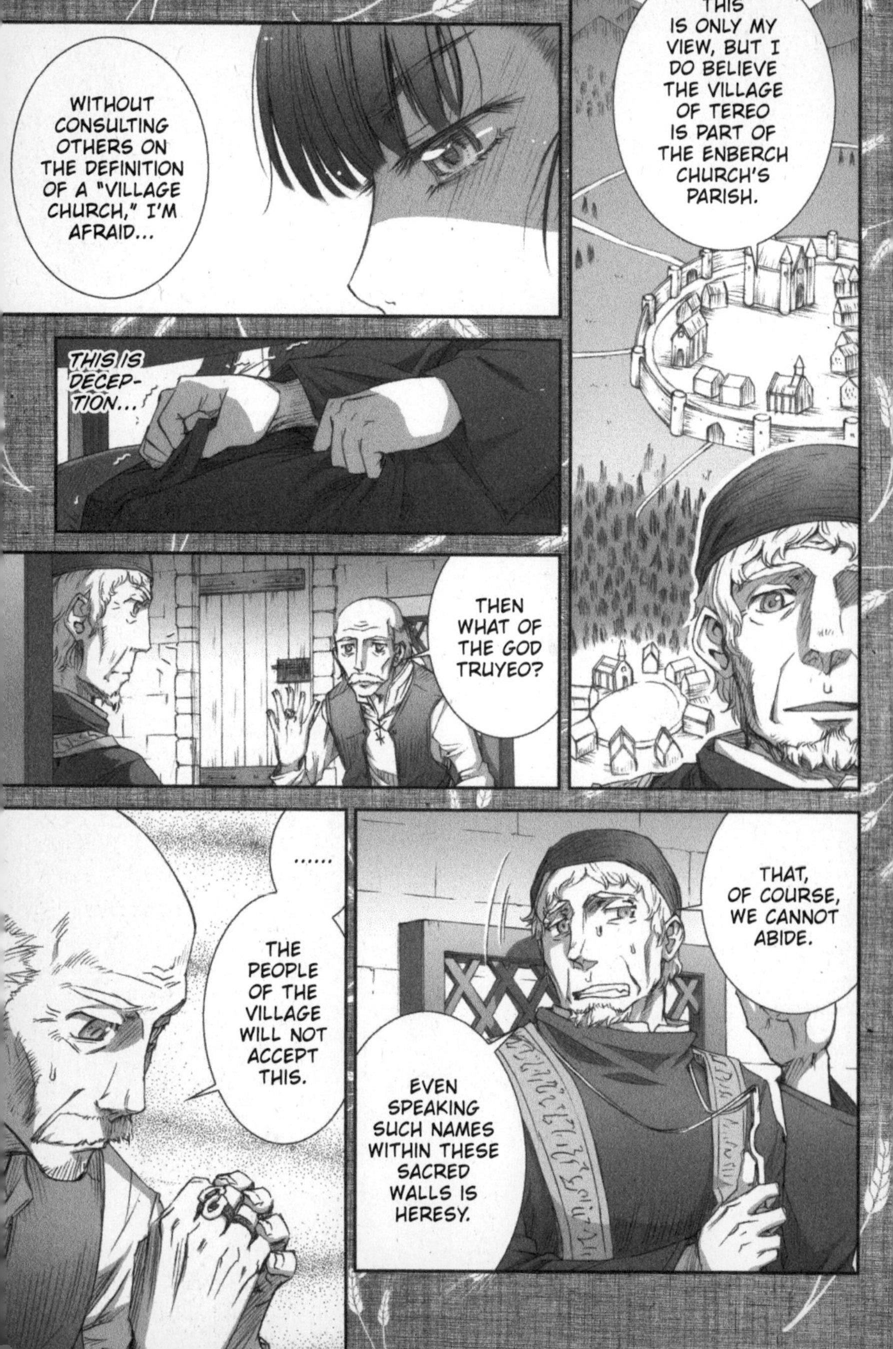
THIS IS ONLY MY VIEW, BUT I DO BELIEVE THE VILLAGE OF TEREO IS PART OF THE ENBERCH CHURCH'S PARISH.
WITHOUT CONSULTING OTHERS ON THE DEFINITION OF A "VILLAGE CHURCH," I'M AFRAID...
THIS IS DECEPTION...
THEN WHAT OF THE GOD TRUYEO?
THAT, OF COURSE, WE CANNOT ABIDE.
EVEN SPEAKING SUCH NAMES WITHIN THESE SACRED WALLS IS HERESY.
......
THE PEOPLE OF THE VILLAGE WILL NOT ACCEPT THIS.

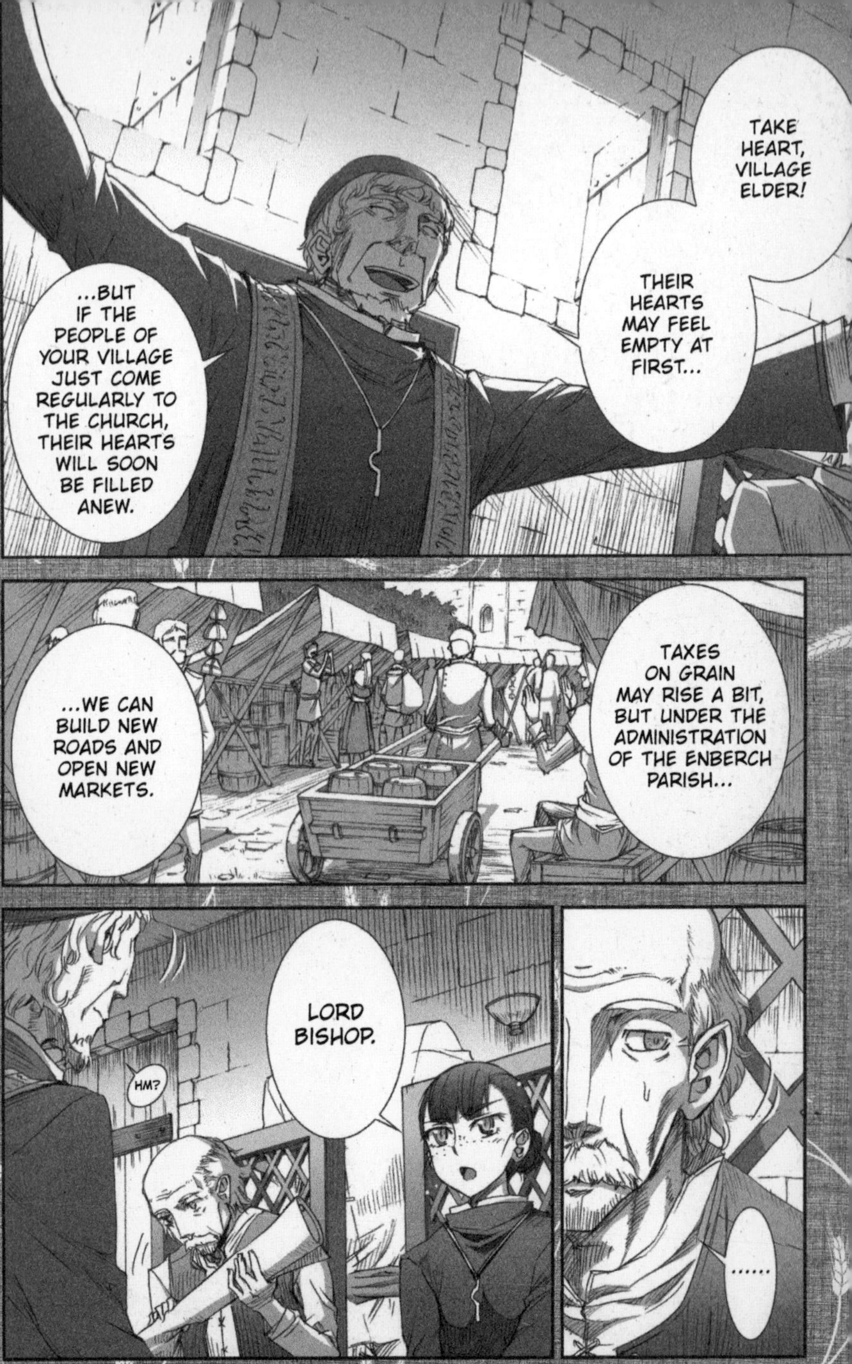
TAKE HEART, VILLAGE ELDER!
THEIR HEARTS MAY FEEL EMPTY AT FIRST...
...BUT IF THE PEOPLE OF YOUR VILLAGE JUST COME REGULARLY TO THE CHURCH, THEIR HEARTS WILL SOON BE FILLED ANEW.
TAXES ON GRAIN MAY RISE A BIT, BUT UNDER THE ADMINISTRATION OF THE ENBERCH PARISH...
...WE CAN BUILD NEW ROADS AND OPEN NEW MARKETS.
......
LORD BISHOP.
HM?

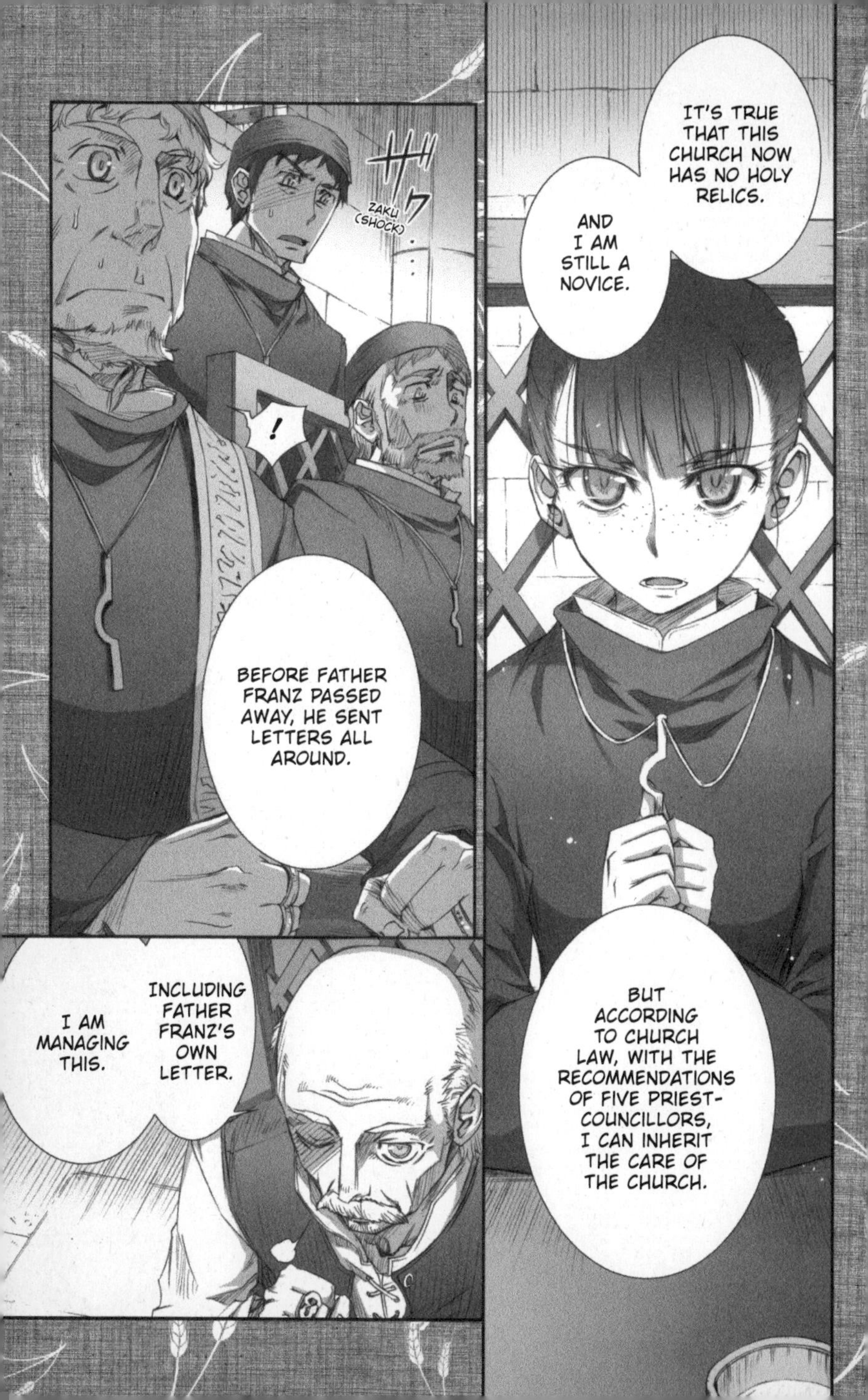
IT'S TRUE THAT THIS CHURCH NOW HAS NO HOLY RELICS.
AND I AM STILL A NOVICE.
BUT ACCORDING TO CHURCH LAW, WITH THE RECOMMENDATIONS OF FIVE PRIEST-COUNCILLORS, I CAN INHERIT THE CARE OF THE CHURCH.
ザク
ZAKU (SHOCK)
!
BEFORE FATHER FRANZ PASSED AWAY, HE SENT LETTERS ALL AROUND.
INCLUDING FATHER FRANZ'S OWN LETTER.
I AM MANAGING THIS.

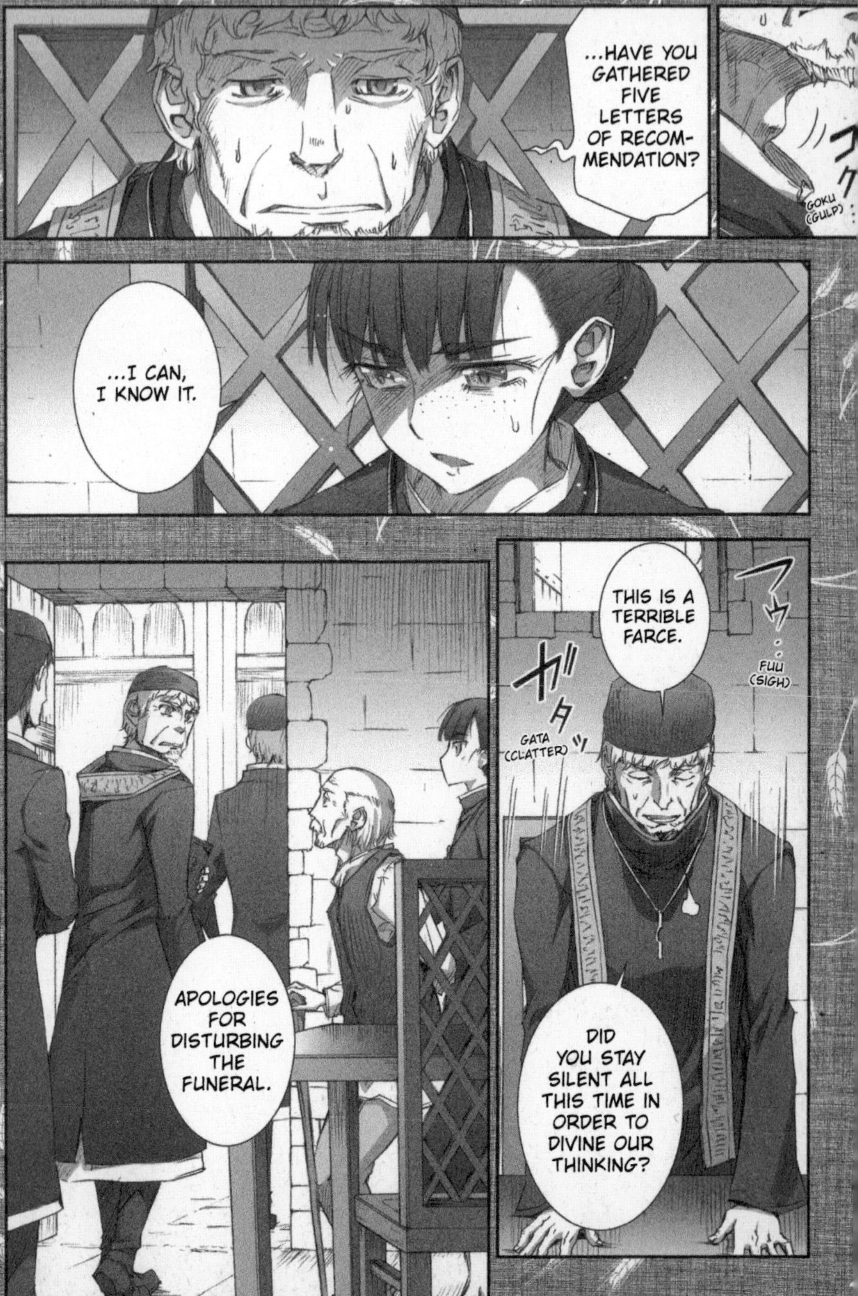
GOKU (GULP)
...HAVE YOU GATHERED FIVE LETTERS OF RECOM-MENDATION?
...I CAN, I KNOW IT.
FUU (SIGH)
THIS IS A TERRIBLE FARCE.
GATA (CLATTER)
DID YOU STAY SILENT ALL THIS TIME IN ORDER TO DIVINE OUR THINKING?
APOLOGIES FOR DISTURBING THE FUNERAL.

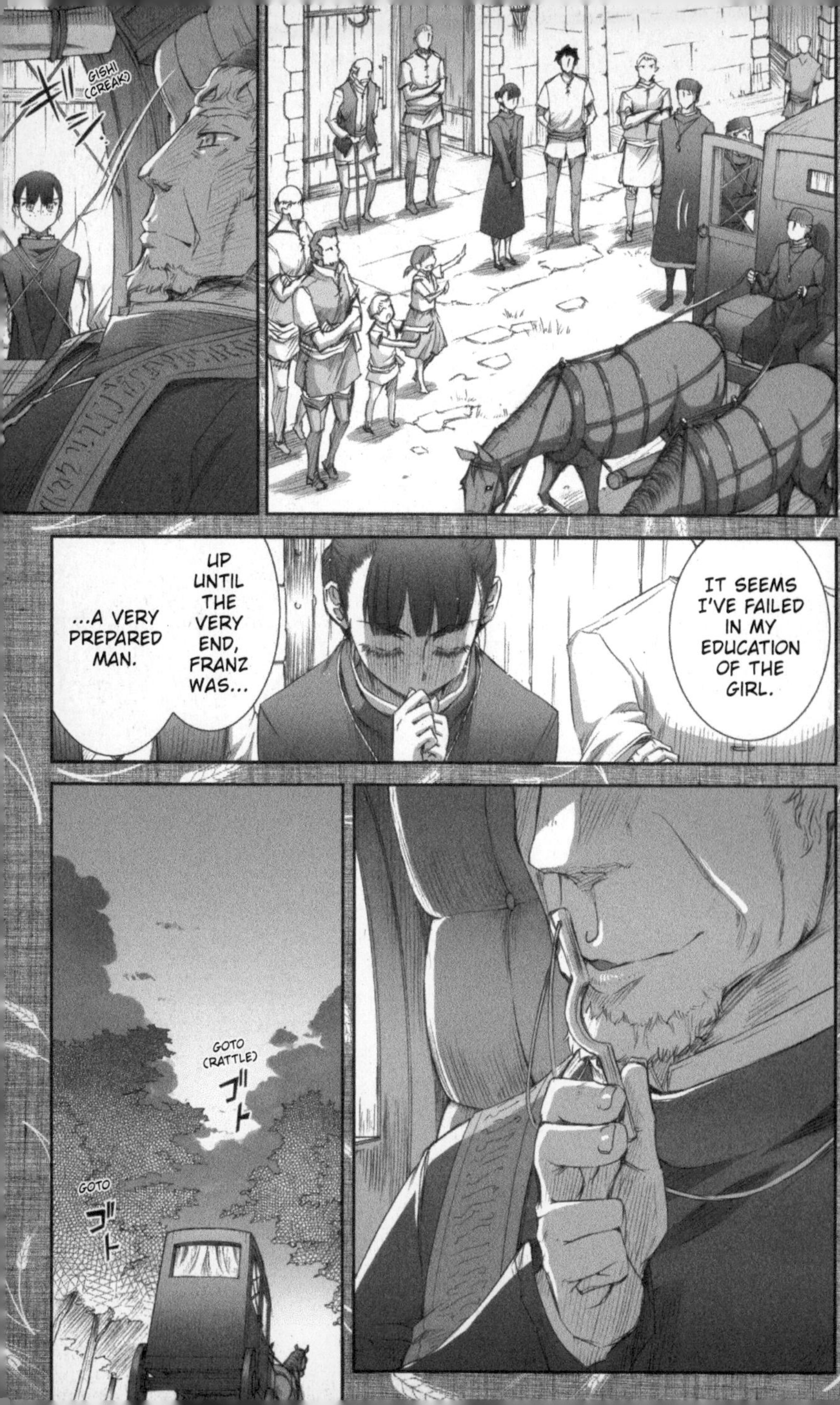
GISHI (CREAK)
ギシ
IT SEEMS I'VE FAILED IN MY EDUCATION OF THE GIRL.
UP UNTIL THE VERY END, FRANZ WAS...
...A VERY PREPARED MAN.
GOTO (RATTLE)
ゴト
GOTO
ゴト

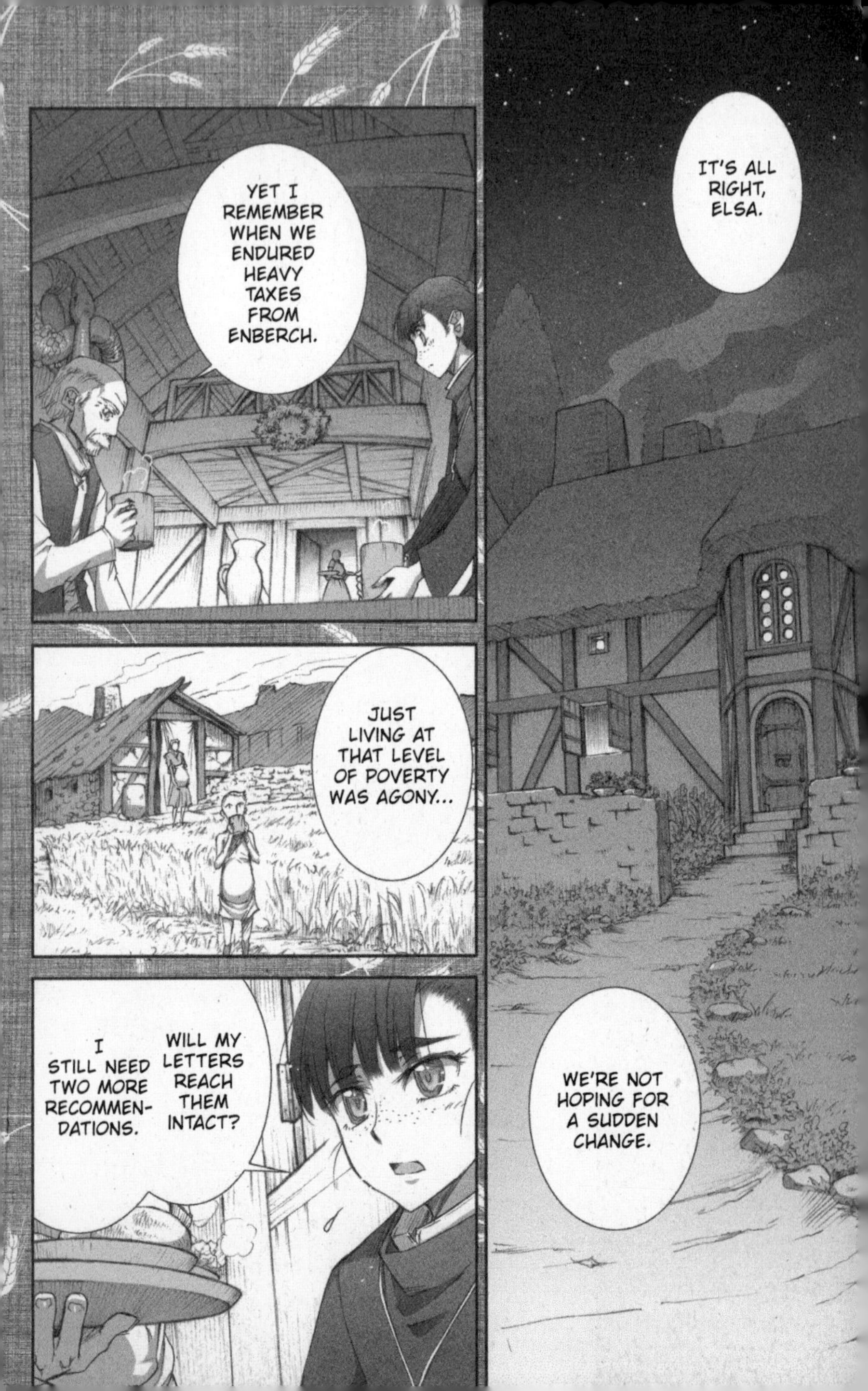
IT'S ALL RIGHT, ELSA.
WE'RE NOT HOPING FOR A SUDDEN CHANGE.
YET I REMEMBER WHEN WE ENDURED HEAVY TAXES FROM ENBERCH.
JUST LIVING AT THAT LEVEL OF POVERTY WAS AGONY...
WILL MY LETTERS REACH THEM INTACT?
I STILL NEED TWO MORE RECOMMEN-DATIONS.

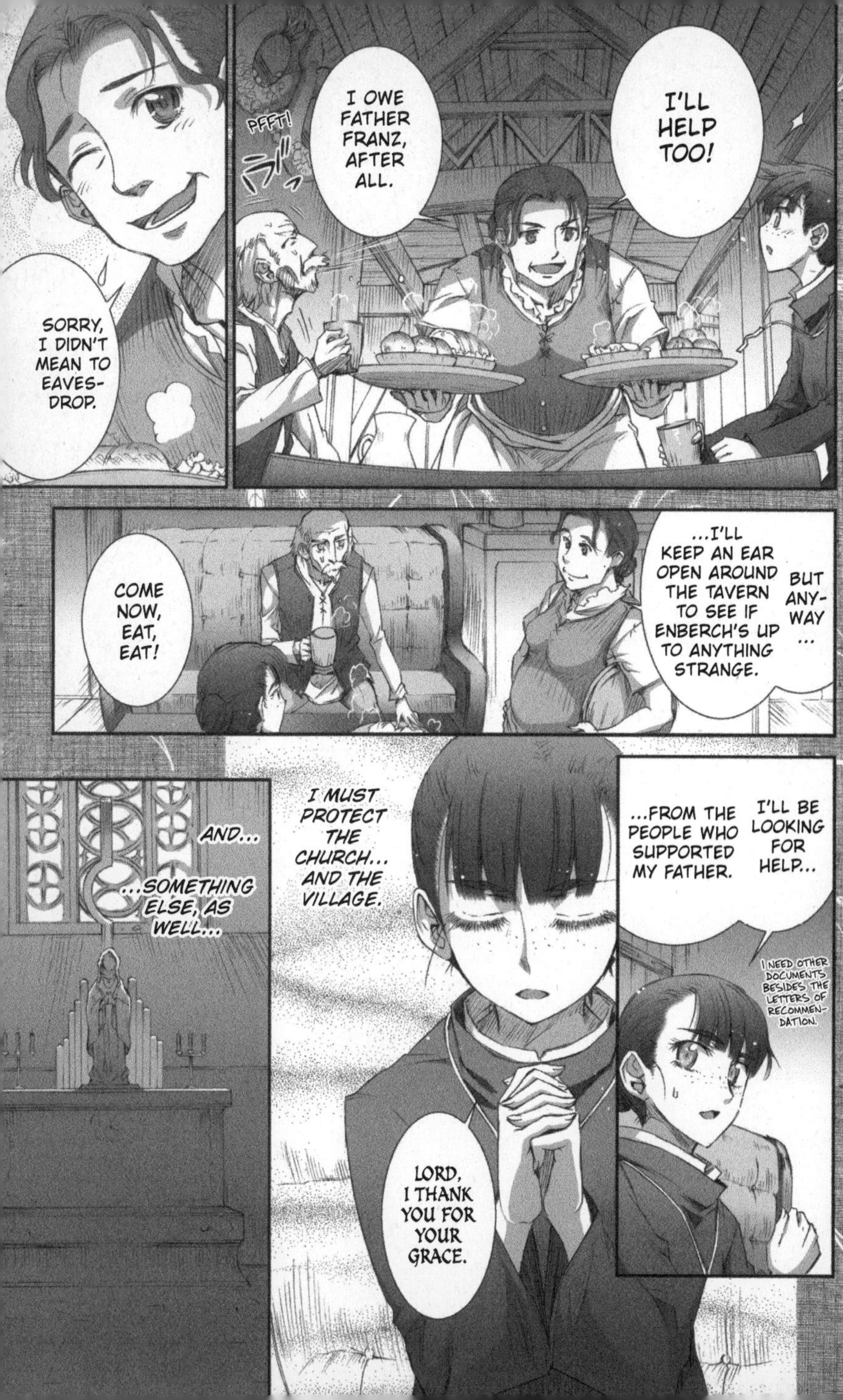
I'LL HELP TOO!
I OWE FATHER FRANZ, AFTER ALL.
PFFT!
SORRY, I DIDN'T MEAN TO EAVES-DROP.
BUT ANY-WAY...
...I'LL KEEP AN EAR OPEN AROUND THE TAVERN TO SEE IF ENBERCH'S UP TO ANYTHING STRANGE.
COME NOW, EAT, EAT!
I'LL BE LOOKING FOR HELP...
...FROM THE PEOPLE WHO SUPPORTED MY FATHER.
I NEED OTHER DOCUMENTS BESIDES THE LETTERS OF RECOMMEN-DATION.
I MUST PROTECT THE CHURCH... AND THE VILLAGE.
LORD, I THANK YOU FOR YOUR GRACE.
AND...
...SOMETHING ELSE, AS WELL...

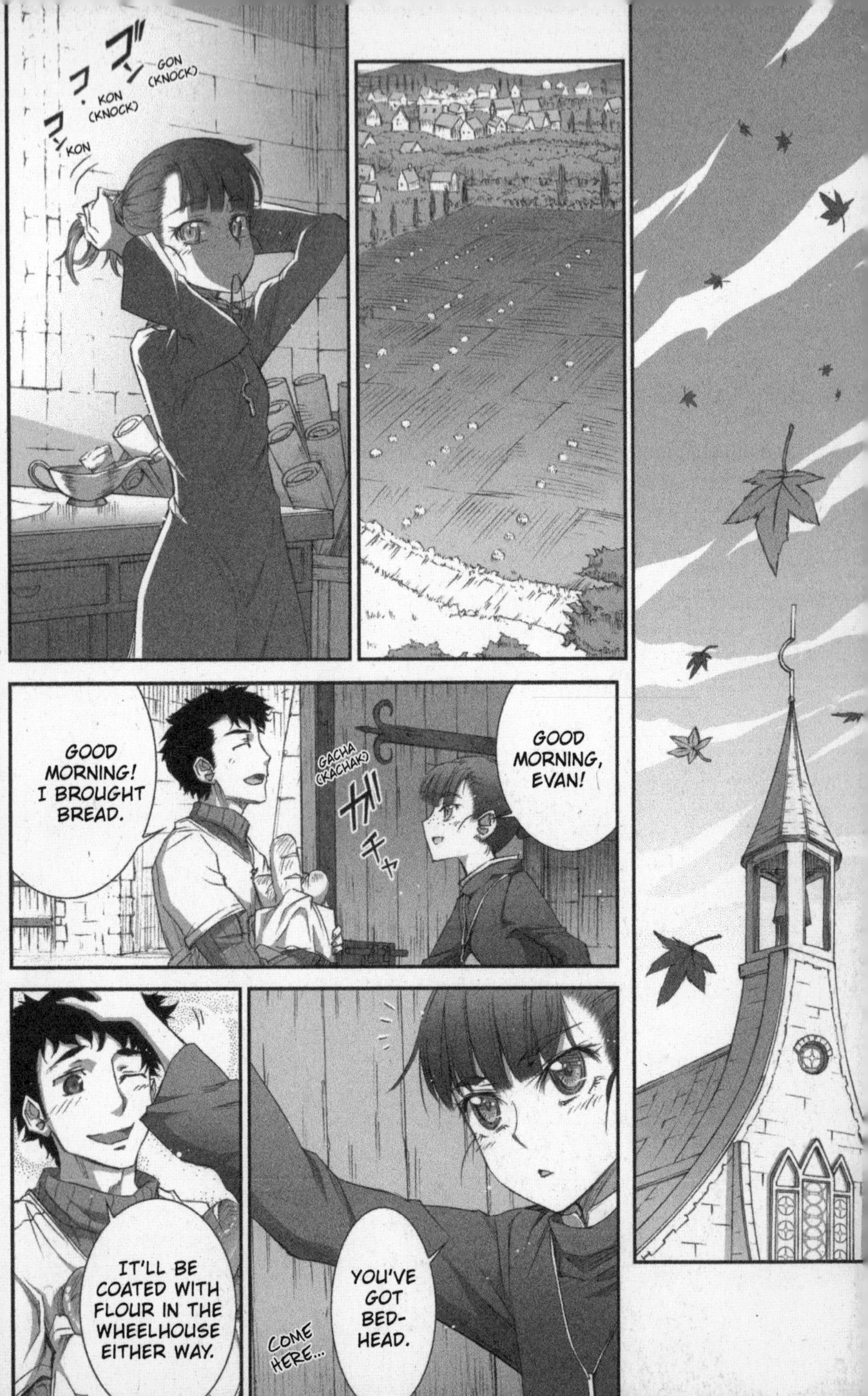
GON (KNOCK)
KON (KNOCK)
KON
GOOD MORNING, EVAN!
GACHA (KACHAK)
GOOD MORNING! I BROUGHT BREAD.
YOU'VE GOT BED-HEAD.
COME HERE...
IT'LL BE COATED WITH FLOUR IN THE WHEELHOUSE EITHER WAY.

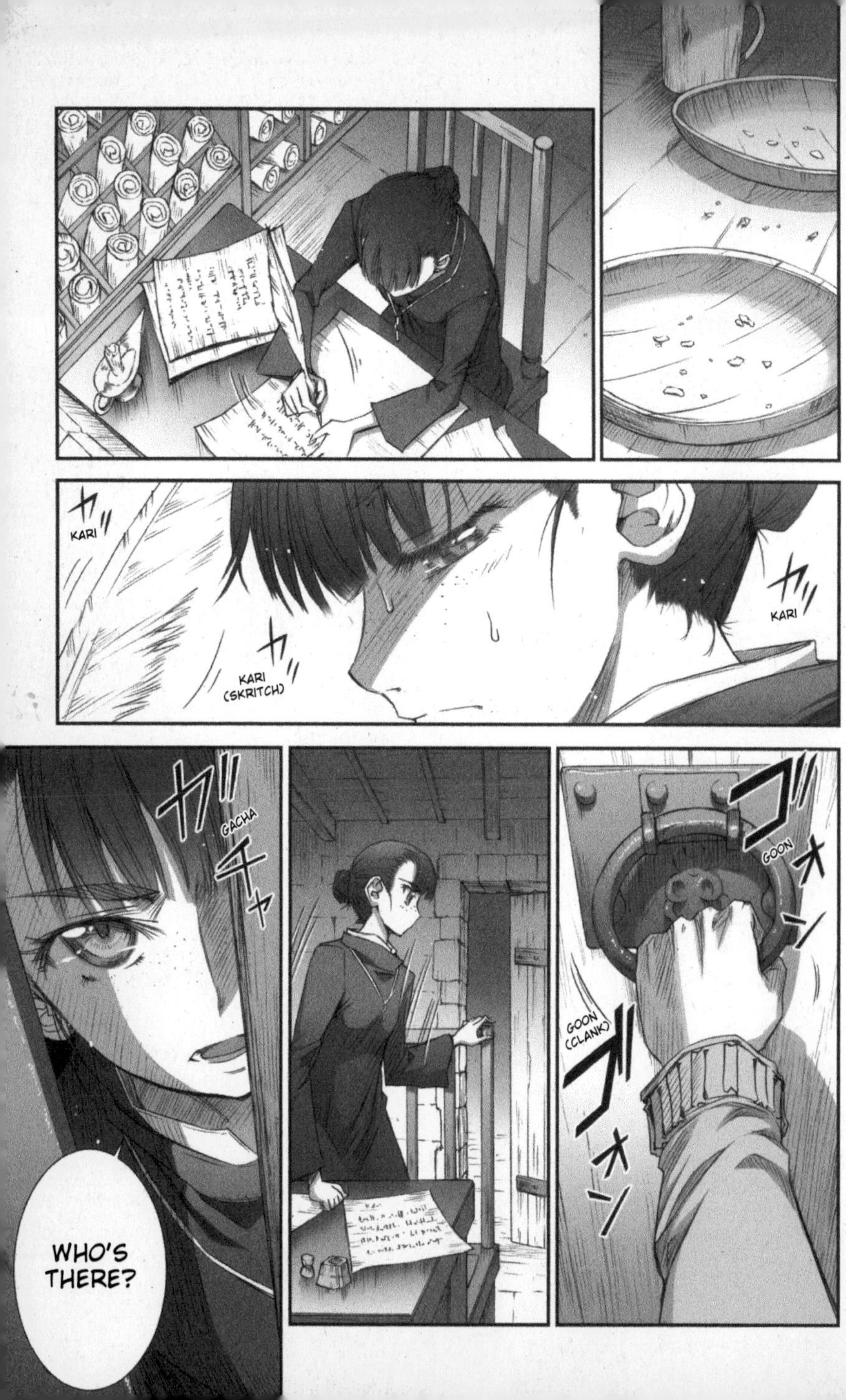
KARI
KARI
KARI (SKRITCH)
GOON
GOON (CLANK)
GACHA
WHO'S THERE?

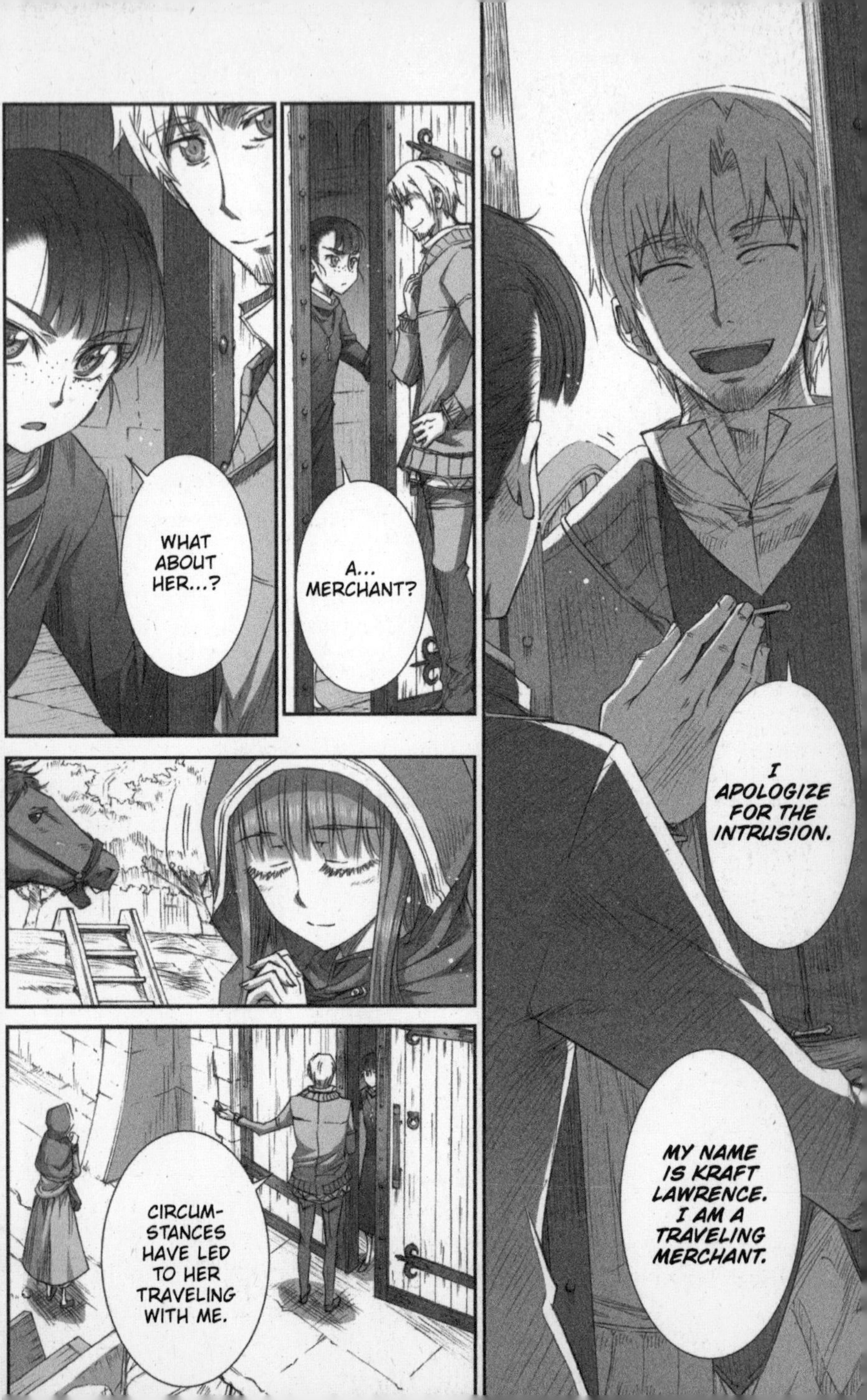
I APOLOGIZE FOR THE INTRUSION.
MY NAME IS KRAFT LAWRENCE. I AM A TRAVELING MERCHANT.
A... MERCHANT?
WHAT ABOUT HER...?
CIRCUM-STANCES HAVE LED TO HER TRAVELING WITH ME.

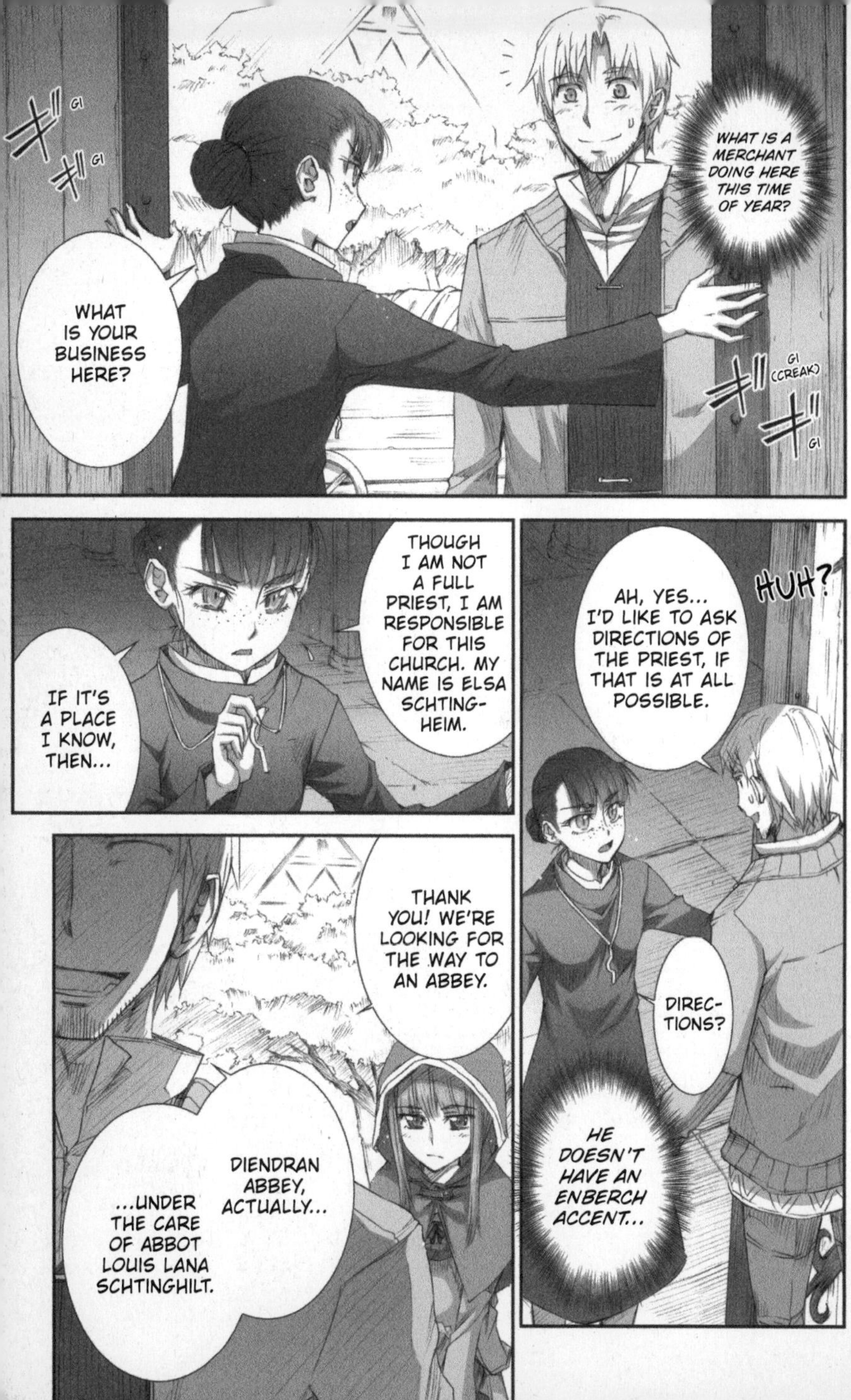
WHAT IS A MERCHANT DOING HERE THIS TIME OF YEAR?
GI
GI
WHAT IS YOUR BUSINESS HERE?
GI (CREAK)
GI
HUH?
AH, YES... I'D LIKE TO ASK DIRECTIONS OF THE PRIEST, IF THAT IS AT ALL POSSIBLE.
DIREC-TIONS?
HE DOESN'T HAVE AN ENBERCH ACCENT...
THOUGH I AM NOT A FULL PRIEST, I AM RESPONSIBLE FOR THIS CHURCH. MY NAME IS ELSA SCHTING-HEIM.
IF IT'S A PLACE I KNOW, THEN...
THANK YOU! WE'RE LOOKING FOR THE WAY TO AN ABBEY.
DIENDRAN ABBEY, ACTUALLY...
...UNDER THE CARE OF ABBOT LOUIS LANA SCHTINGHILT.

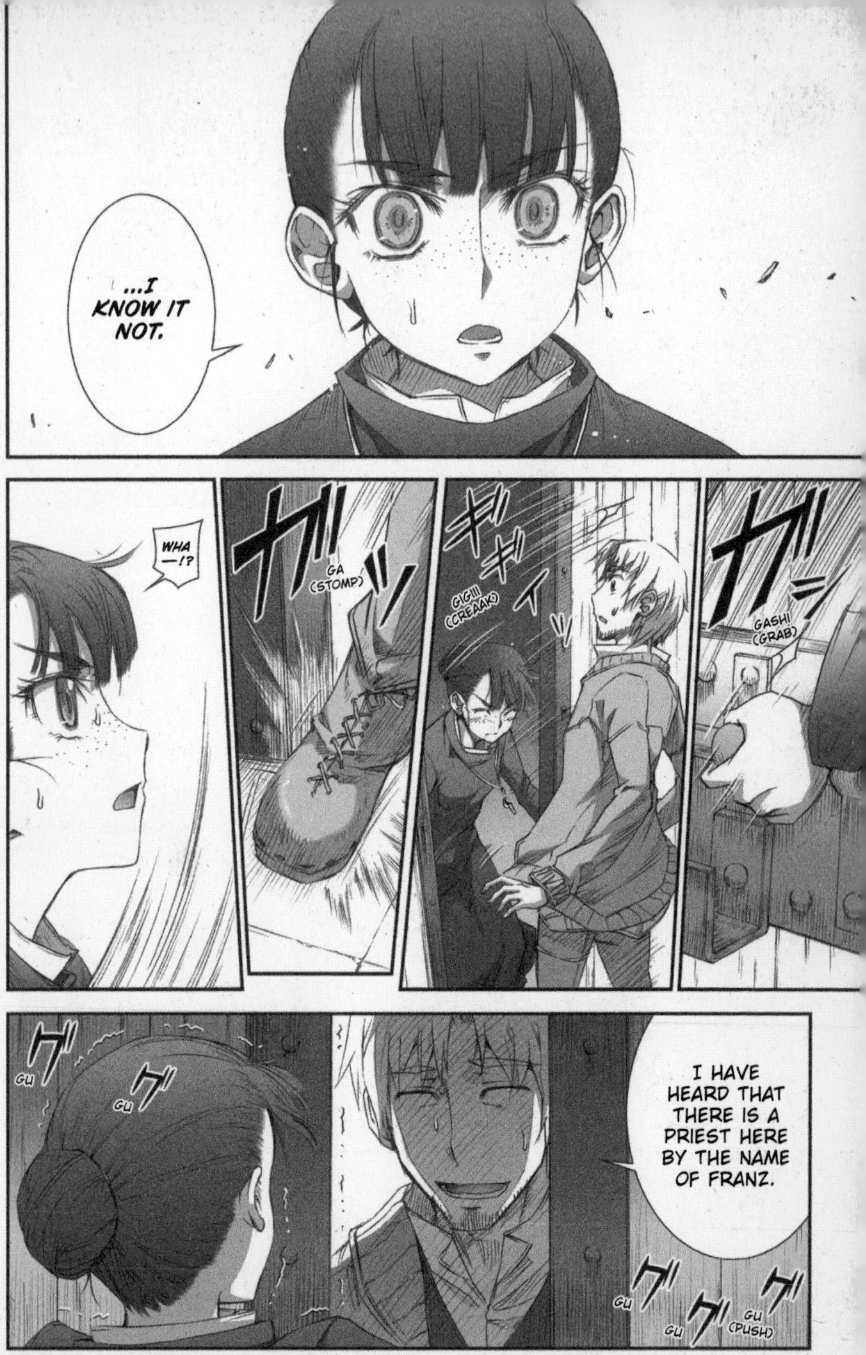
...I KNOW IT NOT.
GASHI (GRAB)
GIGIII (CREAAK)
GA (STOMP)
WHA—!?
I HAVE HEARD THAT THERE IS A PRIEST HERE BY THE NAME OF FRANZ.
GU GU GU (PUSH)
GU
GU

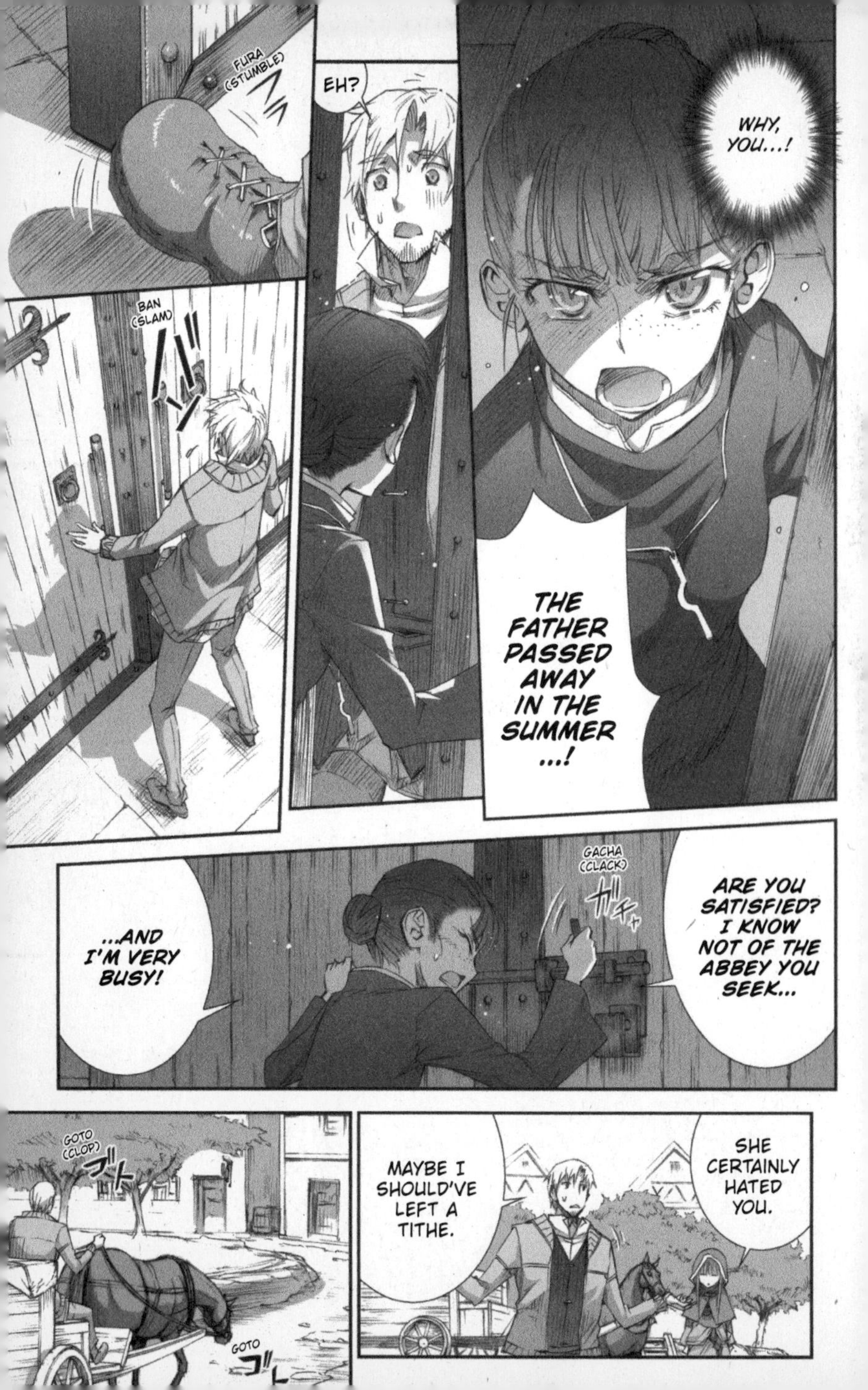
WHY, YOU...!
THE FATHER PASSED AWAY IN THE SUMMER...!
EH?
FURA (STUMBLE)
BAN (SLAM)
ARE YOU SATISFIED? I KNOW NOT OF THE ABBEY YOU SEEK...
GACHA (CLACK)
...AND I'M VERY BUSY!
SHE CERTAINLY HATED YOU.
MAYBE I SHOULD'VE LEFT A TITHE.
GOTO (CLOP)
GOTO

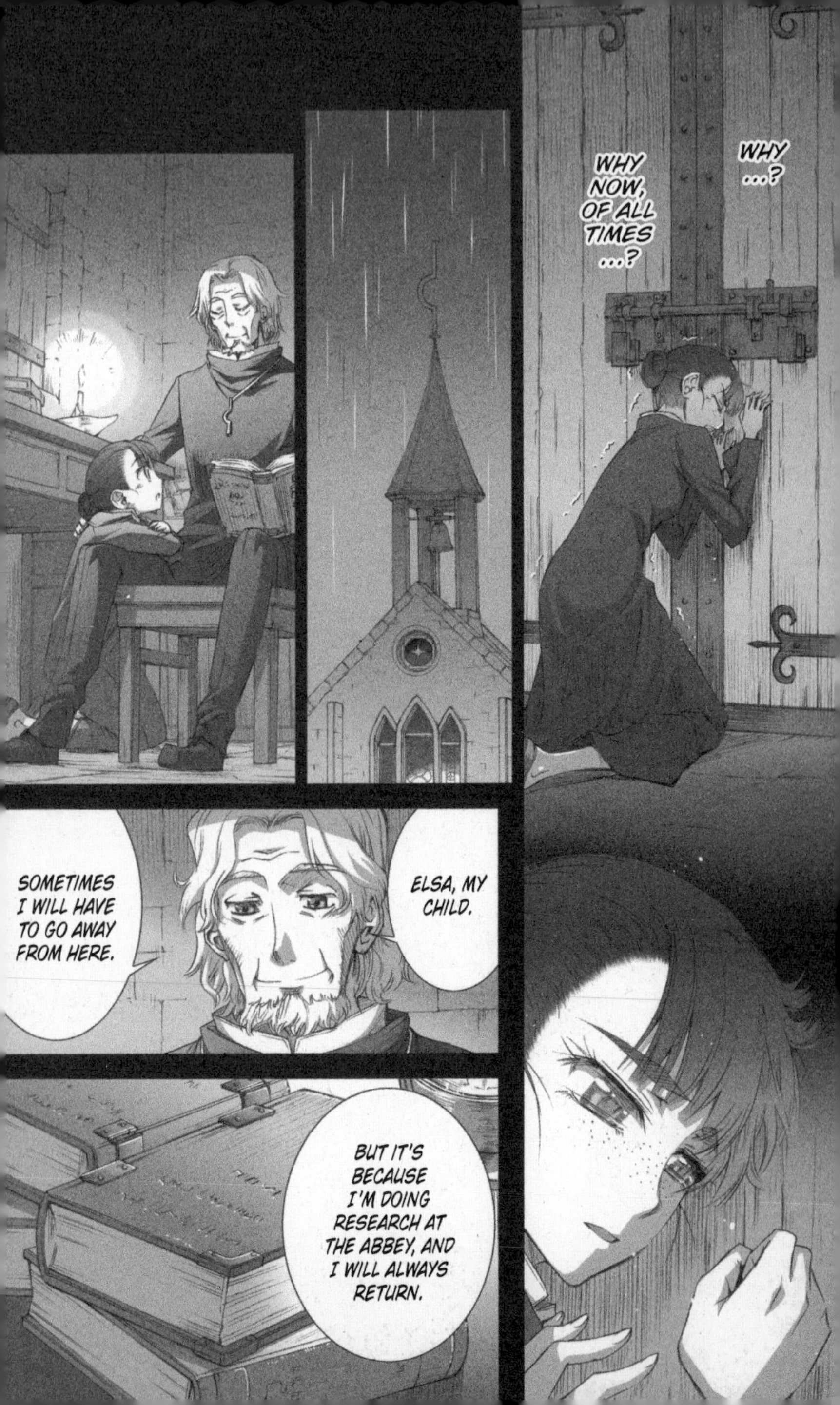
WHY ...?
WHY NOW, OF ALL TIMES ...?
ELSA, MY CHILD.
SOMETIMES I WILL HAVE TO GO AWAY FROM HERE.
BUT IT'S BECAUSE I'M DOING RESEARCH AT THE ABBEY, AND I WILL ALWAYS RETURN.

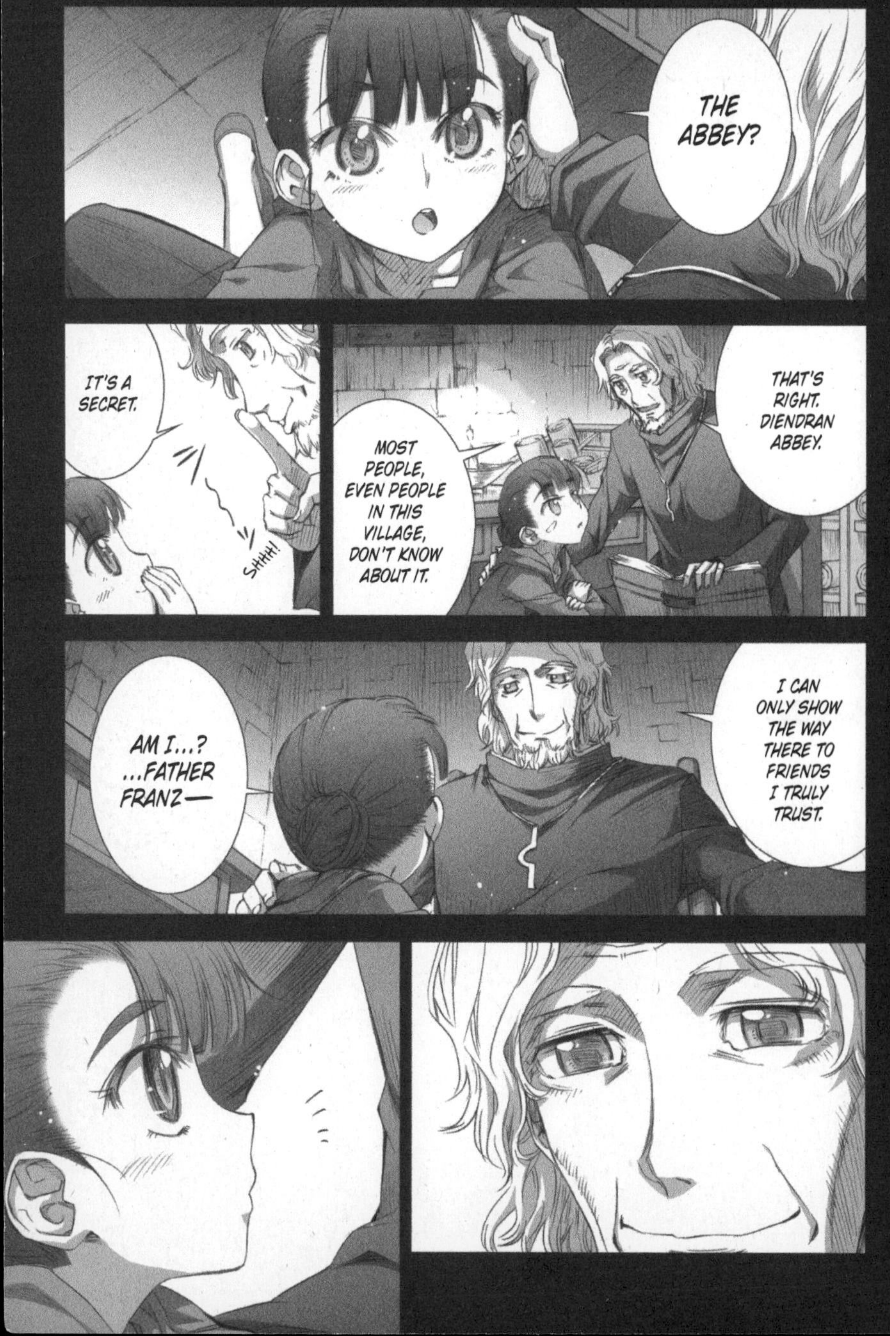
THE ABBEY?
THAT'S RIGHT. DIENDRAN ABBEY.
MOST PEOPLE, EVEN PEOPLE IN THIS VILLAGE, DON'T KNOW ABOUT IT.
IT'S A SECRET.
SHHH!
I CAN ONLY SHOW THE WAY THERE TO FRIENDS I TRULY TRUST.
AM I...? ...FATHER FRANZ—

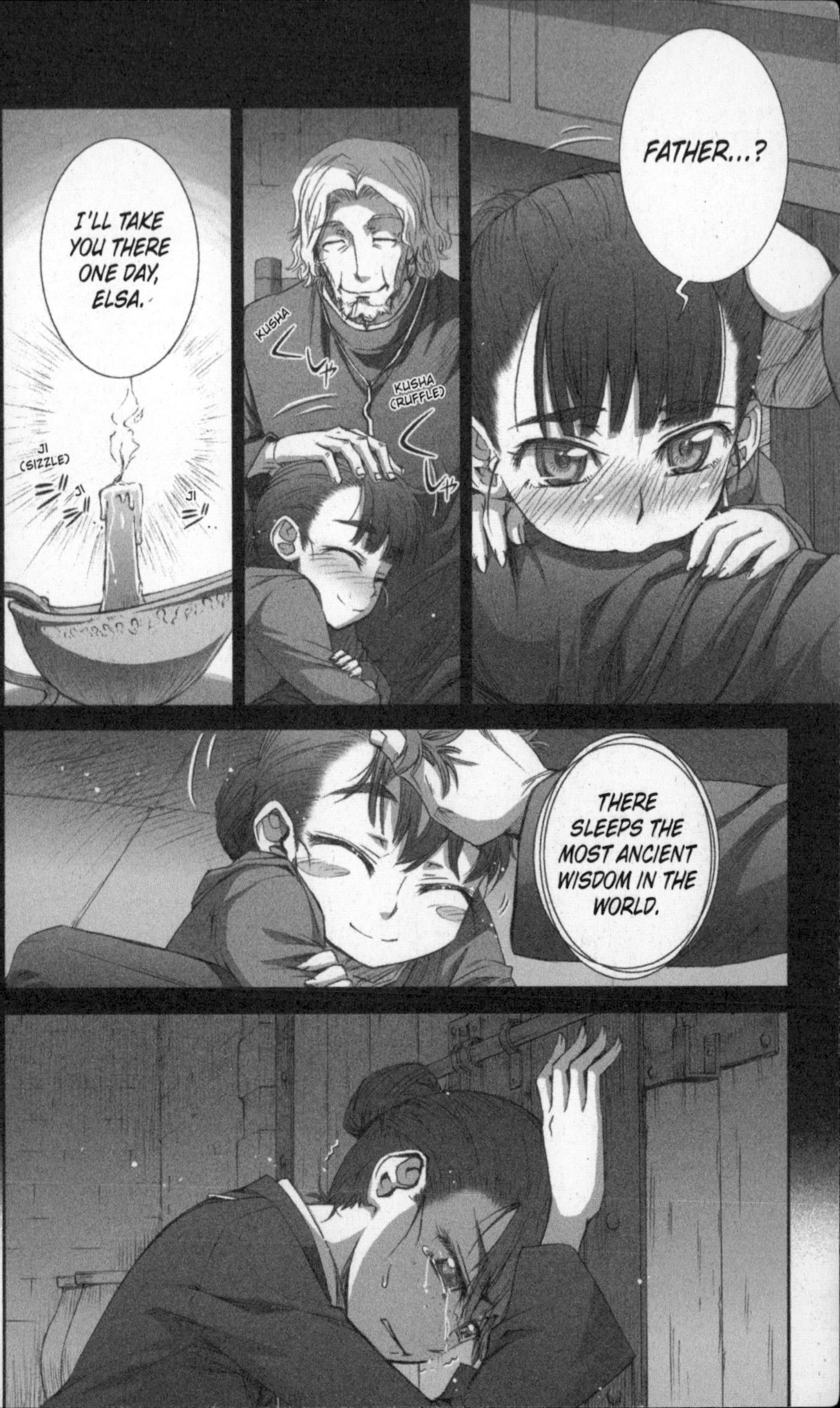
FATHER...?
KUSHA
KUSHA (RUFFLE)
I'LL TAKE YOU THERE ONE DAY, ELSA.
JI (SIZZLE)
JI
JI
THERE SLEEPS THE MOST ANCIENT WISDOM IN THE WORLD.

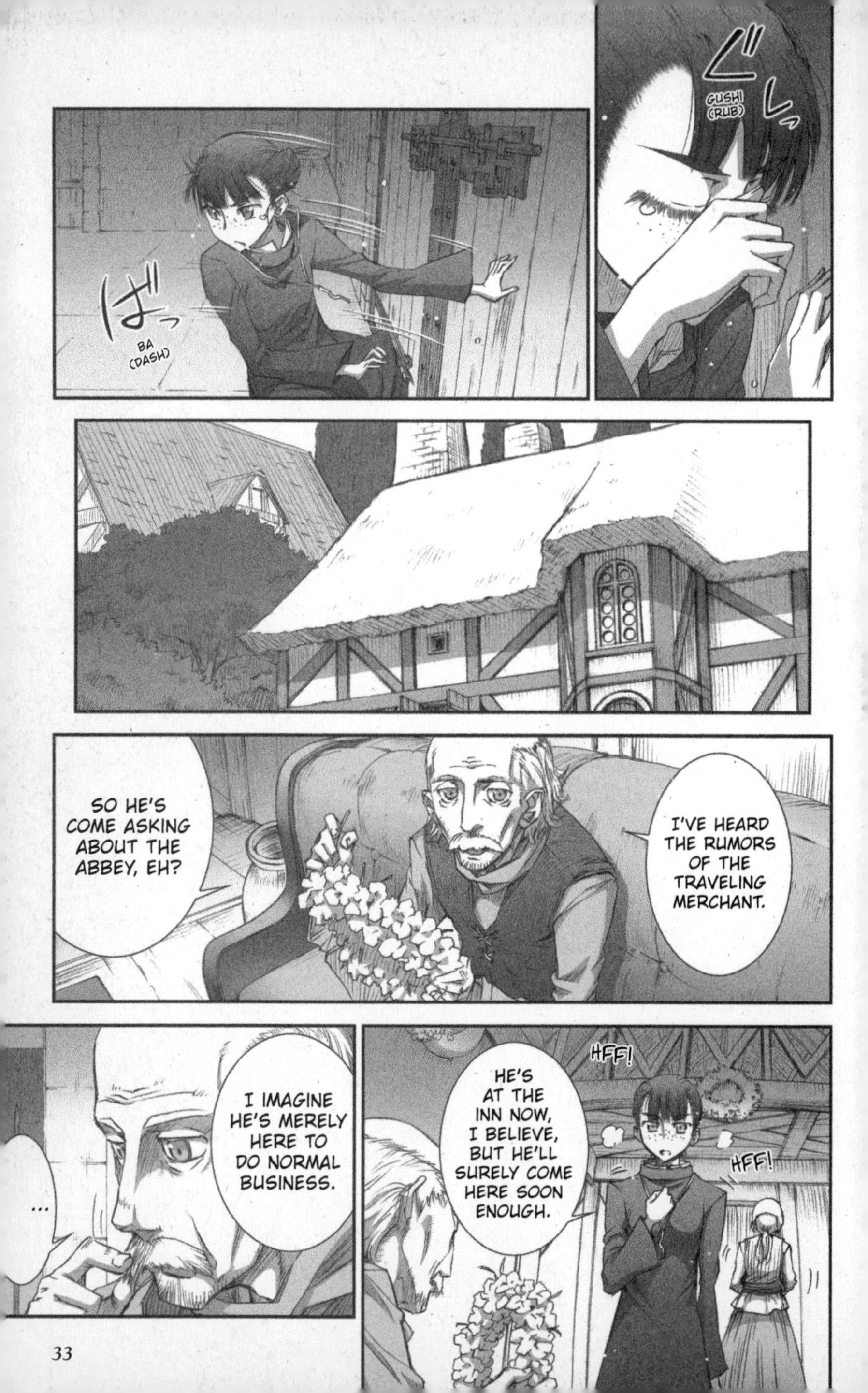
GUSHI (RUB)
BA (DASH)
I'VE HEARD THE RUMORS OF THE TRAVELING MERCHANT.
SO HE'S COME ASKING ABOUT THE ABBEY, EH?
HFF!
HFF!
HE'S AT THE INN NOW, I BELIEVE, BUT HE'LL SURELY COME HERE SOON ENOUGH.
I IMAGINE HE'S MERELY HERE TO DO NORMAL BUSINESS.
...

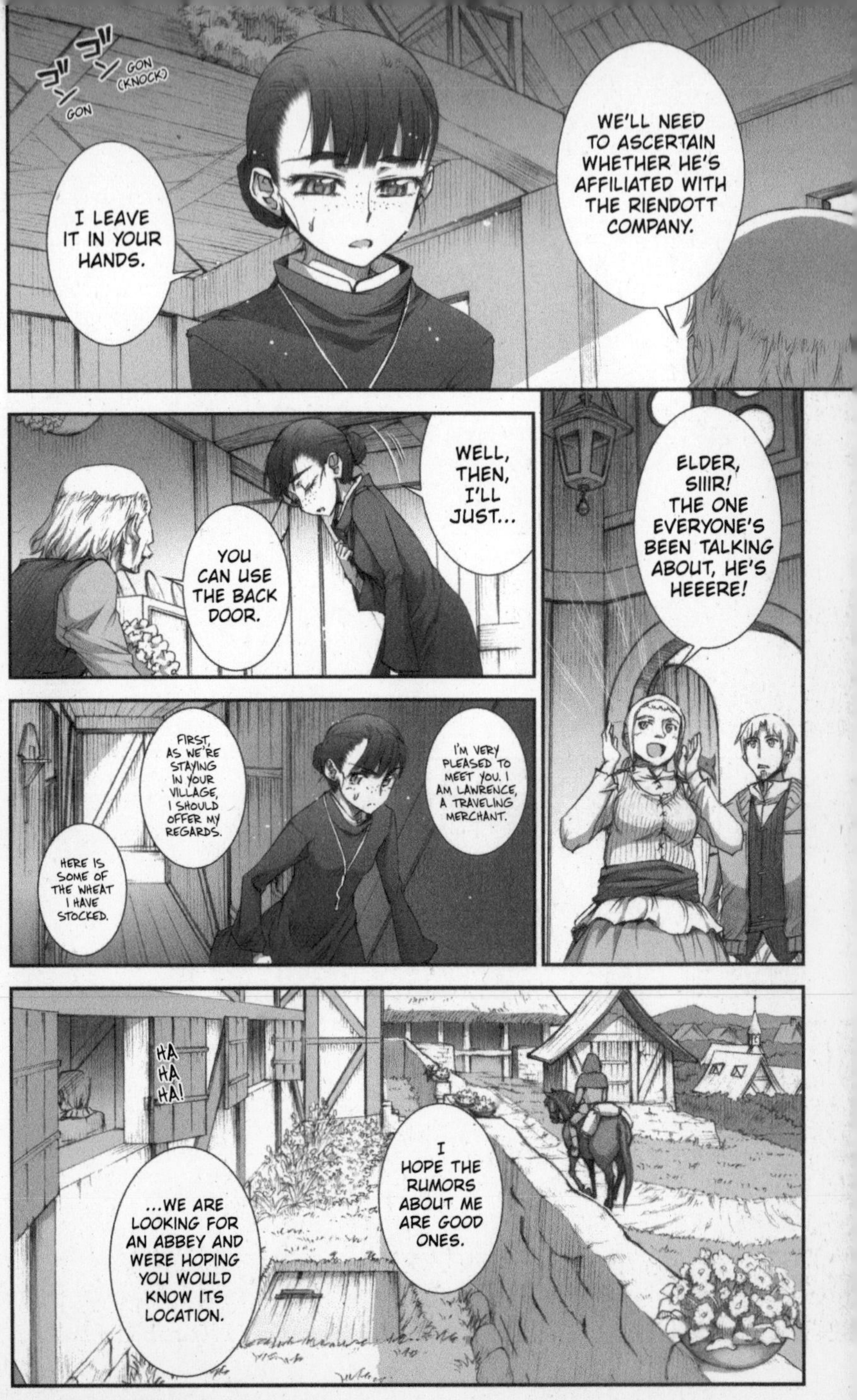
WE'LL NEED TO ASCERTAIN WHETHER HE'S AFFILIATED WITH THE RIENDOTT COMPANY.
ゴン GON (KNOCK)
ゴン GON
I LEAVE IT IN YOUR HANDS.
ELDER, SIIIR! THE ONE EVERYONE'S BEEN TALKING ABOUT, HE'S HEEERE!
WELL, THEN, I'LL JUST...
YOU CAN USE THE BACK DOOR.
I'M VERY PLEASED TO MEET YOU. I AM LAWRENCE, A TRAVELING MERCHANT.
FIRST, AS WE'RE STAYING IN YOUR VILLAGE, I SHOULD OFFER MY REGARDS.
HERE IS SOME OF THE WHEAT I HAVE STOCKED.
I HOPE THE RUMORS ABOUT ME ARE GOOD ONES.
HA HA HA!
...WE ARE LOOKING FOR AN ABBEY AND WERE HOPING YOU WOULD KNOW ITS LOCATION.

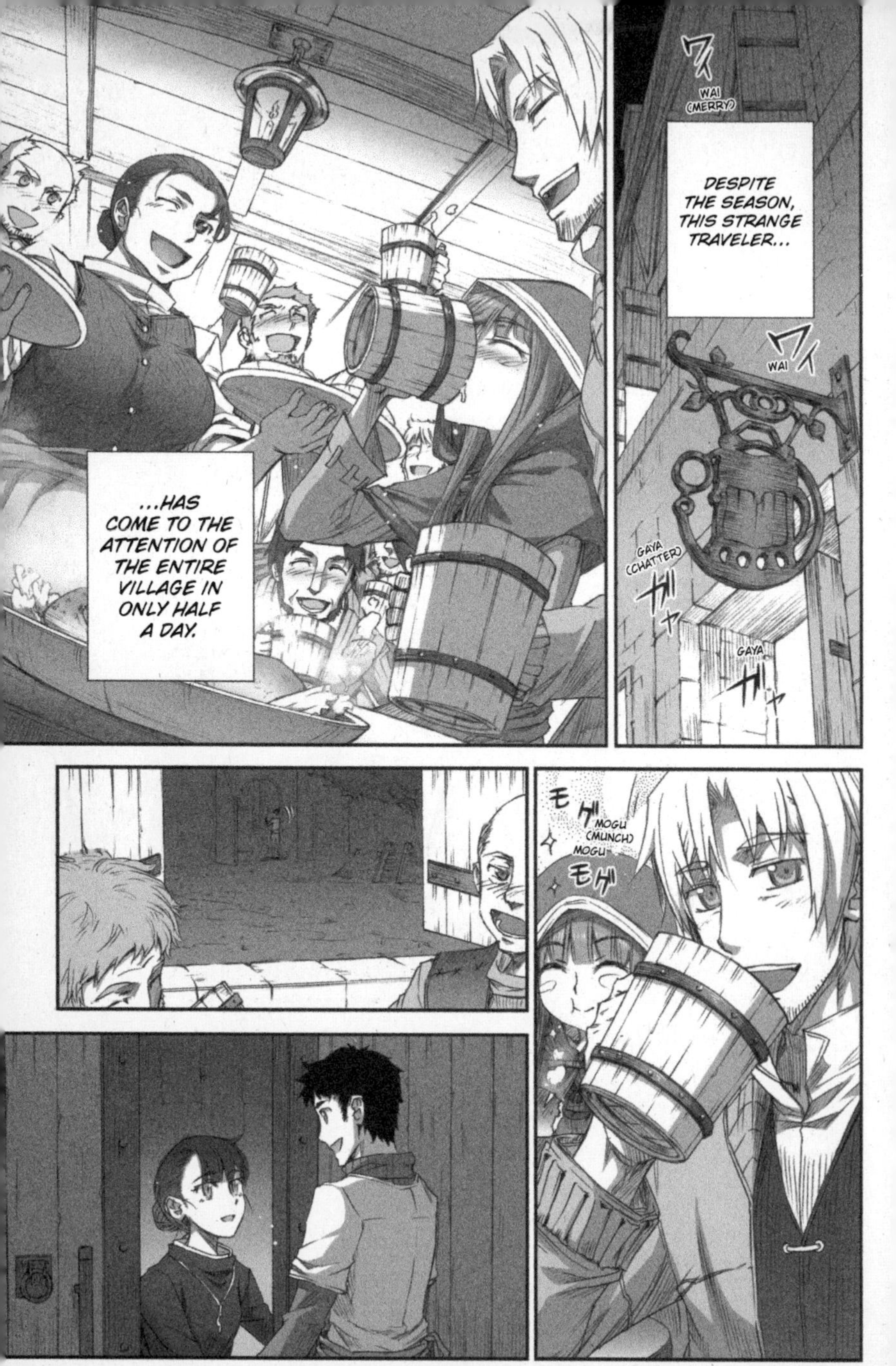
ワイ
WAI (MERRY)
DESPITE THE SEASON, THIS STRANGE TRAVELER...
ワイ
WAI
GAYA (CHATTER)
ガヤ
GAYA
ガヤ
...HAS COME TO THE ATTENTION OF THE ENTIRE VILLAGE IN ONLY HALF A DAY.
モグ
MOGU (MUNCH)
MOGU
モグ

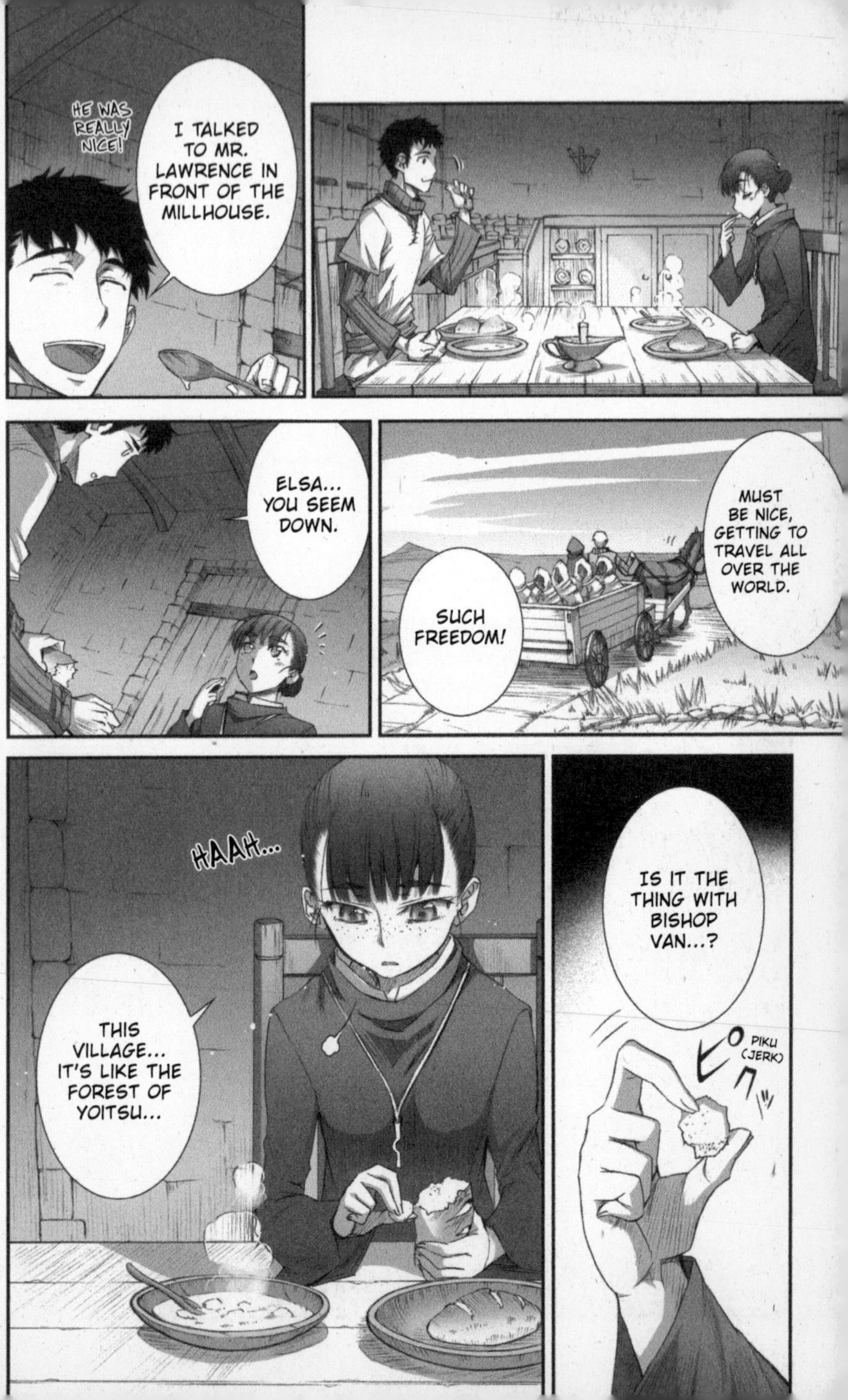
I TALKED TO MR. LAWRENCE IN FRONT OF THE MILLHOUSE.
HE WAS REALLY NICE!
MUST BE NICE, GETTING TO TRAVEL ALL OVER THE WORLD.
SUCH FREEDOM!
ELSA... YOU SEEM DOWN.
IS IT THE THING WITH BISHOP VAN...?
PIKU (JERK)
HAAH...
THIS VILLAGE... IT'S LIKE THE FOREST OF YOITSU...

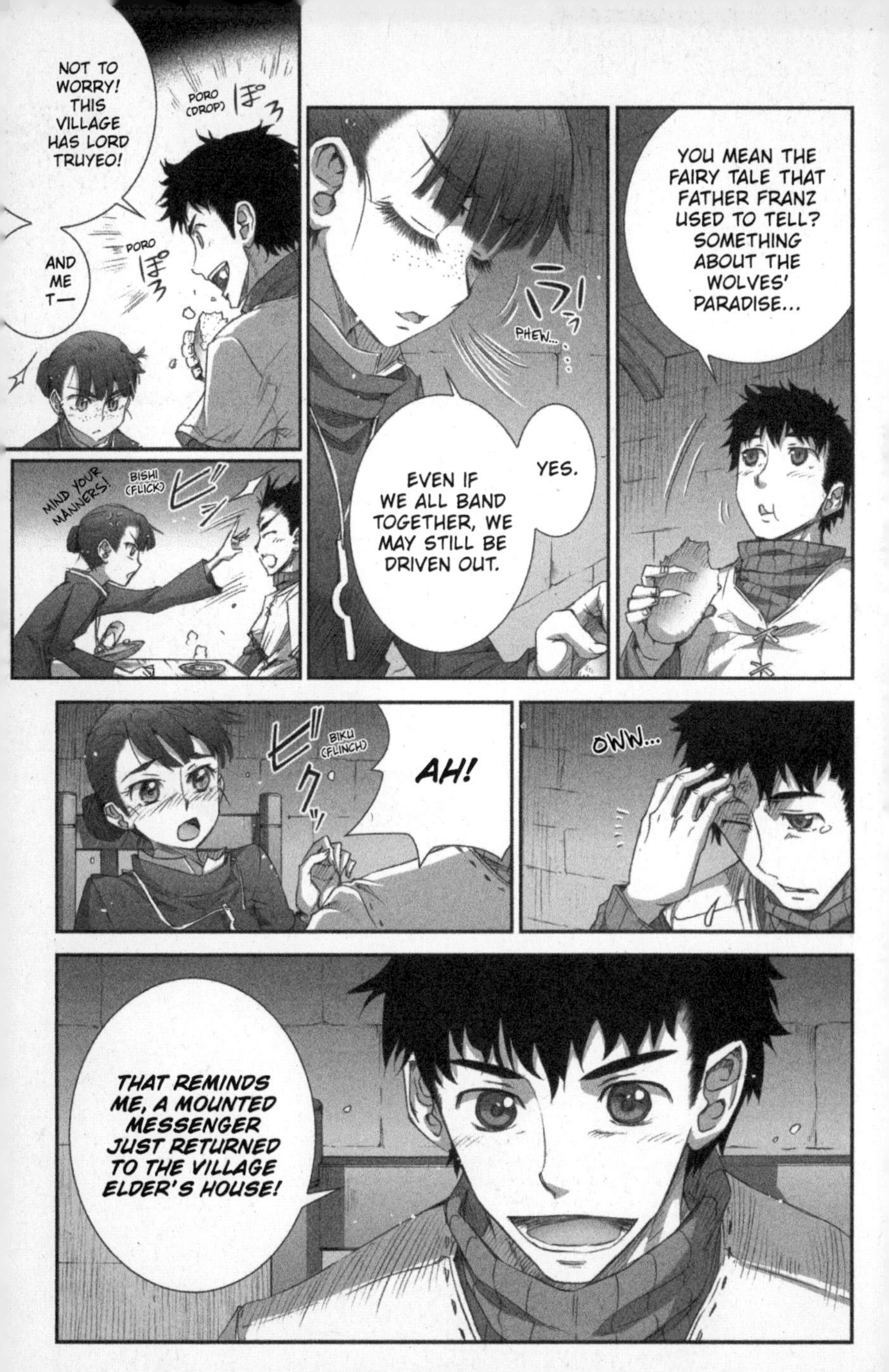
YOU MEAN THE FAIRY TALE THAT FATHER FRANZ USED TO TELL? SOMETHING ABOUT THE WOLVES' PARADISE...
YES.
EVEN IF WE ALL BAND TOGETHER, WE MAY STILL BE DRIVEN OUT.
PHEW...
NOT TO WORRY! THIS VILLAGE HAS LORD TRUYEO!
PORO (DROP)
AND ME T—
PORO
MIND YOUR MANNERS!
BISHI (FLICK)
OWW...
AH!
BIKU (FLINCH)
THAT REMINDS ME, A MOUNTED MESSENGER JUST RETURNED TO THE VILLAGE ELDER'S HOUSE!

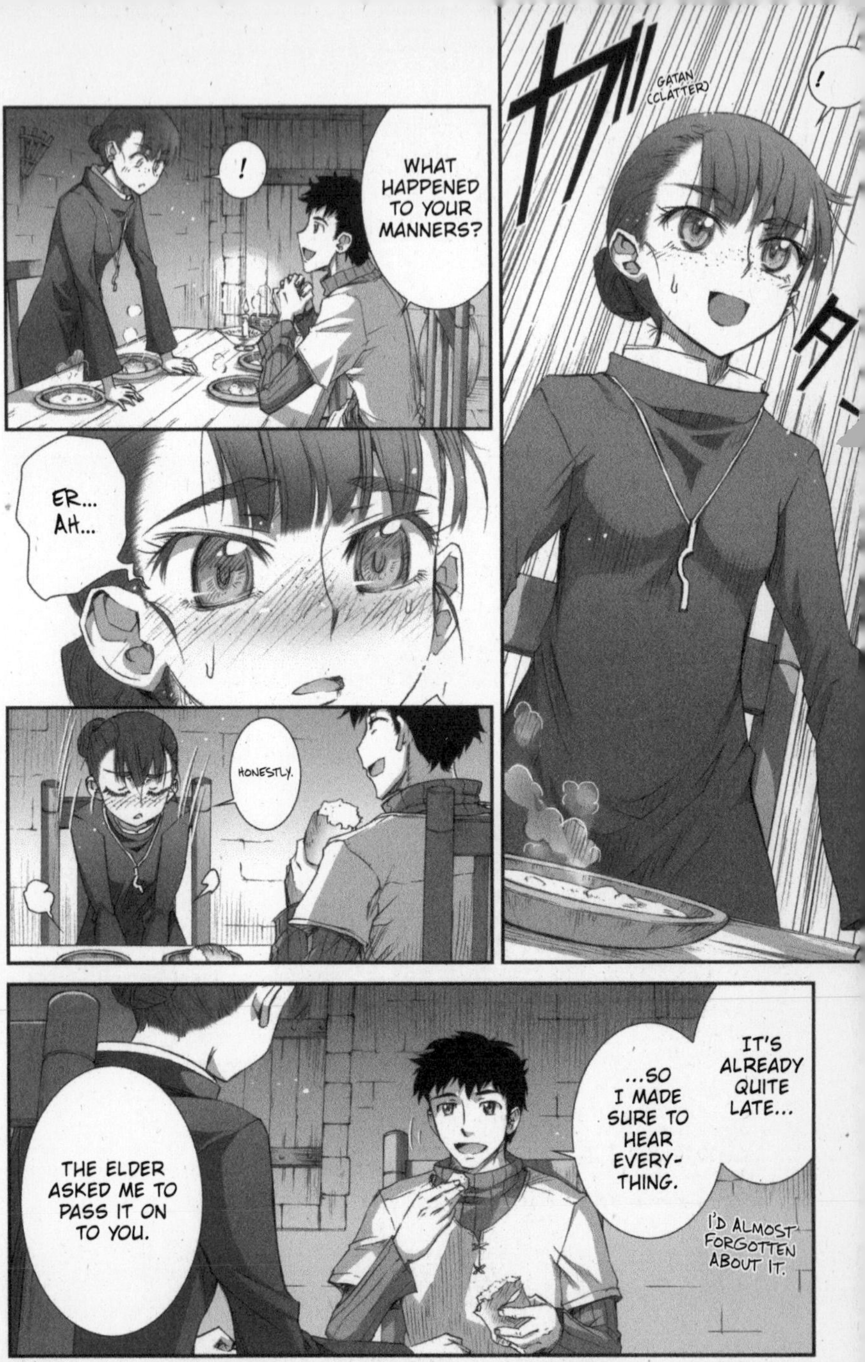
GATAN (CLATTER)
!
!
WHAT HAPPENED TO YOUR MANNERS?
ER... AH...
HONESTLY.
IT'S ALREADY QUITE LATE...
...SO I MADE SURE TO HEAR EVERY-THING.
I'D ALMOST FORGOTTEN ABOUT IT.
THE ELDER ASKED ME TO PASS IT ON TO YOU.

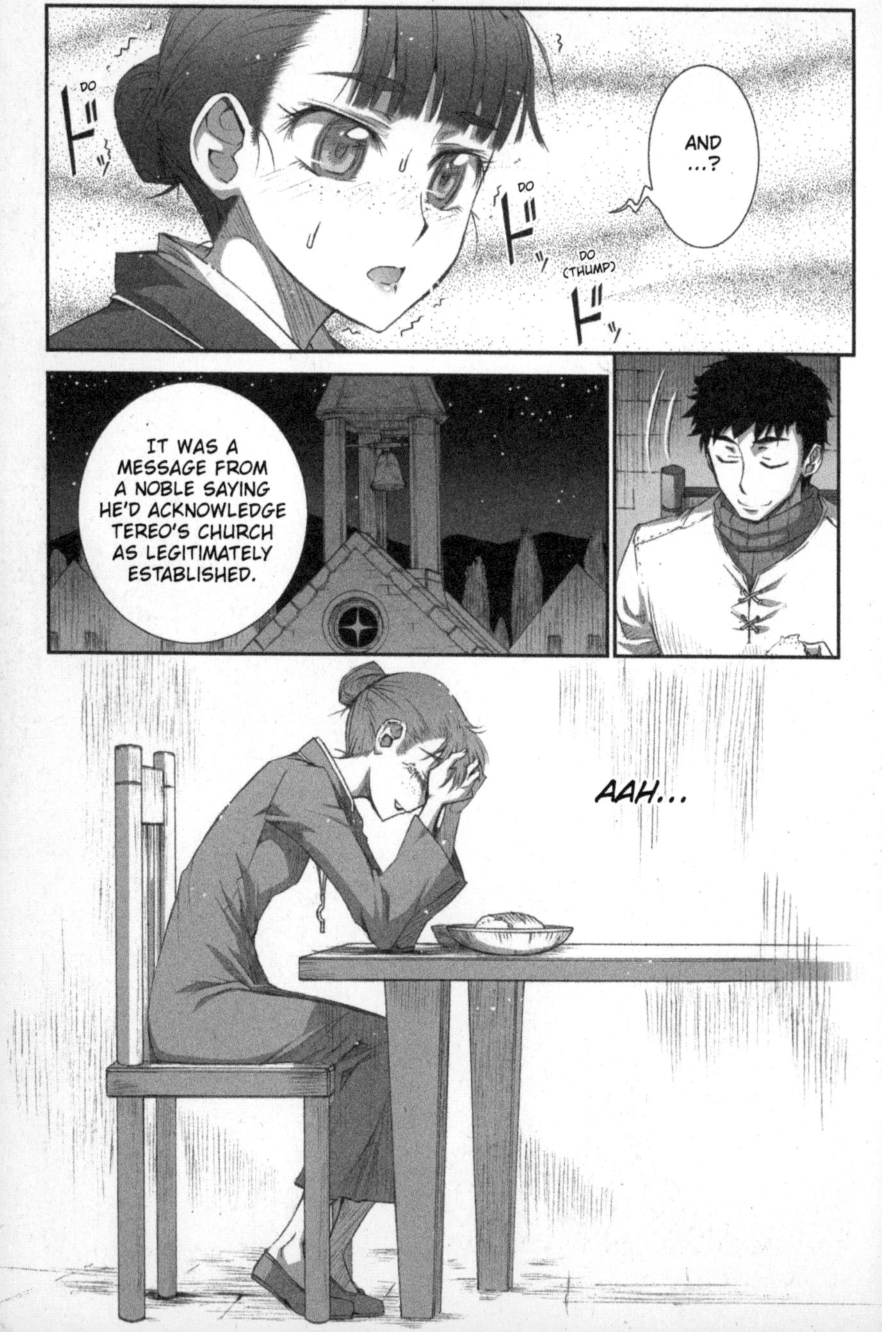
AND ...?
DO
DO
DO (THUMP)
IT WAS A MESSAGE FROM A NOBLE SAYING HE'D ACKNOWLEDGE TEREO'S CHURCH AS LEGITIMATELY ESTABLISHED.
AAH...

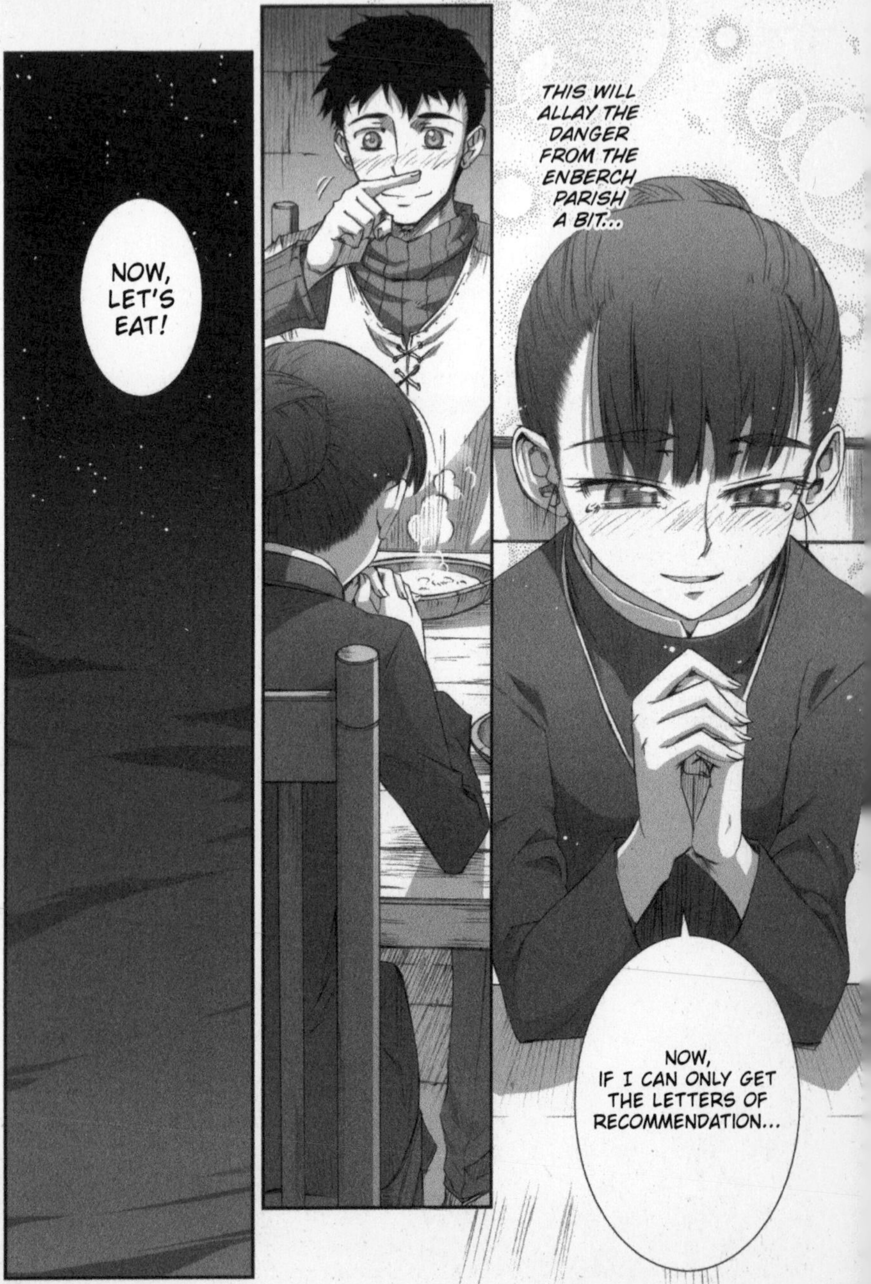
THIS WILL ALLAY THE DANGER FROM THE ENBERCH PARISH A BIT...
NOW, IF I CAN ONLY GET THE LETTERS OF RECOMMENDATION...
NOW, LET'S EAT!

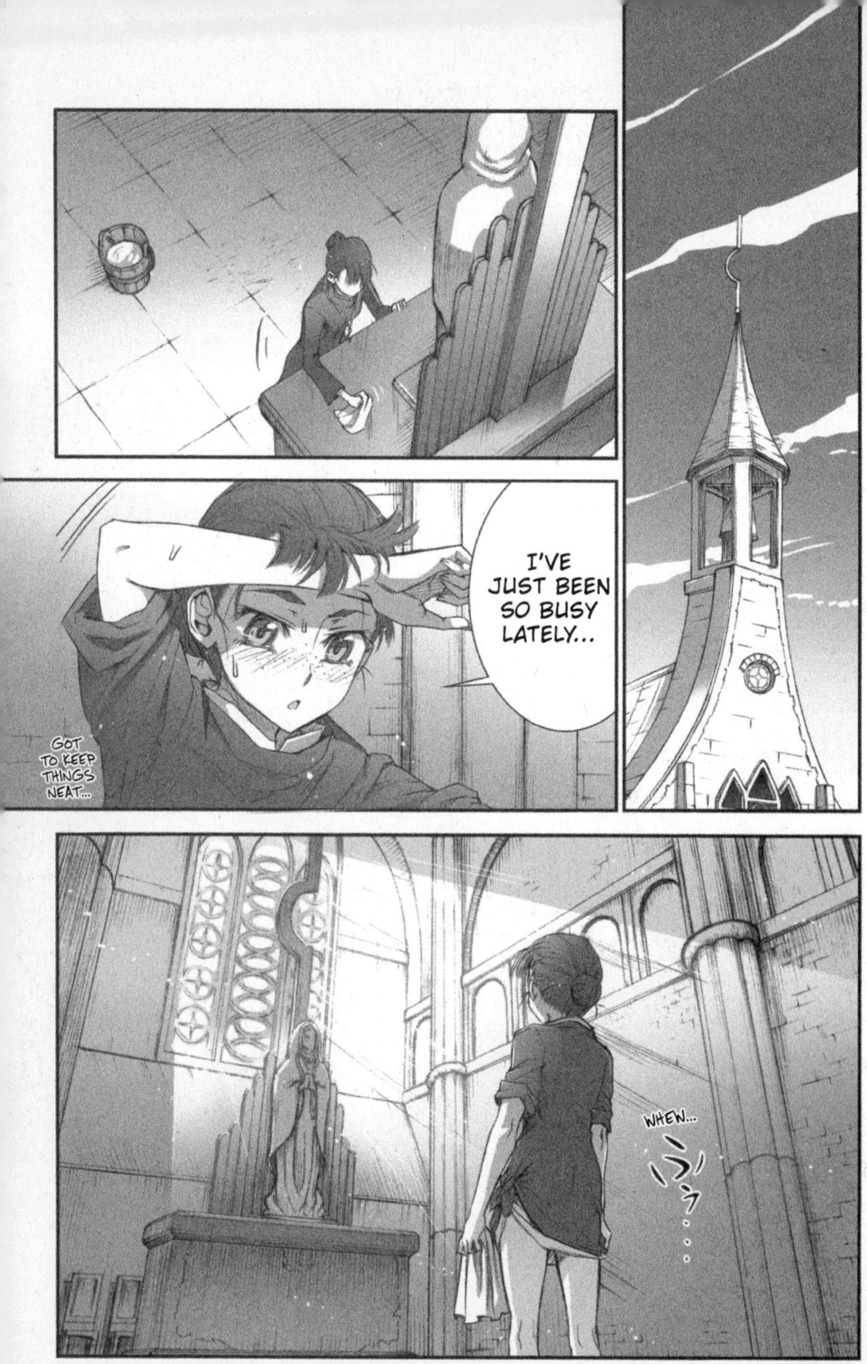
I'VE JUST BEEN SO BUSY LATELY...
GOT TO KEEP THINGS NEAT...
WHEW...
ふう・・・

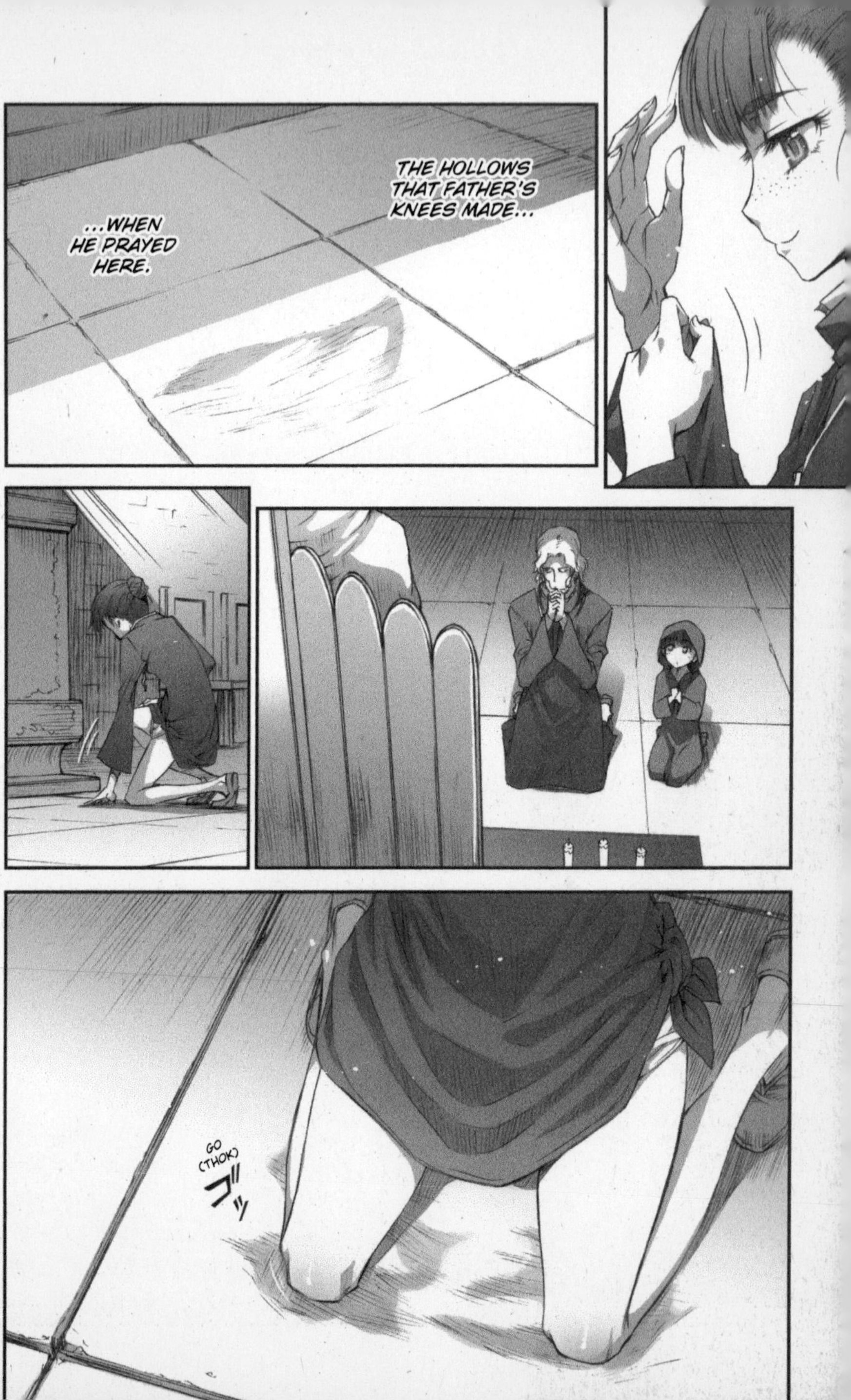
THE HOLLOWS THAT FATHER'S KNEES MADE...
...WHEN HE PRAYED HERE.
GO (THOK)
ゴッ

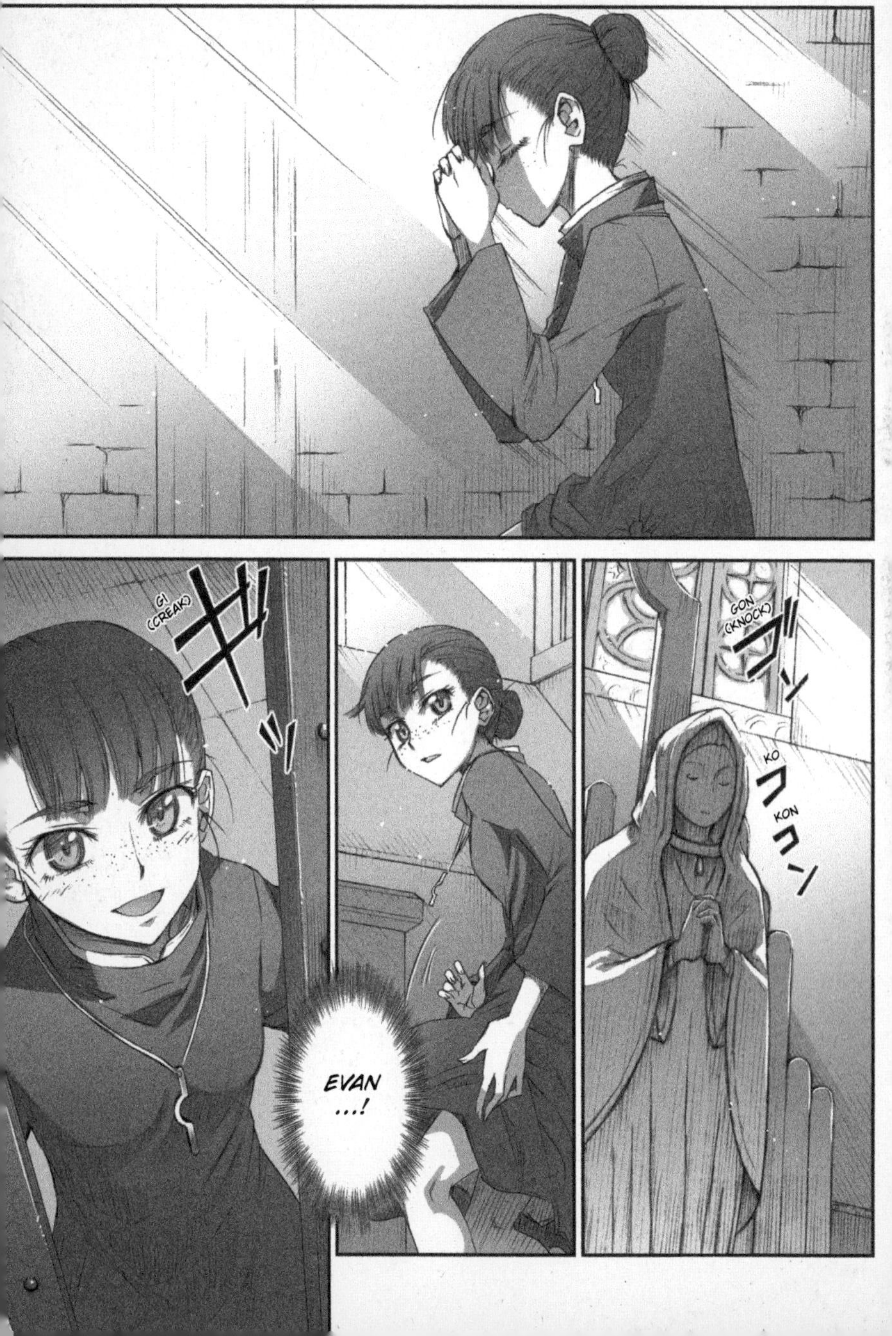
GON (KNOCK)
KO KON
GI (CREAK)
EVAN ...!

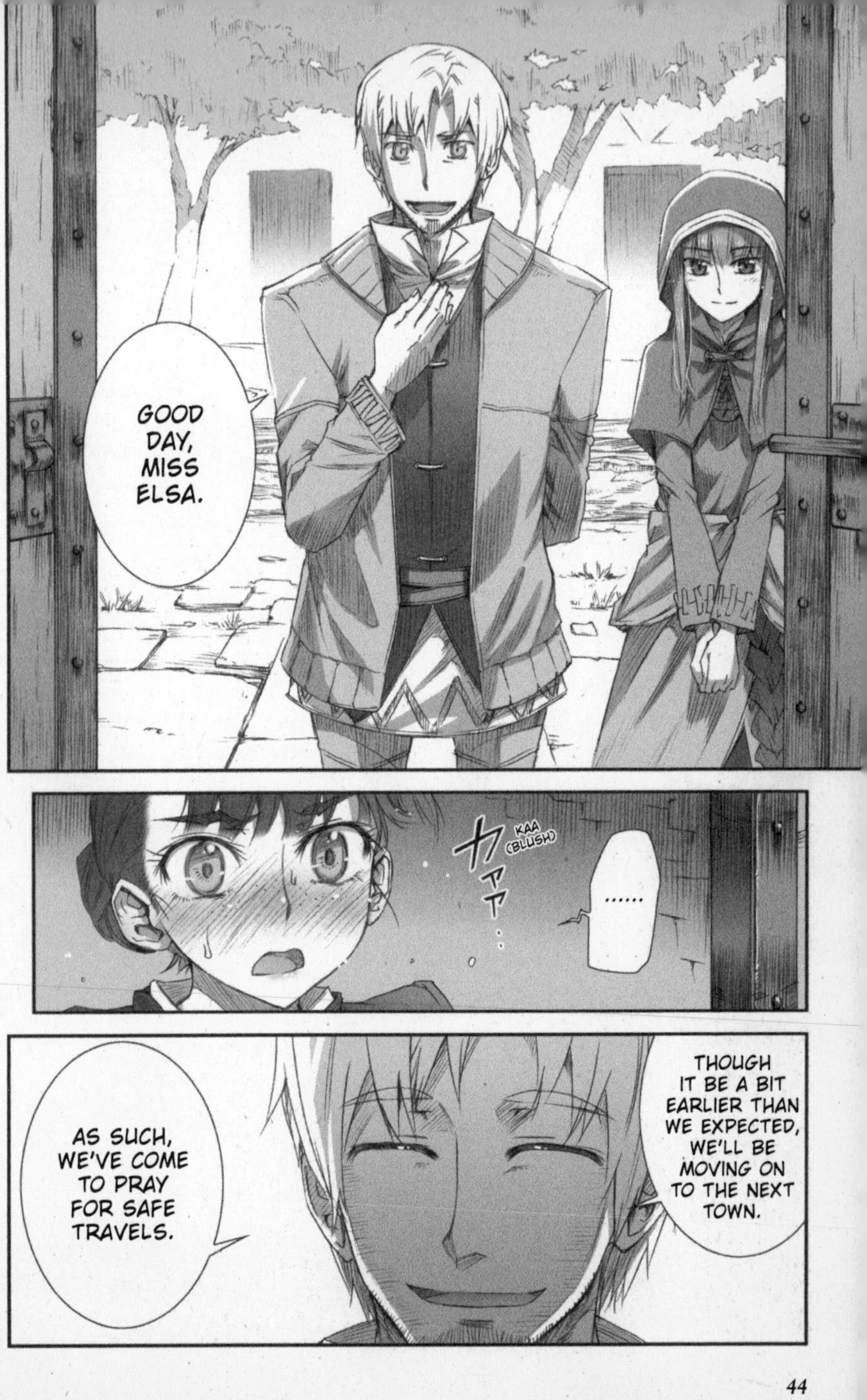
GOOD DAY, MISS ELSA.
KAA (BLUSH)
......
THOUGH IT BE A BIT EARLIER THAN WE EXPECTED, WE'LL BE MOVING ON TO THE NEXT TOWN.
AS SUCH, WE'VE COME TO PRAY FOR SAFE TRAVELS.

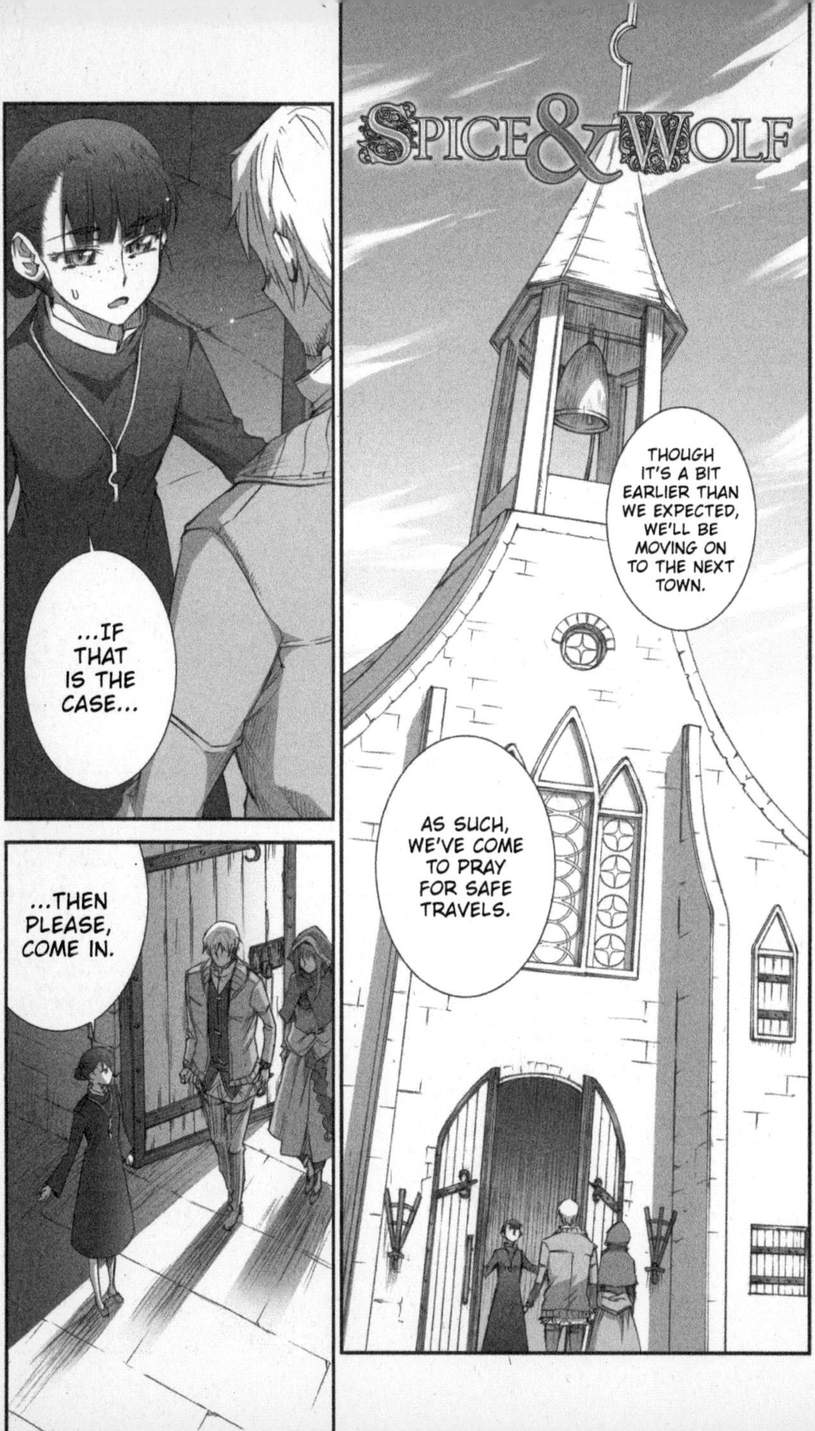
SPICE & WOLF
THOUGH IT'S A BIT EARLIER THAN WE EXPECTED, WE'LL BE MOVING ON TO THE NEXT TOWN.
AS SUCH, WE'VE COME TO PRAY FOR SAFE TRAVELS.
...IF THAT IS THE CASE...
...THEN PLEASE, COME IN.

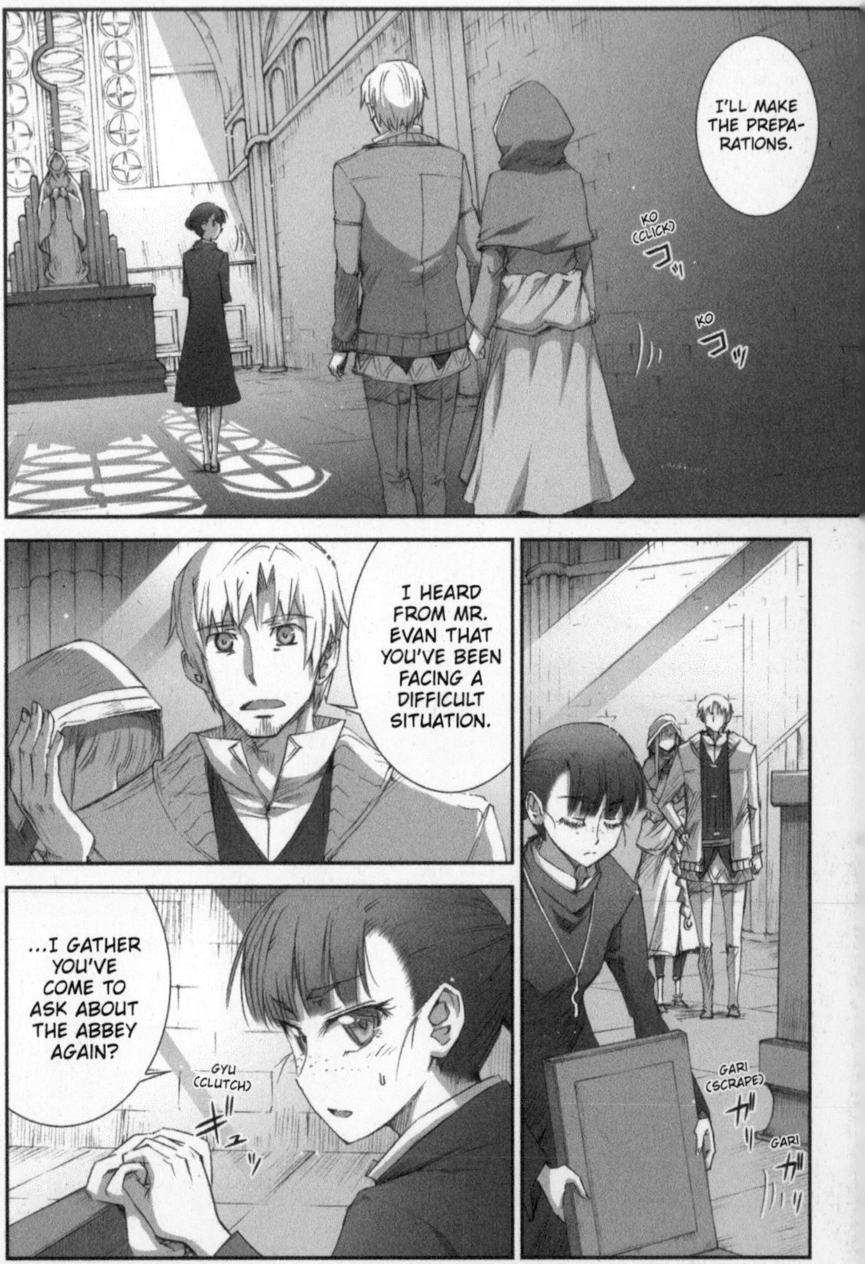
I'LL MAKE THE PREPA-RATIONS.
KO (CLICK)
KO
GARI (SCRAPE)
GARI
I HEARD FROM MR. EVAN THAT YOU'VE BEEN FACING A DIFFICULT SITUATION.
...I GATHER YOU'VE COME TO ASK ABOUT THE ABBEY AGAIN?
GYU (CLUTCH)

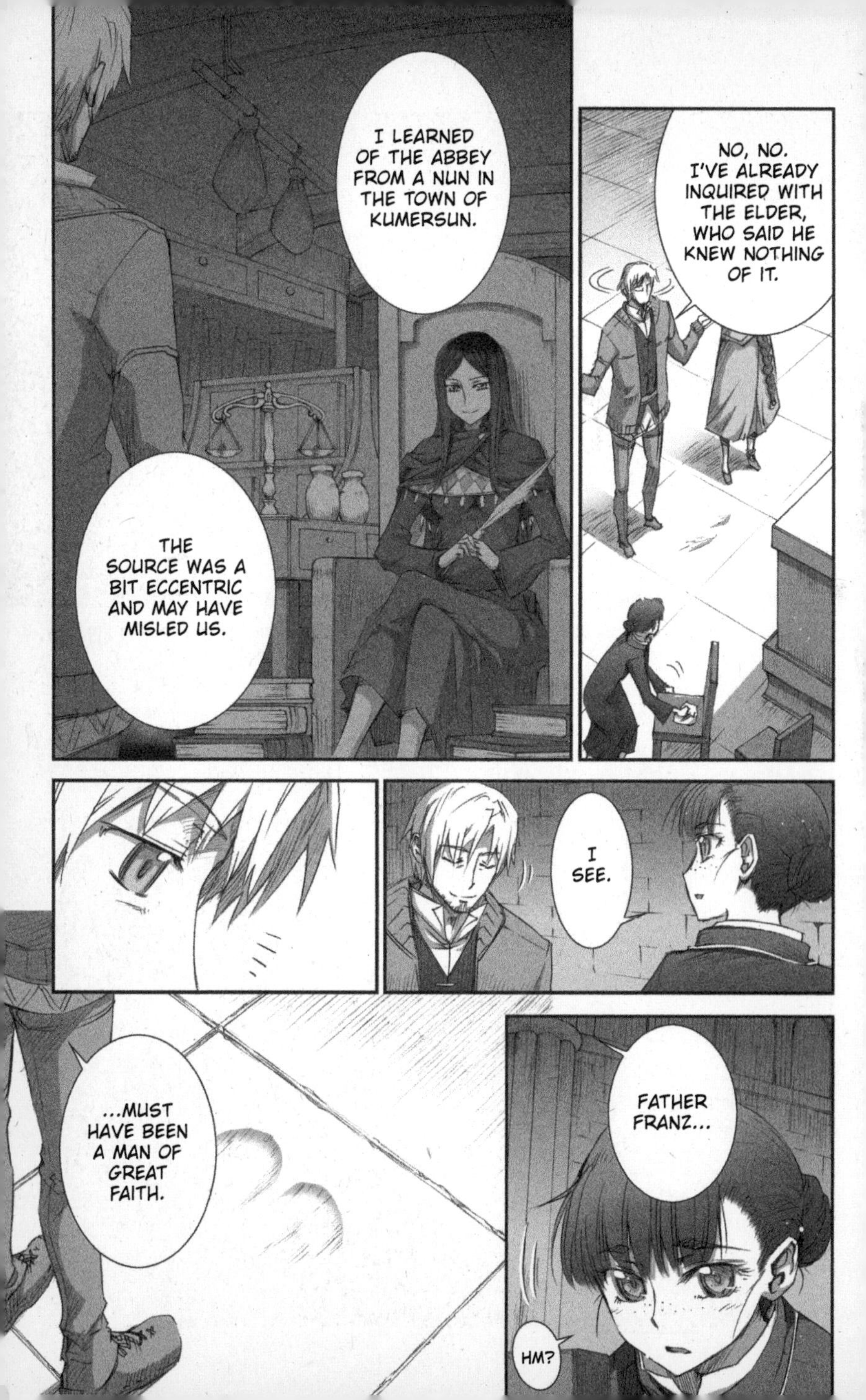
NO, NO. I'VE ALREADY INQUIRED WITH THE ELDER, WHO SAID HE KNEW NOTHING OF IT.
I LEARNED OF THE ABBEY FROM A NUN IN THE TOWN OF KUMERSUN.
THE SOURCE WAS A BIT ECCENTRIC AND MAY HAVE MISLED US.
I SEE.
FATHER FRANZ...
HM?
...MUST HAVE BEEN A MAN OF GREAT FAITH.

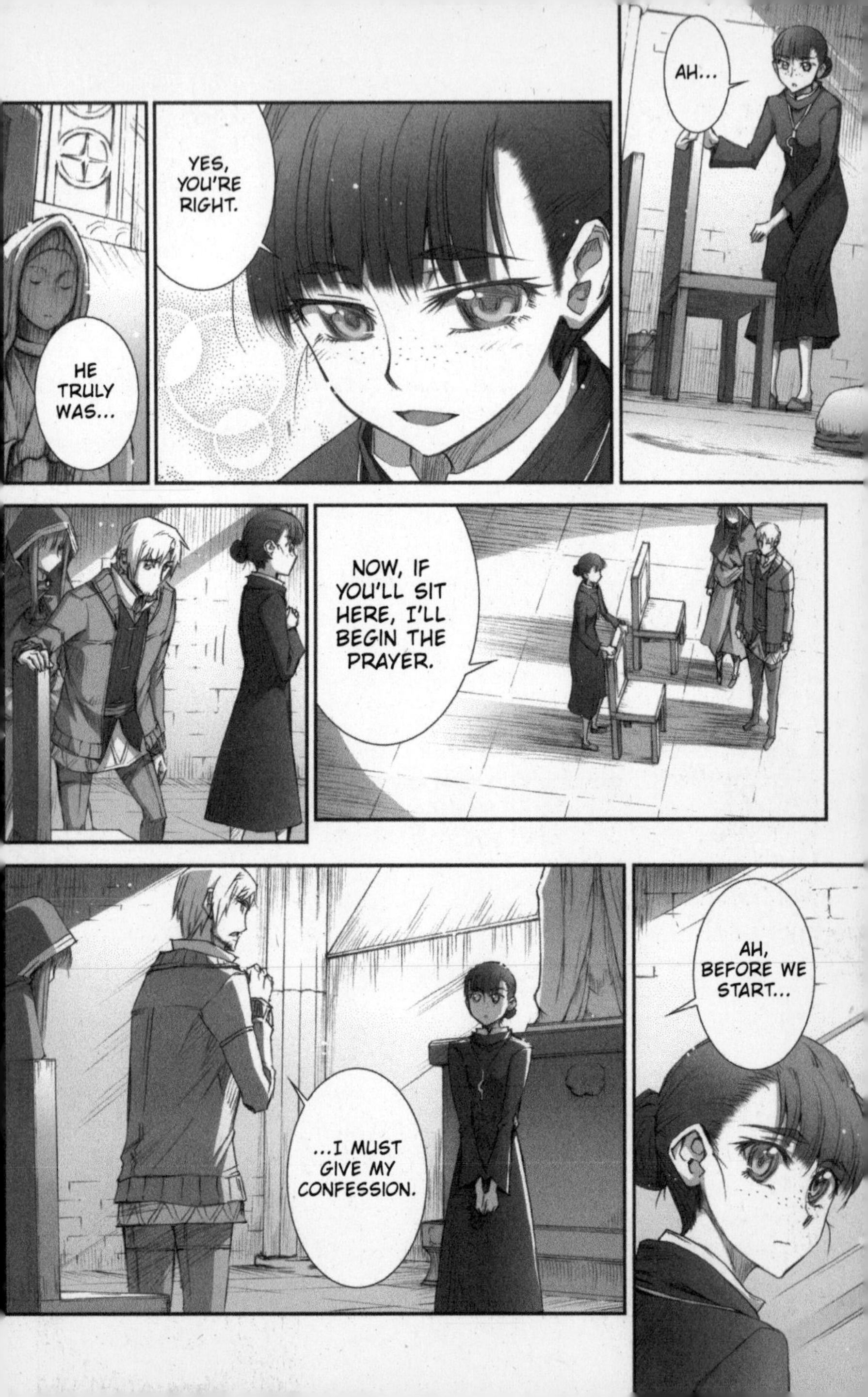
AH...
YES, YOU'RE RIGHT.
HE TRULY WAS...
NOW, IF YOU'LL SIT HERE, I'LL BEGIN THE PRAYER.
AH, BEFORE WE START...
...I MUST GIVE MY CONFESSION.

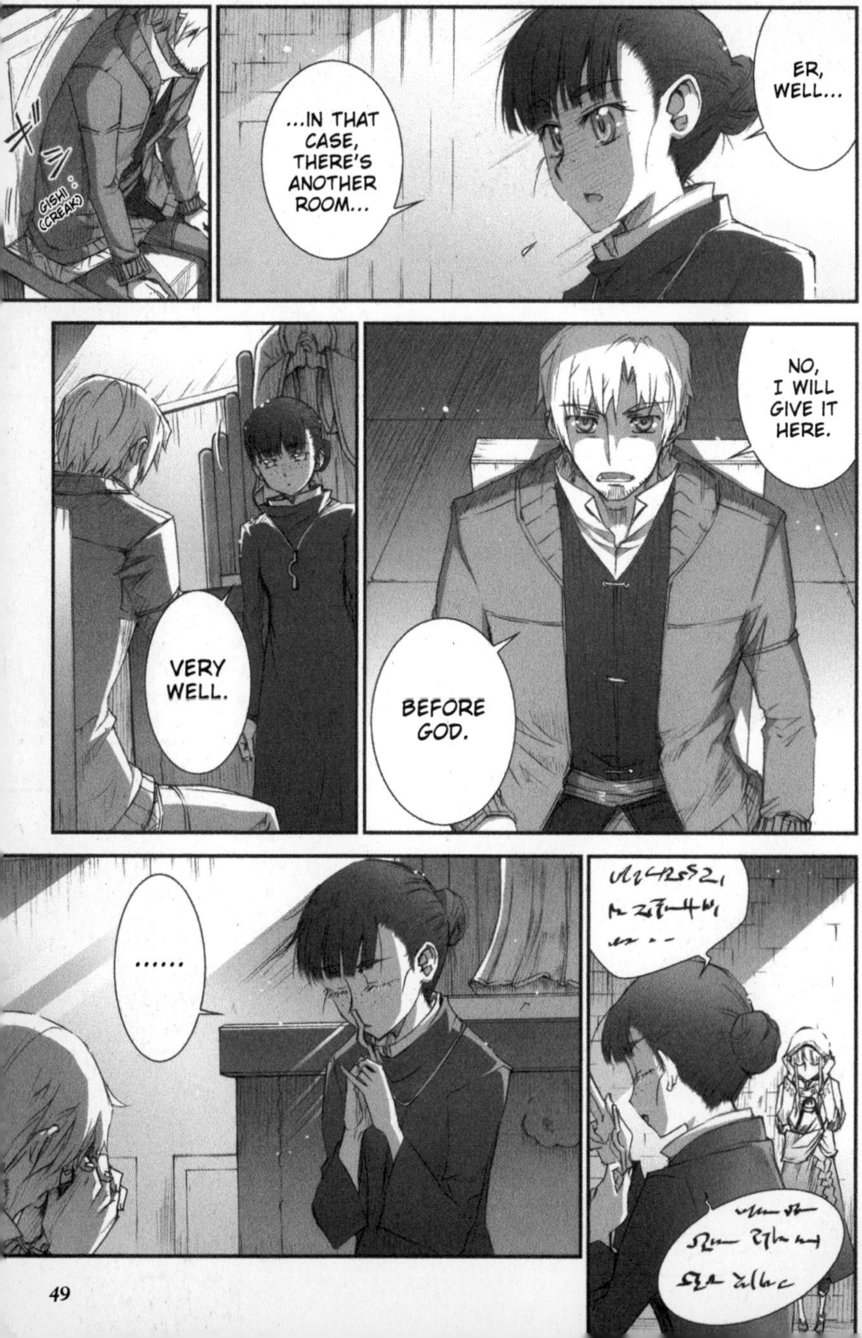
ER, WELL...
...IN THAT CASE, THERE'S ANOTHER ROOM...
GISHI (CREAK)
NO, I WILL GIVE IT HERE.
BEFORE GOD.
VERY WELL.
......

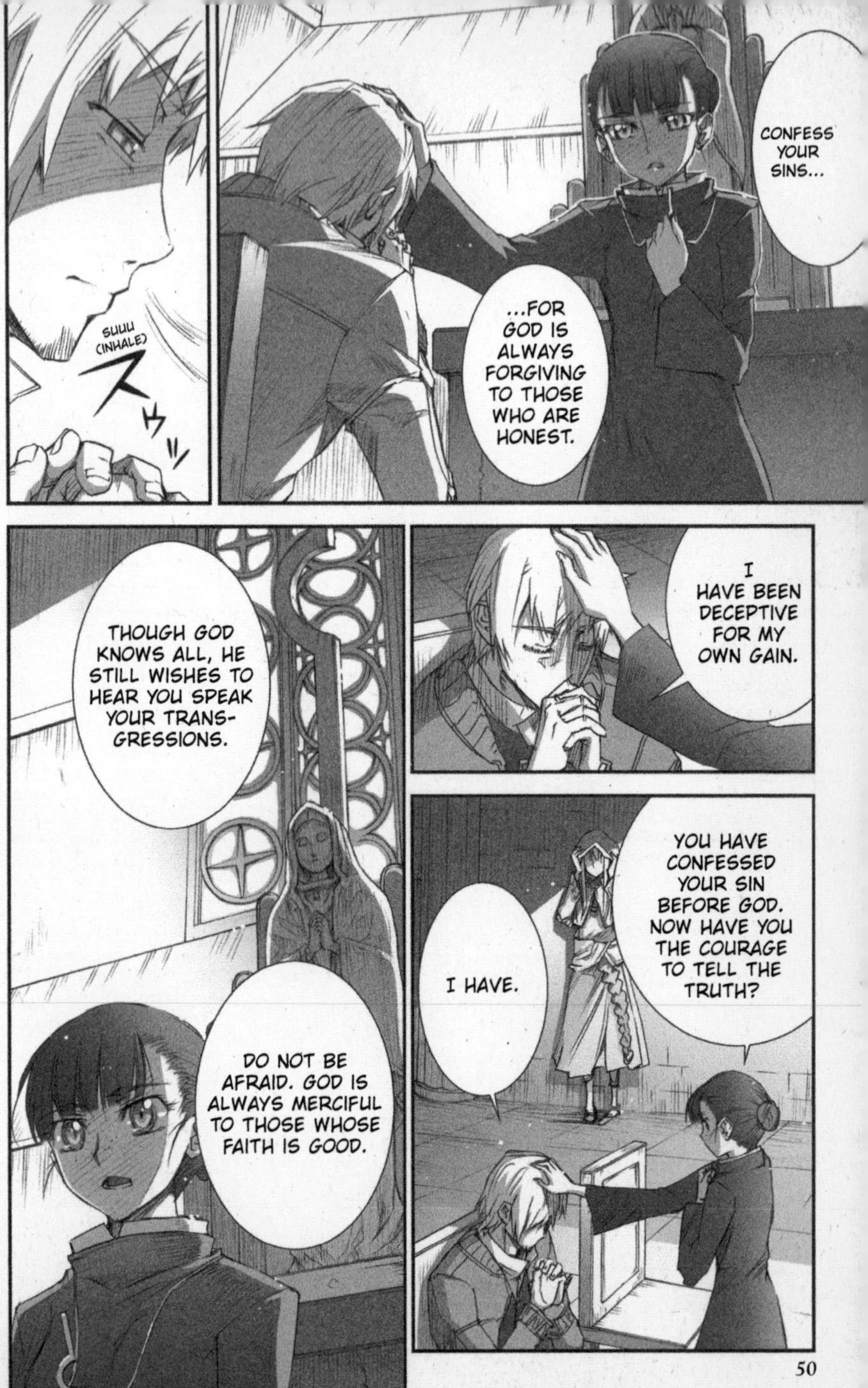
CONFESS YOUR SINS...
...FOR GOD IS ALWAYS FORGIVING TO THOSE WHO ARE HONEST.
SUUU (INHALE)
I HAVE BEEN DECEPTIVE FOR MY OWN GAIN.
THOUGH GOD KNOWS ALL, HE STILL WISHES TO HEAR YOU SPEAK YOUR TRANS-GRESSIONS.
YOU HAVE CONFESSED YOUR SIN BEFORE GOD. NOW HAVE YOU THE COURAGE TO TELL THE TRUTH?
I HAVE.
DO NOT BE AFRAID. GOD IS ALWAYS MERCIFUL TO THOSE WHOSE FAITH IS GOOD.

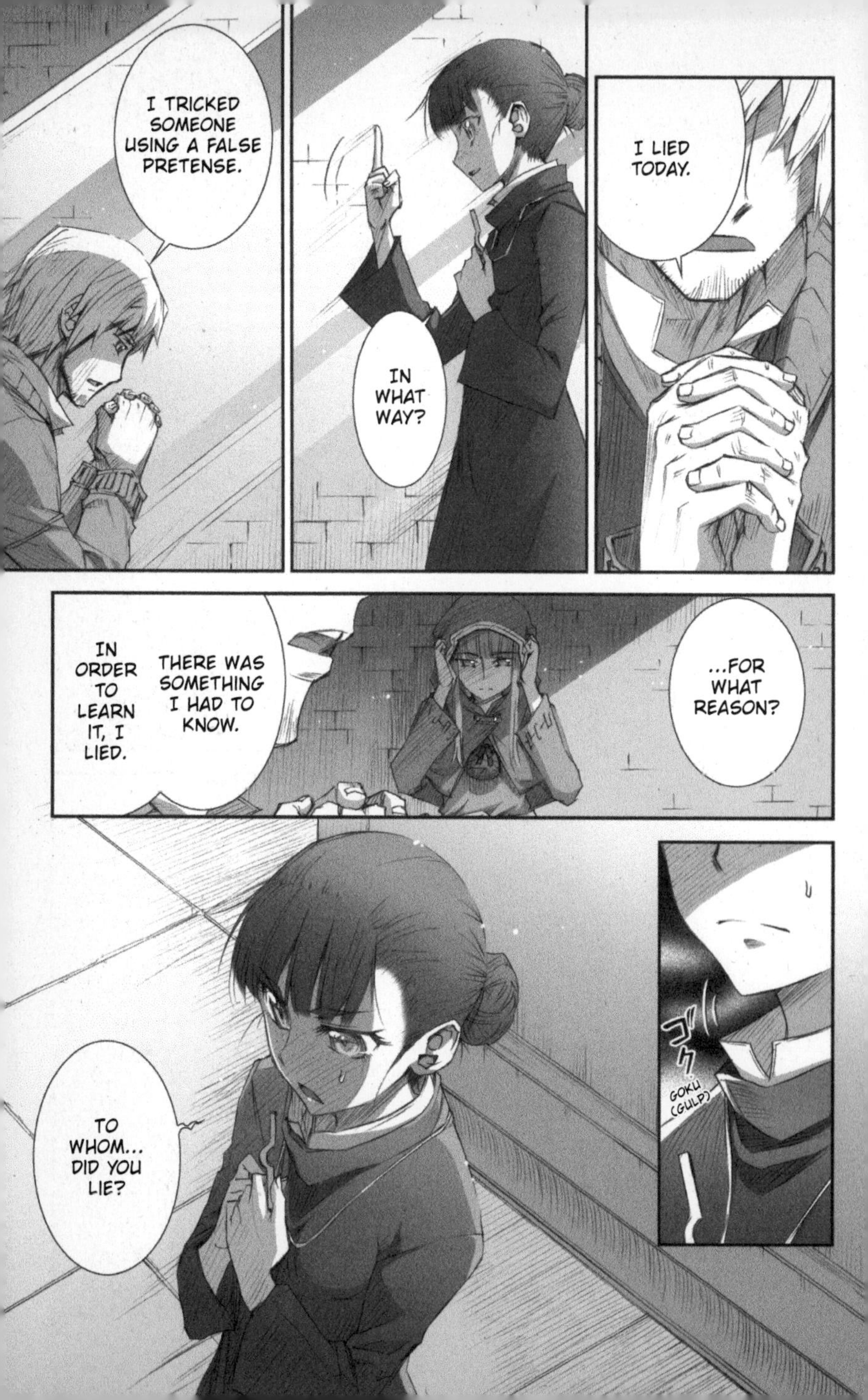
I LIED TODAY.
IN WHAT WAY?
I TRICKED SOMEONE USING A FALSE PRETENSE.
...FOR WHAT REASON?
THERE WAS SOMETHING I HAD TO KNOW.
IN ORDER TO LEARN IT, I LIED.
ゴク
GOKU (GULP)
TO WHOM... DID YOU LIE?

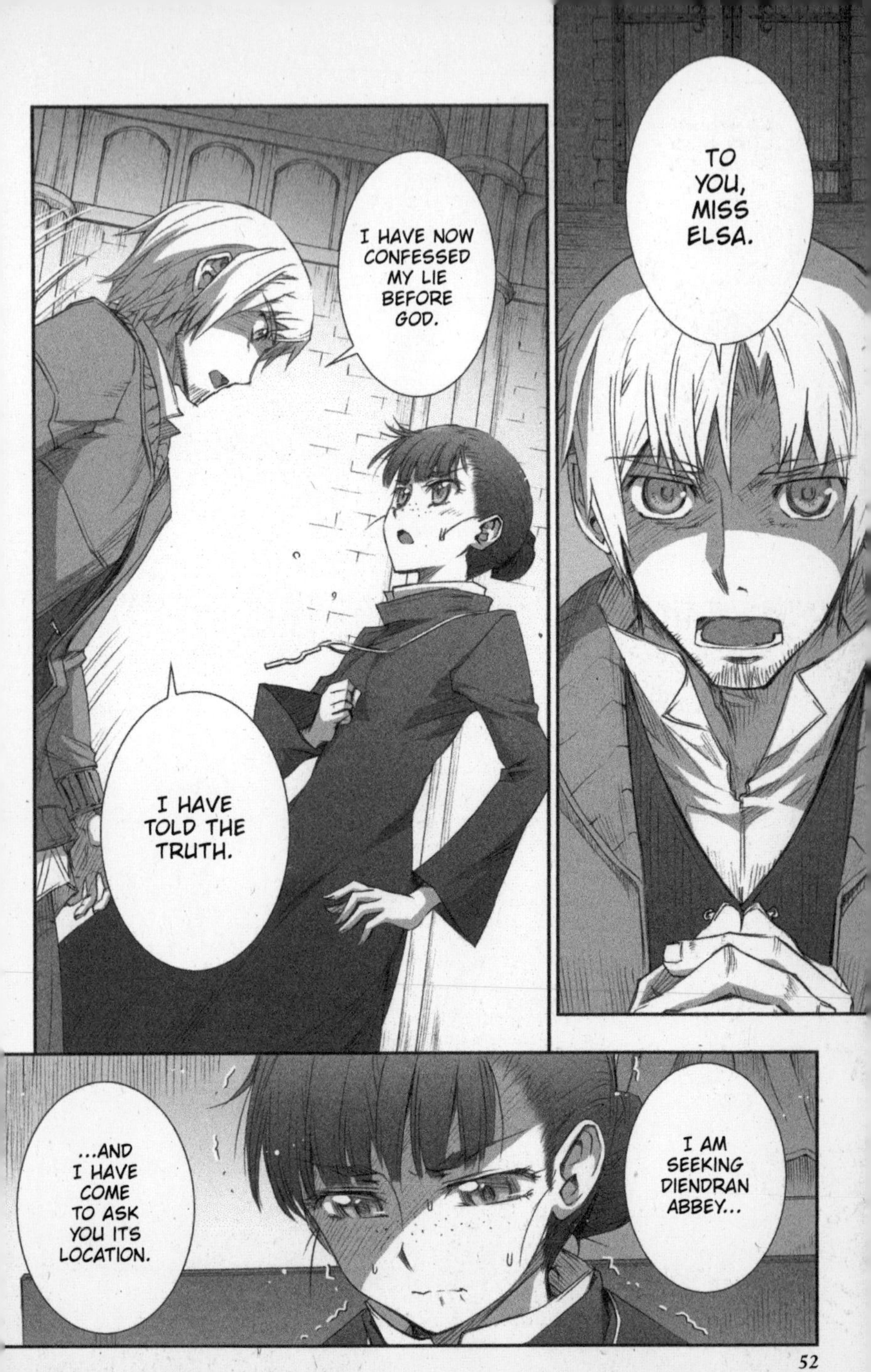
TO YOU, MISS ELSA.
I HAVE NOW CONFESSED MY LIE BEFORE GOD.
I HAVE TOLD THE TRUTH.
I AM SEEKING DIENDRAN ABBEY...
...AND I HAVE COME TO ASK YOU ITS LOCATION.

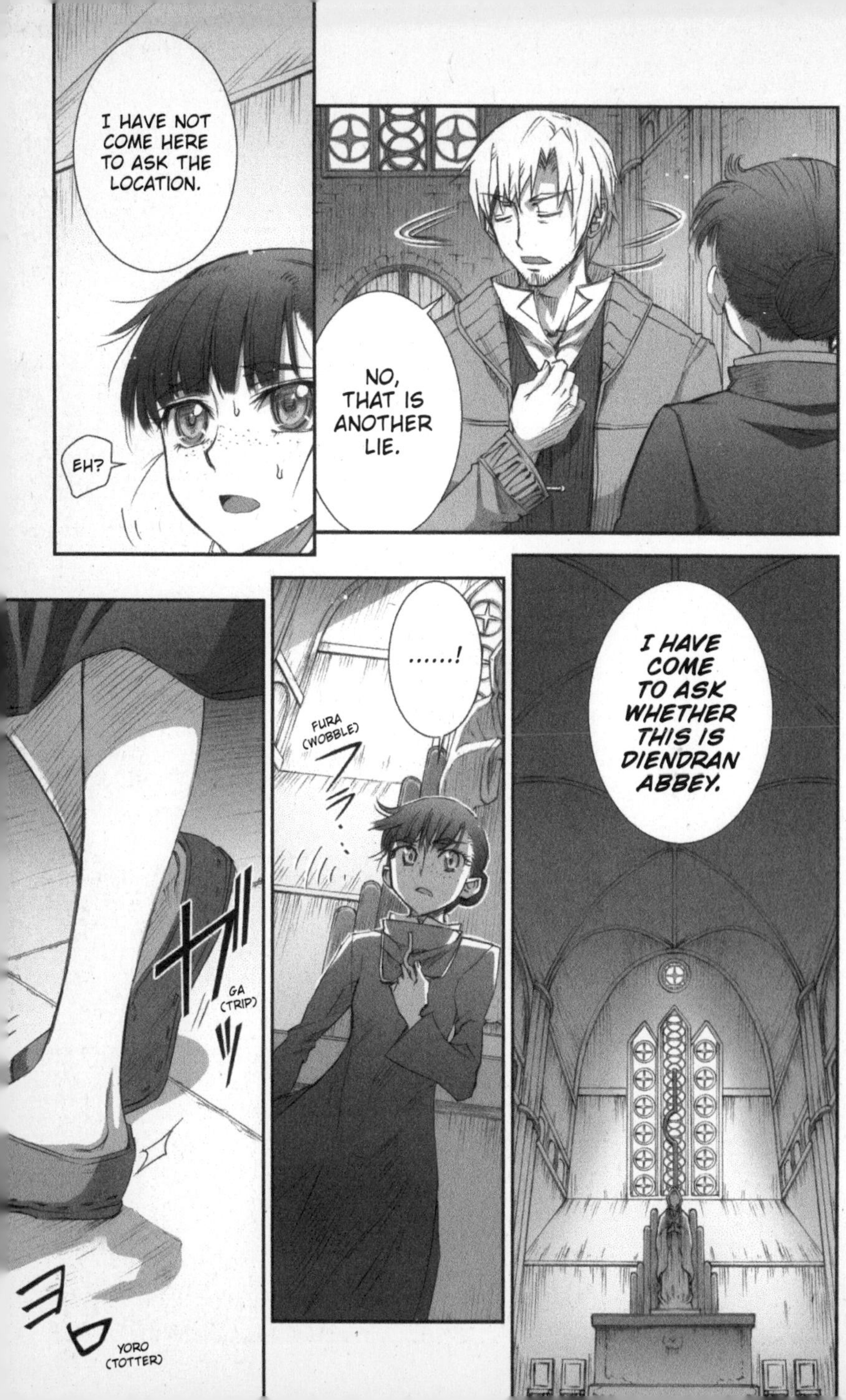
NO, THAT IS ANOTHER LIE.
I HAVE NOT COME HERE TO ASK THE LOCATION.
EH?
I HAVE COME TO ASK WHETHER THIS IS DIENDRAN ABBEY.
......!
FURA (WOBBLE)
GA (TRIP)
YORO (TOTTER)

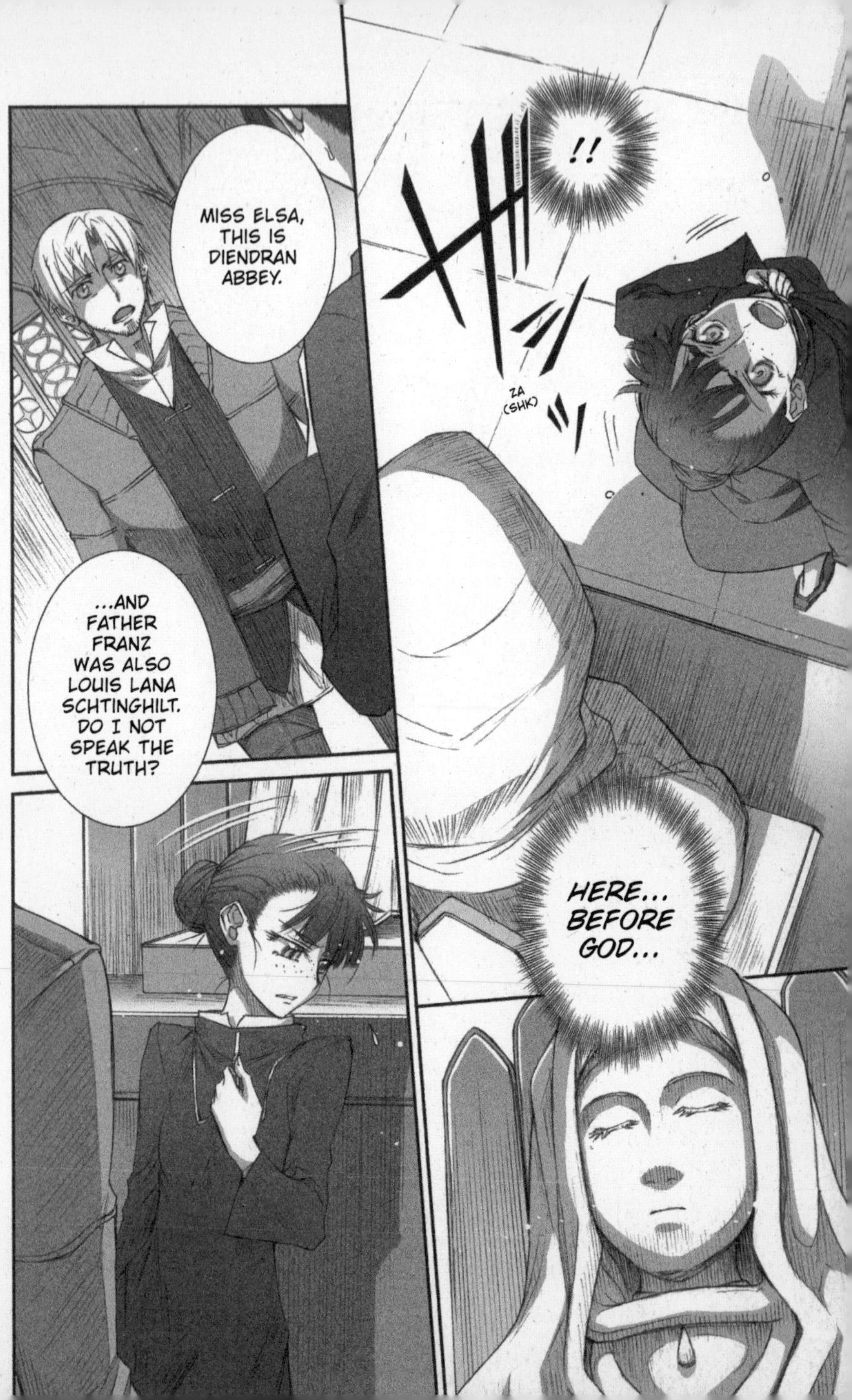
!!
ZA (SHK)
MISS ELSA, THIS IS DIENDRAN ABBEY.
...AND FATHER FRANZ WAS ALSO LOUIS LANA SCHTINGHILT. DO I NOT SPEAK THE TRUTH?
HERE... BEFORE GOD...

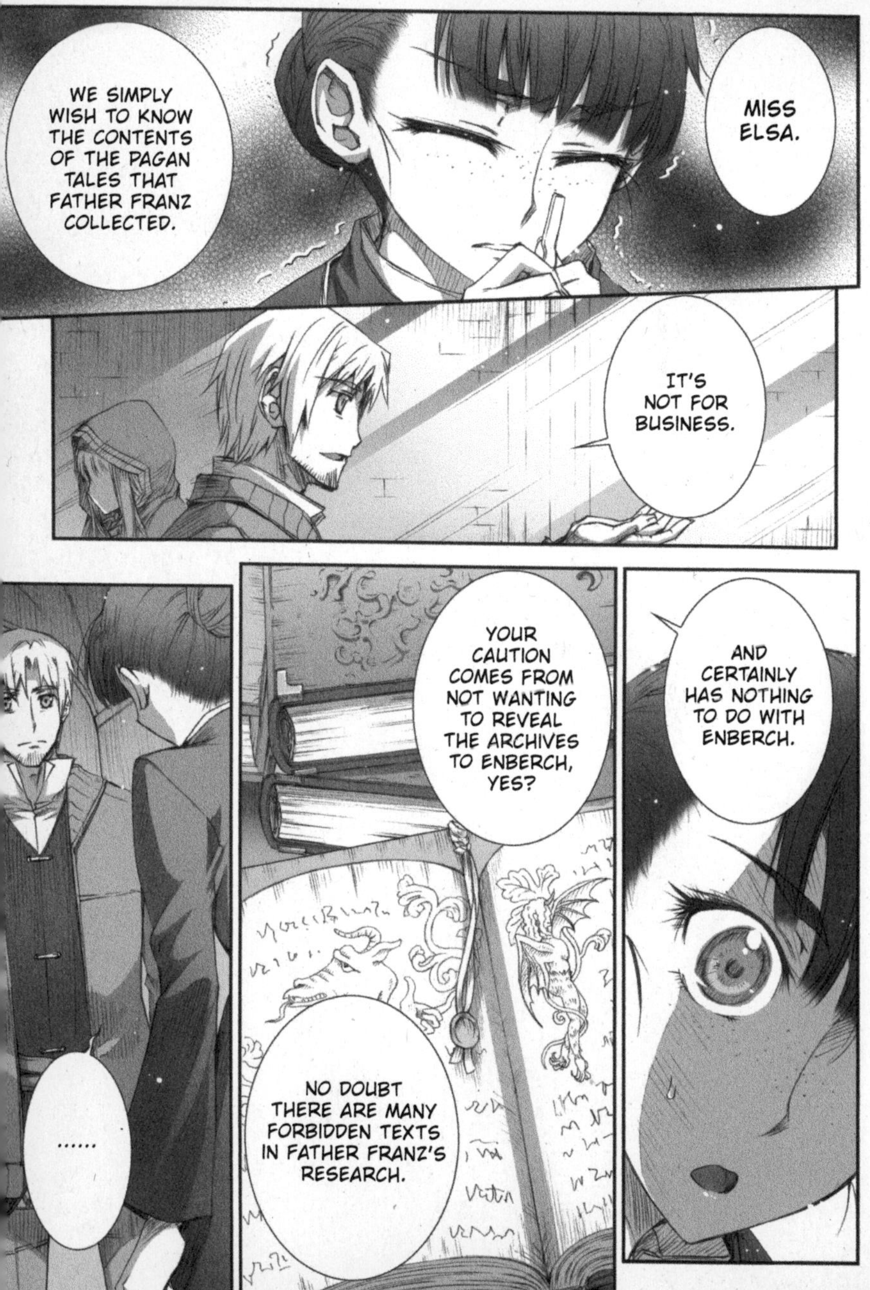
MISS ELSA.
WE SIMPLY WISH TO KNOW THE CONTENTS OF THE PAGAN TALES THAT FATHER FRANZ COLLECTED.
IT'S NOT FOR BUSINESS.
AND CERTAINLY HAS NOTHING TO DO WITH ENBERCH.
YOUR CAUTION COMES FROM NOT WANTING TO REVEAL THE ARCHIVES TO ENBERCH, YES?
NO DOUBT THERE ARE MANY FORBIDDEN TEXTS IN FATHER FRANZ'S RESEARCH.
......

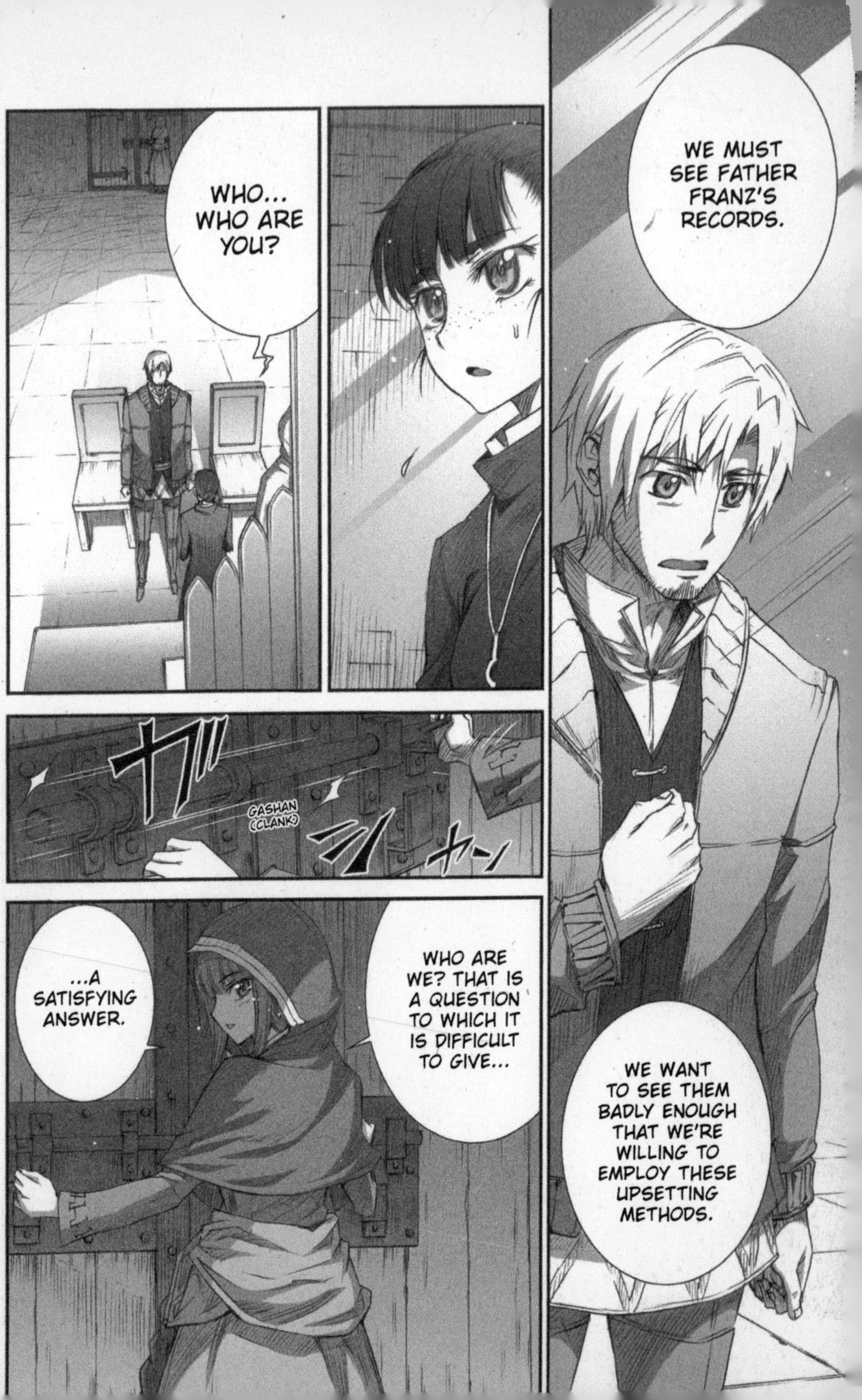
WE MUST SEE FATHER FRANZ'S RECORDS.
WE WANT TO SEE THEM BADLY ENOUGH THAT WE'RE WILLING TO EMPLOY THESE UPSETTING METHODS.
WHO... WHO ARE YOU?
GASHAN (CLANK)
WHO ARE WE? THAT IS A QUESTION TO WHICH IT IS DIFFICULT TO GIVE...
...A SATISFYING ANSWER.

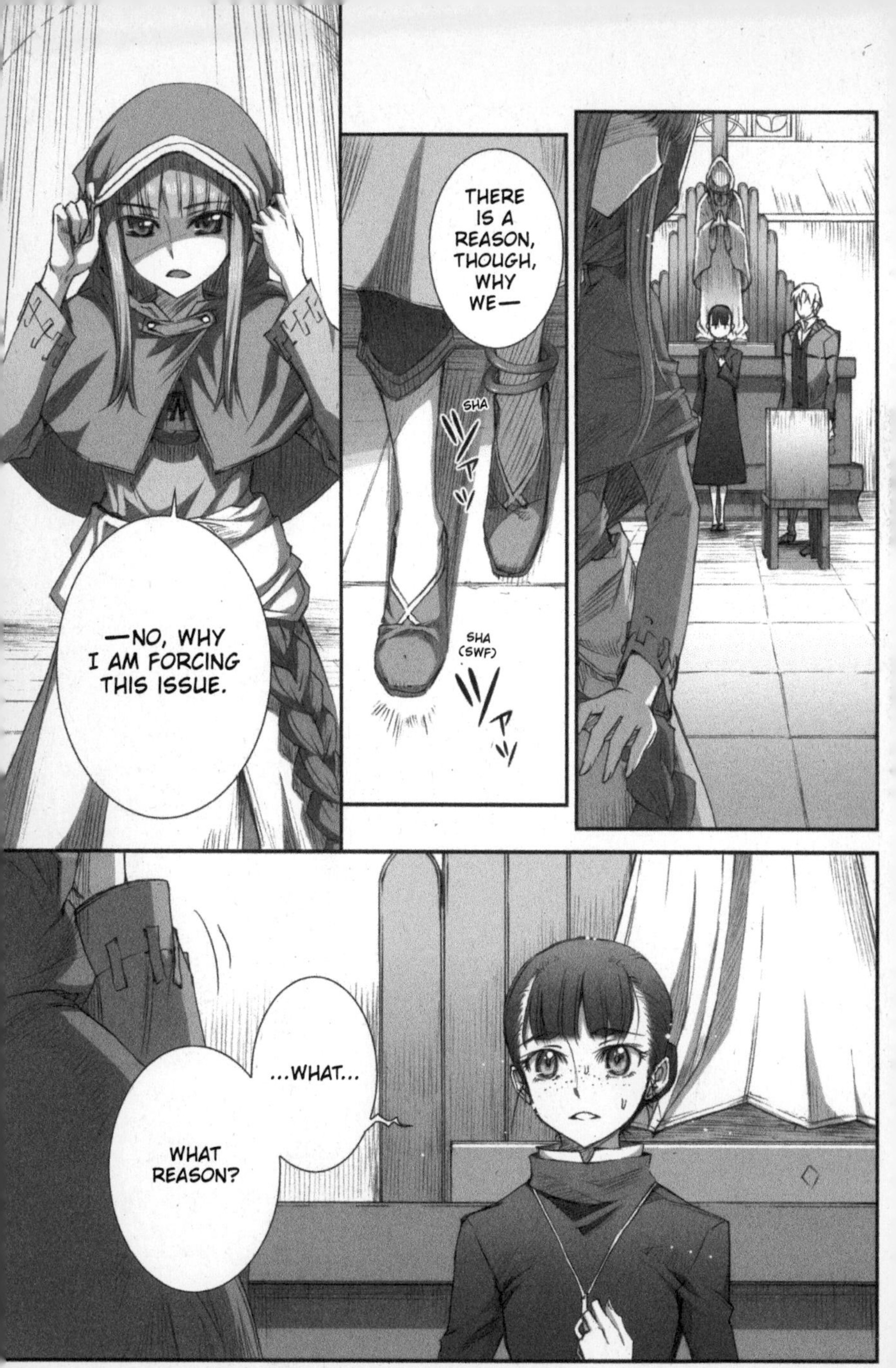
THERE IS A REASON, THOUGH, WHY WE—
SHA
SHA (SWF)
—NO, WHY I AM FORCING THIS ISSUE.
...WHAT...
WHAT REASON?

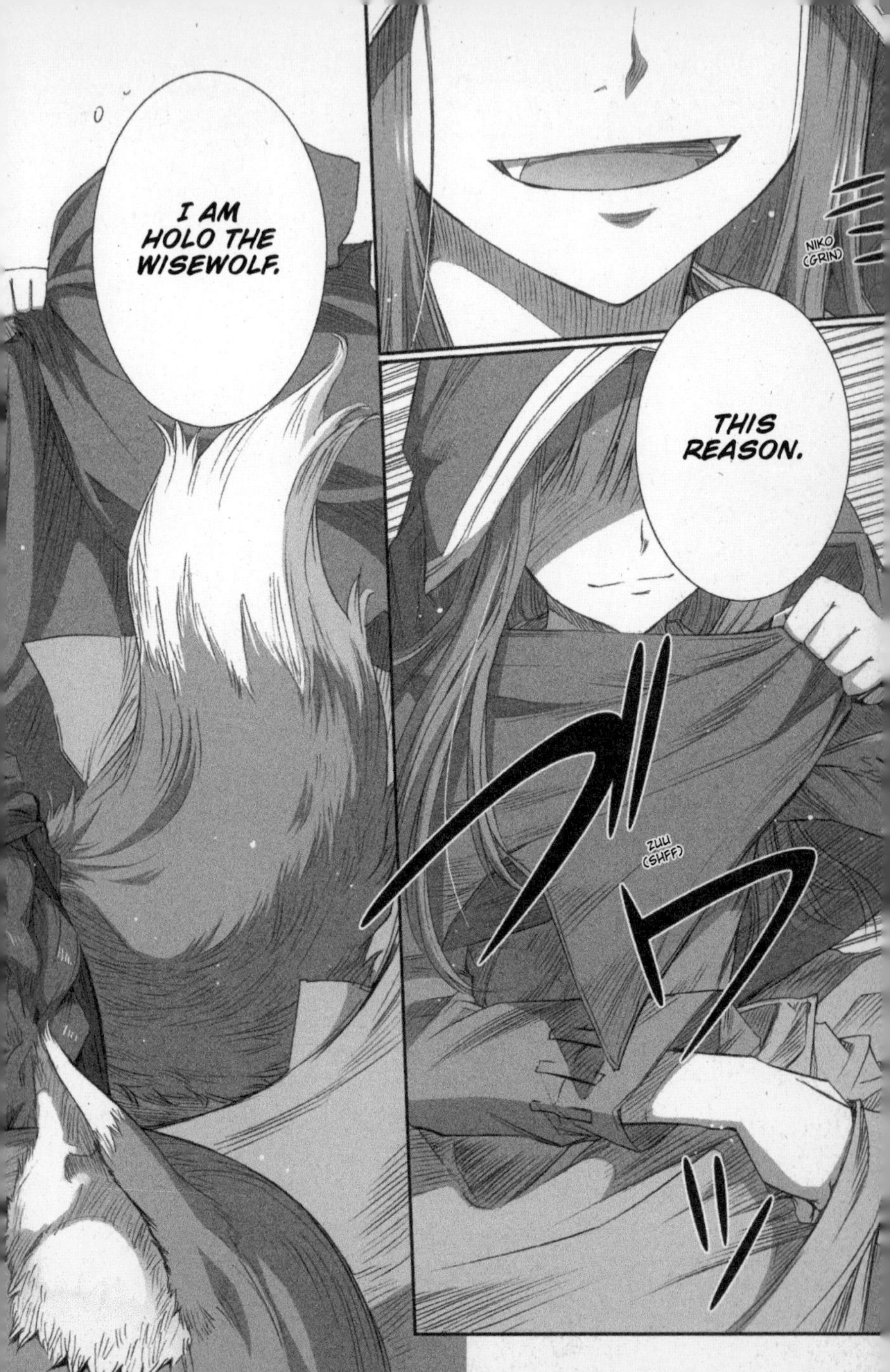
NIKO
(GRIN)
THIS REASON.
ZUU
(SHFF)
I AM HOLO THE WISEWOLF.

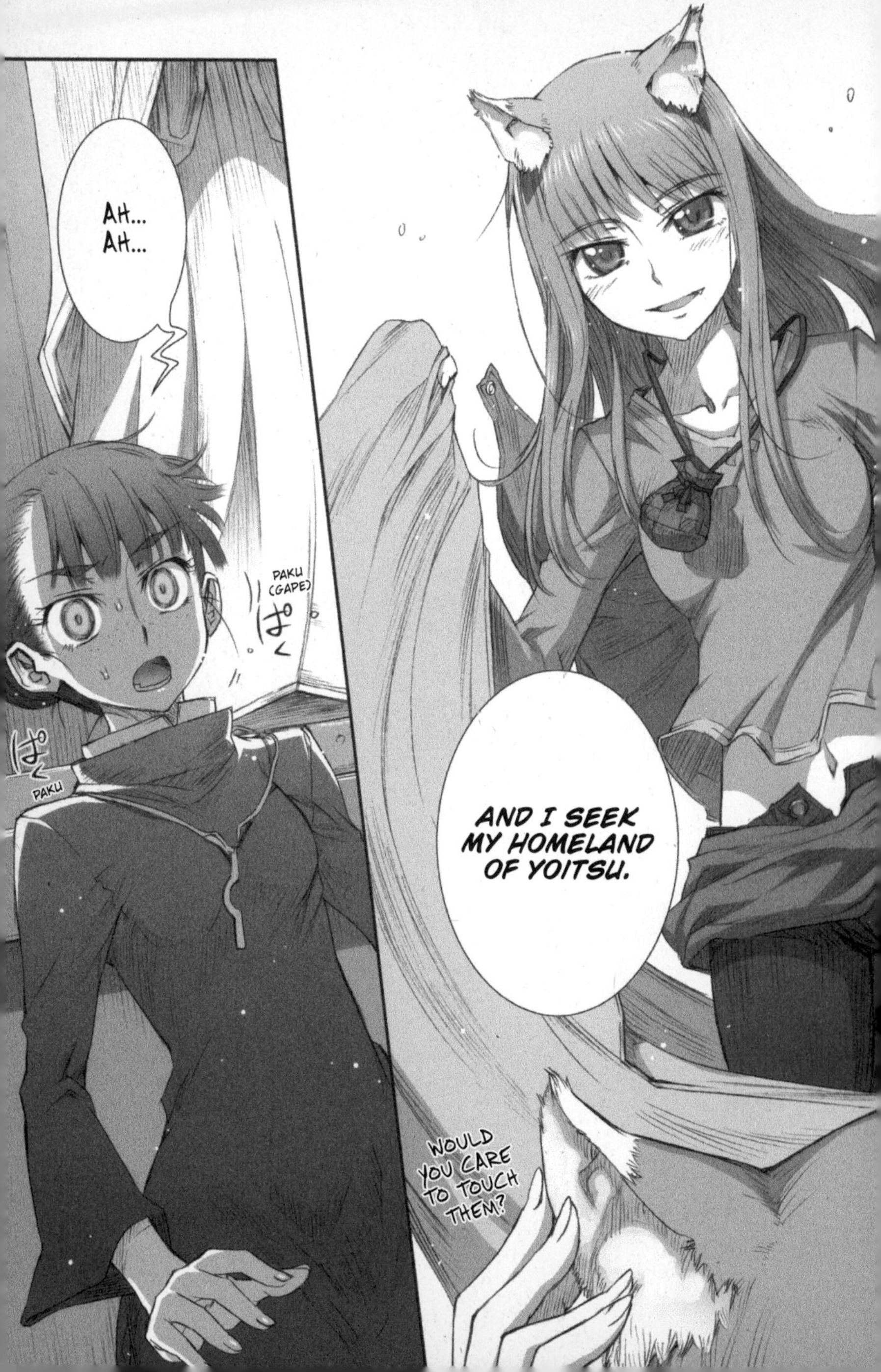
AND I SEEK MY HOMELAND OF YOITSU.
WOULD YOU CARE TO TOUCH THEM?
AH... AH...
ぱく
PAKU (GAPE)
ぱく
PAKU

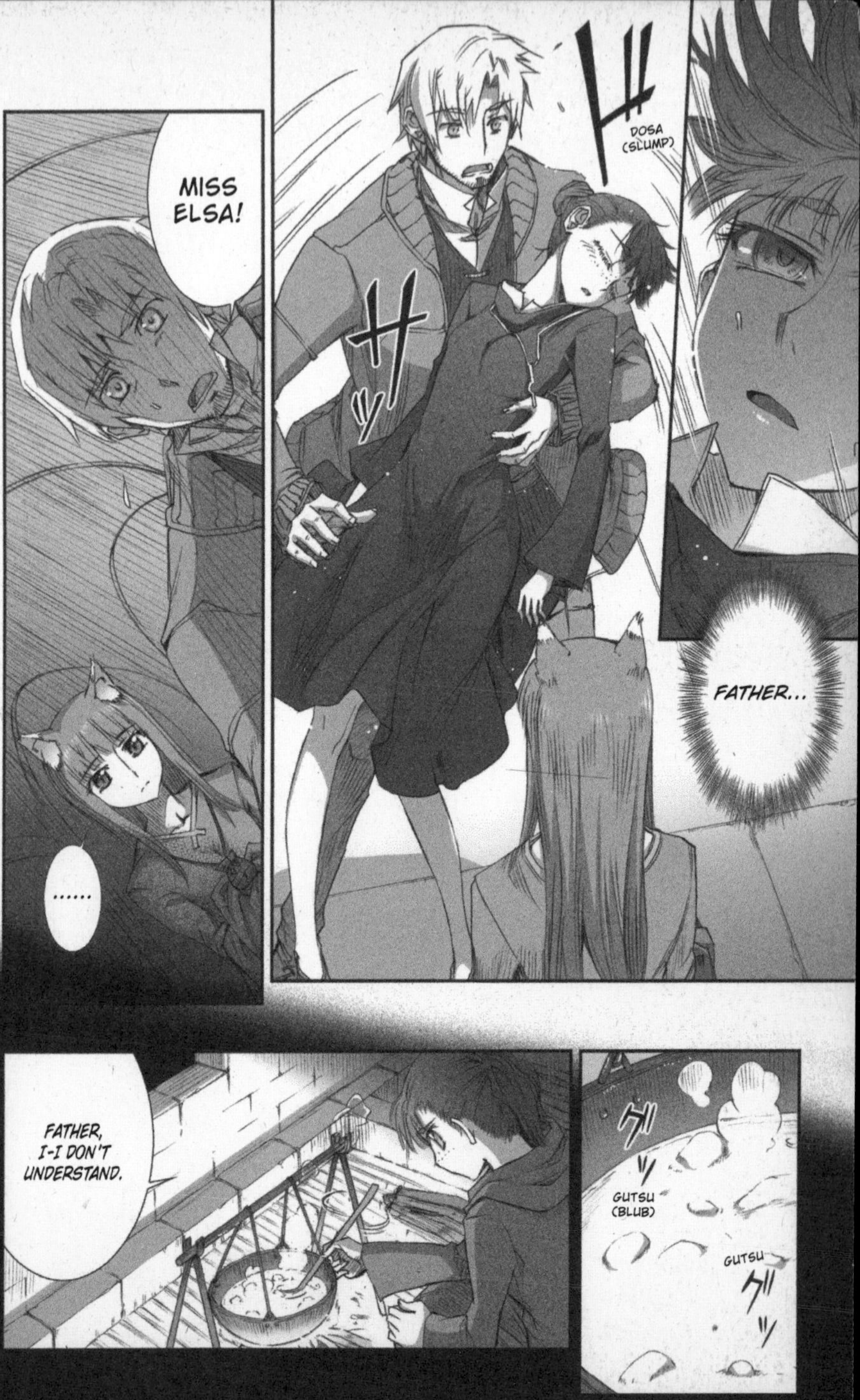
FATHER...
DOSA (SLUMP)
MISS ELSA!
......
GUTSU (BLUB)
GUTSU
FATHER, I-I DON'T UNDERSTAND.

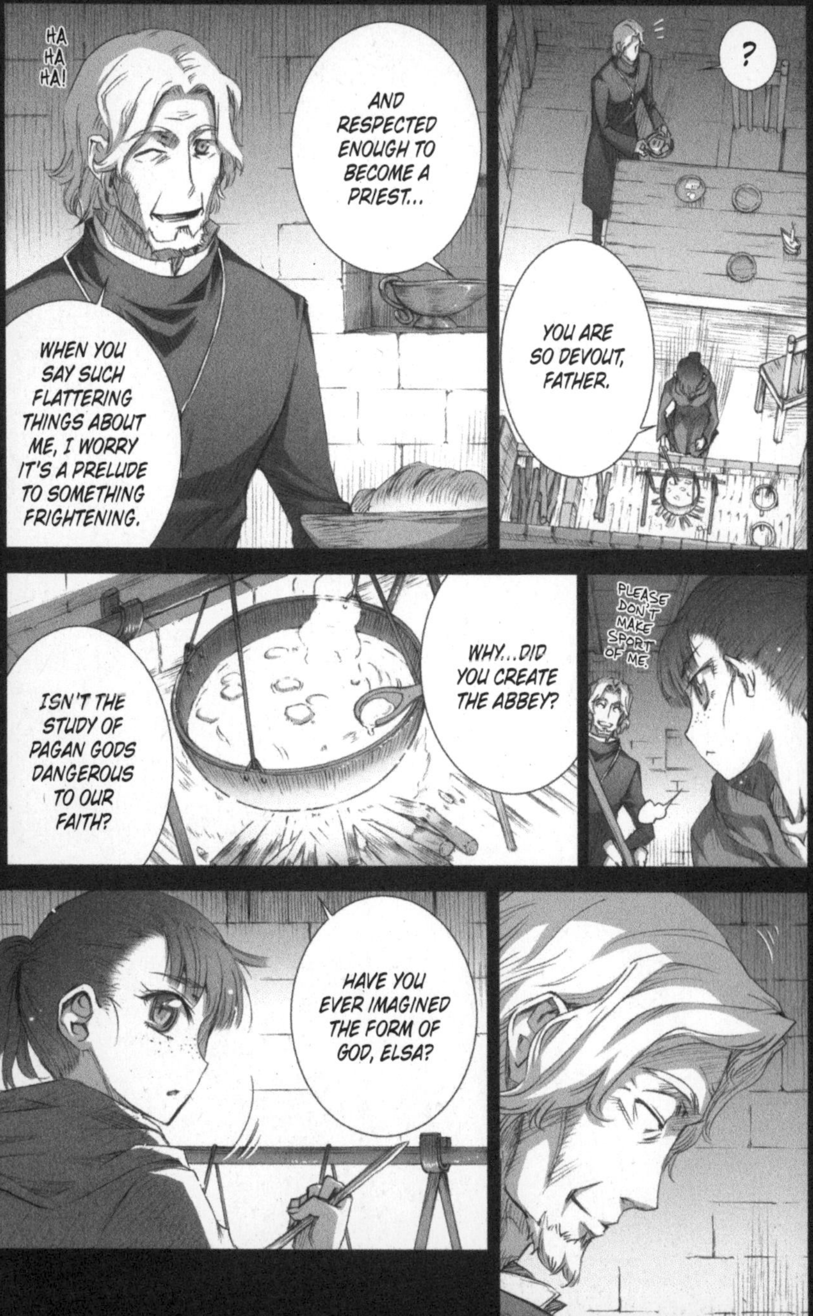
?
YOU ARE SO DEVOUT, FATHER.
AND RESPECTED ENOUGH TO BECOME A PRIEST...
HA HA HA!
WHEN YOU SAY SUCH FLATTERING THINGS ABOUT ME, I WORRY IT'S A PRELUDE TO SOMETHING FRIGHTENING.
PLEASE DON'T MAKE SPORT OF ME.
WHY...DID YOU CREATE THE ABBEY?
ISN'T THE STUDY OF PAGAN GODS DANGEROUS TO OUR FAITH?
HAVE YOU EVER IMAGINED THE FORM OF GOD, ELSA?

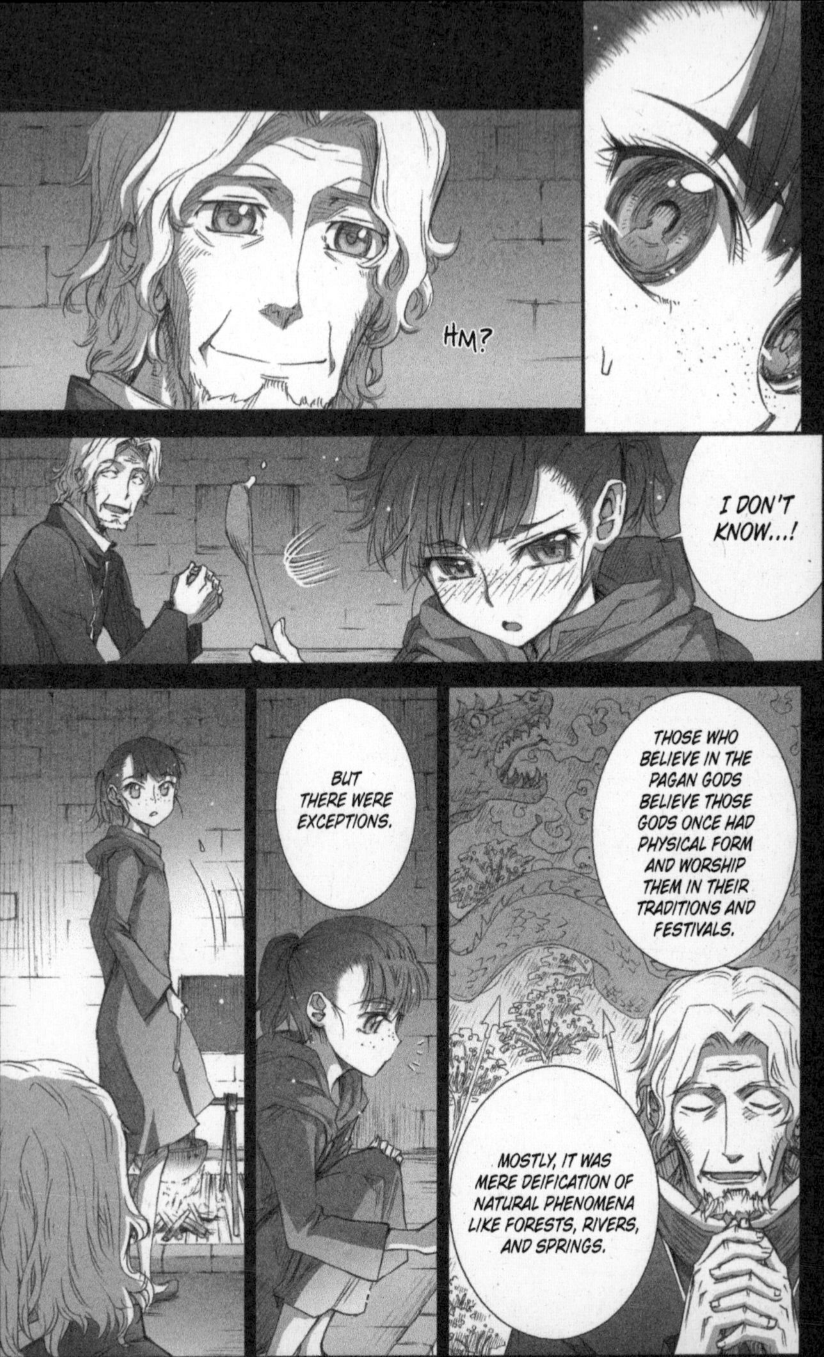
HM?
I DON'T KNOW...!
THOSE WHO BELIEVE IN THE PAGAN GODS BELIEVE THOSE GODS ONCE HAD PHYSICAL FORM AND WORSHIP THEM IN THEIR TRADITIONS AND FESTIVALS.
MOSTLY, IT WAS MERE DEIFICATION OF NATURAL PHENOMENA LIKE FORESTS, RIVERS, AND SPRINGS.
BUT THERE WERE EXCEPTIONS.

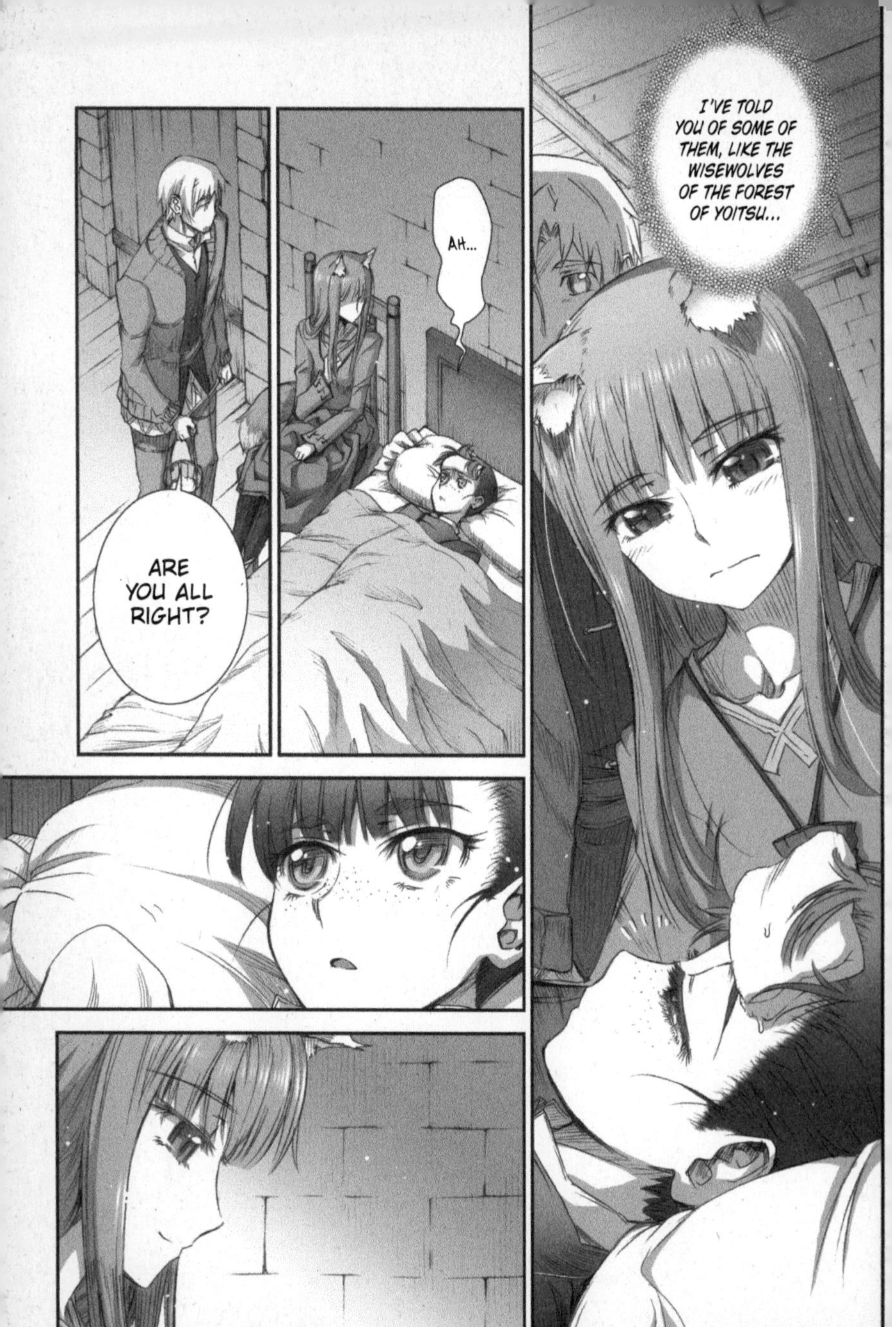
I'VE TOLD YOU OF SOME OF THEM, LIKE THE WISEWOLVES OF THE FOREST OF YOITSU...
AH...
ARE YOU ALL RIGHT?

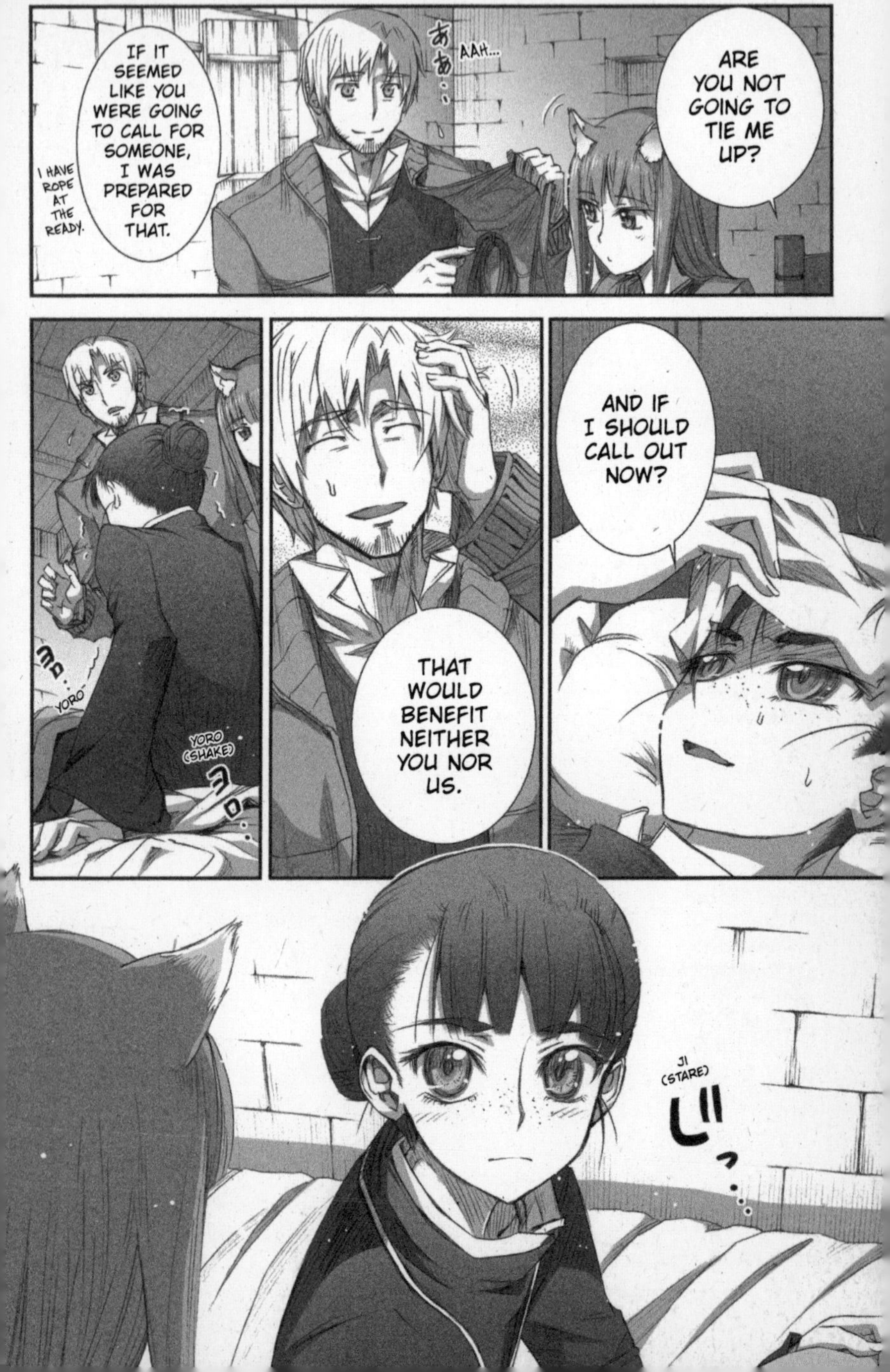
ARE YOU NOT GOING TO TIE ME UP?
ああ・・
AAH...
IF IT SEEMED LIKE YOU WERE GOING TO CALL FOR SOMEONE, I WAS PREPARED FOR THAT.
I HAVE ROPE AT THE READY.
AND IF I SHOULD CALL OUT NOW?
THAT WOULD BENEFIT NEITHER YOU NOR US.
ヨロ…
YORO
YORO (SHAKE)
ヨロ・・
JI (STARE)
じっ・・・

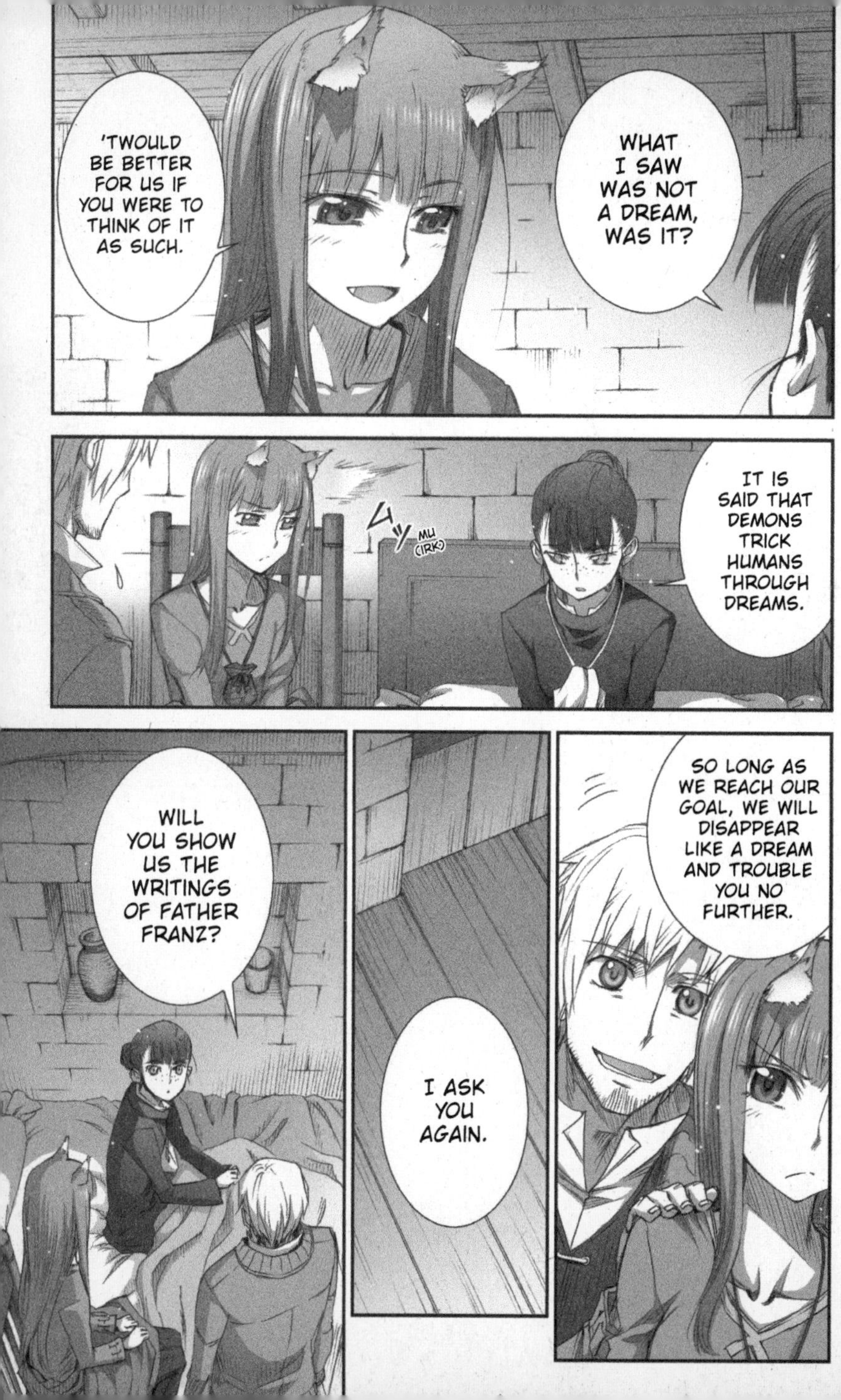
WHAT I SAW WAS NOT A DREAM, WAS IT?
'TWOULD BE BETTER FOR US IF YOU WERE TO THINK OF IT AS SUCH.
IT IS SAID THAT DEMONS TRICK HUMANS THROUGH DREAMS.
MU (IRK)
SO LONG AS WE REACH OUR GOAL, WE WILL DISAPPEAR LIKE A DREAM AND TROUBLE YOU NO FURTHER.
I ASK YOU AGAIN.
WILL YOU SHOW US THE WRITINGS OF FATHER FRANZ?

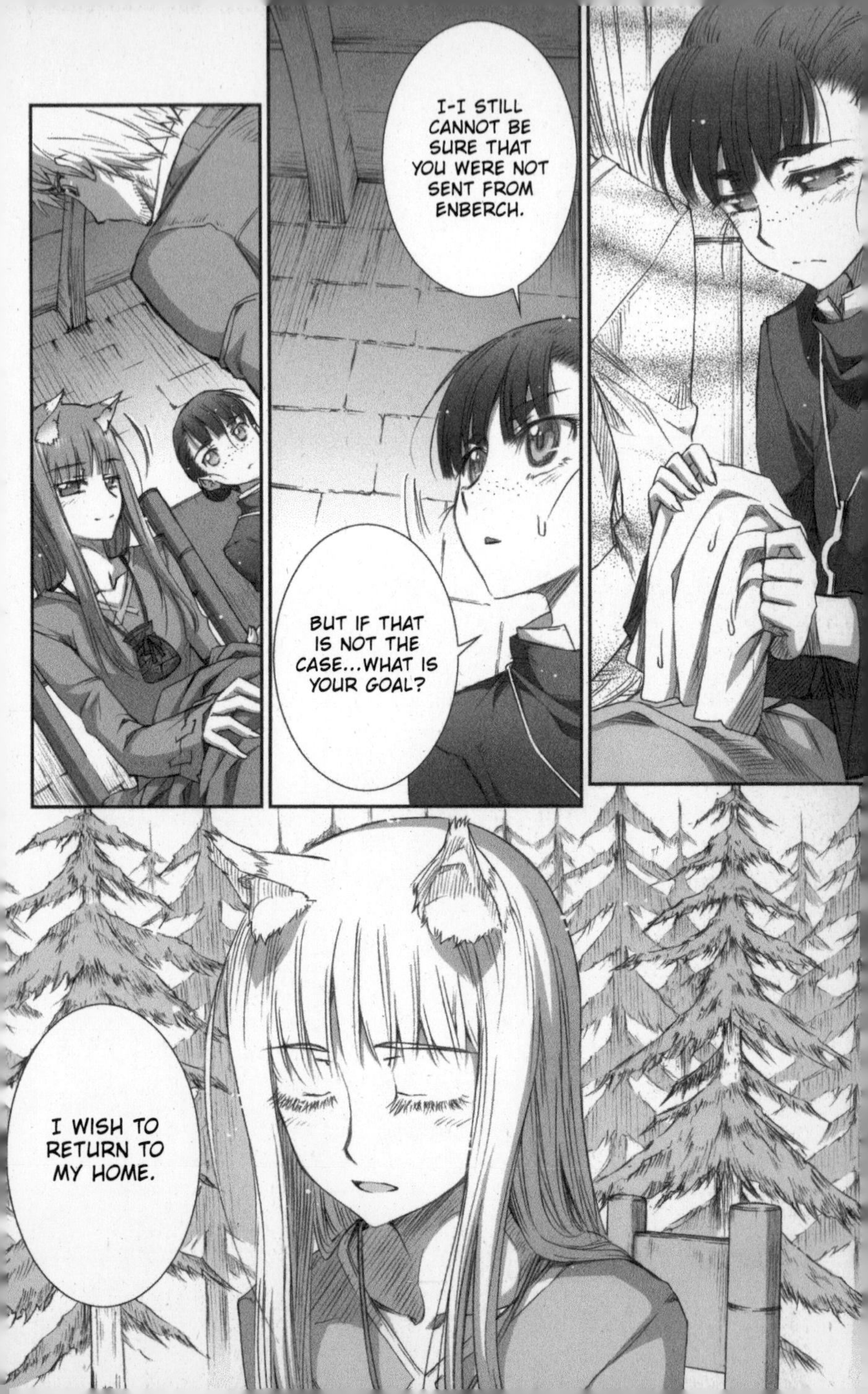
I-I STILL CANNOT BE SURE THAT YOU WERE NOT SENT FROM ENBERCH.
BUT IF THAT IS NOT THE CASE...WHAT IS YOUR GOAL?
I WISH TO RETURN TO MY HOME.

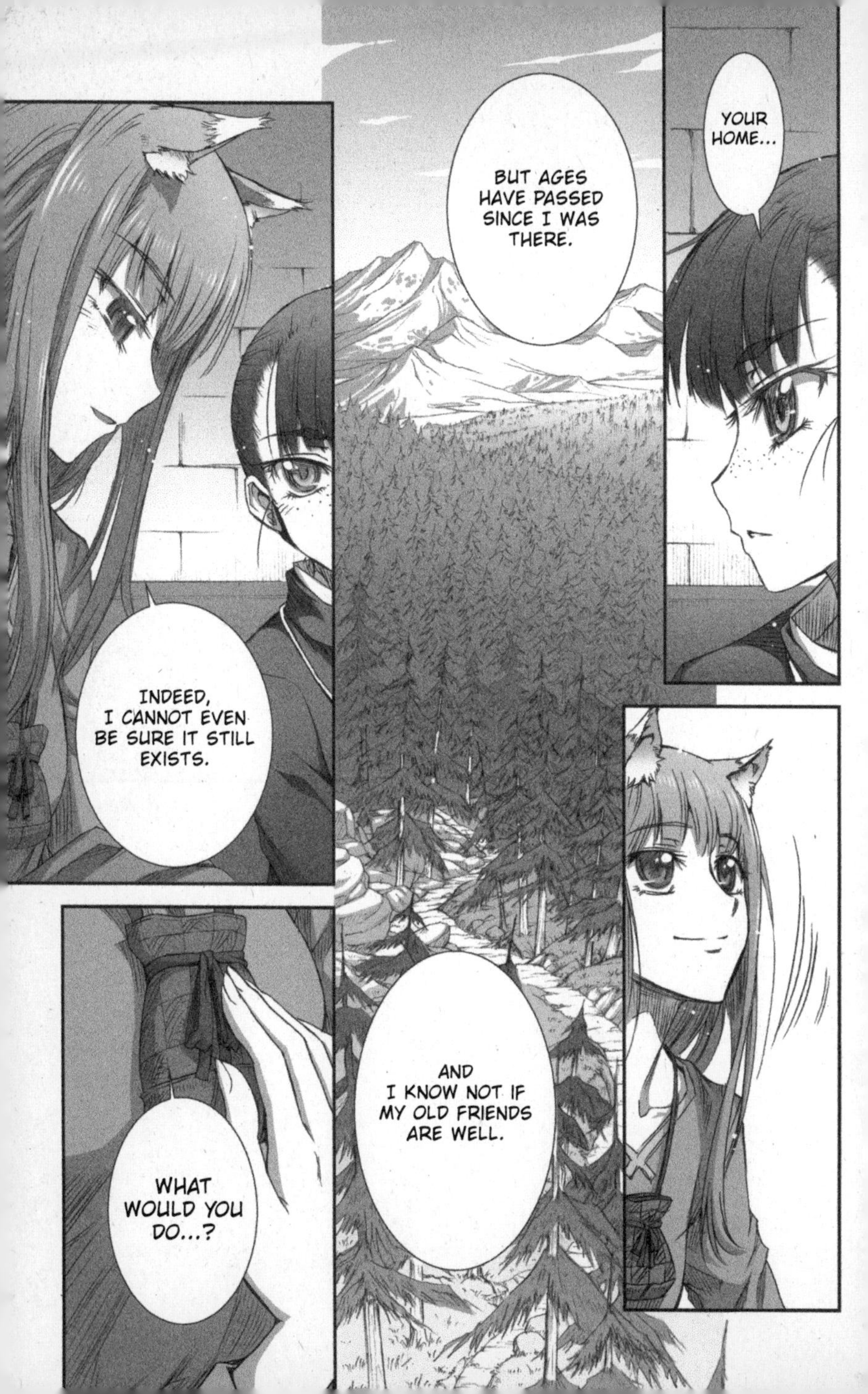
YOUR HOME...
BUT AGES HAVE PASSED SINCE I WAS THERE.
INDEED, I CANNOT EVEN BE SURE IT STILL EXISTS.
AND I KNOW NOT IF MY OLD FRIENDS ARE WELL.
WHAT WOULD YOU DO...?

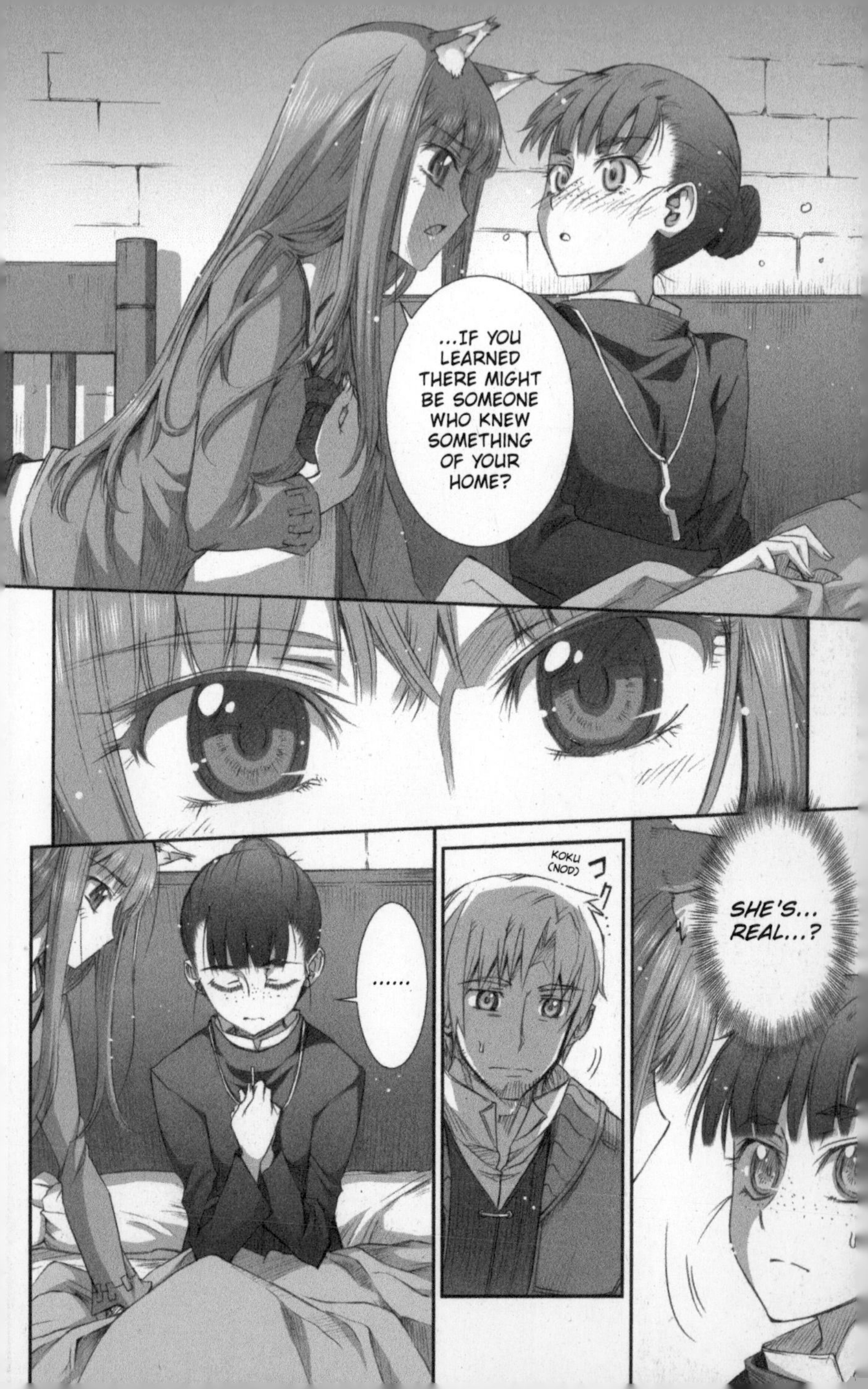
...IF YOU LEARNED THERE MIGHT BE SOMEONE WHO KNEW SOMETHING OF YOUR HOME?
SHE'S... REAL...?
KOKU (NOD)
......

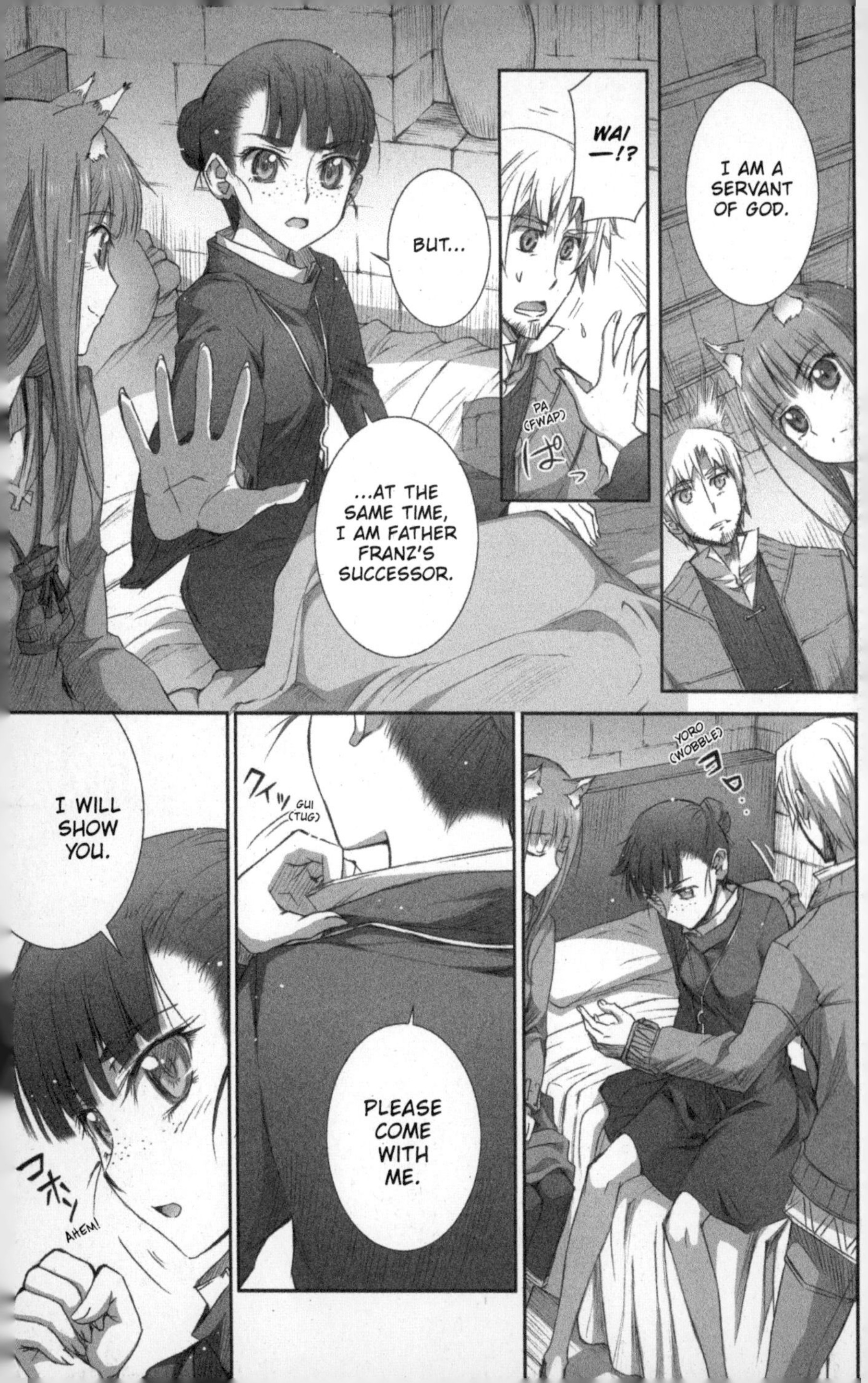
I AM A SERVANT OF GOD.
WAI —!?
PA (FWAP)
ぱっ
BUT...
...AT THE SAME TIME, I AM FATHER FRANZ'S SUCCESSOR.
YORO (WOBBLE)
ヨロ
グイッ
GUI (TUG)
PLEASE COME WITH ME.
I WILL SHOW YOU.
コホン
AHEM!

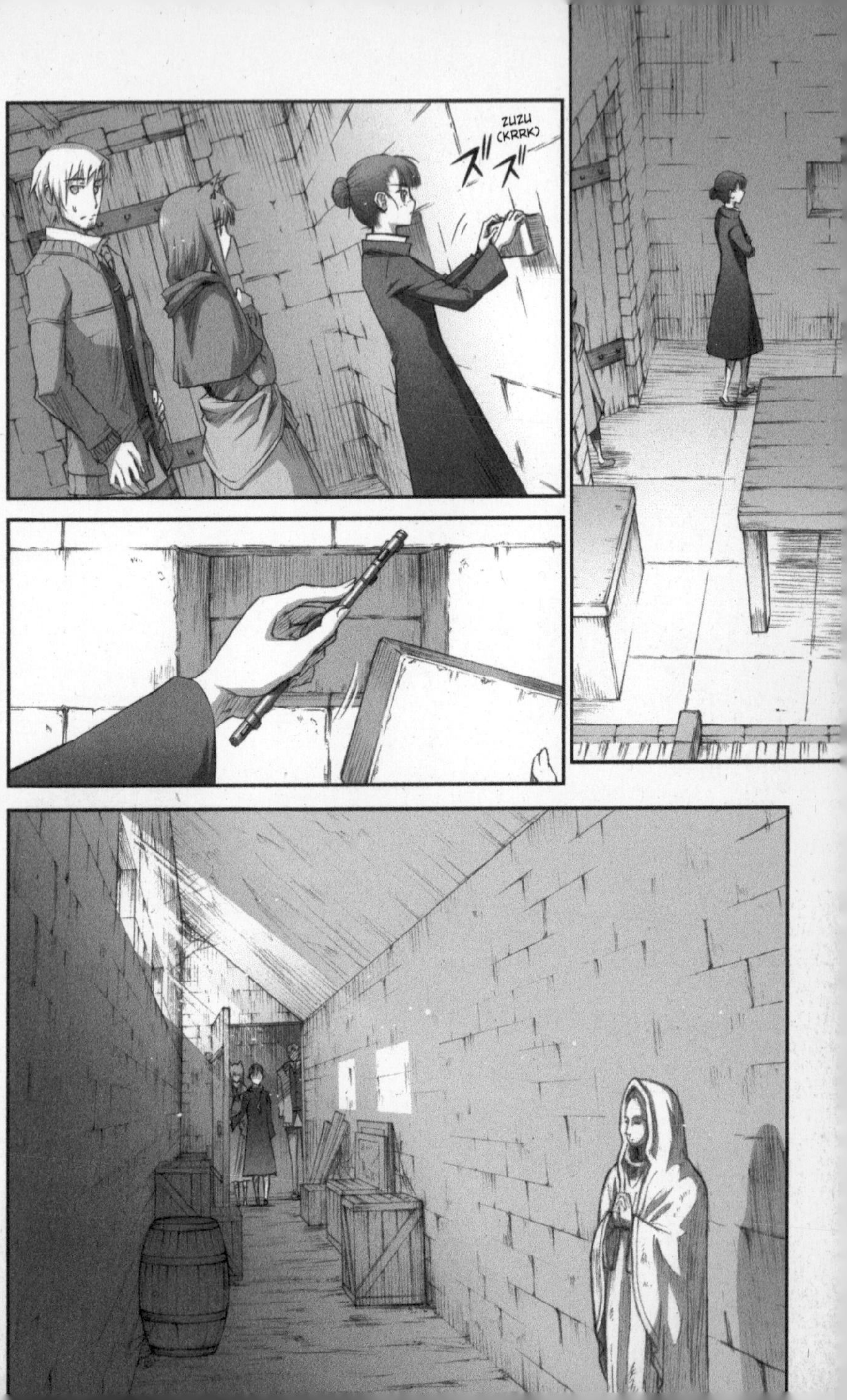
ZUZU (KRRK)
ズズ

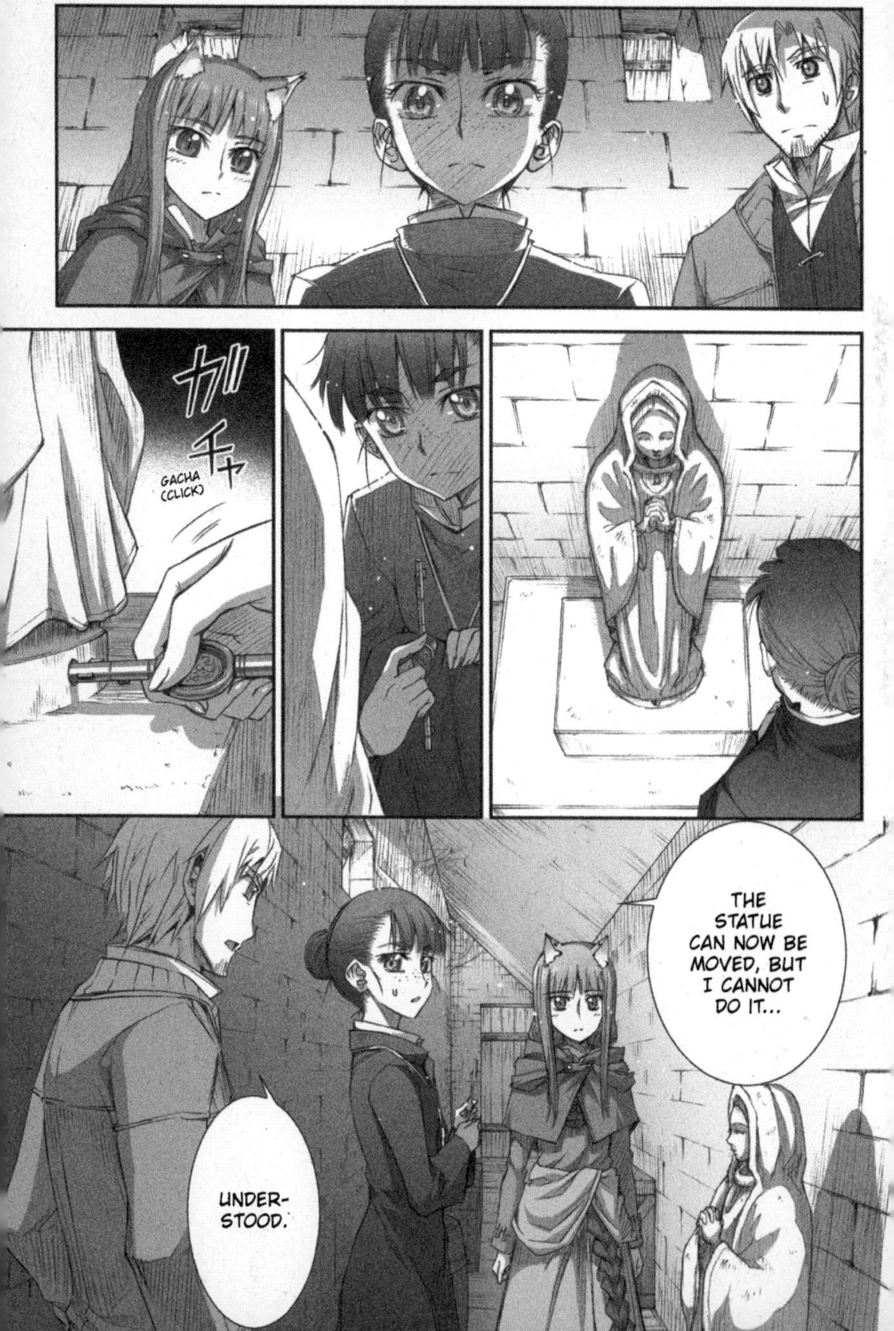
ガチャ
GACHA (CLICK)
THE STATUE CAN NOW BE MOVED, BUT I CANNOT DO IT...
UNDER-STOOD.

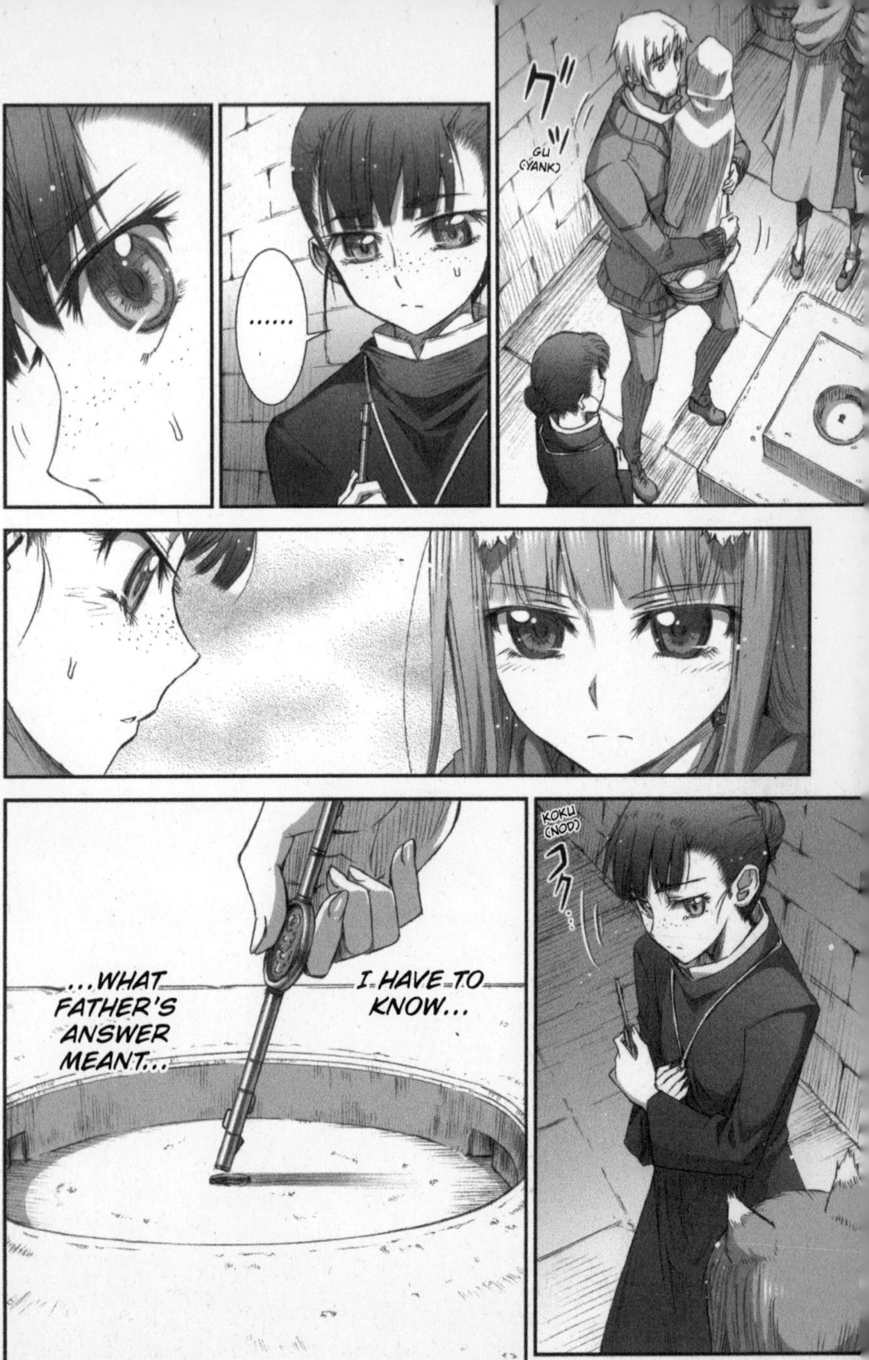

グッ
GU (YANK)
......
KOKU (NOD)
コク...
I HAVE TO KNOW...
...WHAT FATHER'S ANSWER MEANT...

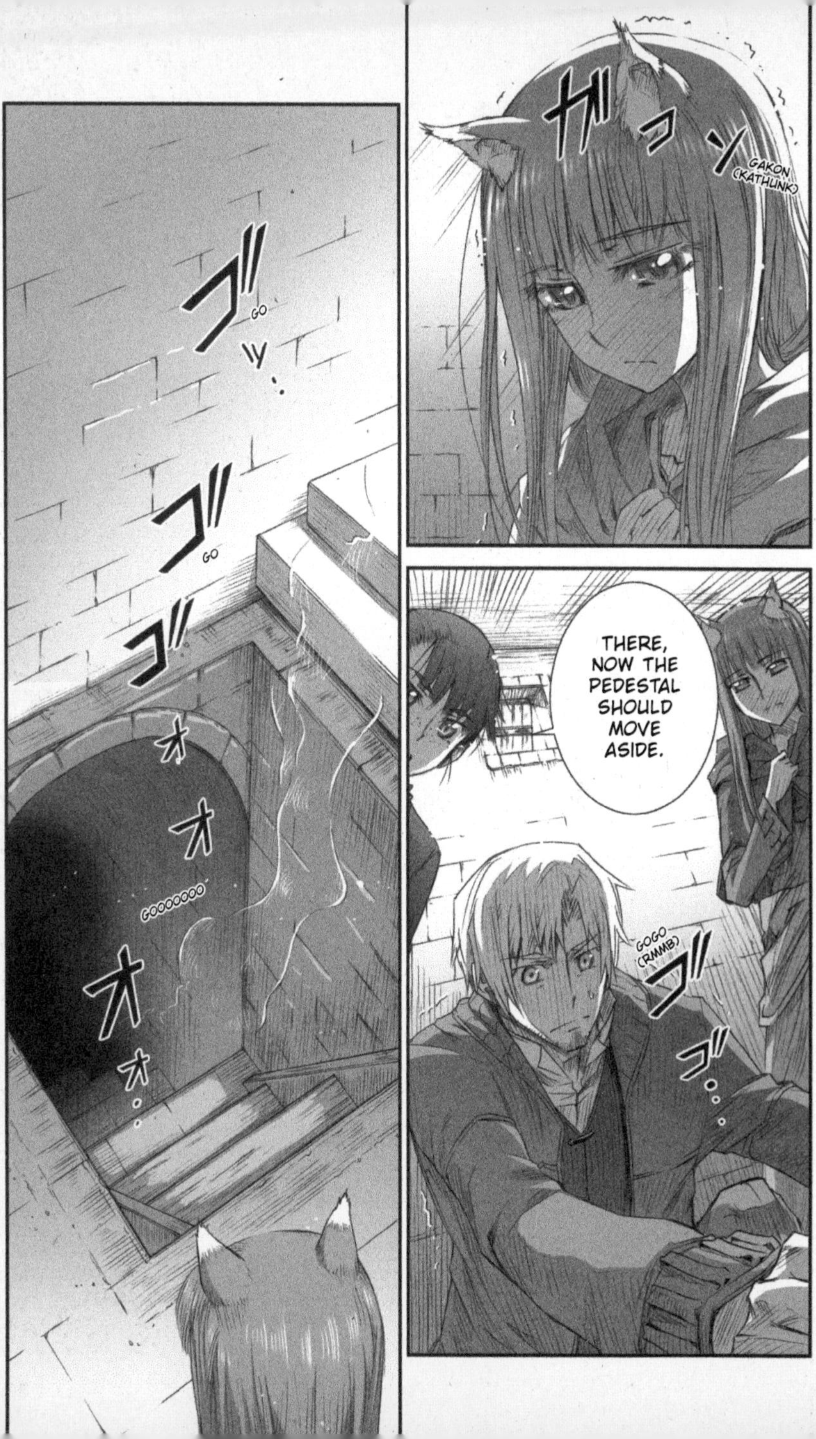
ガコン
GAKON (KATHUNK)
THERE, NOW THE PEDESTAL SHOULD MOVE ASIDE.
ゴゴ
GOGO (RMMB)
ゴッ
GO
ゴ
GO
ゴオオオオ
GOOOOOOO

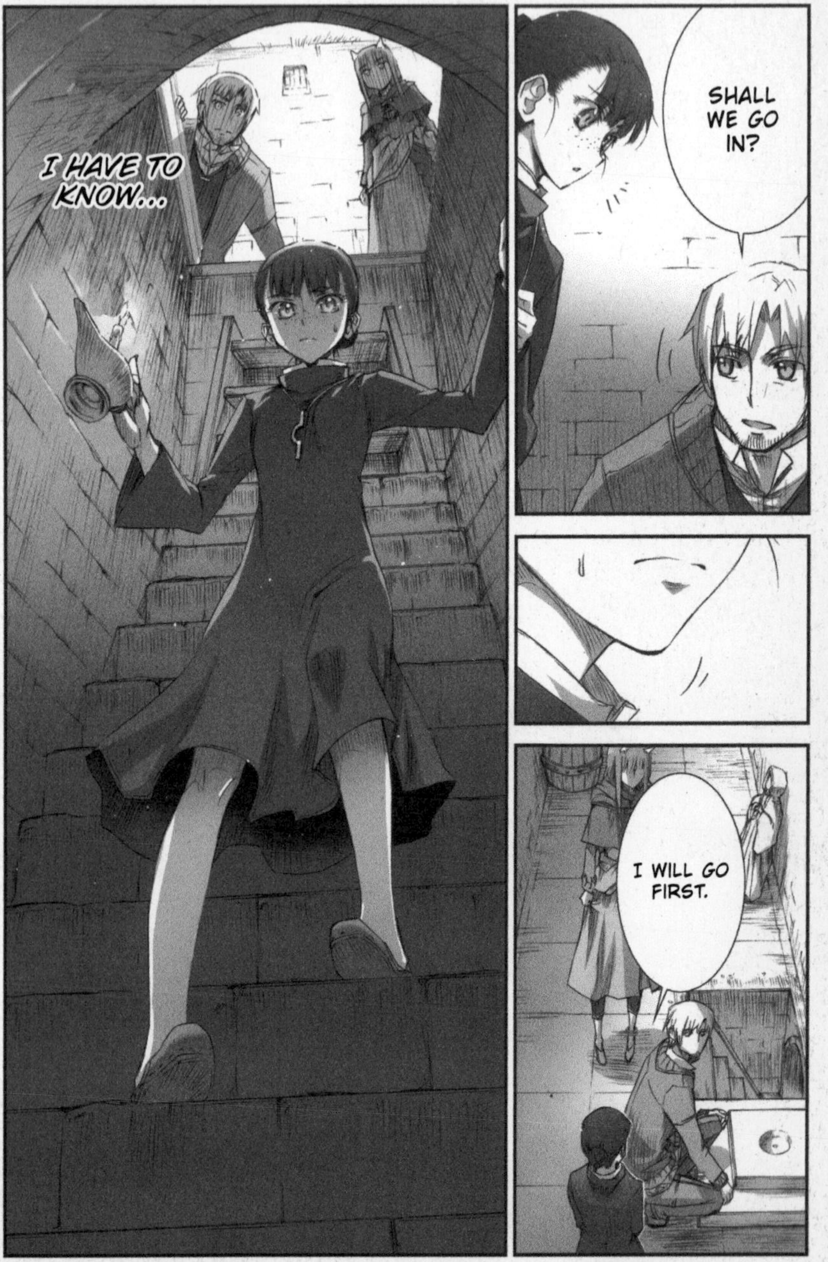
SHALL WE GO IN?
I WILL GO FIRST.
I HAVE TO KNOW...

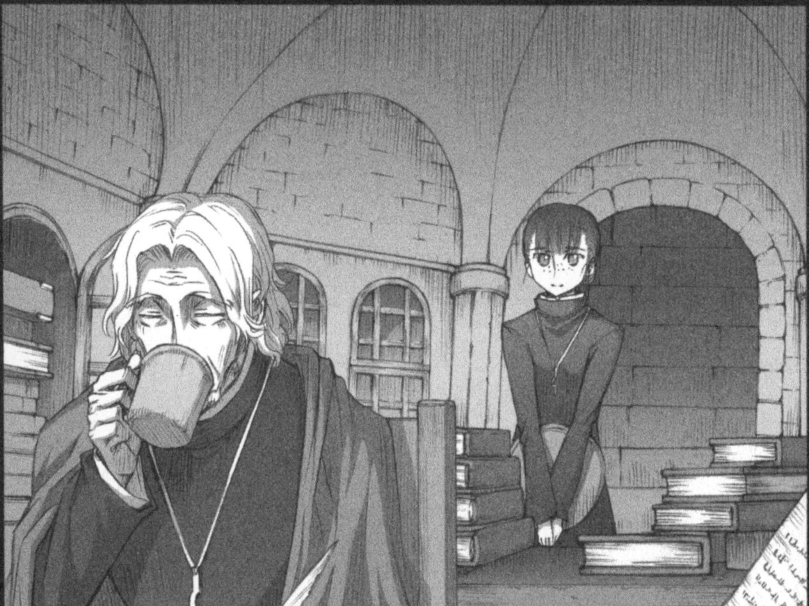
SPICE & WOLF
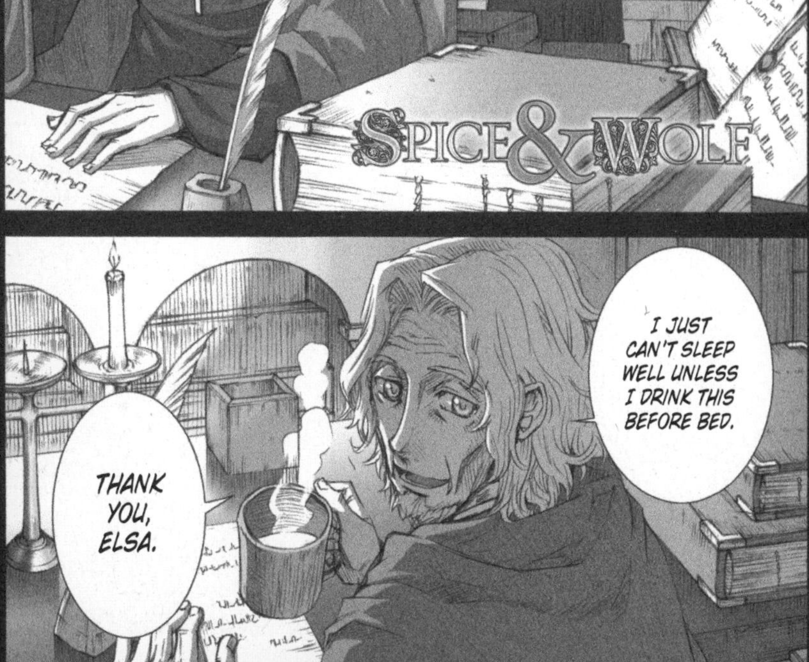
I JUST CAN'T SLEEP WELL UNLESS I DRINK THIS BEFORE BED.
THANK YOU, ELSA.

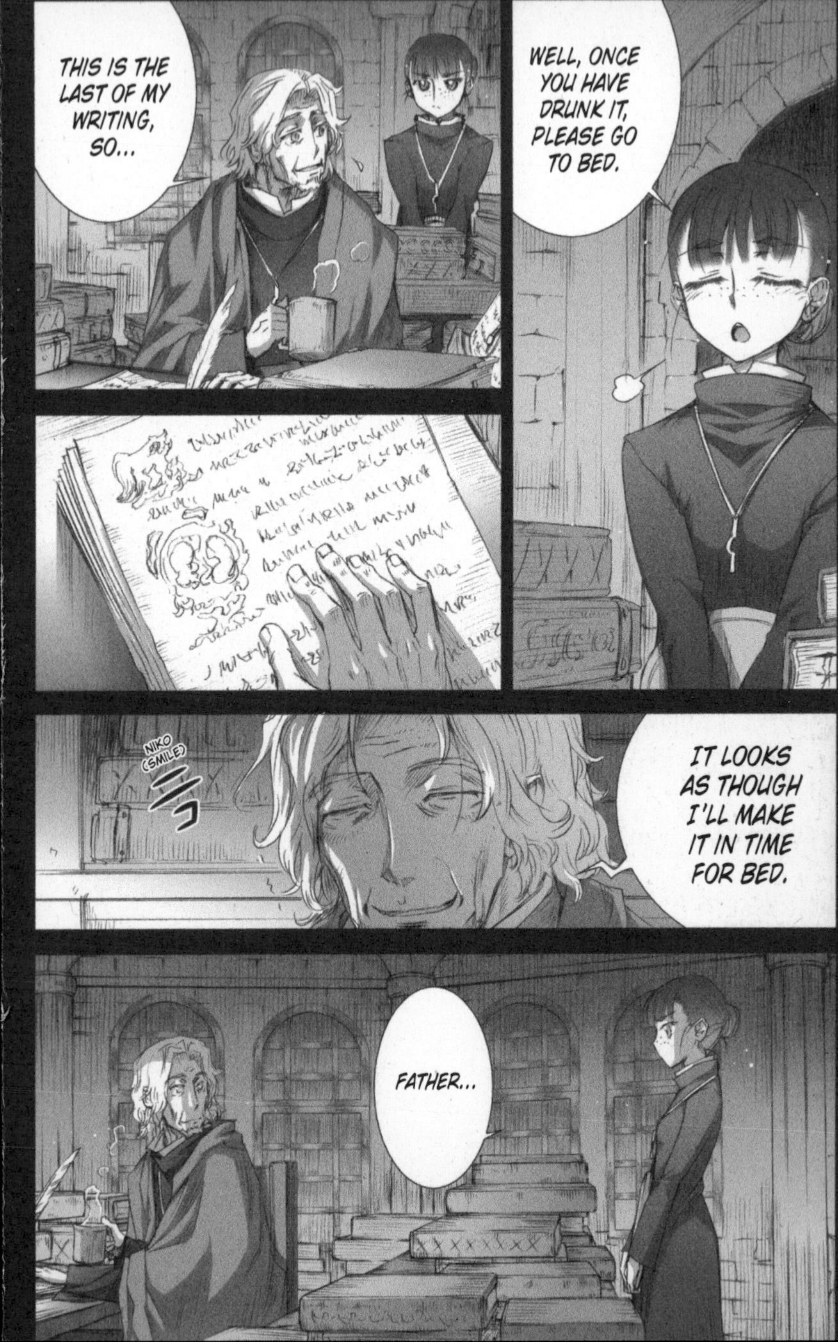
WELL, ONCE YOU HAVE DRUNK IT, PLEASE GO TO BED.
THIS IS THE LAST OF MY WRITING, SO...
IT LOOKS AS THOUGH I'LL MAKE IT IN TIME FOR BED.
NIKO (SMILE)
FATHER...

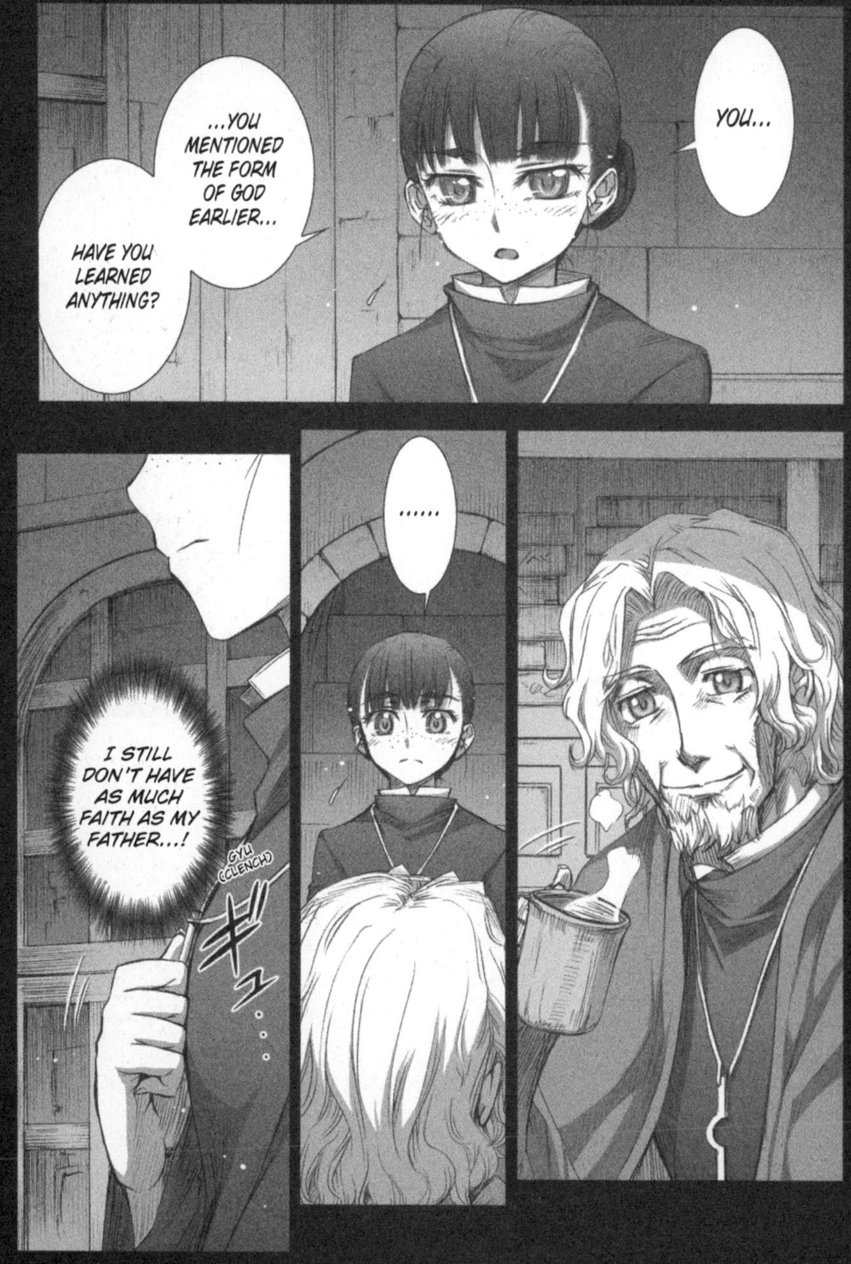
YOU...
...YOU MENTIONED THE FORM OF GOD EARLIER...
HAVE YOU LEARNED ANYTHING?
......
I STILL DON'T HAVE AS MUCH FAITH AS MY FATHER...!
GYU (CLENCH)

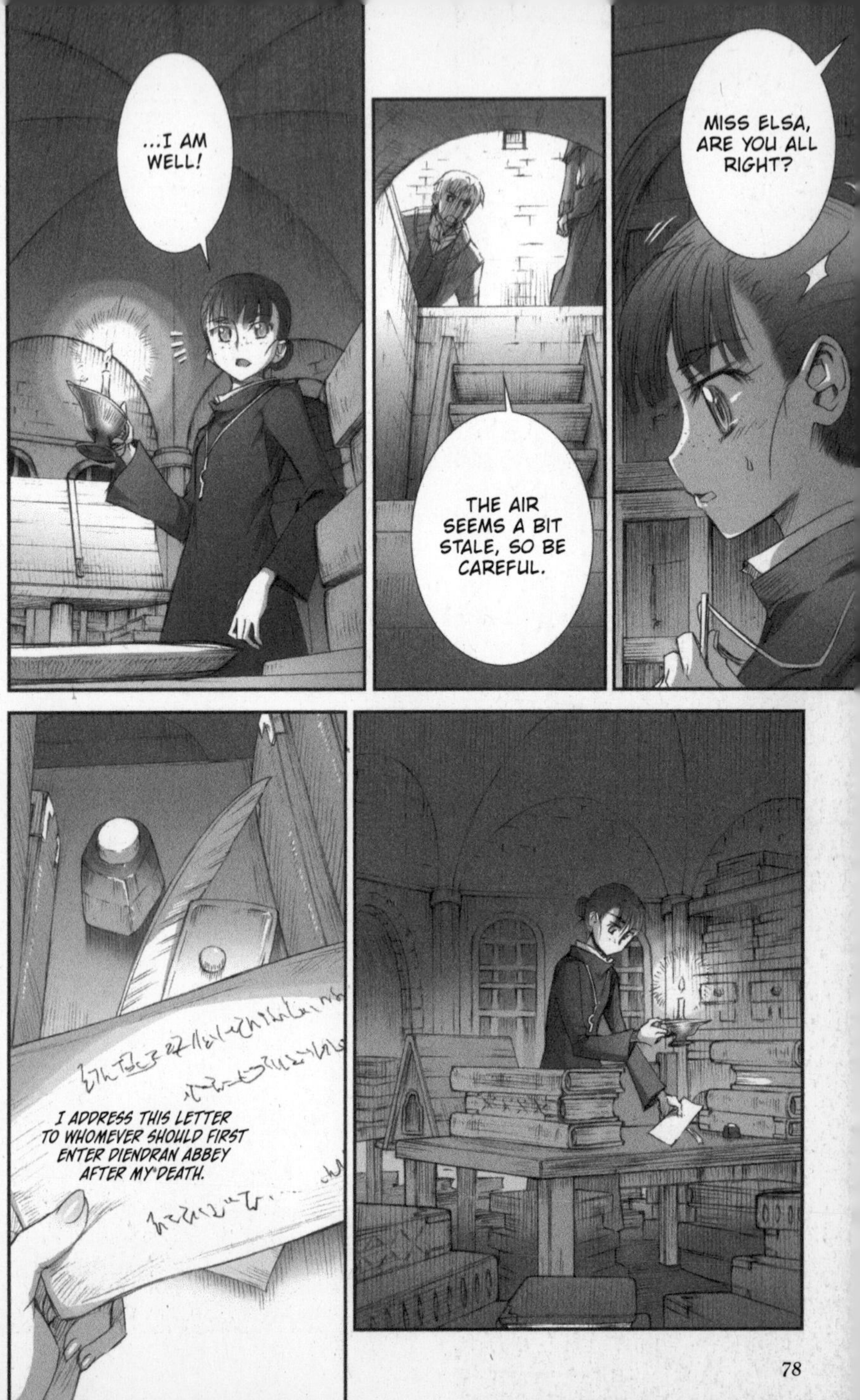
MISS ELSA, ARE YOU ALL RIGHT?
THE AIR SEEMS A BIT STALE, SO BE CAREFUL.
...I AM WELL!
I ADDRESS THIS LETTER TO WHOMEVER SHOULD FIRST ENTER DIENDRAN ABBEY AFTER MY DEATH.

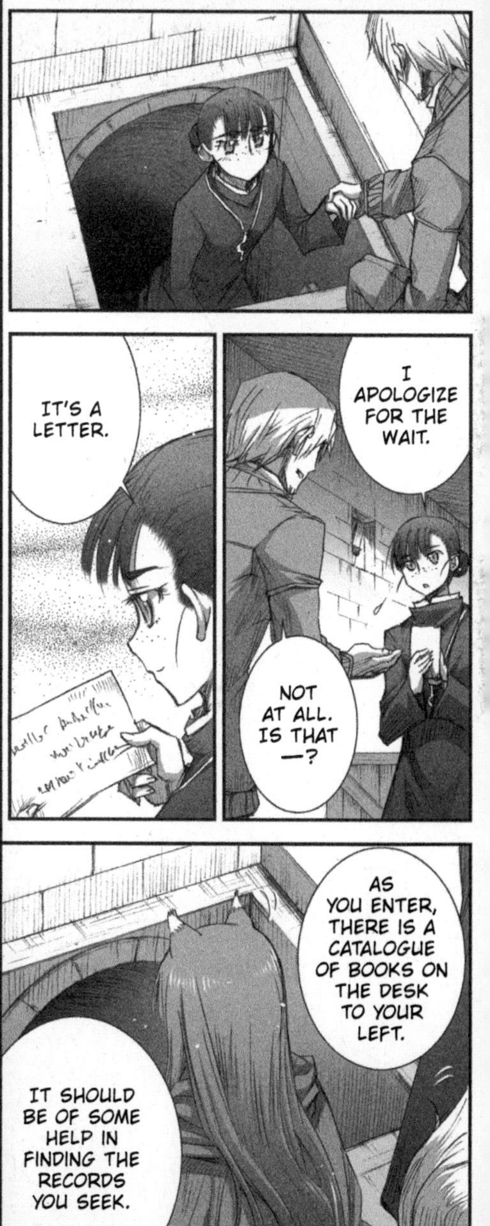
I APOLOGIZE FOR THE WAIT.
NOT AT ALL. IS THAT —?
IT'S A LETTER.
AS YOU ENTER, THERE IS A CATALOGUE OF BOOKS ON THE DESK TO YOUR LEFT.
IT SHOULD BE OF SOME HELP IN FINDING THE RECORDS YOU SEEK.
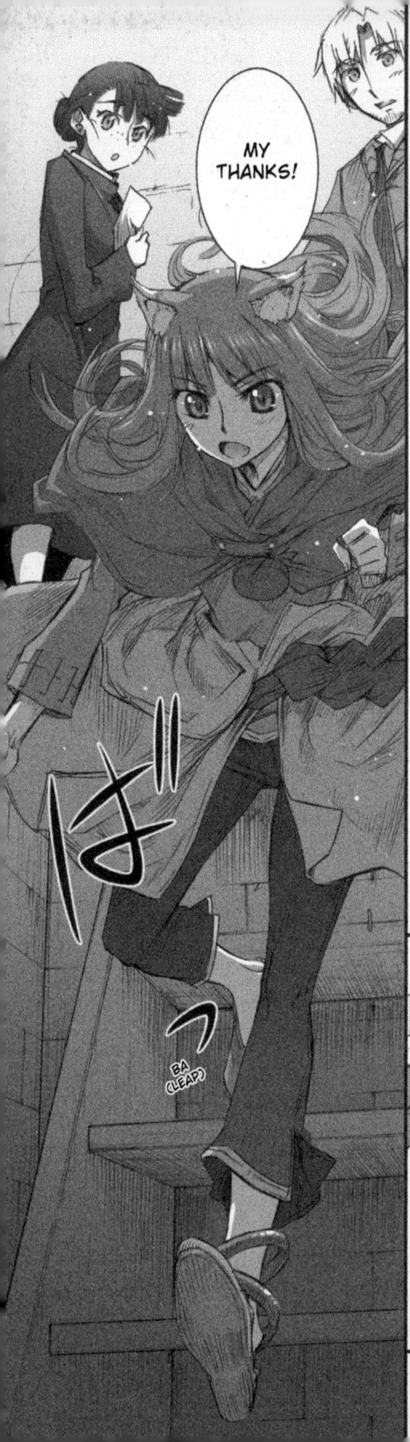
MY THANKS!
BA (LEAP)

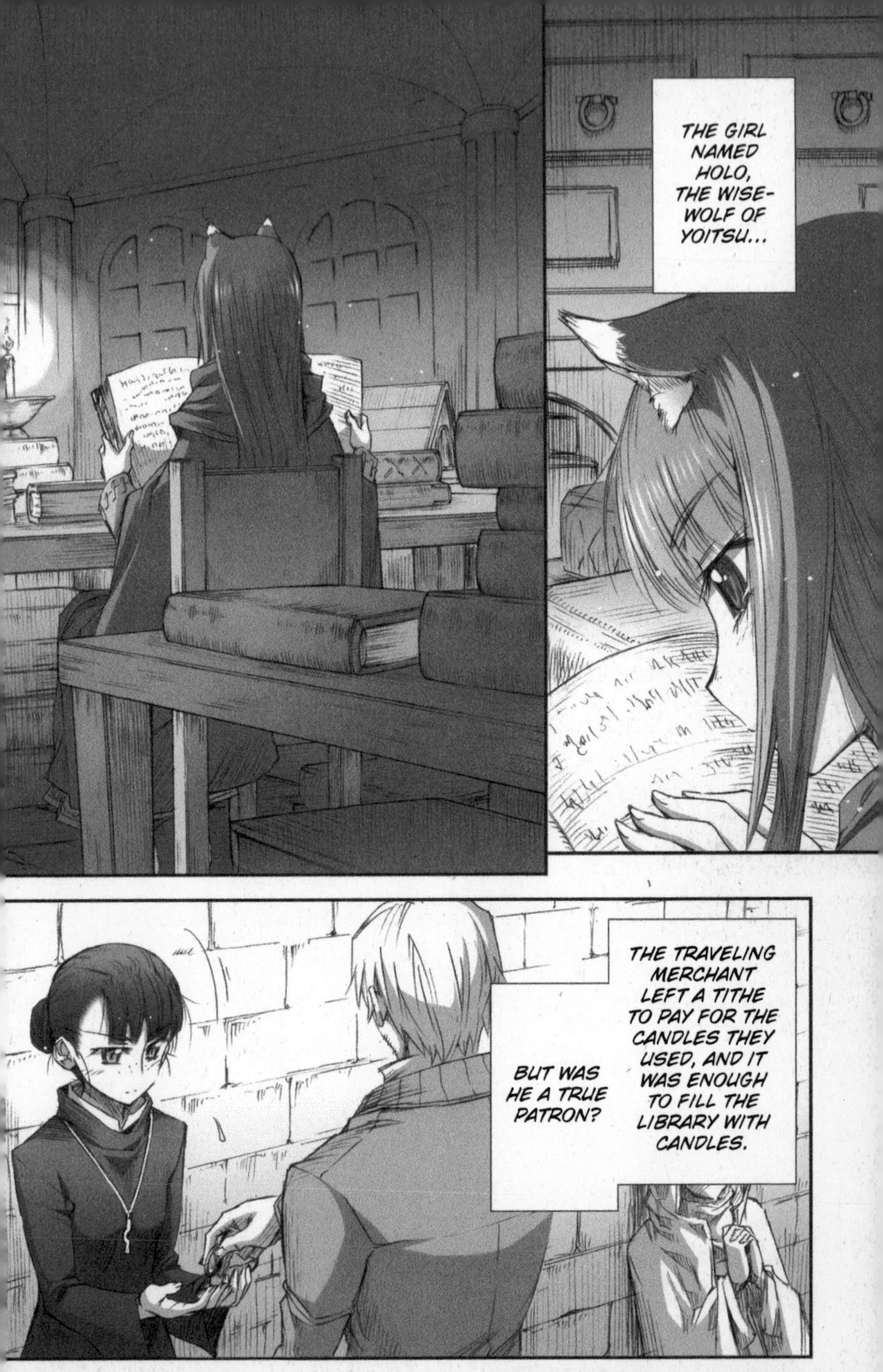
THE GIRL NAMED HOLO, THE WISE-WOLF OF YOITSU...
THE TRAVELING MERCHANT LEFT A TITHE TO PAY FOR THE CANDLES THEY USED, AND IT WAS ENOUGH TO FILL THE LIBRARY WITH CANDLES.
BUT WAS HE A TRUE PATRON?

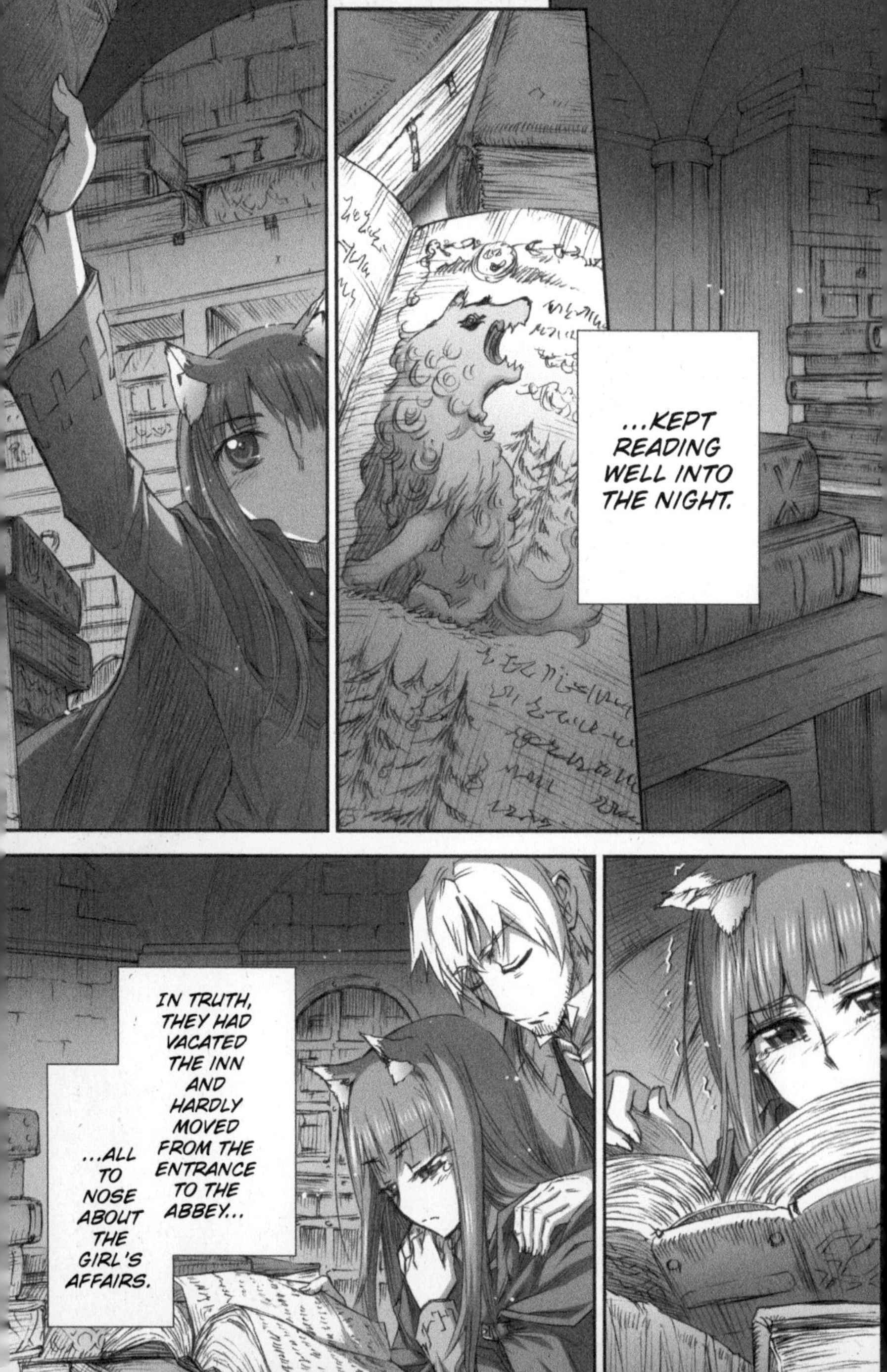
...KEPT READING WELL INTO THE NIGHT.
IN TRUTH, THEY HAD VACATED THE INN AND HARDLY MOVED FROM THE ENTRANCE TO THE ABBEY...
...ALL TO NOSE ABOUT THE GIRL'S AFFAIRS.

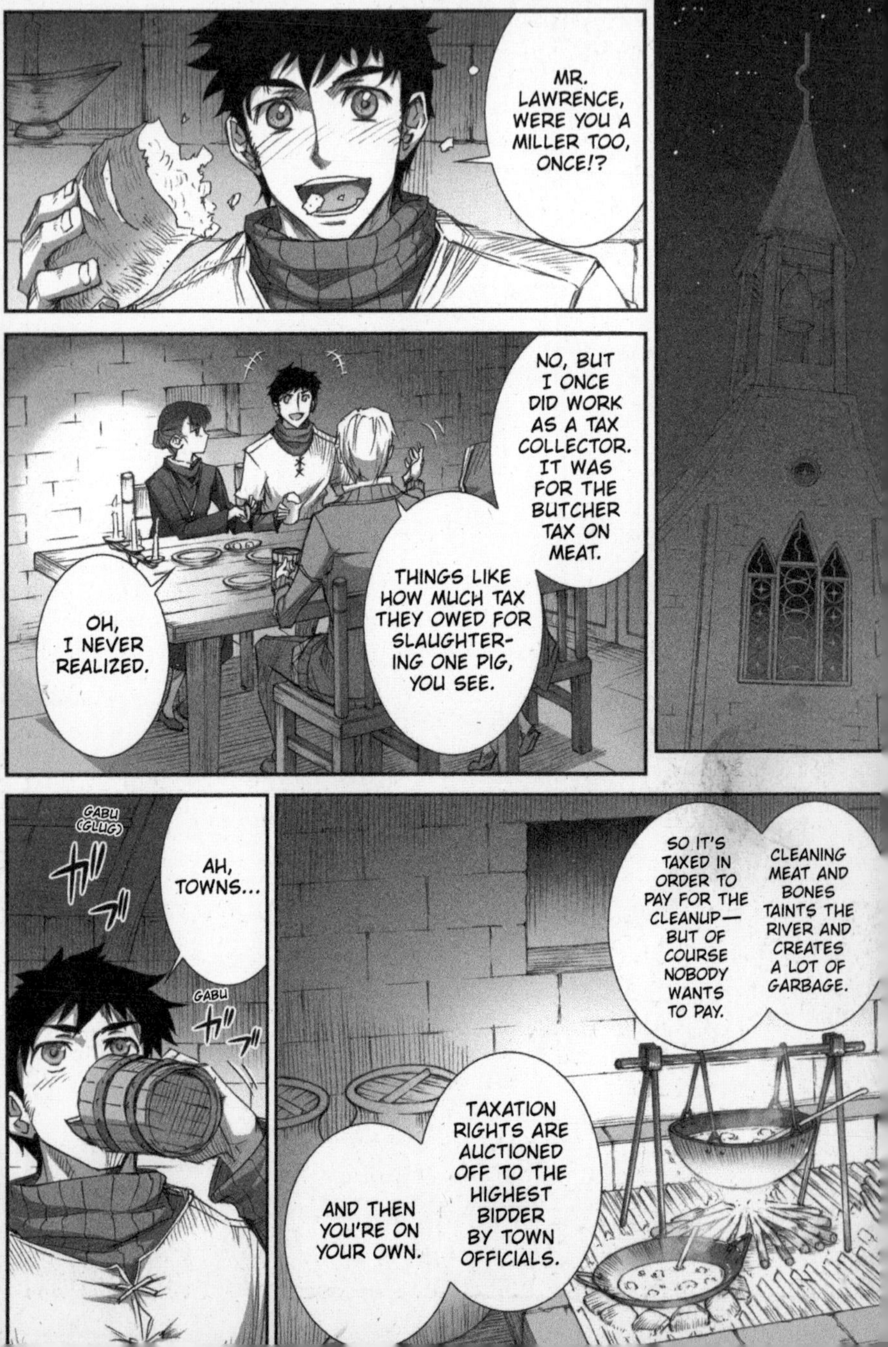
MR. LAWRENCE, WERE YOU A MILLER TOO, ONCE!?
NO, BUT I ONCE DID WORK AS A TAX COLLECTOR. IT WAS FOR THE BUTCHER TAX ON MEAT.
THINGS LIKE HOW MUCH TAX THEY OWED FOR SLAUGHTER-ING ONE PIG, YOU SEE.
OH, I NEVER REALIZED.
CLEANING MEAT AND BONES TAINTS THE RIVER AND CREATES A LOT OF GARBAGE.
SO IT'S TAXED IN ORDER TO PAY FOR THE CLEANUP—BUT OF COURSE NOBODY WANTS TO PAY.
TAXATION RIGHTS ARE AUCTIONED OFF TO THE HIGHEST BIDDER BY TOWN OFFICIALS.
AND THEN YOU'RE ON YOUR OWN.
GABU (GLUG)
AH, TOWNS...
GABU

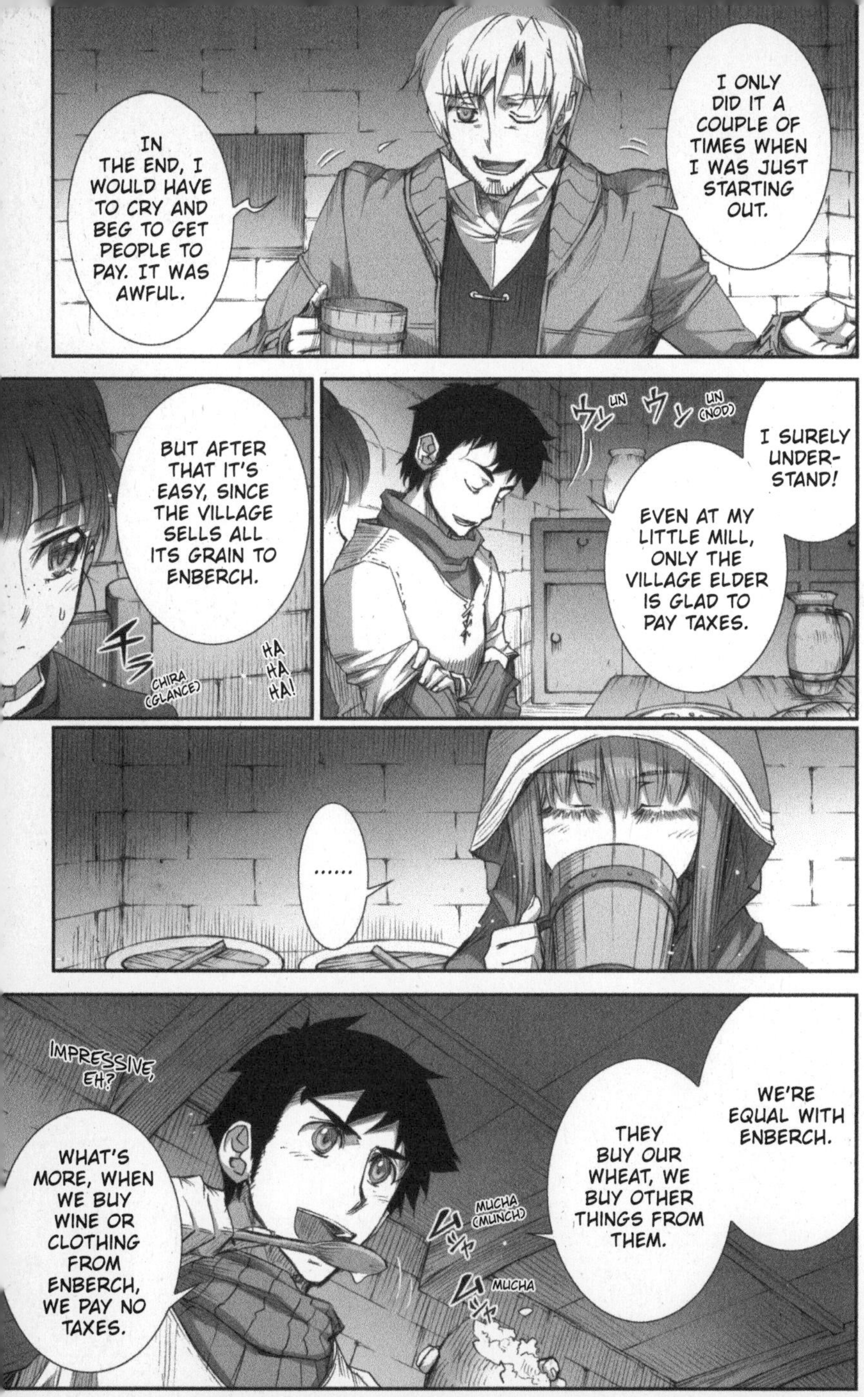
I ONLY DID IT A COUPLE OF TIMES WHEN I WAS JUST STARTING OUT.
IN THE END, I WOULD HAVE TO CRY AND BEG TO GET PEOPLE TO PAY. IT WAS AWFUL.
UN UN (NOD)
I SURELY UNDER-STAND!
EVEN AT MY LITTLE MILL, ONLY THE VILLAGE ELDER IS GLAD TO PAY TAXES.
BUT AFTER THAT IT'S EASY, SINCE THE VILLAGE SELLS ALL ITS GRAIN TO ENBERCH.
HA HA HA!
CHIRA (GLANCE)
......
WE'RE EQUAL WITH ENBERCH.
THEY BUY OUR WHEAT, WE BUY OTHER THINGS FROM THEM.
MUCHA (MUNCH)
MUCHA
IMPRESSIVE, EH?
WHAT'S MORE, WHEN WE BUY WINE OR CLOTHING FROM ENBERCH, WE PAY NO TAXES.

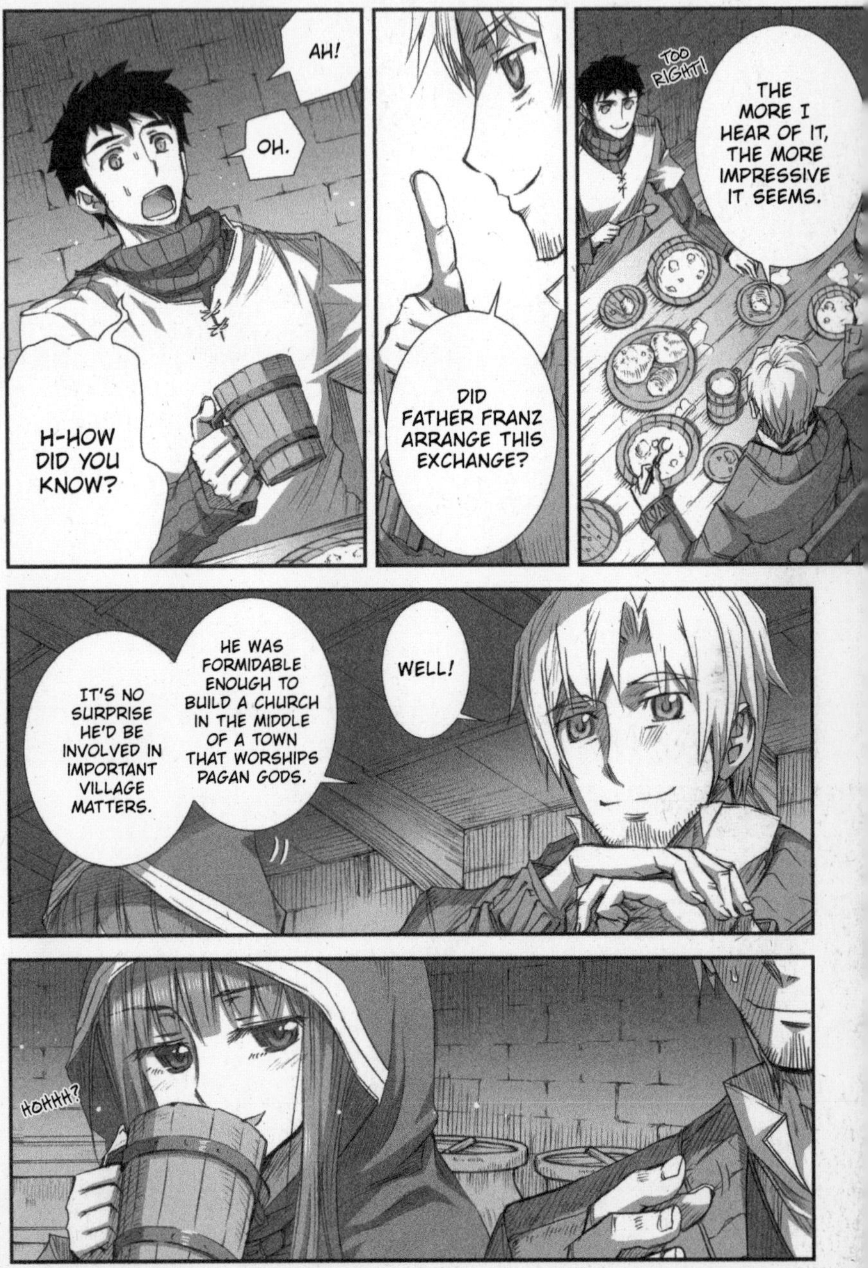
TOO RIGHT!
THE MORE I HEAR OF IT, THE MORE IMPRESSIVE IT SEEMS.
DID FATHER FRANZ ARRANGE THIS EXCHANGE?
AH!
OH.
H-HOW DID YOU KNOW?
WELL!
HE WAS FORMIDABLE ENOUGH TO BUILD A CHURCH IN THE MIDDLE OF A TOWN THAT WORSHIPS PAGAN GODS.
IT'S NO SURPRISE HE'D BE INVOLVED IN IMPORTANT VILLAGE MATTERS.
HOHHH?

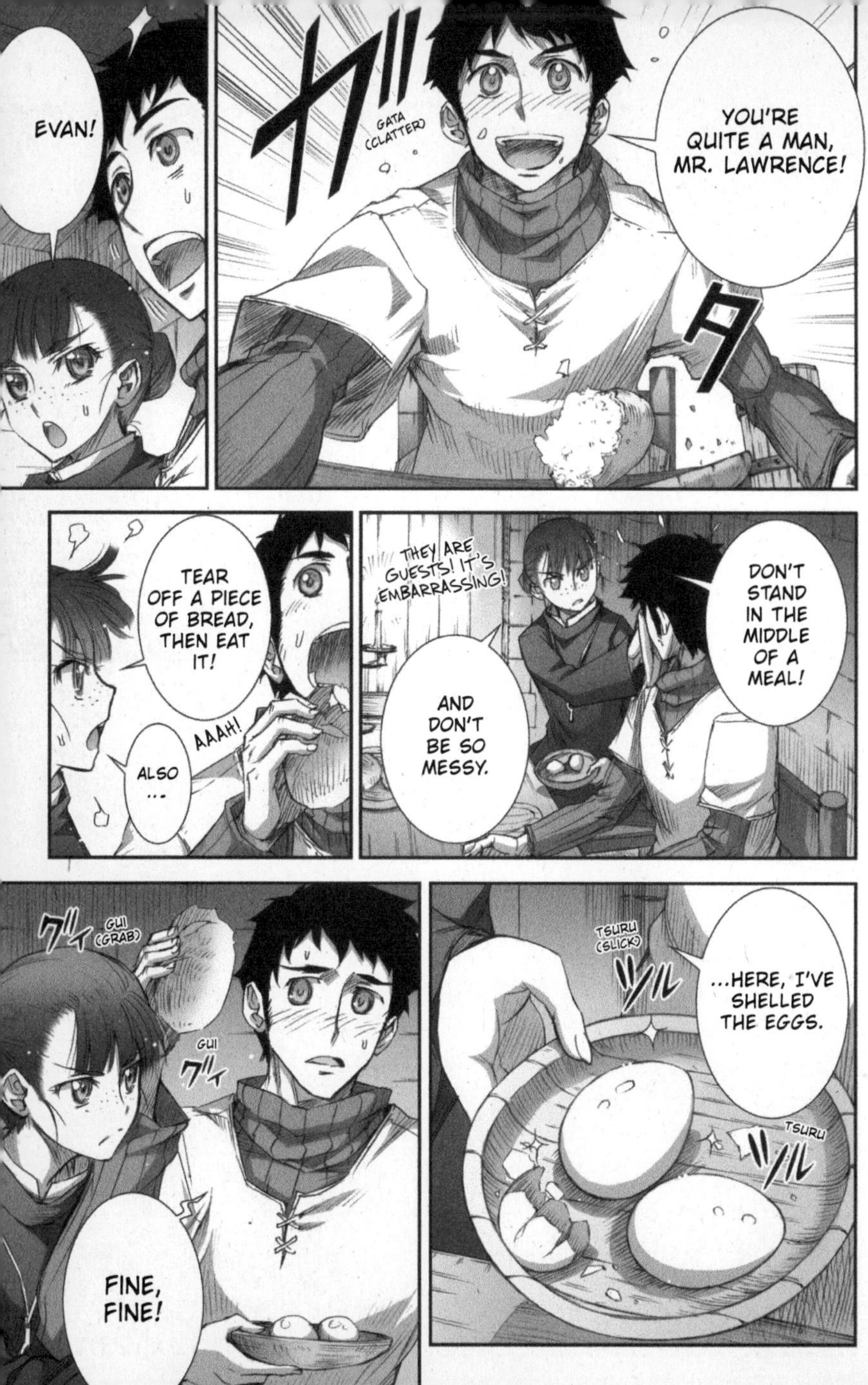
YOU'RE QUITE A MAN, MR. LAWRENCE!
GATA (CLATTER)
EVAN!
DON'T STAND IN THE MIDDLE OF A MEAL!
THEY ARE GUESTS! IT'S EMBARRASSING!
AND DON'T BE SO MESSY.
TEAR OFF A PIECE OF BREAD, THEN EAT IT!
AAAH!
ALSO...
...HERE, I'VE SHELLED THE EGGS.
TSURU (SLICK)
TSURU
GUI (GRAB)
GUI
FINE, FINE!

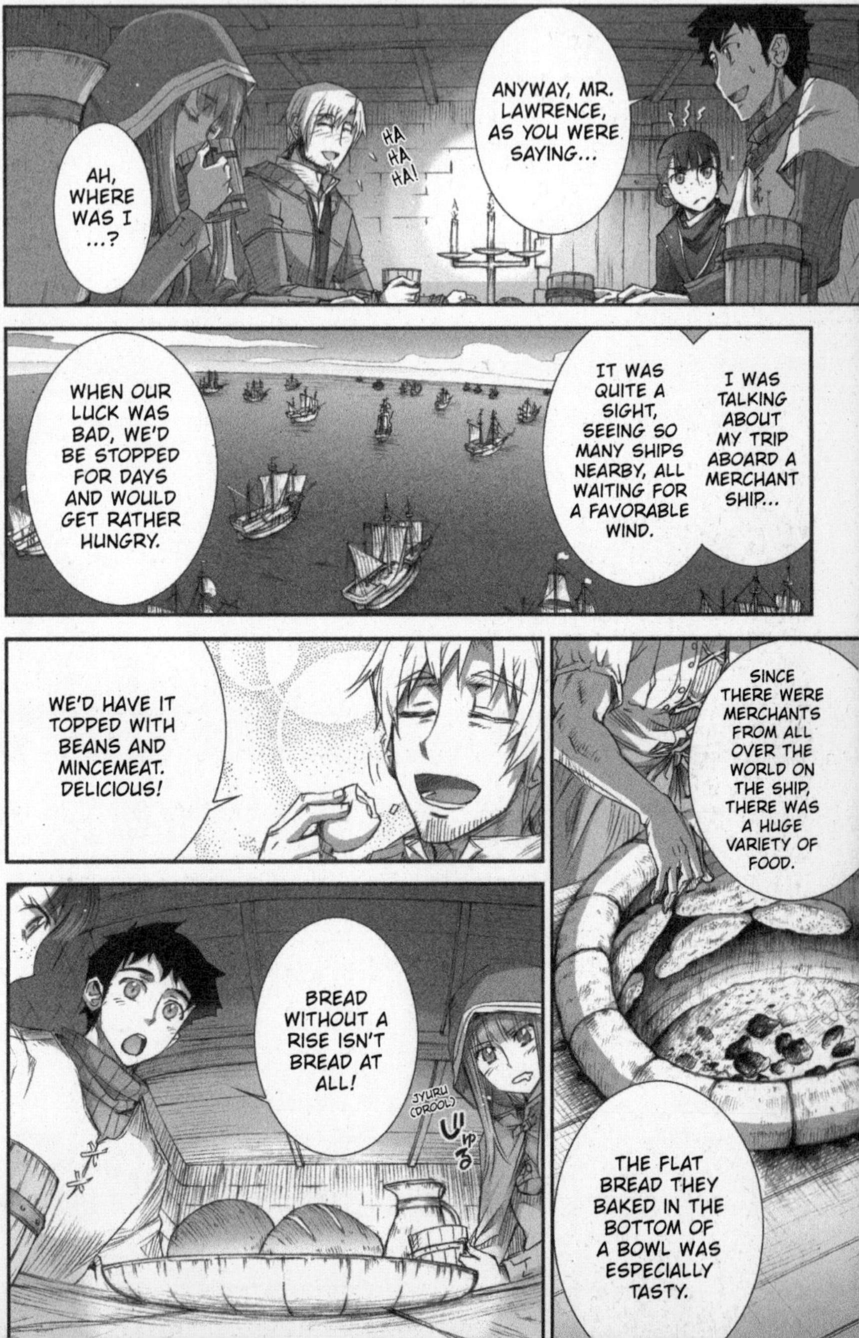
ANYWAY, MR. LAWRENCE, AS YOU WERE SAYING...
HA HA HA!
AH, WHERE WAS I ...?
I WAS TALKING ABOUT MY TRIP ABOARD A MERCHANT SHIP...
IT WAS QUITE A SIGHT, SEEING SO MANY SHIPS NEARBY, ALL WAITING FOR A FAVORABLE WIND.
WHEN OUR LUCK WAS BAD, WE'D BE STOPPED FOR DAYS AND WOULD GET RATHER HUNGRY.
SINCE THERE WERE MERCHANTS FROM ALL OVER THE WORLD ON THE SHIP, THERE WAS A HUGE VARIETY OF FOOD.
THE FLAT BREAD THEY BAKED IN THE BOTTOM OF A BOWL WAS ESPECIALLY TASTY.
WE'D HAVE IT TOPPED WITH BEANS AND MINCEMEAT. DELICIOUS!
BREAD WITHOUT A RISE ISN'T BREAD AT ALL!
JYURU (DROOL)

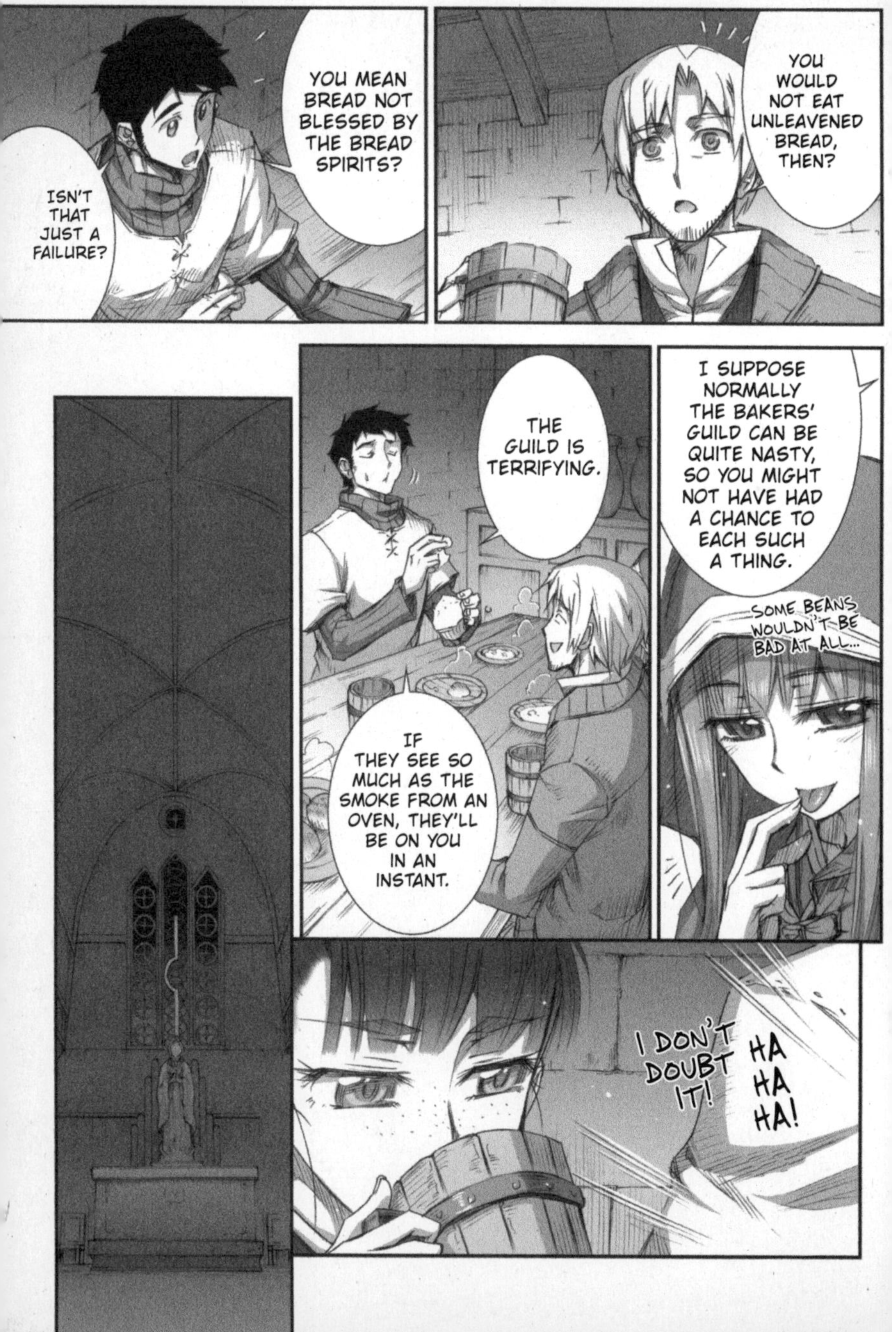

YOU WOULD NOT EAT UNLEAVENED BREAD, THEN?
YOU MEAN BREAD NOT BLESSED BY THE BREAD SPIRITS?
ISN'T THAT JUST A FAILURE?
I SUPPOSE NORMALLY THE BAKERS' GUILD CAN BE QUITE NASTY, SO YOU MIGHT NOT HAVE HAD A CHANCE TO EACH SUCH A THING.
SOME BEANS WOULDN'T BE BAD AT ALL...
THE GUILD IS TERRIFYING.
IF THEY SEE SO MUCH AS THE SMOKE FROM AN OVEN, THEY'LL BE ON YOU IN AN INSTANT.
I DON'T DOUBT IT!
HA HA HA!

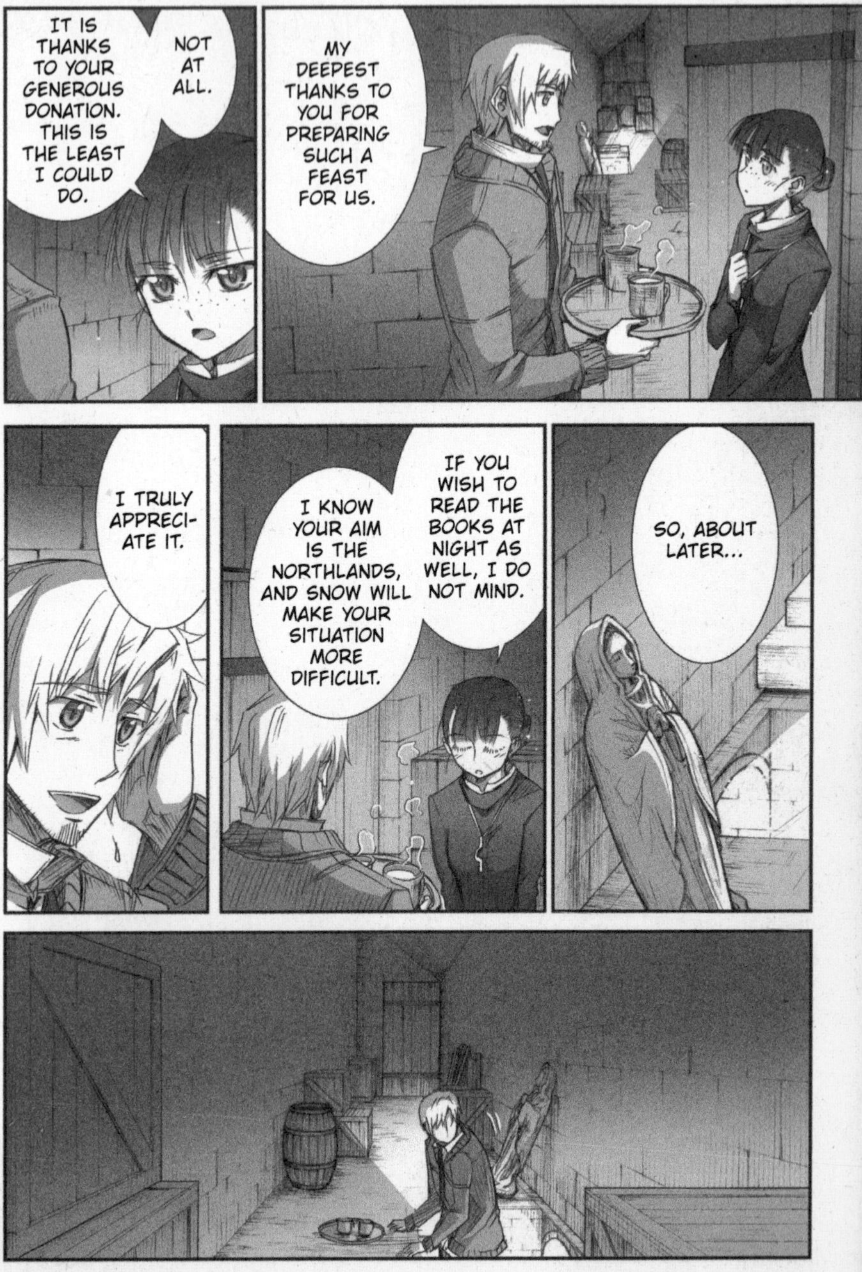
MY DEEPEST THANKS TO YOU FOR PREPARING SUCH A FEAST FOR US.
NOT AT ALL.
IT IS THANKS TO YOUR GENEROUS DONATION. THIS IS THE LEAST I COULD DO.
SO, ABOUT LATER...
IF YOU WISH TO READ THE BOOKS AT NIGHT AS WELL, I DO NOT MIND.
I KNOW YOUR AIM IS THE NORTHLANDS, AND SNOW WILL MAKE YOUR SITUATION MORE DIFFICULT.
I TRULY APPRECI-ATE IT.

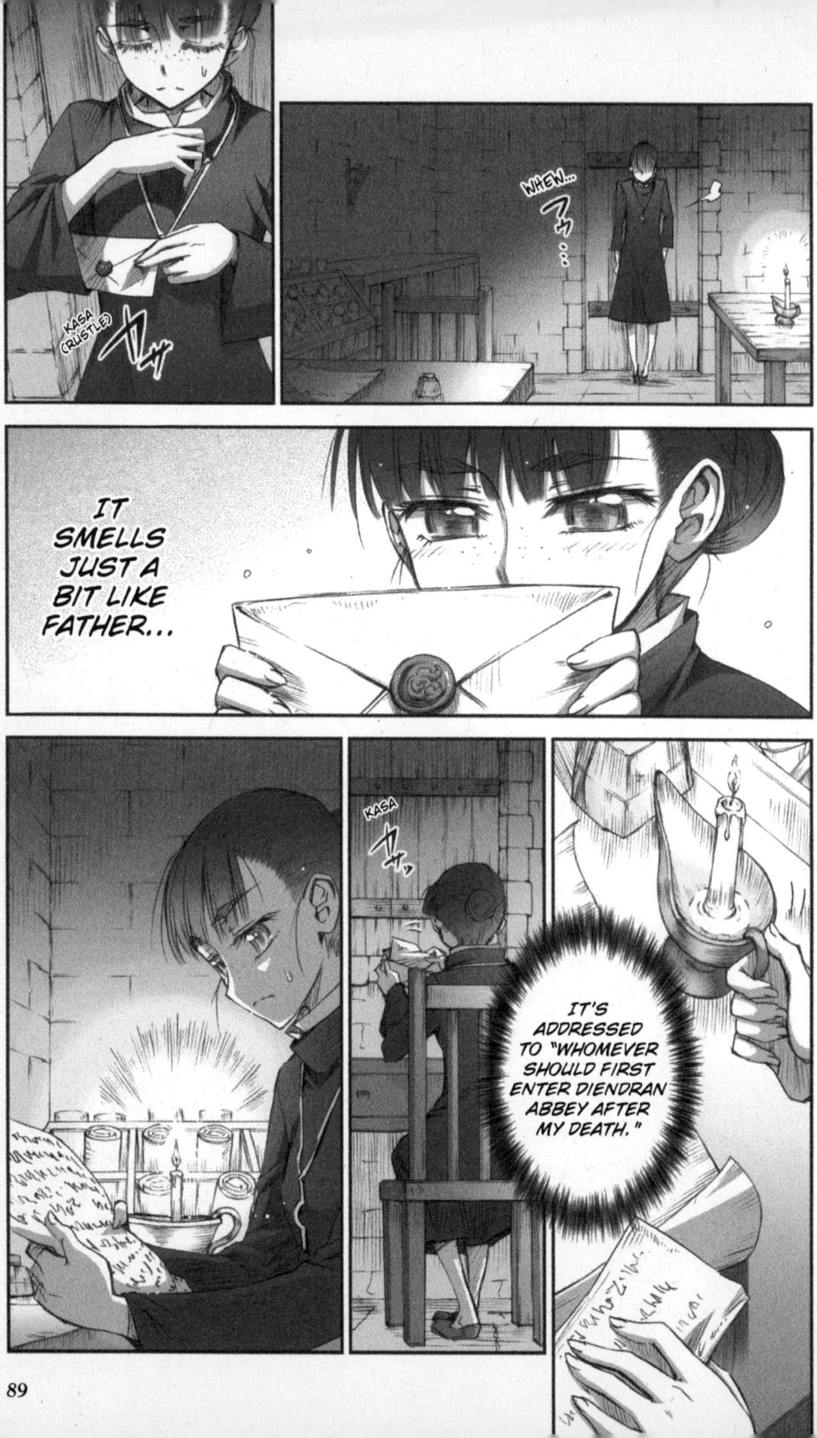
WHEW...
KASA (RUSTLE)
IT SMELLS JUST A BIT LIKE FATHER...
IT'S ADDRESSED TO "WHOMEVER SHOULD FIRST ENTER DIENDRAN ABBEY AFTER MY DEATH."
KASA

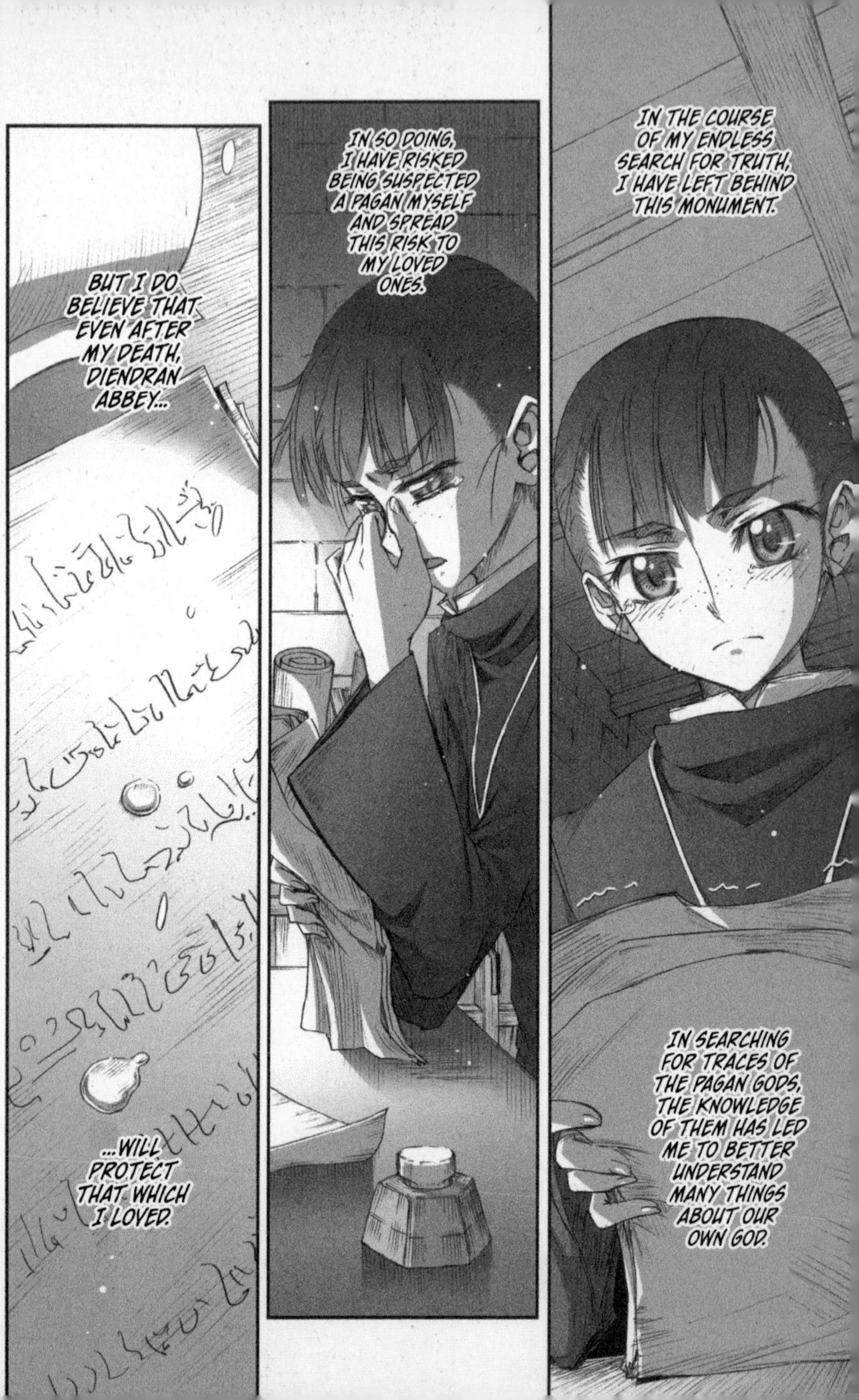
IN THE COURSE OF MY ENDLESS SEARCH FOR TRUTH, I HAVE LEFT BEHIND THIS MONUMENT.
IN SEARCHING FOR TRACES OF THE PAGAN GODS, THE KNOWLEDGE OF THEM HAS LED ME TO BETTER UNDERSTAND MANY THINGS ABOUT OUR OWN GOD.
IN SO DOING, I HAVE RISKED BEING SUSPECTED A PAGAN MYSELF AND SPREAD THIS RISK TO MY LOVED ONES.
BUT I DO BELIEVE THAT EVEN AFTER MY DEATH, DIENDRAN ABBEY...
...WILL PROTECT THAT WHICH I LOVED.

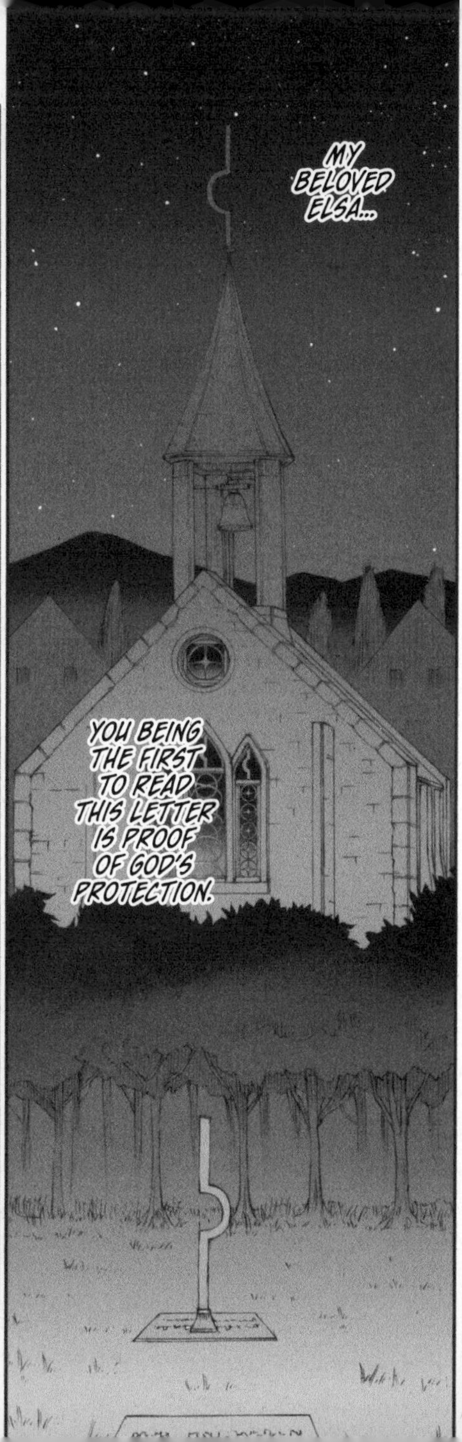
MY BELOVED ELSA...
YOU BEING THE FIRST TO READ THIS LETTER IS PROOF OF GOD'S PROTECTION.
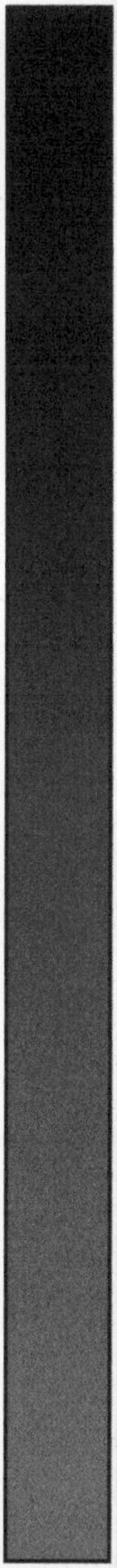
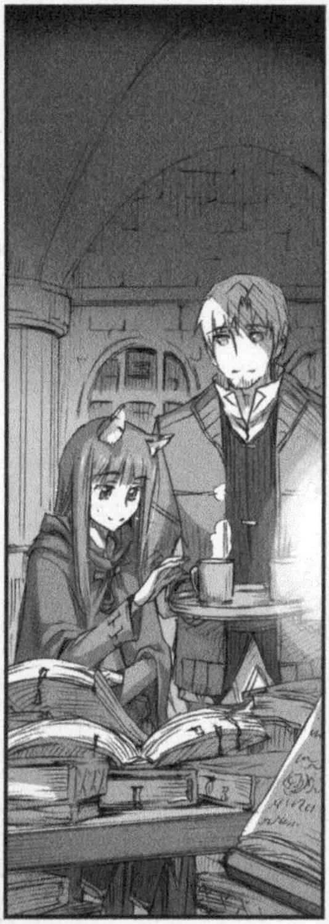
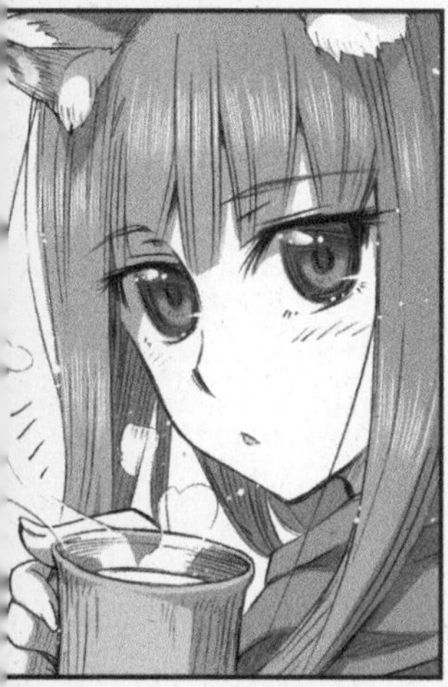

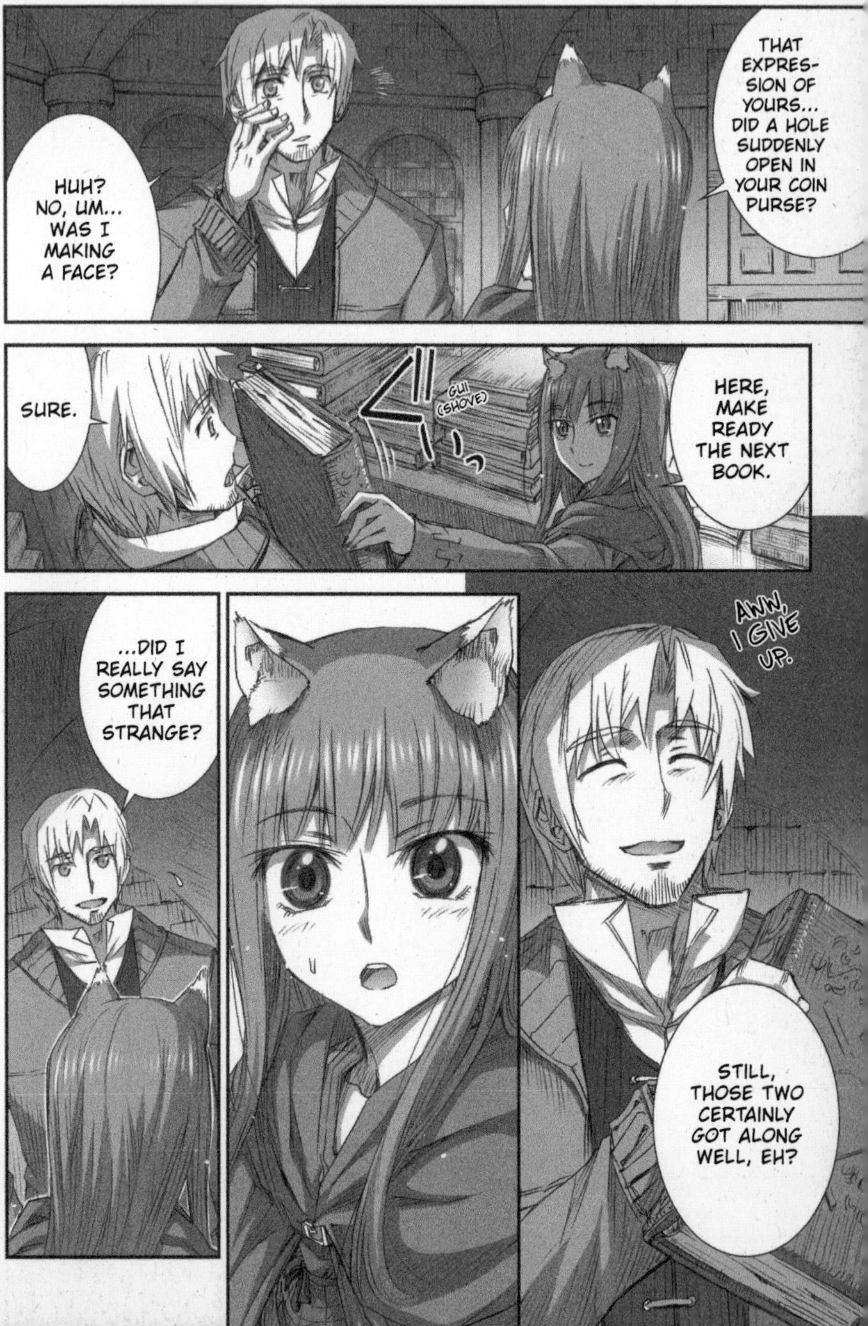
THAT EXPRES-SION OF YOURS... DID A HOLE SUDDENLY OPEN IN YOUR COIN PURSE?
HUH? NO, UM... WAS I MAKING A FACE?
HERE, MAKE READY THE NEXT BOOK.
GUI (SHOVE)
SURE.
AWW, I GIVE UP.
STILL, THOSE TWO CERTAINLY GOT ALONG WELL, EH?
...DID I REALLY SAY SOMETHING THAT STRANGE?

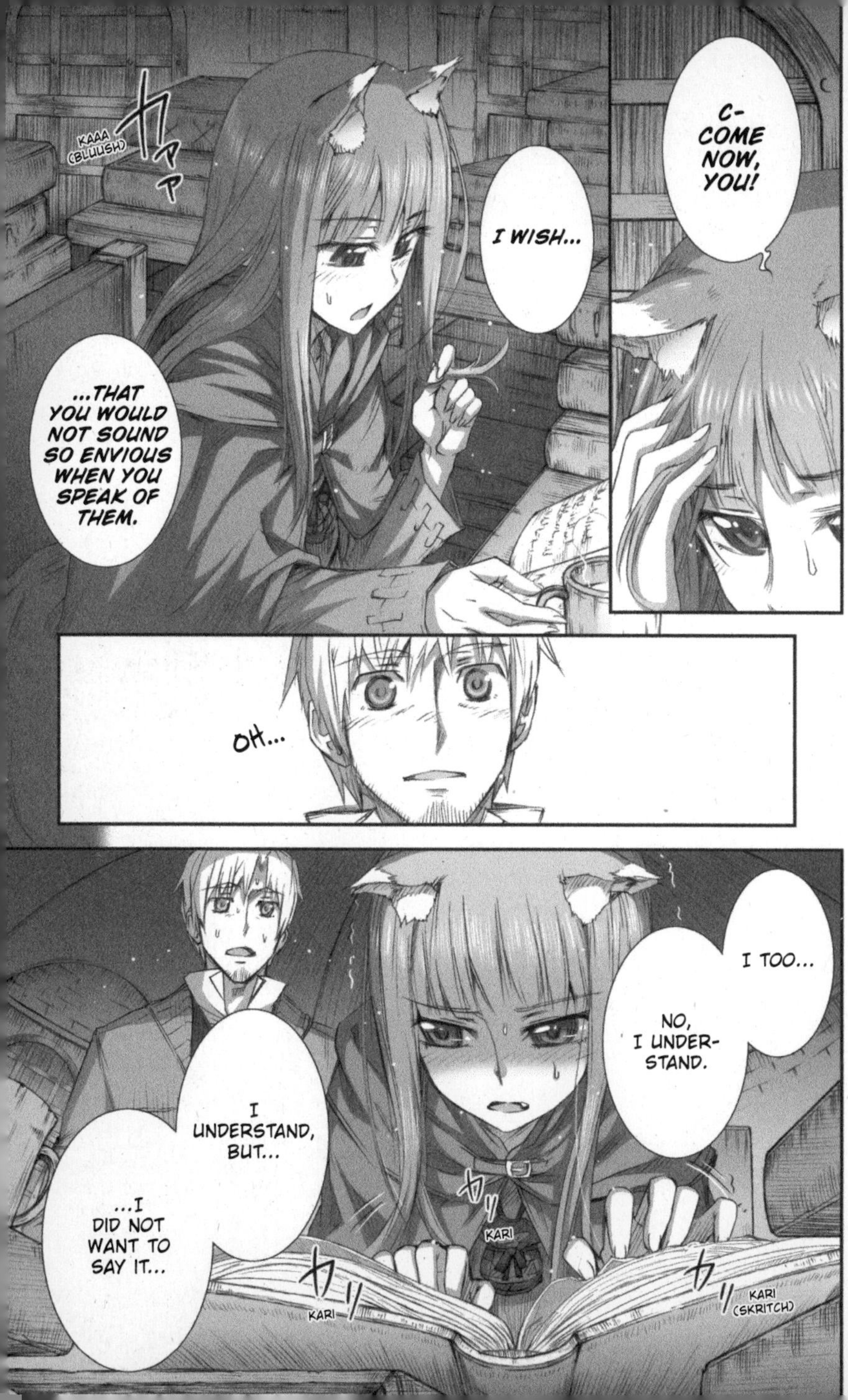

C-COME NOW, YOU!
I WISH...
カァァ
KAAA (BLUUSH)
...THAT YOU WOULD NOT SOUND SO ENVIOUS WHEN YOU SPEAK OF THEM.
OH...
I TOO...
NO, I UNDER-STAND.
カリ
KARI (SKRITCH)
カリ
KARI
I UNDERSTAND, BUT...
...I DID NOT WANT TO SAY IT...
カリ
KARI

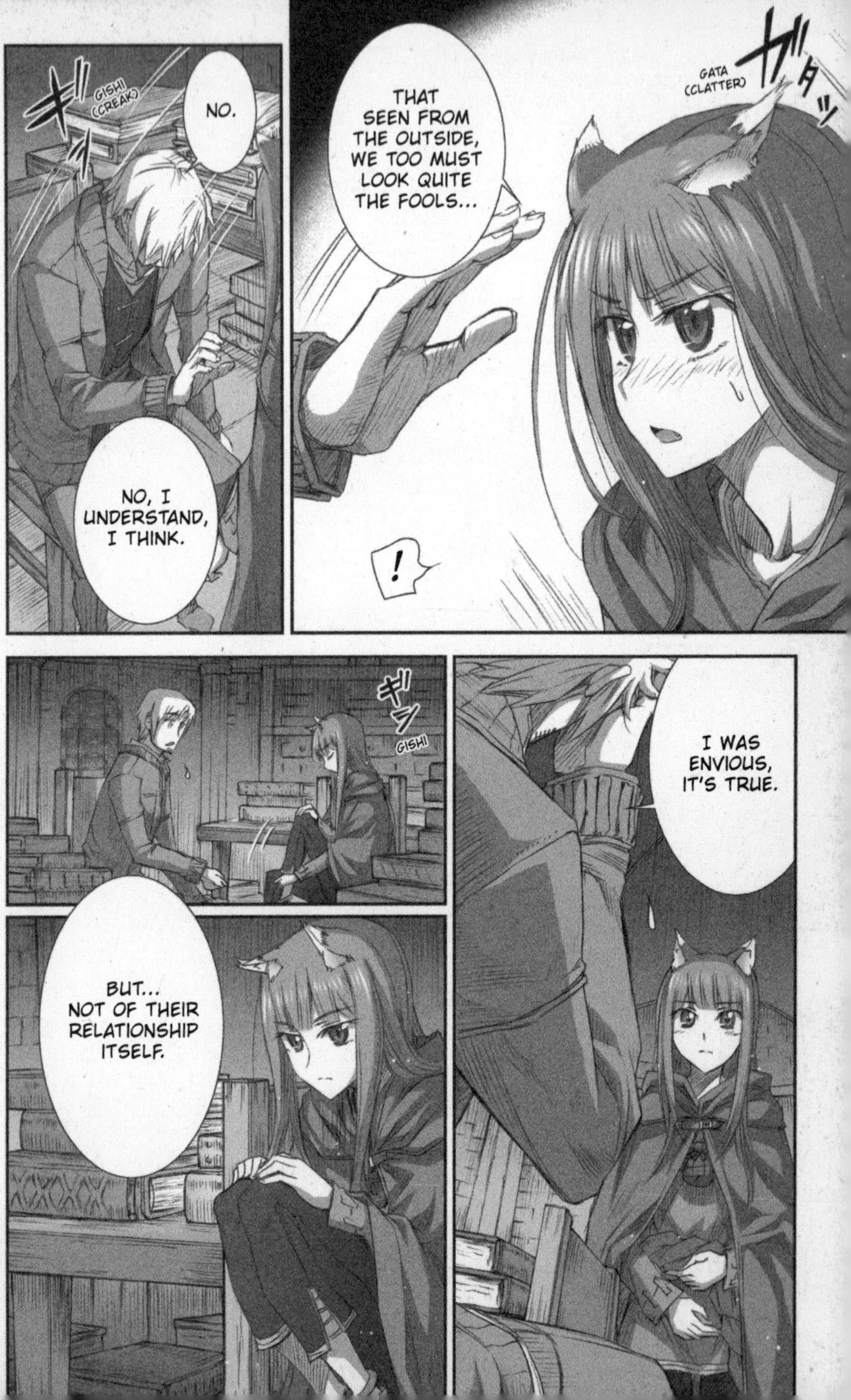
GATA (CLATTER)
THAT SEEN FROM THE OUTSIDE, WE TOO MUST LOOK QUITE THE FOOLS...
!
GISHI (CREAK)
NO.
NO, I UNDERSTAND, I THINK.
I WAS ENVIOUS, IT'S TRUE.
GISHI
BUT... NOT OF THEIR RELATIONSHIP ITSELF.

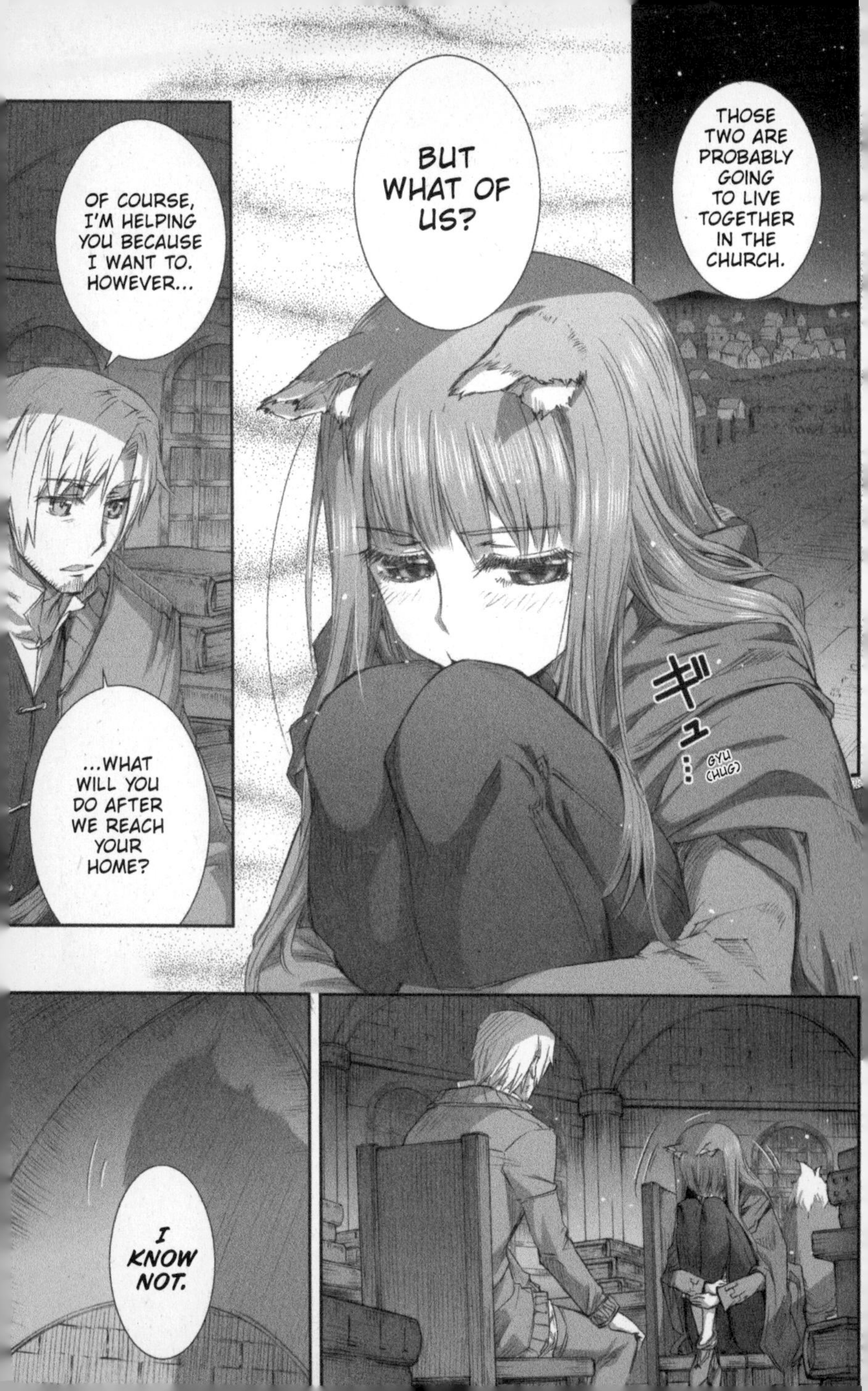
THOSE TWO ARE PROBABLY GOING TO LIVE TOGETHER IN THE CHURCH.
BUT WHAT OF US?
ギュ…
GYU (HUG)
OF COURSE, I'M HELPING YOU BECAUSE I WANT TO. HOWEVER...
...WHAT WILL YOU DO AFTER WE REACH YOUR HOME?
I KNOW NOT.

JIJI
(CRACKLE)

THERE IS
NO POINT
IN SPECU-
LATION.

NO,
FORGET
IT. I AM
SORRY.

I AM...

...HOLO
THE WISE-
WOLF.

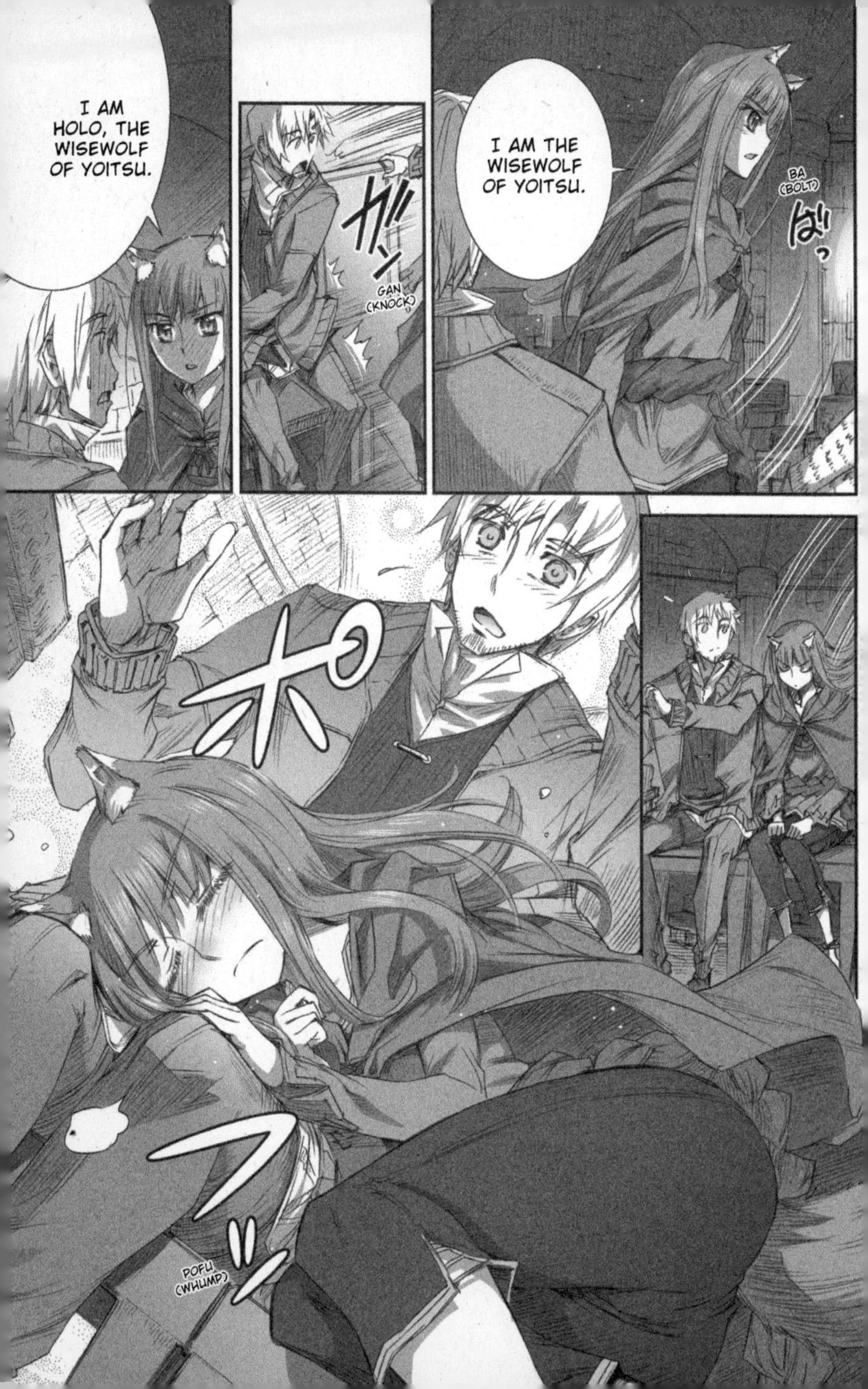
I AM THE WISEWOLF OF YOITSU.
BA (BOLT)
GAN (KNOCK)
I AM HOLO, THE WISEWOLF OF YOITSU.
POFU (WHUMP)

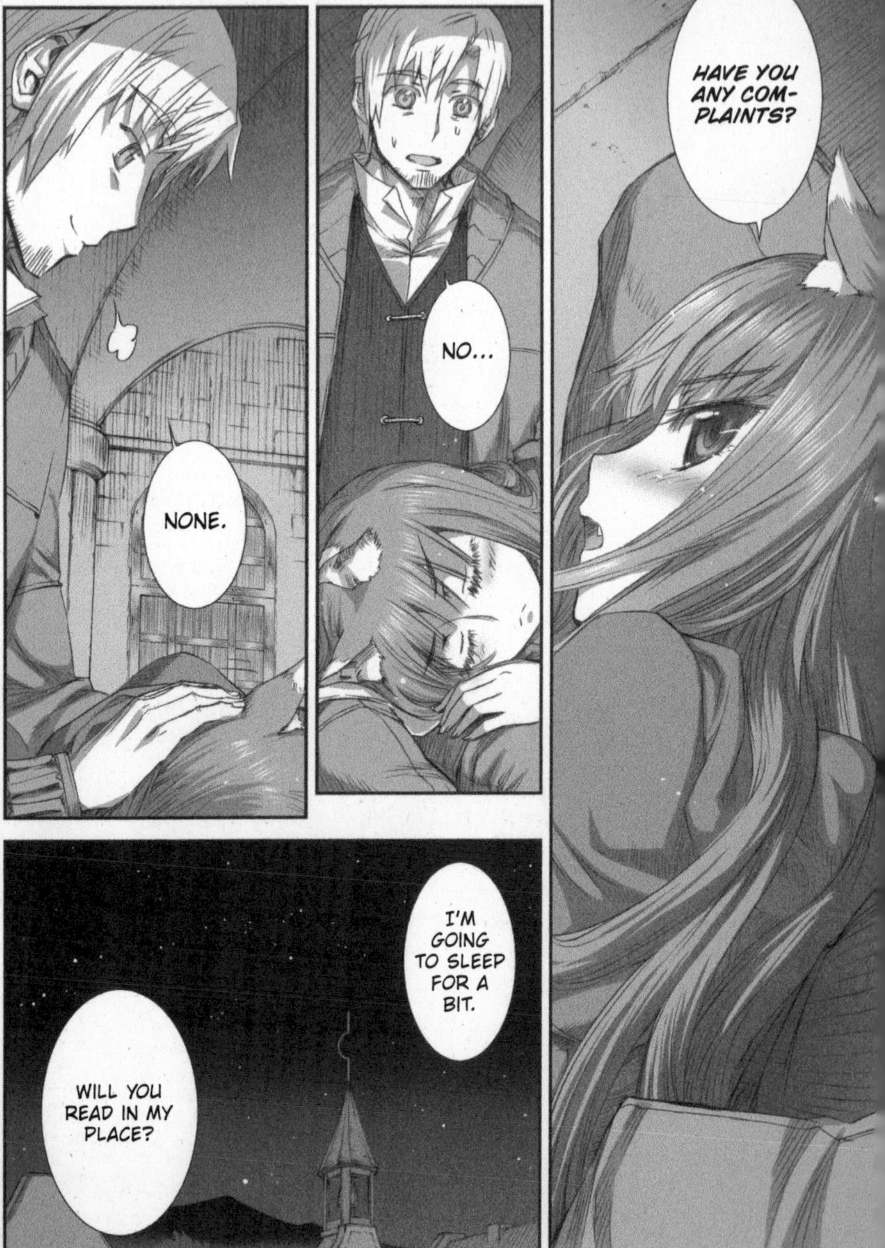
HAVE YOU ANY COM-PLAINTS?
NO...
NONE.
I'M GOING TO SLEEP FOR A BIT.
WILL YOU READ IN MY PLACE?

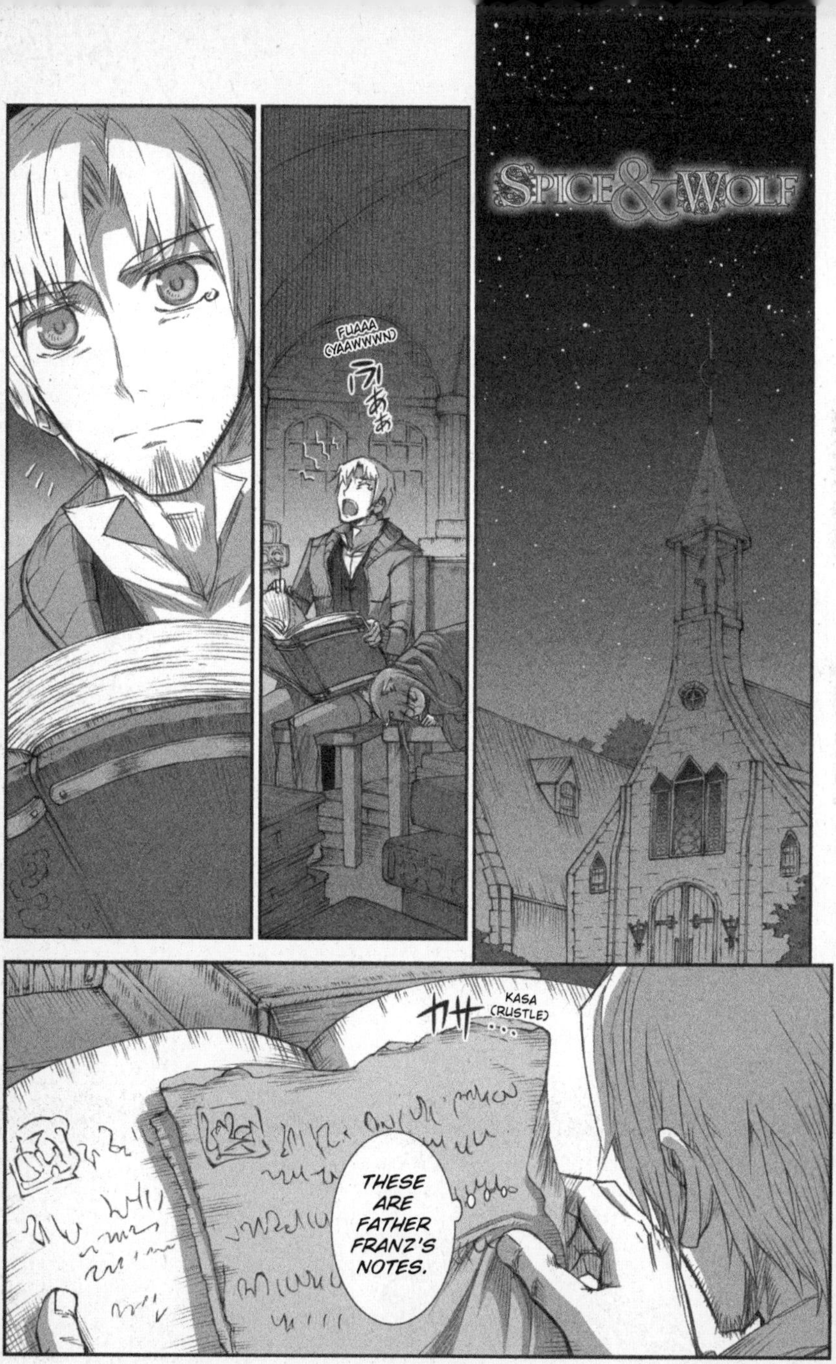
SPICE & WOLF
FUAAA (YAAWWWN)
ふぁああ
カサ
KASA (RUSTLE)
...
THESE ARE FATHER FRANZ'S NOTES.

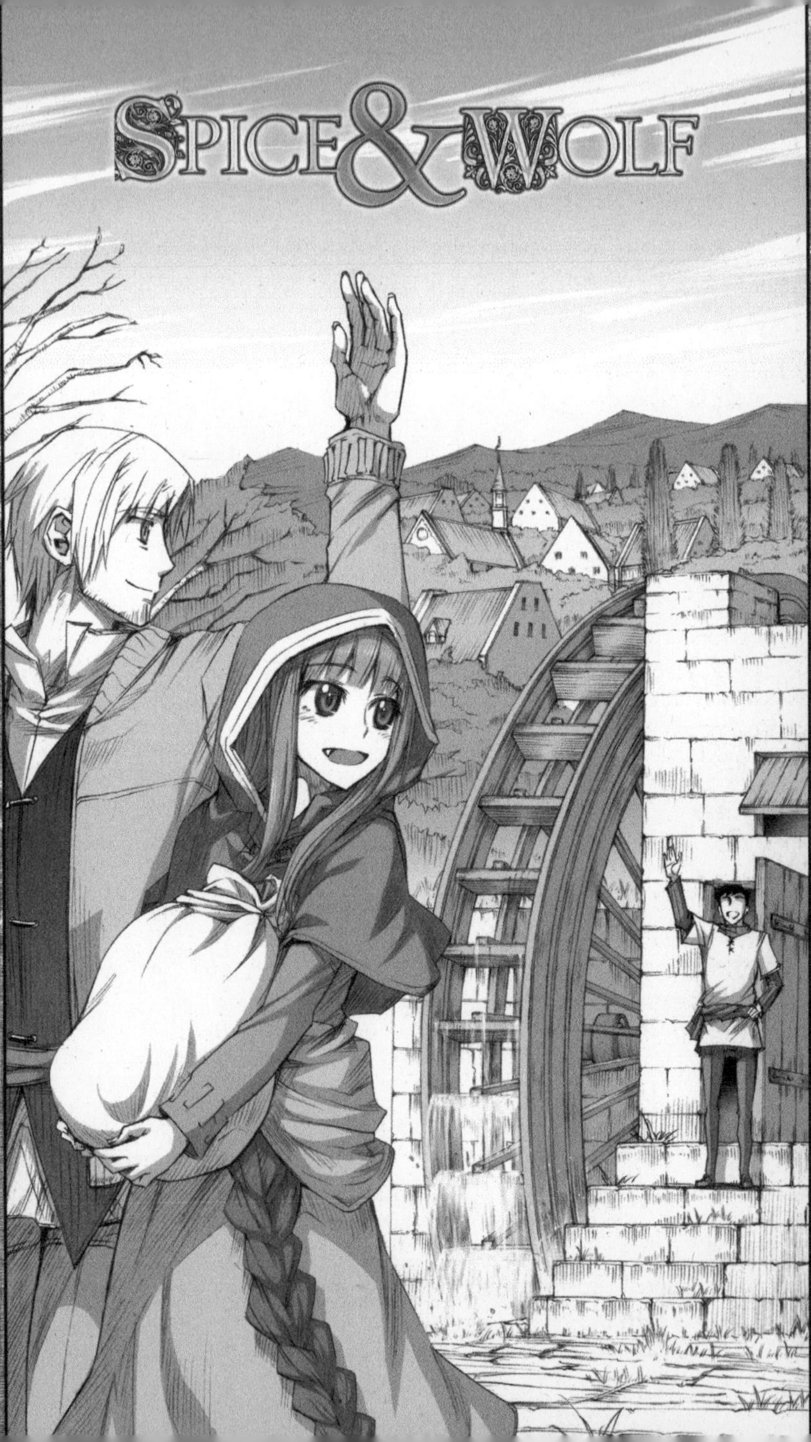
SPICE&WOLF

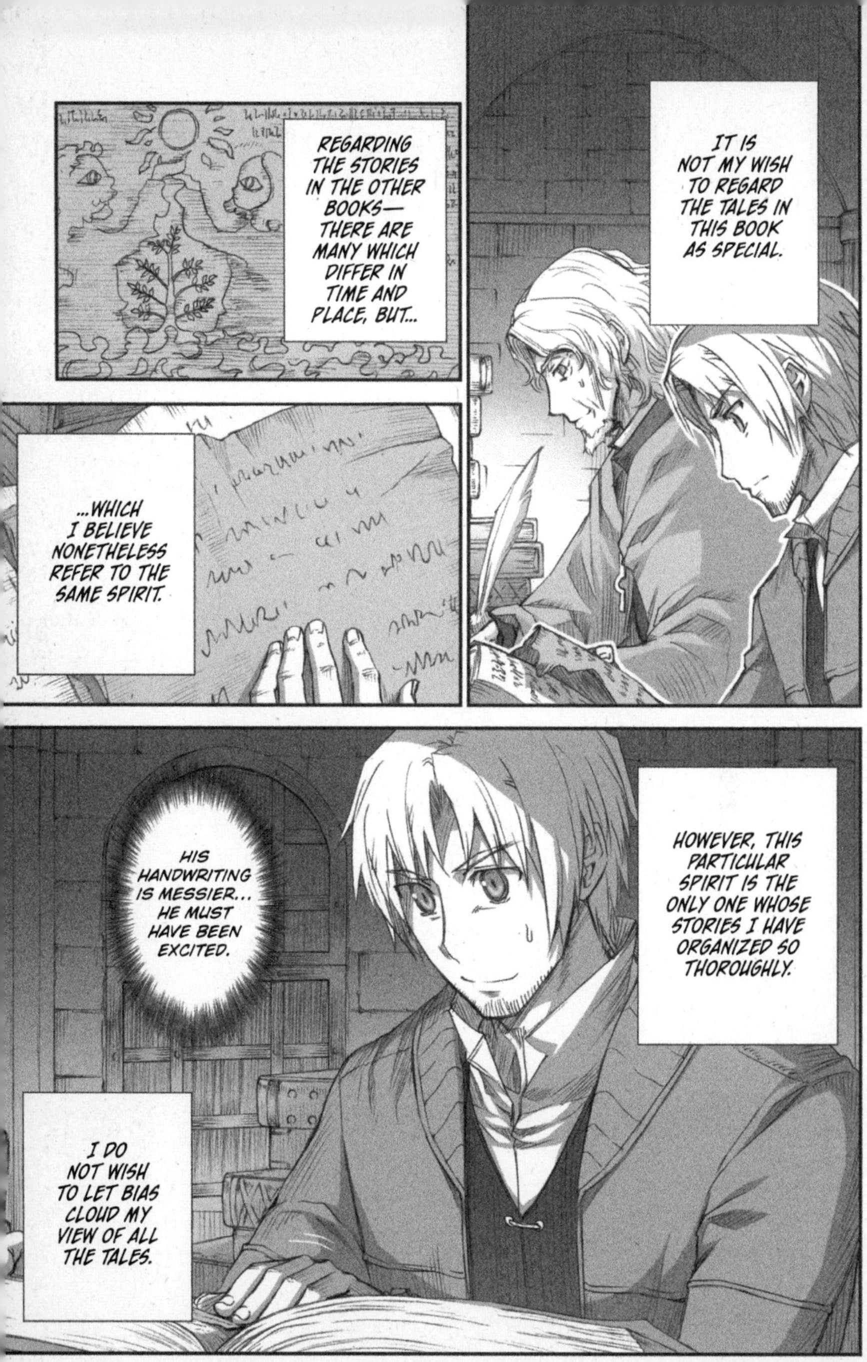
IT IS NOT MY WISH TO REGARD THE TALES IN THIS BOOK AS SPECIAL.
REGARDING THE STORIES IN THE OTHER BOOKS—THERE ARE MANY WHICH DIFFER IN TIME AND PLACE, BUT...
...WHICH I BELIEVE NONETHELESS REFER TO THE SAME SPIRIT.
HOWEVER, THIS PARTICULAR SPIRIT IS THE ONLY ONE WHOSE STORIES I HAVE ORGANIZED SO THOROUGHLY.
HIS HANDWRITING IS MESSIER... HE MUST HAVE BEEN EXCITED.
I DO NOT WISH TO LET BIAS CLOUD MY VIEW OF ALL THE TALES.

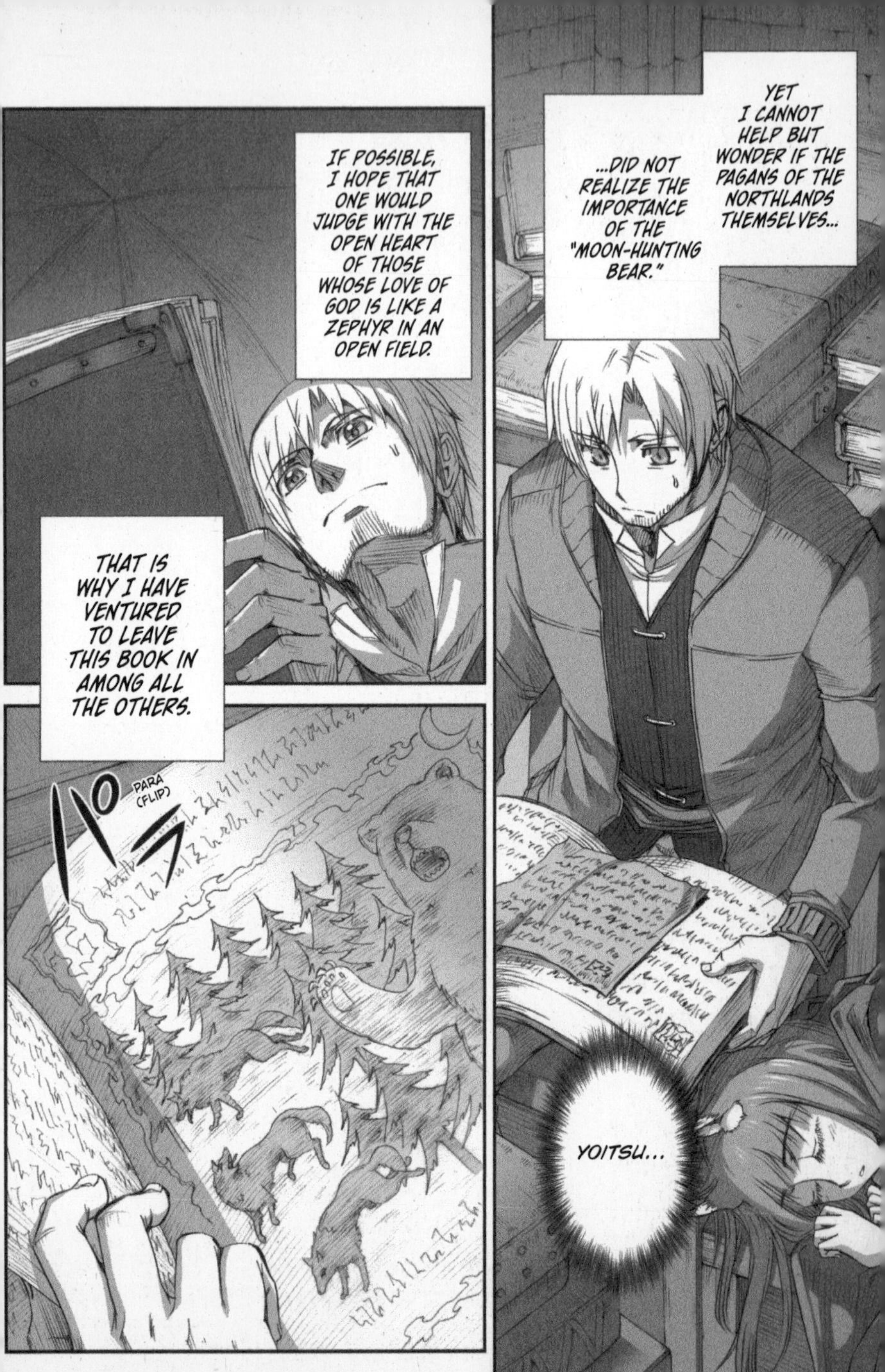
YET I CANNOT HELP BUT WONDER IF THE PAGANS OF THE NORTHLANDS THEMSELVES...
...DID NOT REALIZE THE IMPORTANCE OF THE "MOON-HUNTING BEAR."
YOITSU...
IF POSSIBLE, I HOPE THAT ONE WOULD JUDGE WITH THE OPEN HEART OF THOSE WHOSE LOVE OF GOD IS LIKE A ZEPHYR IN AN OPEN FIELD.
THAT IS WHY I HAVE VENTURED TO LEAVE THIS BOOK IN AMONG ALL THE OTHERS.
PARA (FLIP)

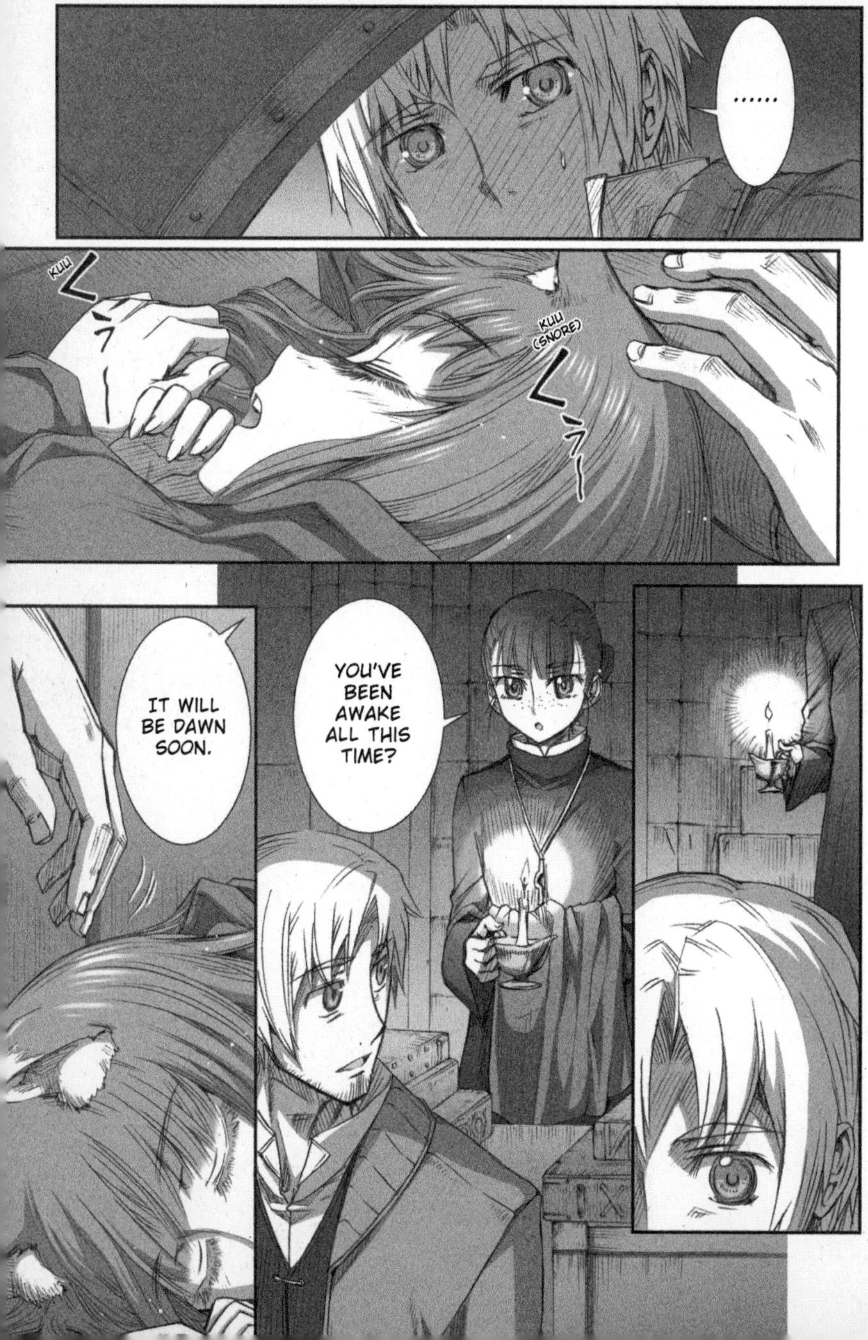
......
KUU (SNORE)
KUU
YOU'VE BEEN AWAKE ALL THIS TIME?
IT WILL BE DAWN SOON.

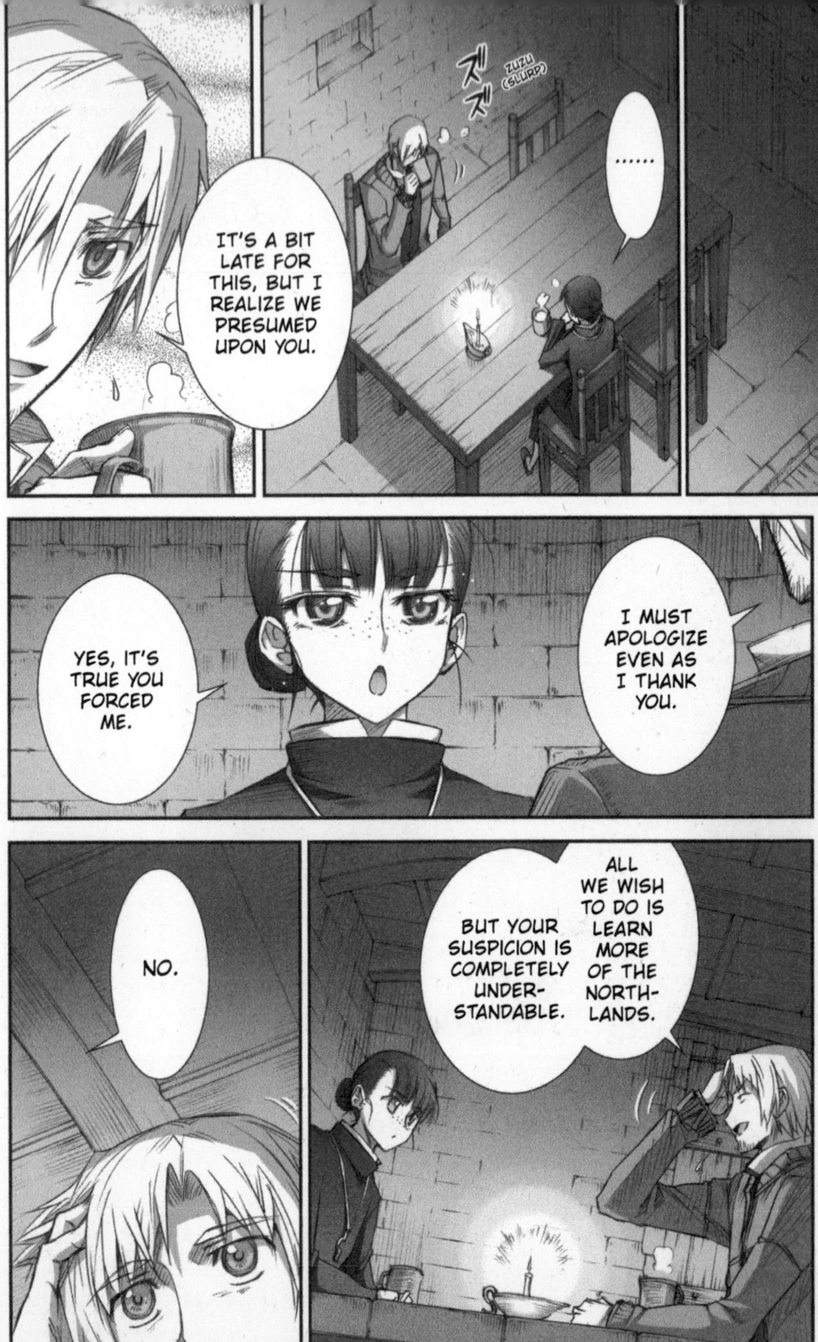
ズズ
ZUZU (SLURP)
......
IT'S A BIT LATE FOR THIS, BUT I REALIZE WE PRESUMED UPON YOU.
I MUST APOLOGIZE EVEN AS I THANK YOU.
YES, IT'S TRUE YOU FORCED ME.
ALL WE WISH TO DO IS LEARN MORE OF THE NORTH-LANDS.
BUT YOUR SUSPICION IS COMPLETELY UNDER-STANDABLE.
NO.

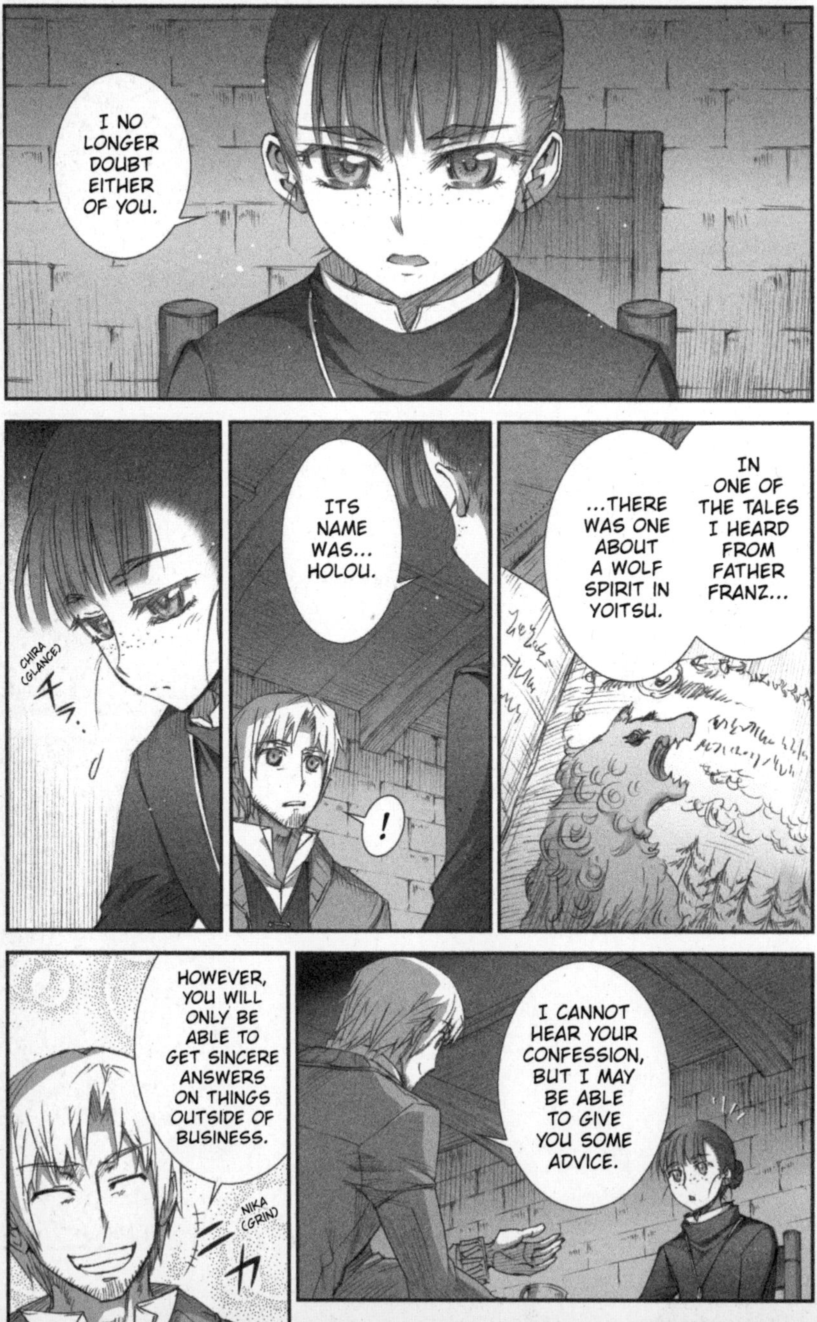
I NO LONGER DOUBT EITHER OF YOU.
IN ONE OF THE TALES I HEARD FROM FATHER FRANZ...
...THERE WAS ONE ABOUT A WOLF SPIRIT IN YOITSU.
ITS NAME WAS... HOLOU.
!
CHIRA (GLANCE)
I CANNOT HEAR YOUR CONFESSION, BUT I MAY BE ABLE TO GIVE YOU SOME ADVICE.
HOWEVER, YOU WILL ONLY BE ABLE TO GET SINCERE ANSWERS ON THINGS OUTSIDE OF BUSINESS.
NIKA (GRIN)

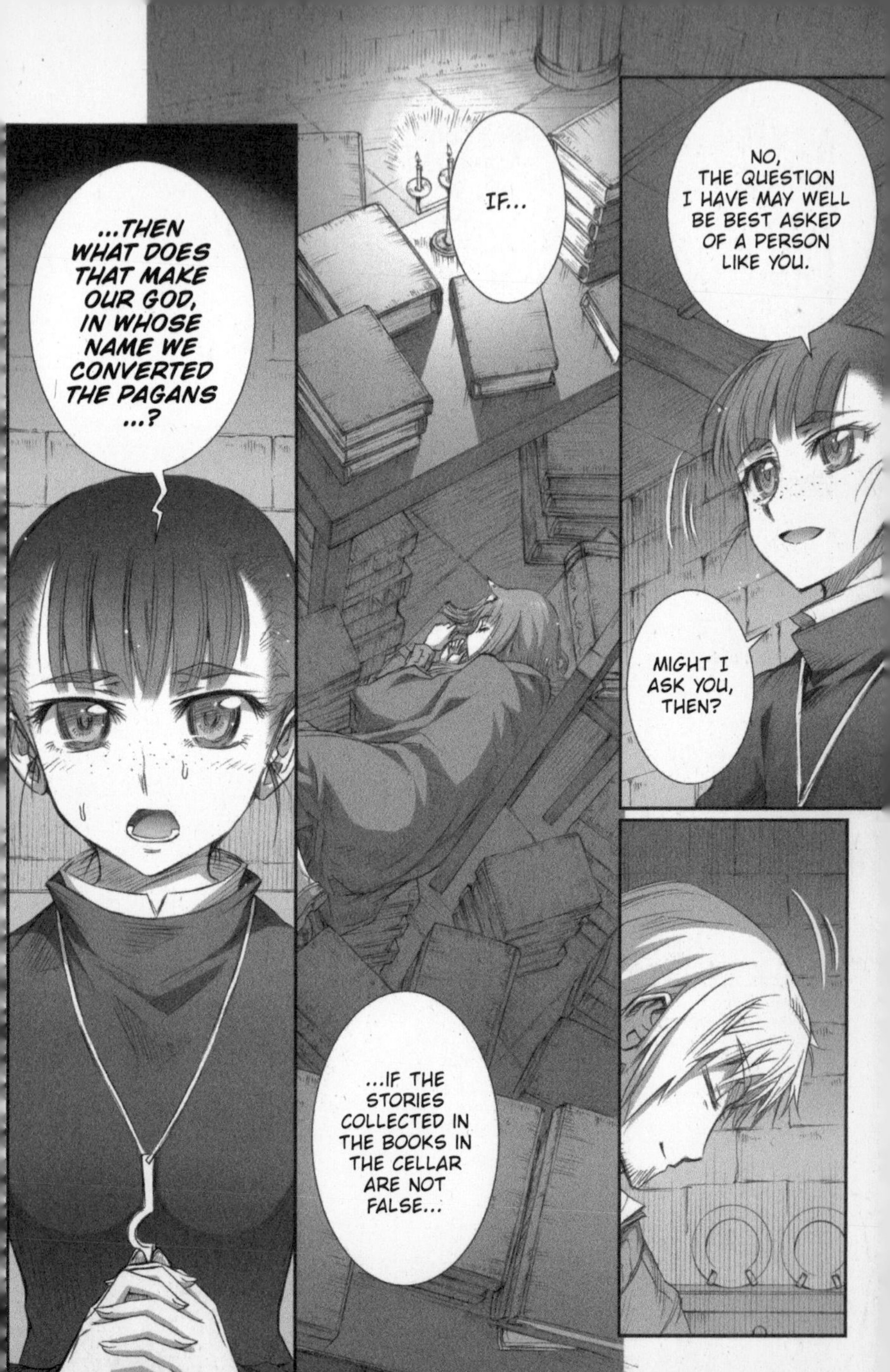
NO, THE QUESTION I HAVE MAY WELL BE BEST ASKED OF A PERSON LIKE YOU.
MIGHT I ASK YOU, THEN?
IF...
...IF THE STORIES COLLECTED IN THE BOOKS IN THE CELLAR ARE NOT FALSE...
...THEN WHAT DOES THAT MAKE OUR GOD, IN WHOSE NAME WE CONVERTED THE PAGANS ...?

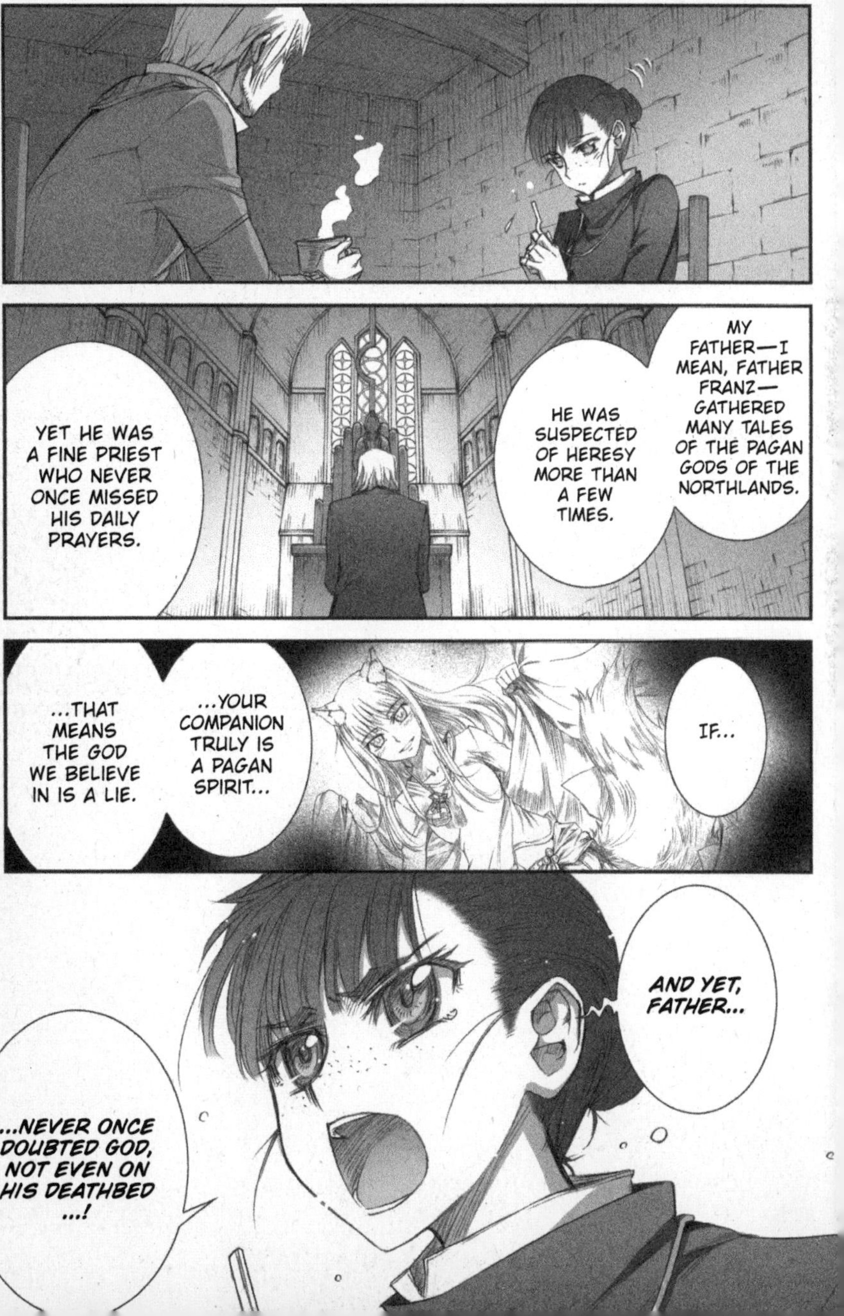
MY FATHER—I MEAN, FATHER FRANZ—GATHERED MANY TALES OF THE PAGAN GODS OF THE NORTHLANDS.
HE WAS SUSPECTED OF HERESY MORE THAN A FEW TIMES.
YET HE WAS A FINE PRIEST WHO NEVER ONCE MISSED HIS DAILY PRAYERS.
IF...
...YOUR COMPANION TRULY IS A PAGAN SPIRIT...
...THAT MEANS THE GOD WE BELIEVE IN IS A LIE.
AND YET, FATHER...
...NEVER ONCE DOUBTED GOD, NOT EVEN ON HIS DEATHBED ...!

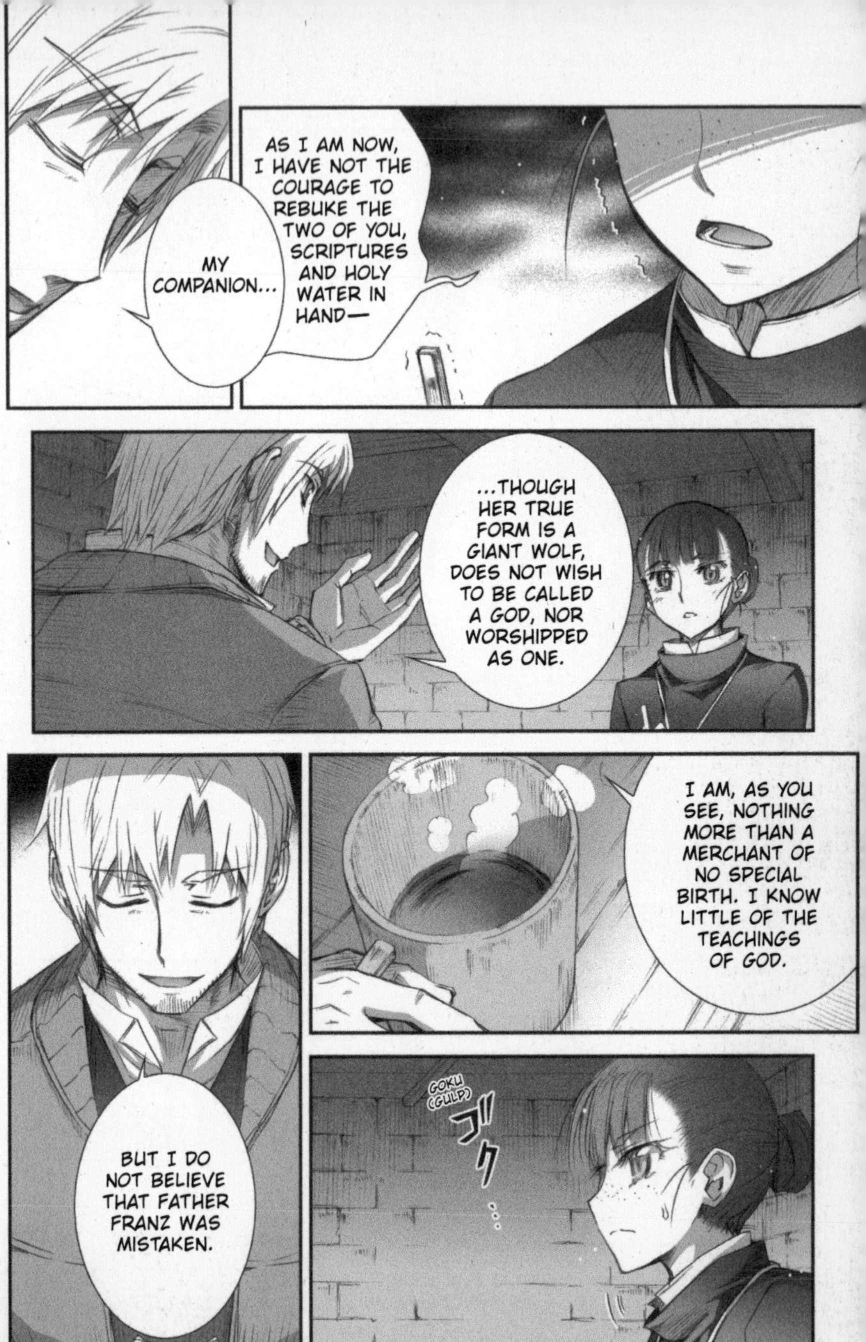
AS I AM NOW, I HAVE NOT THE COURAGE TO REBUKE THE TWO OF YOU, SCRIPTURES AND HOLY WATER IN HAND—
MY COMPANION...
...THOUGH HER TRUE FORM IS A GIANT WOLF, DOES NOT WISH TO BE CALLED A GOD, NOR WORSHIPPED AS ONE.
I AM, AS YOU SEE, NOTHING MORE THAN A MERCHANT OF NO SPECIAL BIRTH. I KNOW LITTLE OF THE TEACHINGS OF GOD.
GOKU (GULP)
ゴク
...
BUT I DO NOT BELIEVE THAT FATHER FRANZ WAS MISTAKEN.

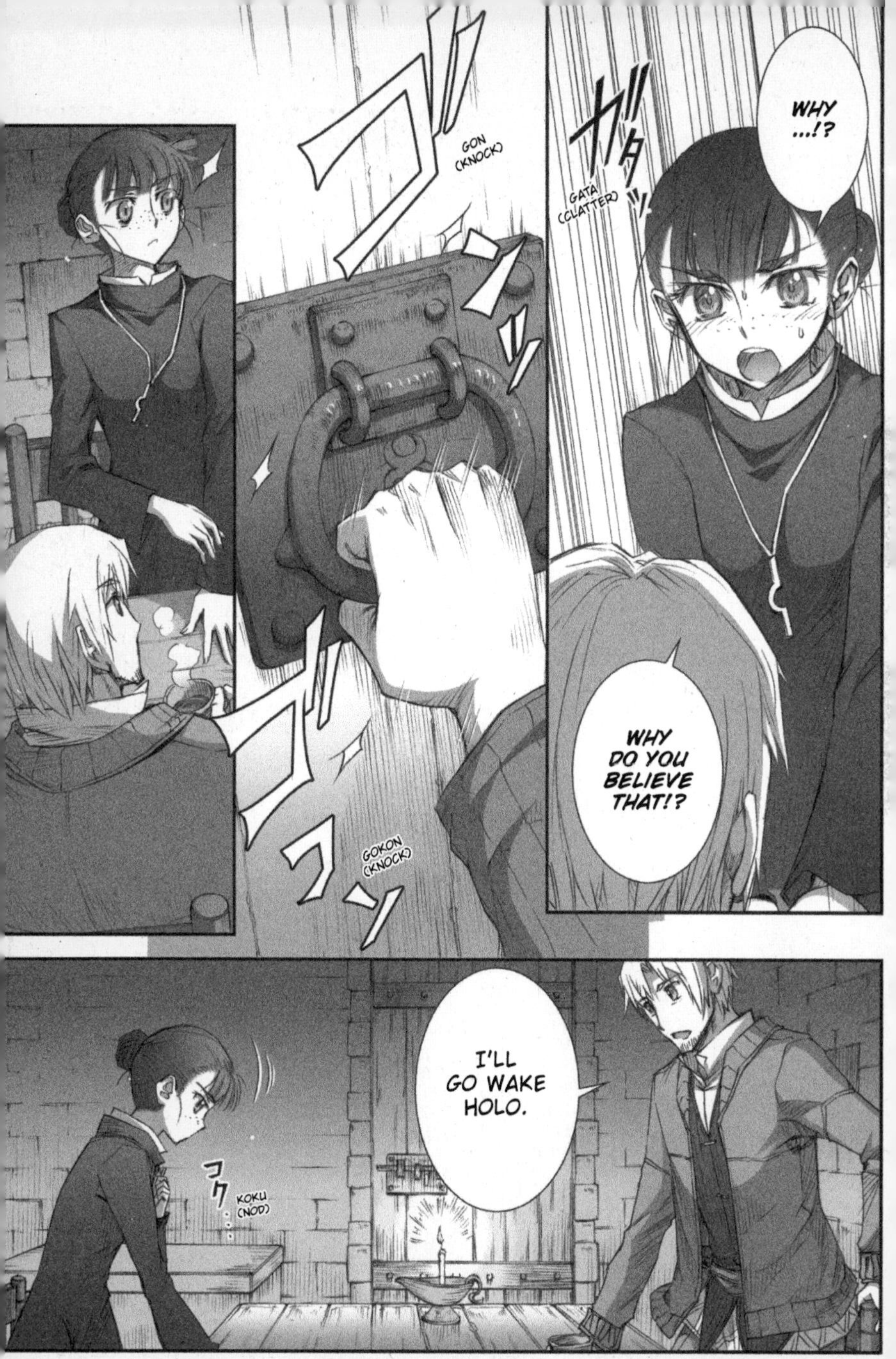
WHY ...!?
GATA (CLATTER)
WHY DO YOU BELIEVE THAT!?
GON (KNOCK)
GOKON (KNOCK)
I'LL GO WAKE HOLO.
KOKU (NOD)

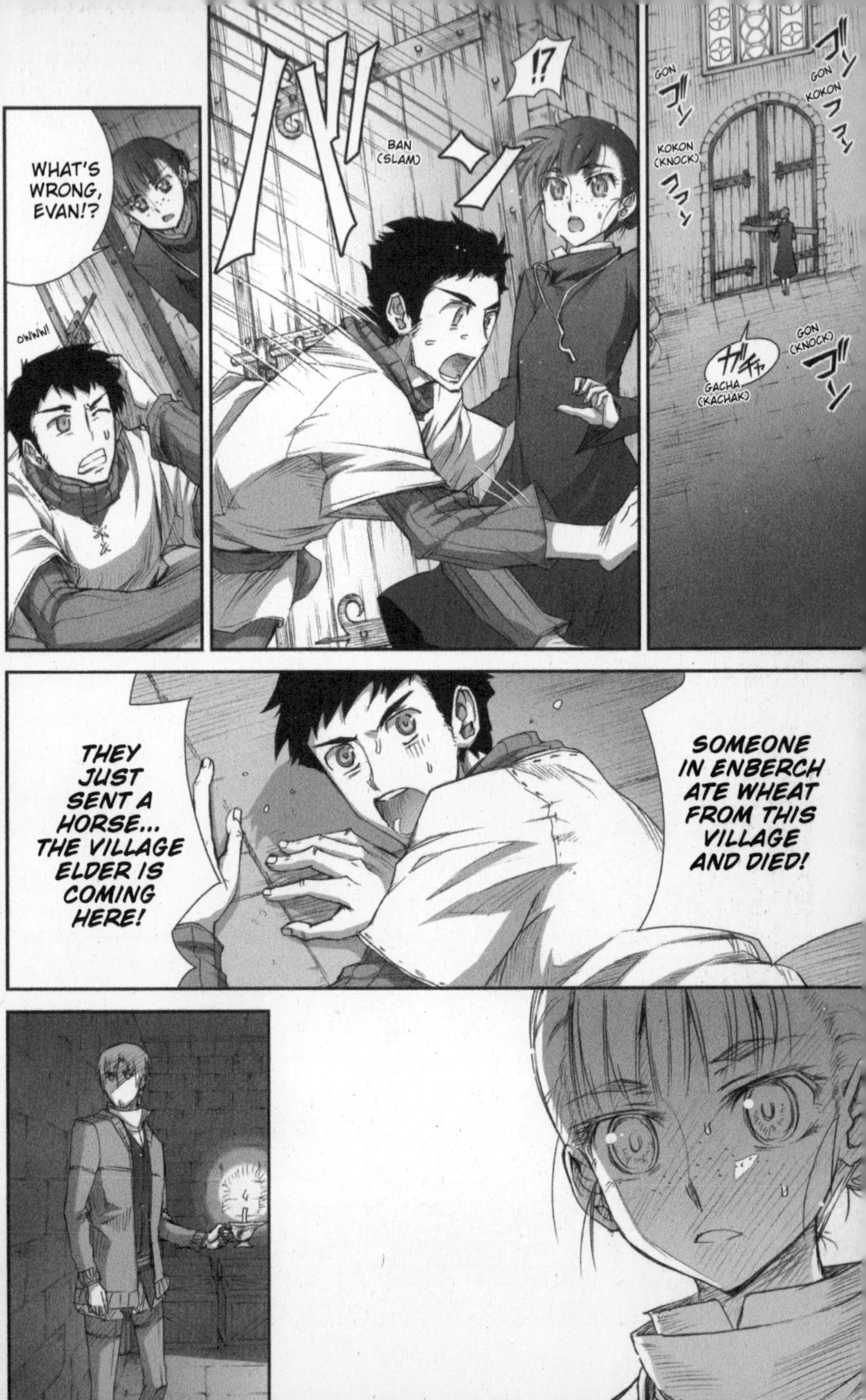
GON
KOKON
GON
KOKON (KNOCK)
GON (KNOCK)
GACHA (KACHAK)
!?
BAN (SLAM)
WHAT'S WRONG, EVAN!?
OWWW!
SOMEONE IN ENBERCH ATE WHEAT FROM THIS VILLAGE AND DIED!
THEY JUST SENT A HORSE... THE VILLAGE ELDER IS COMING HERE!

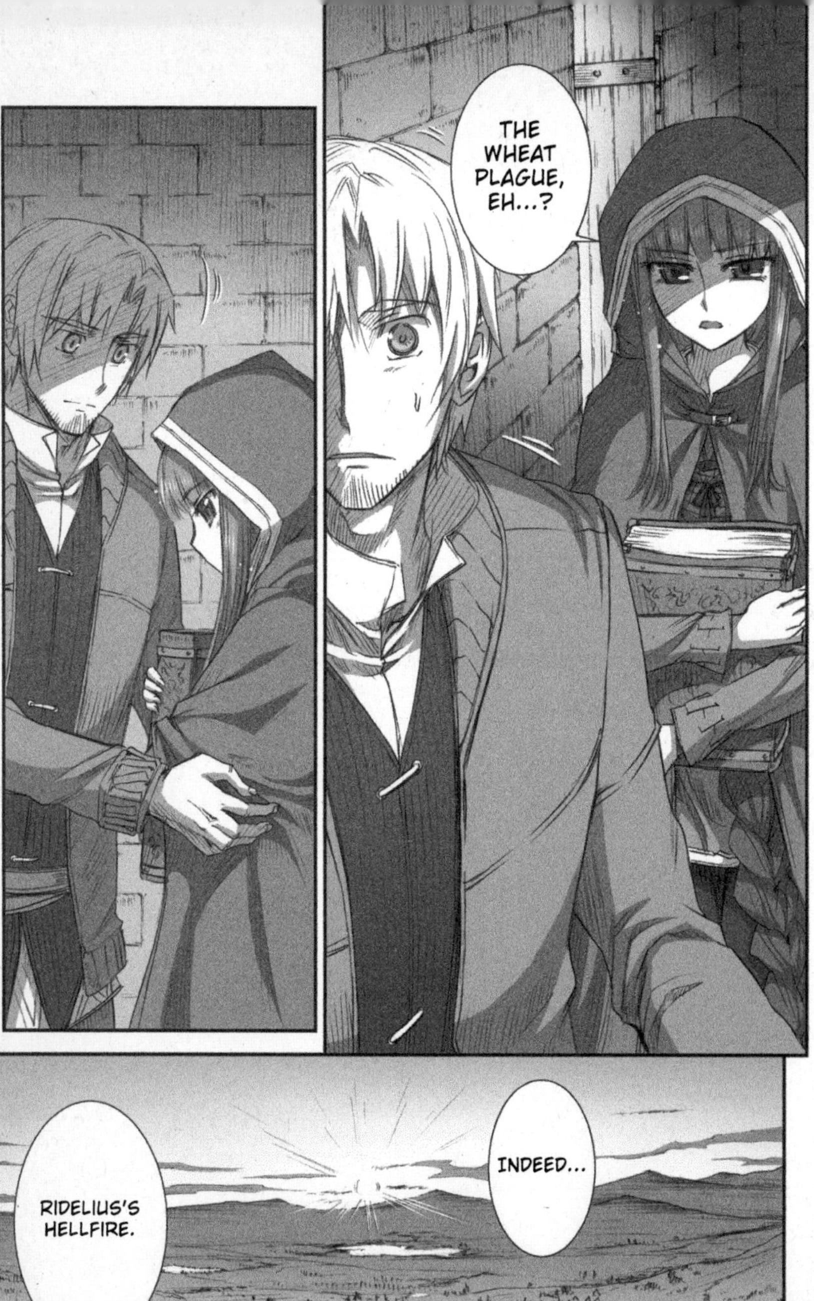
THE WHEAT PLAGUE, EH...?
INDEED...
RIDELIUS'S HELLFIRE.

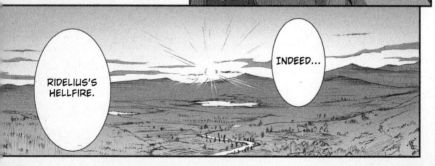

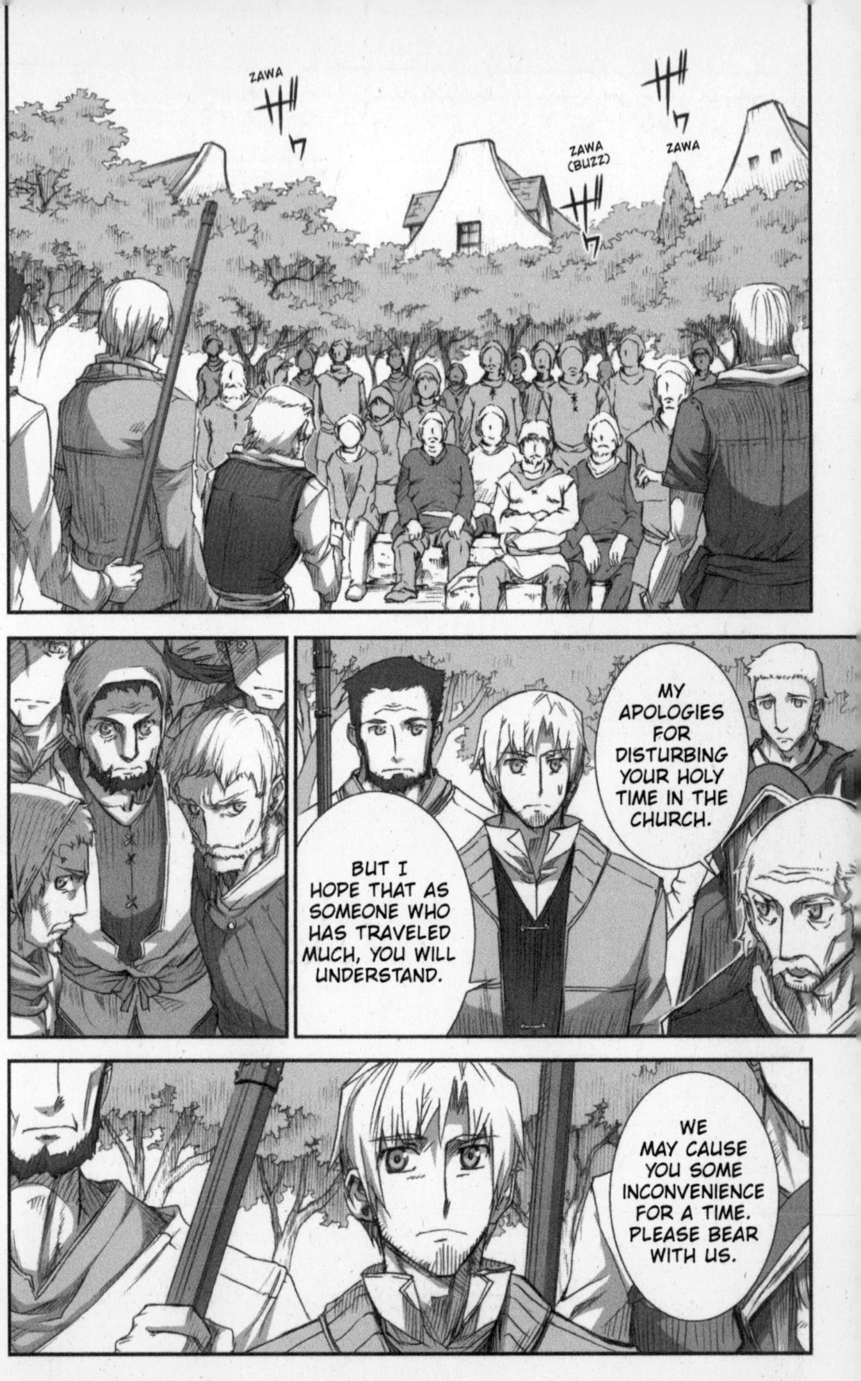
ZAWA
ZAWA (BUZZ)
ZAWA
MY APOLOGIES FOR DISTURBING YOUR HOLY TIME IN THE CHURCH.
BUT I HOPE THAT AS SOMEONE WHO HAS TRAVELED MUCH, YOU WILL UNDERSTAND.
WE MAY CAUSE YOU SOME INCONVENIENCE FOR A TIME. PLEASE BEAR WITH US.

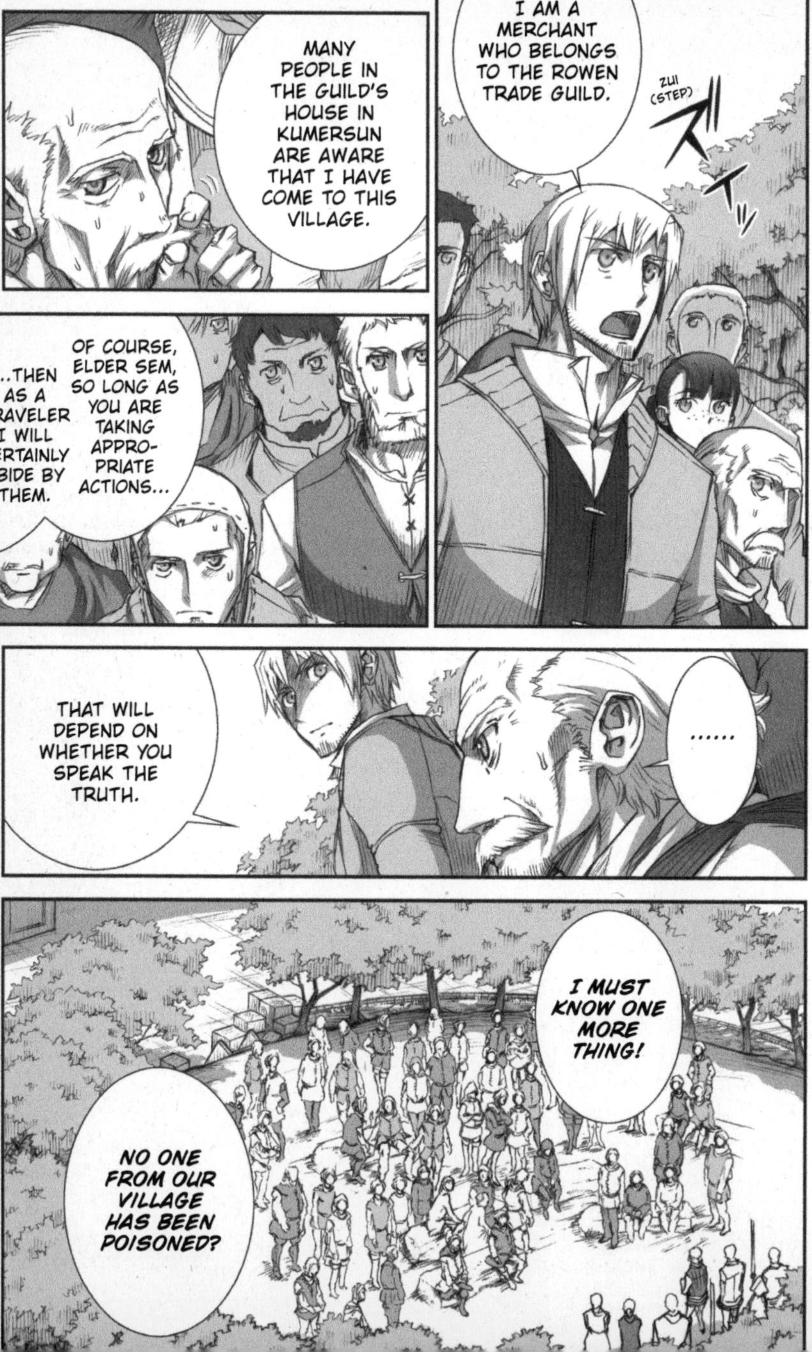
I AM A MERCHANT WHO BELONGS TO THE ROWEN TRADE GUILD.
ZUI (STEP)
MANY PEOPLE IN THE GUILD'S HOUSE IN KUMERSUN ARE AWARE THAT I HAVE COME TO THIS VILLAGE.
OF COURSE, ELDER SEM, SO LONG AS YOU ARE TAKING APPROPRIATE ACTIONS...
...THEN AS A TRAVELER I WILL CERTAINLY ABIDE BY THEM.
......
THAT WILL DEPEND ON WHETHER YOU SPEAK THE TRUTH.
I MUST KNOW ONE MORE THING!
NO ONE FROM OUR VILLAGE HAS BEEN POISONED?

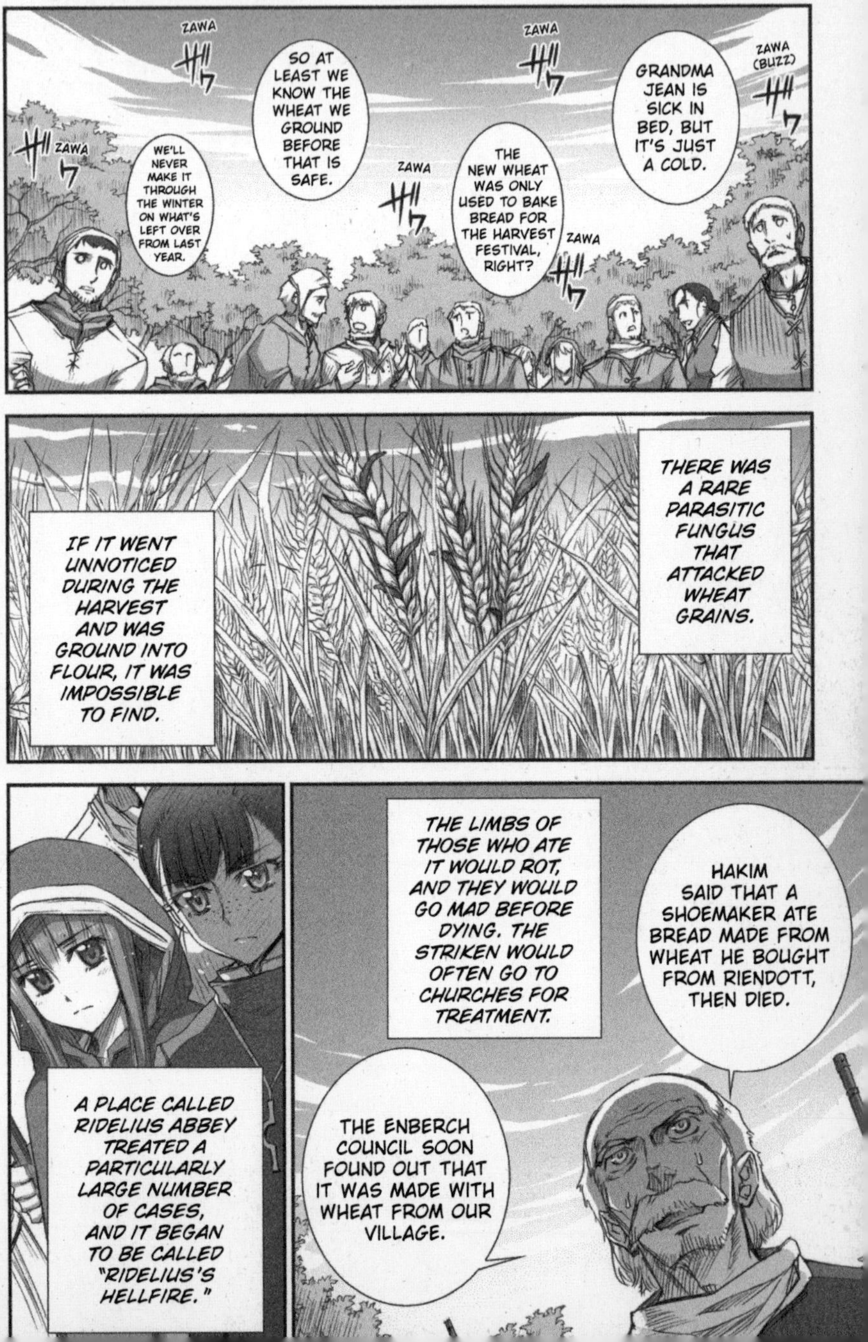
ZAWA (BUZZ)
GRANDMA JEAN IS SICK IN BED, BUT IT'S JUST A COLD.
ZAWA
ZAWA
THE NEW WHEAT WAS ONLY USED TO BAKE BREAD FOR THE HARVEST FESTIVAL, RIGHT?
ZAWA
SO AT LEAST WE KNOW THE WHEAT WE GROUND BEFORE THAT IS SAFE.
ZAWA
WE'LL NEVER MAKE IT THROUGH THE WINTER ON WHAT'S LEFT OVER FROM LAST YEAR.
ZAWA
THERE WAS A RARE PARASITIC FUNGUS THAT ATTACKED WHEAT GRAINS.
IF IT WENT UNNOTICED DURING THE HARVEST AND WAS GROUND INTO FLOUR, IT WAS IMPOSSIBLE TO FIND.
THE LIMBS OF THOSE WHO ATE IT WOULD ROT, AND THEY WOULD GO MAD BEFORE DYING. THE STRIKEN WOULD OFTEN GO TO CHURCHES FOR TREATMENT.
HAKIM SAID THAT A SHOEMAKER ATE BREAD MADE FROM WHEAT HE BOUGHT FROM RIENDOTT, THEN DIED.
THE ENBERCH COUNCIL SOON FOUND OUT THAT IT WAS MADE WITH WHEAT FROM OUR VILLAGE.
A PLACE CALLED RIDELIUS ABBEY TREATED A PARTICULARLY LARGE NUMBER OF CASES, AND IT BEGAN TO BE CALLED "RIDELIUS'S HELLFIRE."

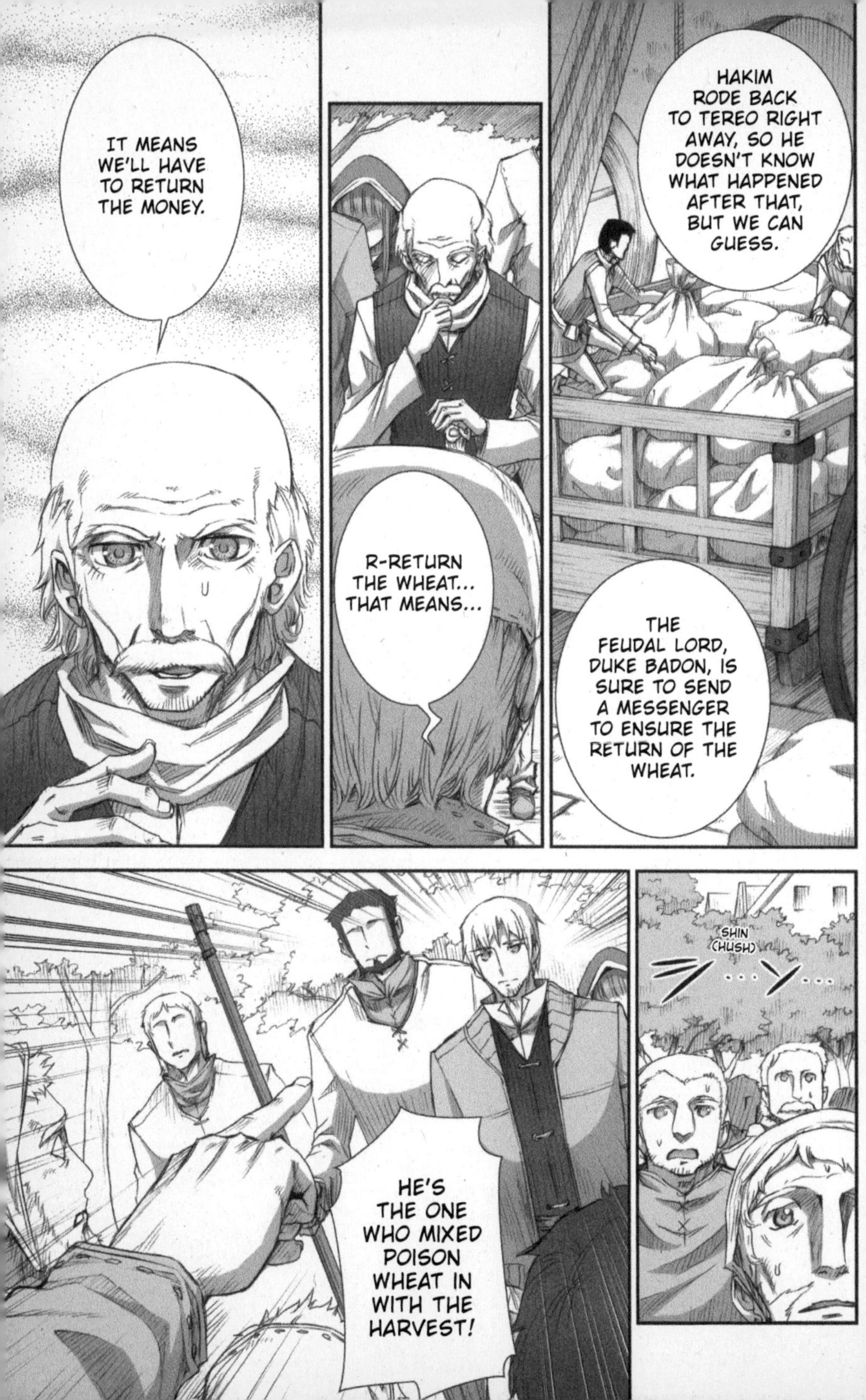
HAKIM RODE BACK TO TEREO RIGHT AWAY, SO HE DOESN'T KNOW WHAT HAPPENED AFTER THAT, BUT WE CAN GUESS.
THE FEUDAL LORD, DUKE BADON, IS SURE TO SEND A MESSENGER TO ENSURE THE RETURN OF THE WHEAT.
R-RETURN THE WHEAT... THAT MEANS...
IT MEANS WE'LL HAVE TO RETURN THE MONEY.
SHIN (HUSH)
HE'S THE ONE WHO MIXED POISON WHEAT IN WITH THE HARVEST!

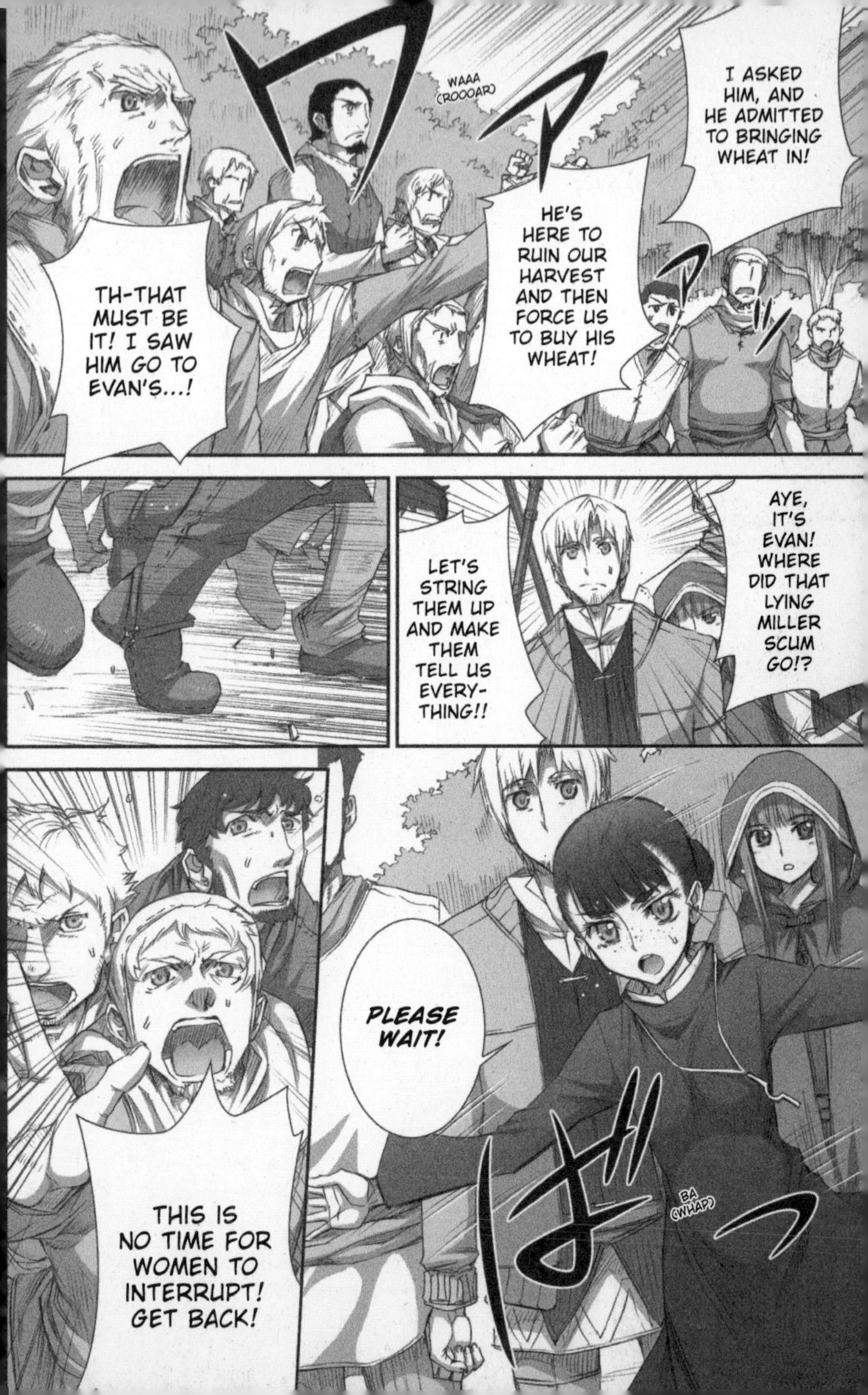
I ASKED HIM, AND HE ADMITTED TO BRINGING WHEAT IN!
WAAA (ROOOAR)
HE'S HERE TO RUIN OUR HARVEST AND THEN FORCE US TO BUY HIS WHEAT!
TH-THAT MUST BE IT! I SAW HIM GO TO EVAN'S...!
AYE, IT'S EVAN! WHERE DID THAT LYING MILLER SCUM GO!?
LET'S STRING THEM UP AND MAKE THEM TELL US EVERY-THING!!
PLEASE WAIT!
BA (WHAP)
THIS IS NO TIME FOR WOMEN TO INTERRUPT! GET BACK!

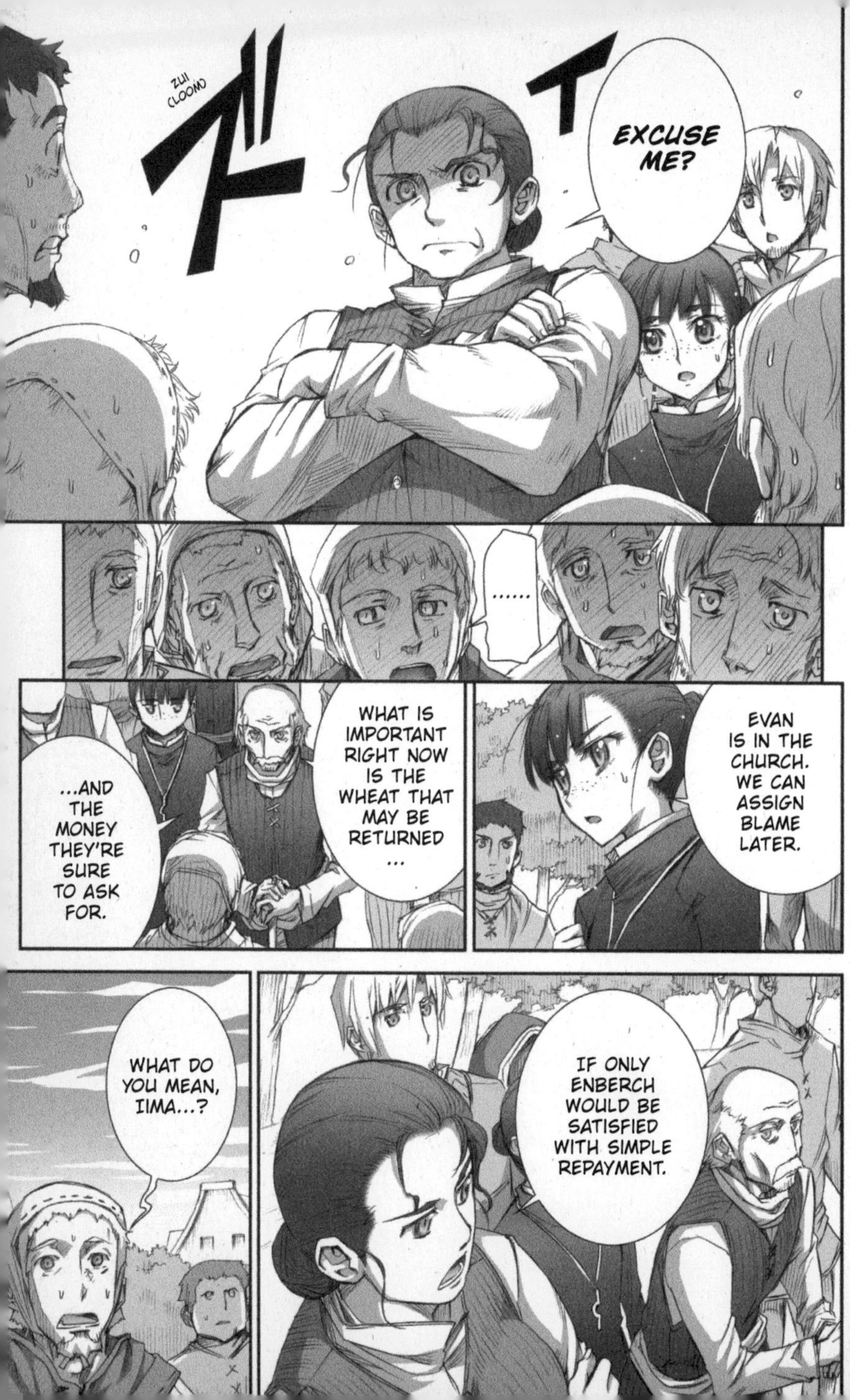
EXCUSE ME?
ZUI (LOOM)
......
EVAN IS IN THE CHURCH. WE CAN ASSIGN BLAME LATER.
WHAT IS IMPORTANT RIGHT NOW IS THE WHEAT THAT MAY BE RETURNED ...
...AND THE MONEY THEY'RE SURE TO ASK FOR.
IF ONLY ENBERCH WOULD BE SATISFIED WITH SIMPLE REPAYMENT.
WHAT DO YOU MEAN, IIMA...?

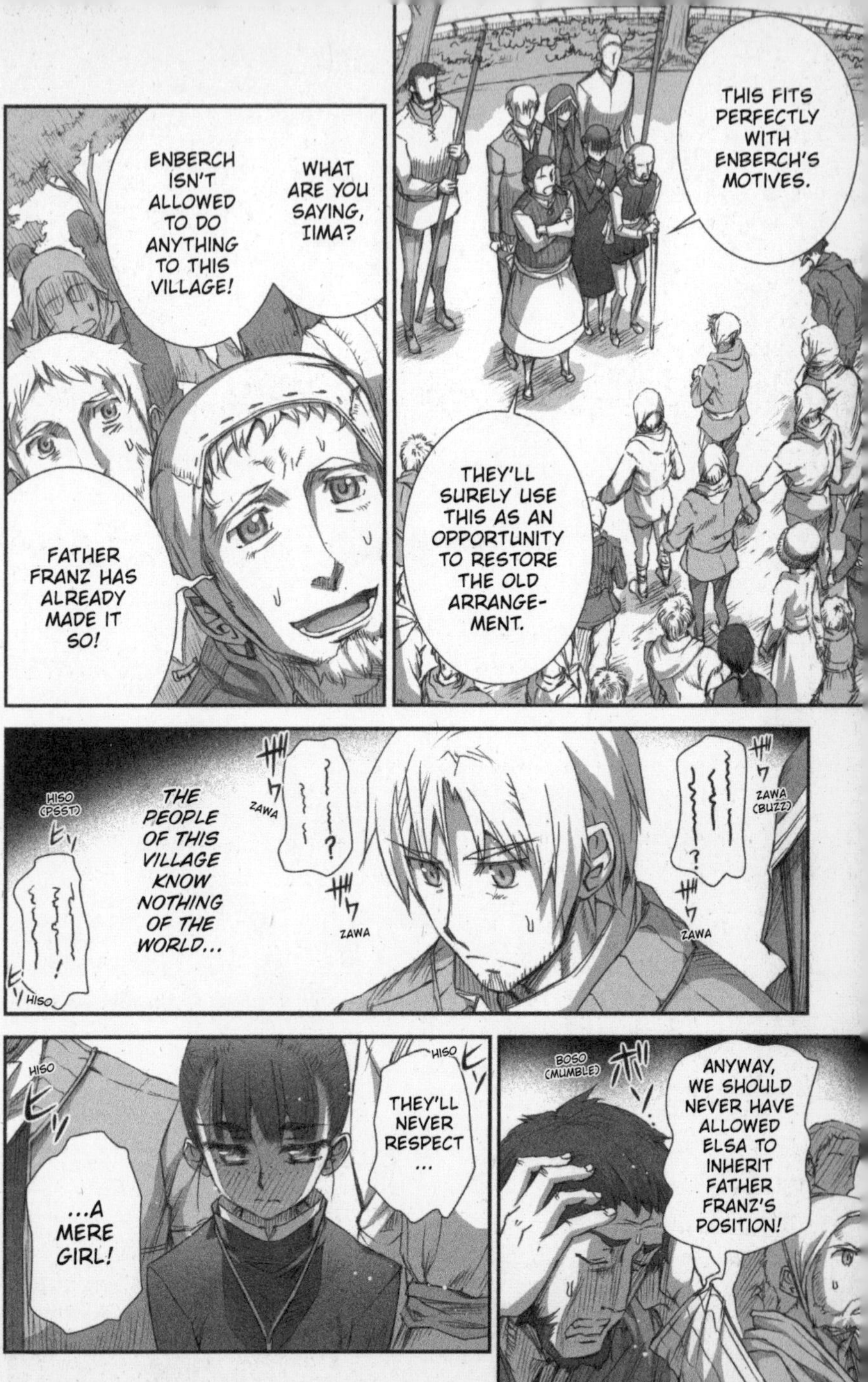
THIS FITS PERFECTLY WITH ENBERCH'S MOTIVES.
THEY'LL SURELY USE THIS AS AN OPPORTUNITY TO RESTORE THE OLD ARRANGE-MENT.
WHAT ARE YOU SAYING, IMA?
ENBERCH ISN'T ALLOWED TO DO ANYTHING TO THIS VILLAGE!
FATHER FRANZ HAS ALREADY MADE IT SO!
ZAWA (BUZZ)
ZAWA
ZAWA
ZAWA
THE PEOPLE OF THIS VILLAGE KNOW NOTHING OF THE WORLD...
HISO (PSST)
HISO
BOSO (MUMBLE)
ANYWAY, WE SHOULD NEVER HAVE ALLOWED ELSA TO INHERIT FATHER FRANZ'S POSITION!
HISO
THEY'LL NEVER RESPECT ...
HISO
...A MERE GIRL!

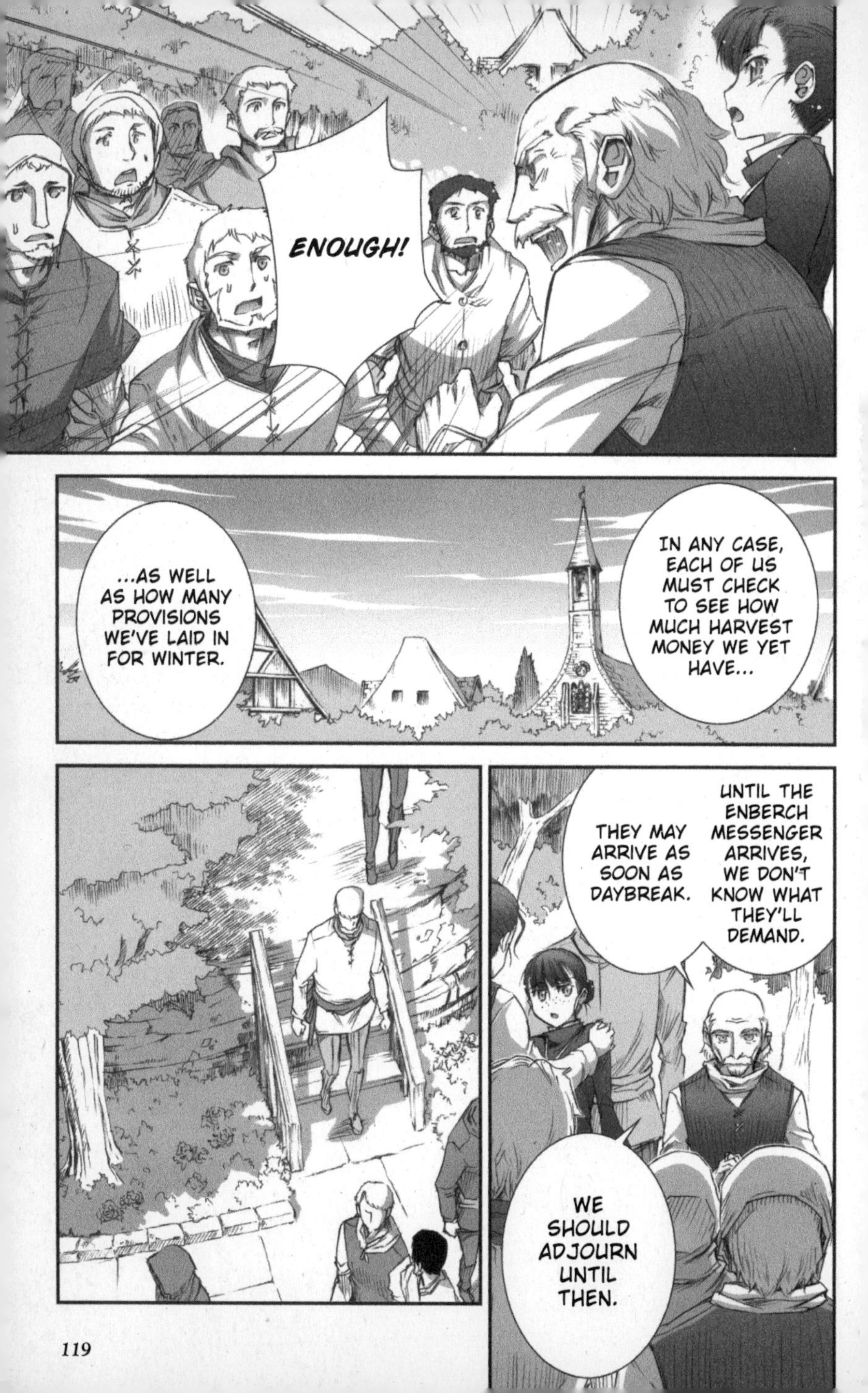
ENOUGH!
IN ANY CASE, EACH OF US MUST CHECK TO SEE HOW MUCH HARVEST MONEY WE YET HAVE...
...AS WELL AS HOW MANY PROVISIONS WE'VE LAID IN FOR WINTER.
UNTIL THE ENBERCH MESSENGER ARRIVES, WE DON'T KNOW WHAT THEY'LL DEMAND.
THEY MAY ARRIVE AS SOON AS DAYBREAK.
WE SHOULD ADJOURN UNTIL THEN.

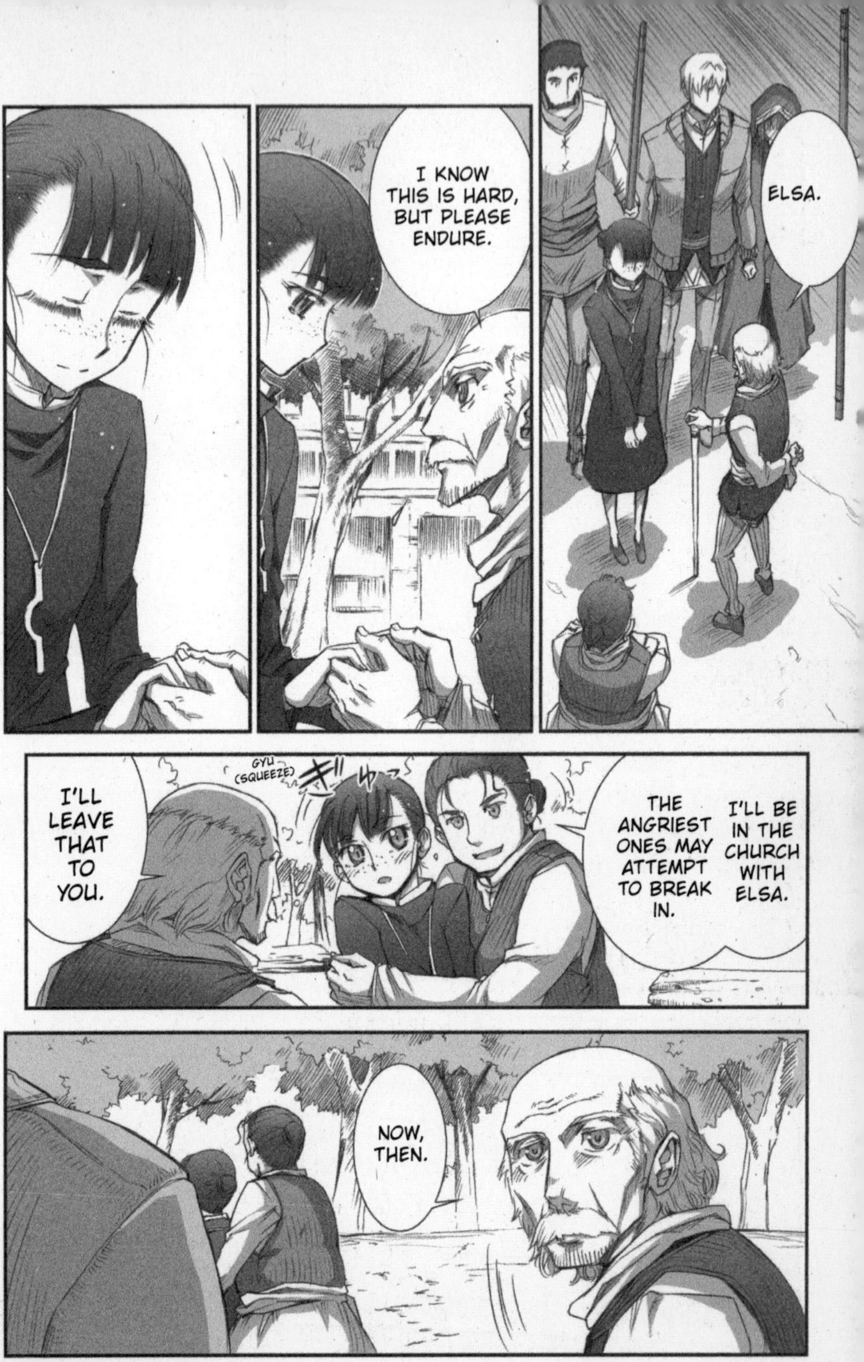
ELSA.
I KNOW THIS IS HARD, BUT PLEASE ENDURE.
I'LL BE IN THE CHURCH WITH ELSA.
THE ANGRIEST ONES MAY ATTEMPT TO BREAK IN.
GYU (SQUEEZE)
I'LL LEAVE THAT TO YOU.
NOW, THEN.

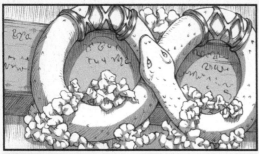

MR. LAWRENCE, I'M AFRAID I WILL HAVE TO ASK YOU TO COME TO MY HOUSE.

JIIII
(STAAARE)

WHAT DO YOU THINK?

I SHOULD'VE GIVEN UP ON THE BOOK AND LEFT THE VILLAGE WITH YOU.

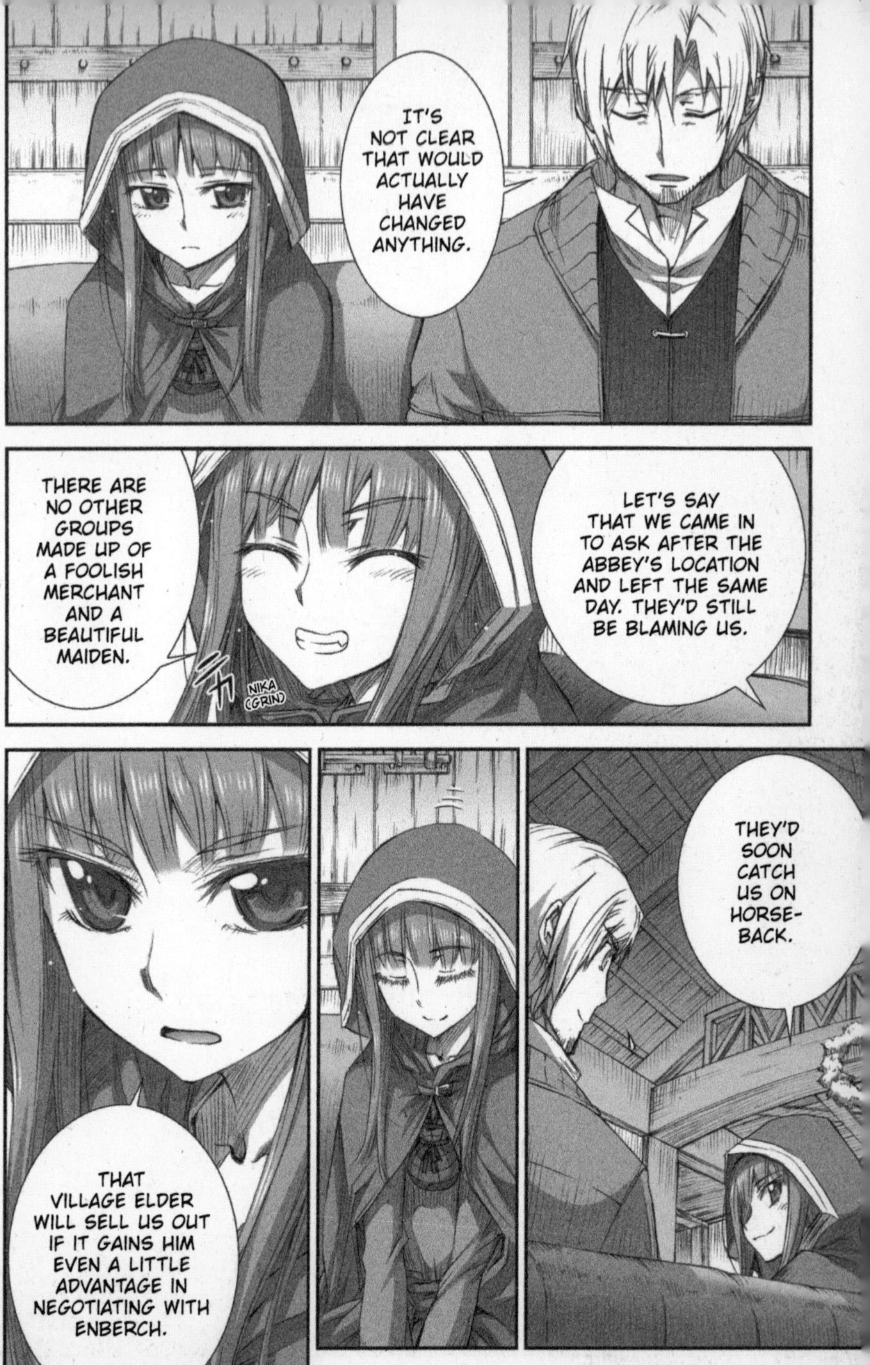
IT'S NOT CLEAR THAT WOULD ACTUALLY HAVE CHANGED ANYTHING.
LET'S SAY THAT WE CAME IN TO ASK AFTER THE ABBEY'S LOCATION AND LEFT THE SAME DAY. THEY'D STILL BE BLAMING US.
THERE ARE NO OTHER GROUPS MADE UP OF A FOOLISH MERCHANT AND A BEAUTIFUL MAIDEN.
NIKA (GRIN)
THEY'D SOON CATCH US ON HORSE-BACK.
THAT VILLAGE ELDER WILL SELL US OUT IF IT GAINS HIM EVEN A LITTLE ADVANTAGE IN NEGOTIATING WITH ENBERCH.

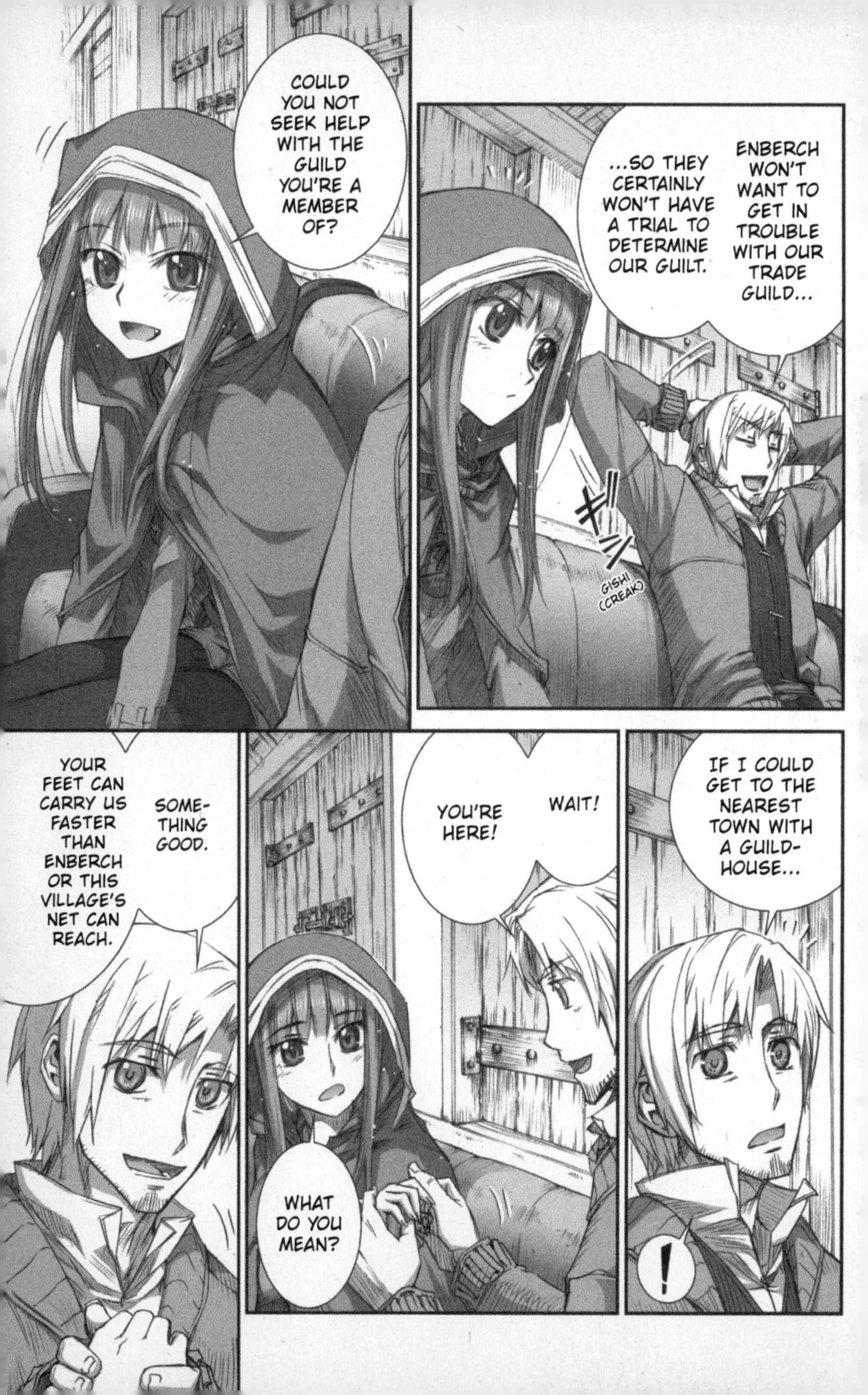

ENBERCH WON'T WANT TO GET IN TROUBLE WITH OUR TRADE GUILD...
...SO THEY CERTAINLY WON'T HAVE A TRIAL TO DETERMINE OUR GUILT.
GISHI (CREAK)
COULD YOU NOT SEEK HELP WITH THE GUILD YOU'RE A MEMBER OF?
IF I COULD GET TO THE NEAREST TOWN WITH A GUILD-HOUSE...
!
WAIT!
YOU'RE HERE!
WHAT DO YOU MEAN?
SOME-THING GOOD.
YOUR FEET CAN CARRY US FASTER THAN ENBERCH OR THIS VILLAGE'S NET CAN REACH.

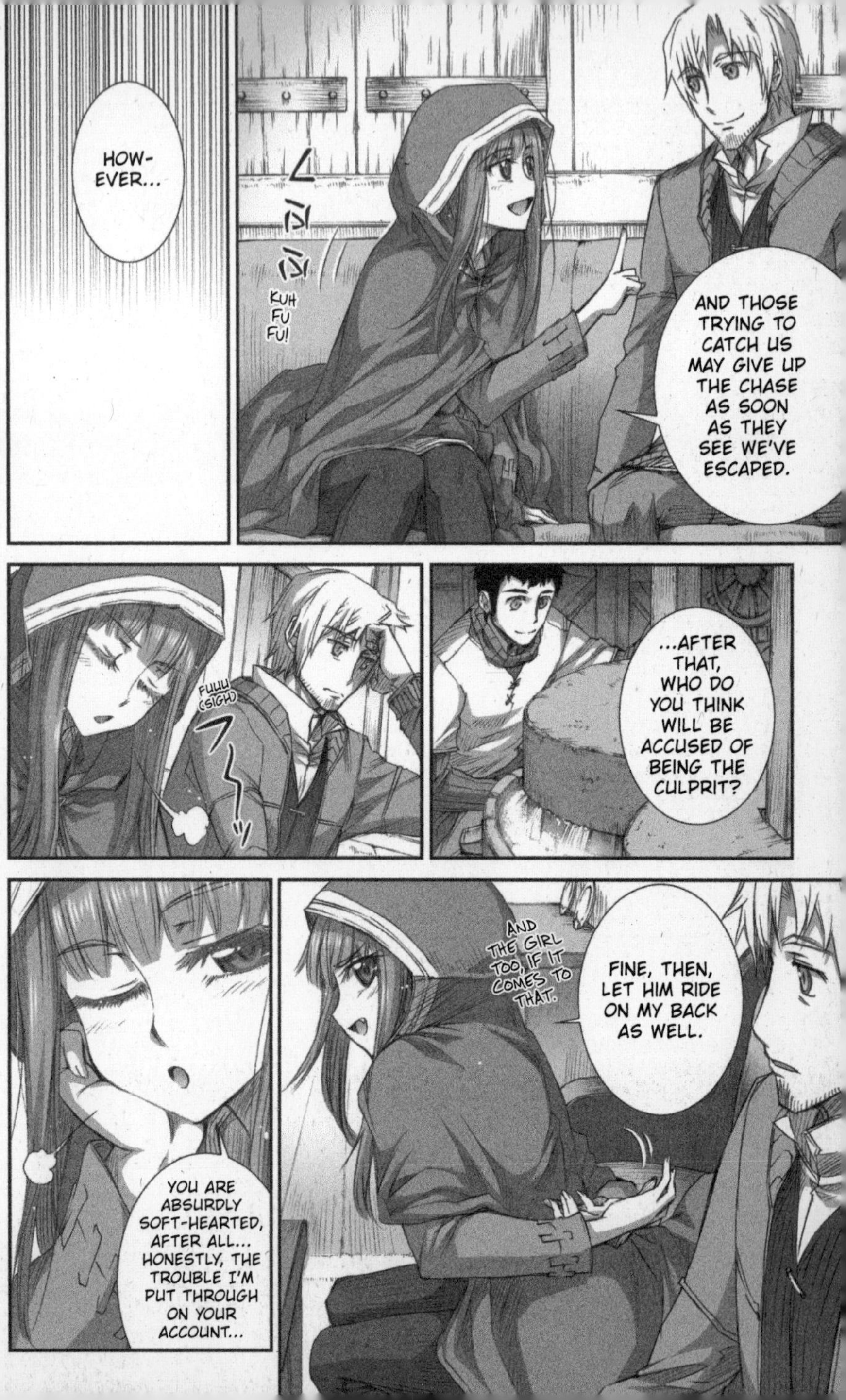
AND THOSE TRYING TO CATCH US MAY GIVE UP THE CHASE AS SOON AS THEY SEE WE'VE ESCAPED.
KUH FU FU!
HOW-EVER...
...AFTER THAT, WHO DO YOU THINK WILL BE ACCUSED OF BEING THE CULPRIT?
FUUU (SIGH)
FINE, THEN, LET HIM RIDE ON MY BACK AS WELL.
AND THE GIRL TOO, IF IT COMES TO THAT.
YOU ARE ABSURDLY SOFT-HEARTED, AFTER ALL... HONESTLY, THE TROUBLE I'M PUT THROUGH ON YOUR ACCOUNT...

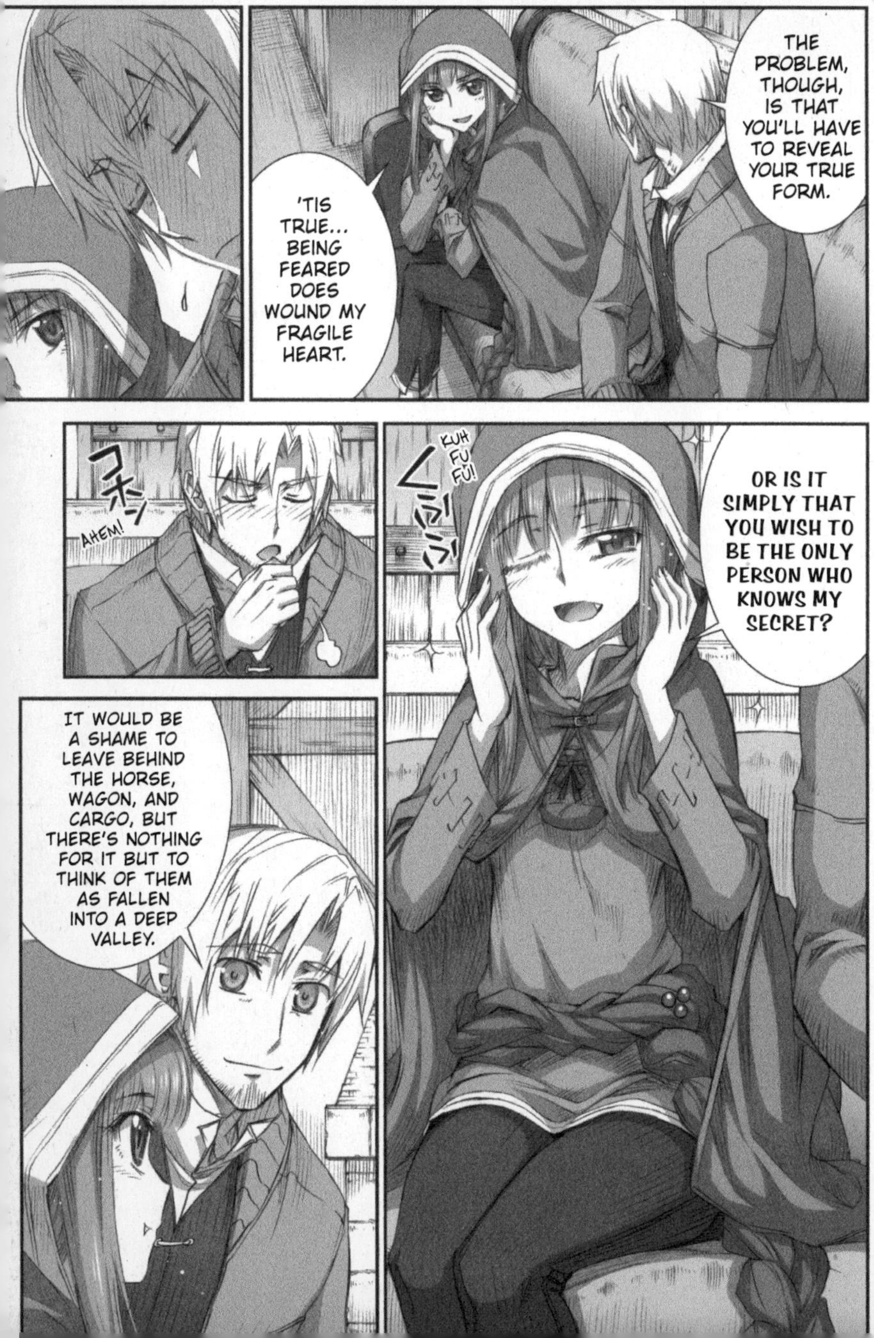
THE PROBLEM, THOUGH, IS THAT YOU'LL HAVE TO REVEAL YOUR TRUE FORM.
'TIS TRUE... BEING FEARED DOES WOUND MY FRAGILE HEART.
OR IS IT SIMPLY THAT YOU WISH TO BE THE ONLY PERSON WHO KNOWS MY SECRET?
KUH FU FU!
AHEM!
IT WOULD BE A SHAME TO LEAVE BEHIND THE HORSE, WAGON, AND CARGO, BUT THERE'S NOTHING FOR IT BUT TO THINK OF THEM AS FALLEN INTO A DEEP VALLEY.

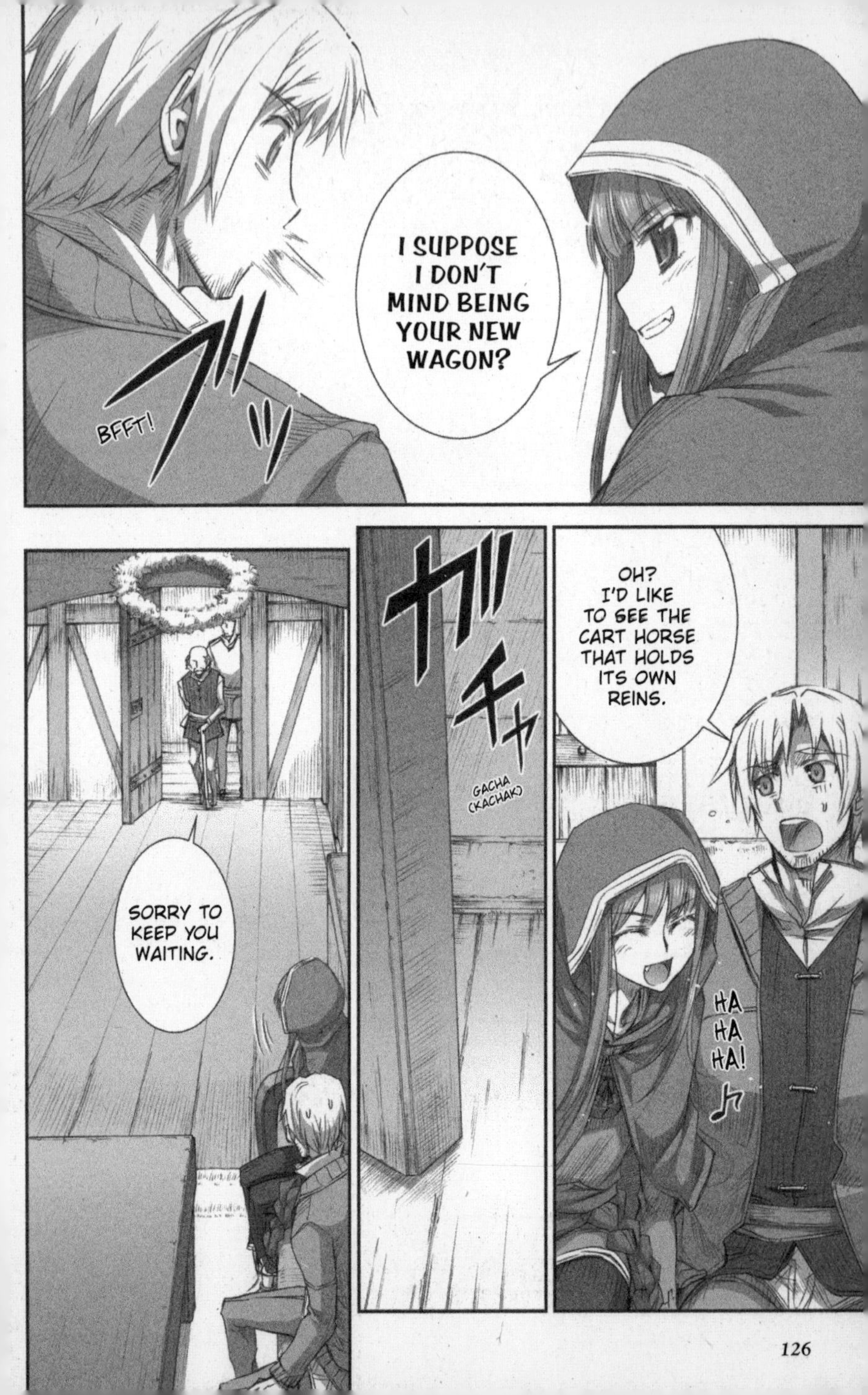
I SUPPOSE I DON'T MIND BEING YOUR NEW WAGON?
BFFT!
OH? I'D LIKE TO SEE THE CART HORSE THAT HOLDS ITS OWN REINS.
HA HA HA! ♪
GACHA (KACHAK)
SORRY TO KEEP YOU WAITING.

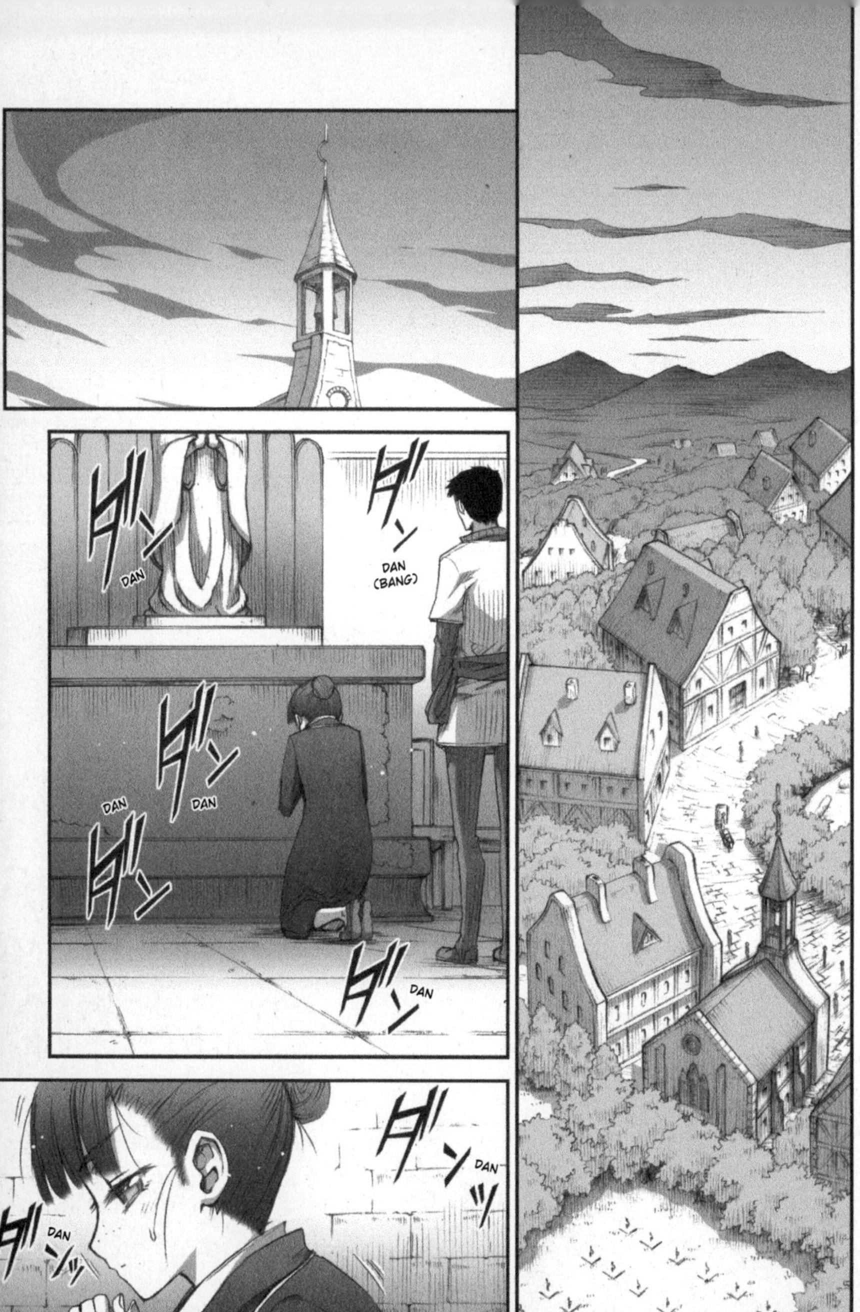
ダン
DAN
(BANG)
ダン
DAN
ダン
DAN
ダン
DAN
ダン
DAN
ダンッ
DAN
ダンッ
DAN

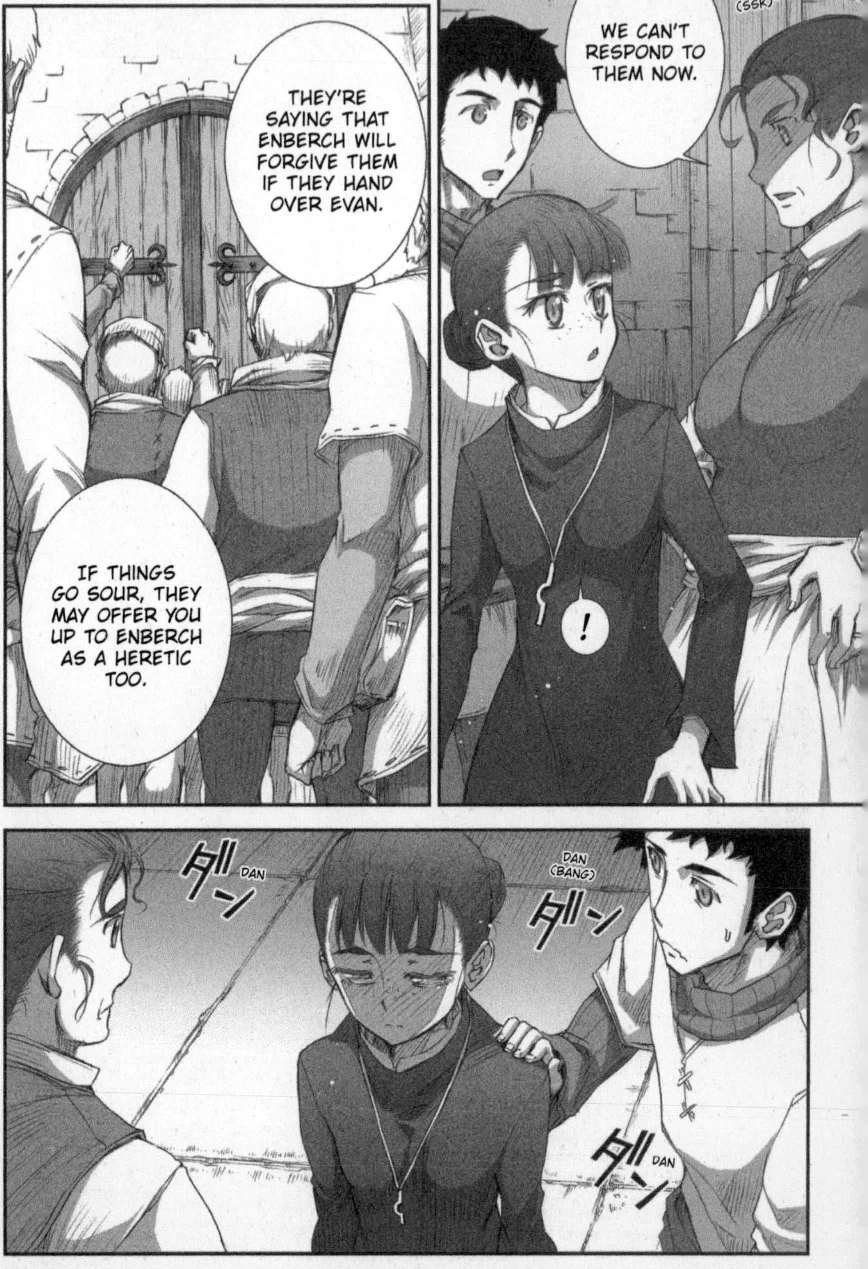
ZUI (SSK)
WE CAN'T RESPOND TO THEM NOW.
!
THEY'RE SAYING THAT ENBERCH WILL FORGIVE THEM IF THEY HAND OVER EVAN.
IF THINGS GO SOUR, THEY MAY OFFER YOU UP TO ENBERCH AS A HERETIC TOO.
DAN (BANG)
DAN
DAN

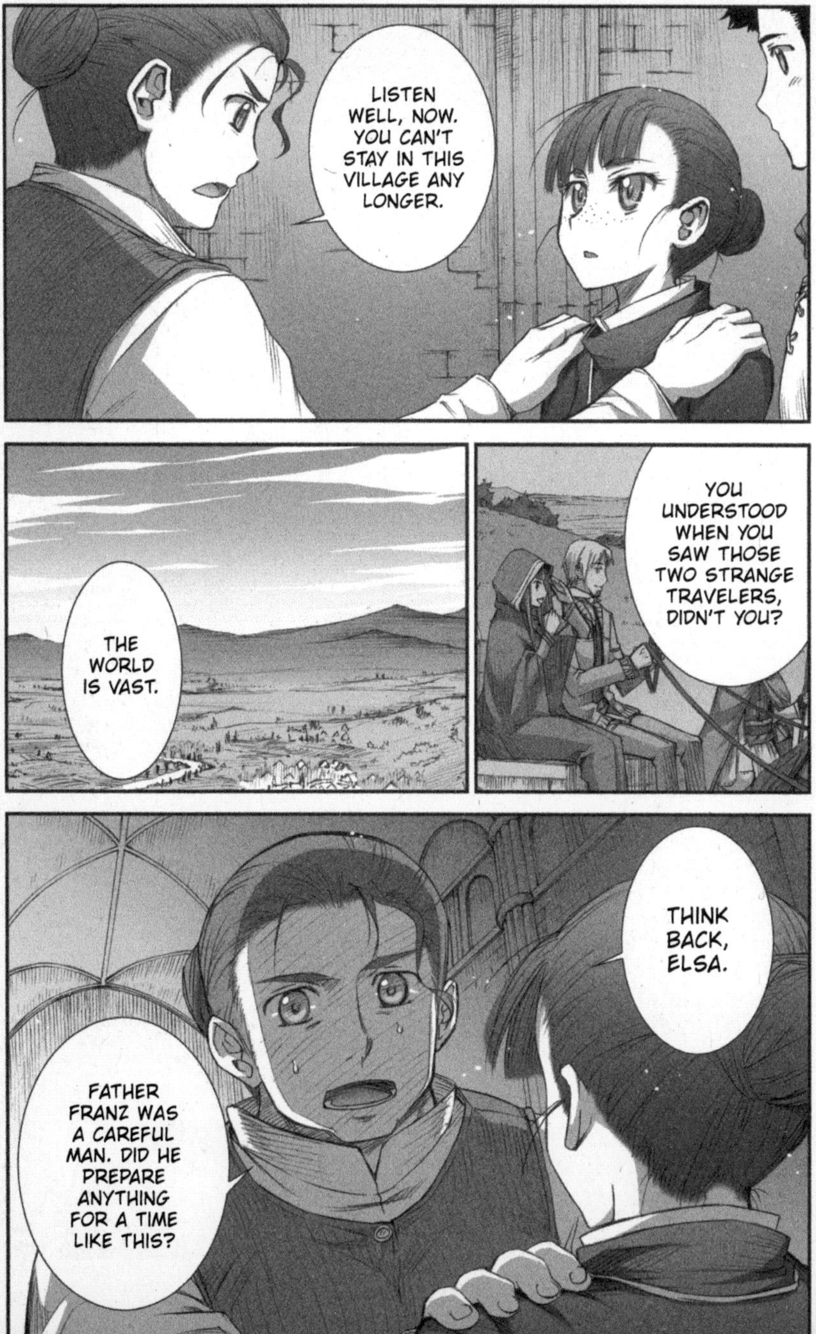
LISTEN WELL, NOW. YOU CAN'T STAY IN THIS VILLAGE ANY LONGER.
YOU UNDERSTOOD WHEN YOU SAW THOSE TWO STRANGE TRAVELERS, DIDN'T YOU?
THE WORLD IS VAST.
THINK BACK, ELSA.
FATHER FRANZ WAS A CAREFUL MAN. DID HE PREPARE ANYTHING FOR A TIME LIKE THIS?

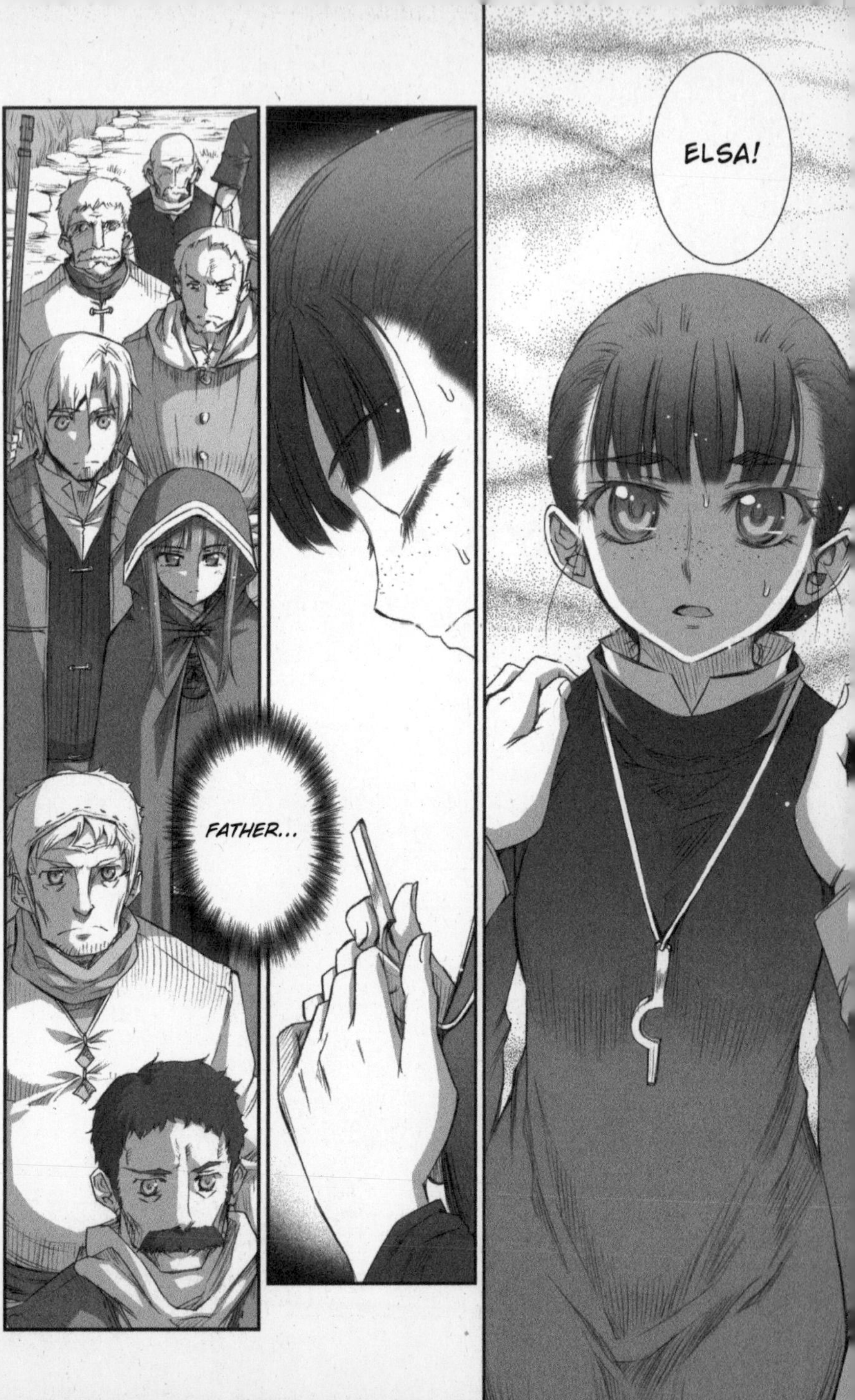
ELSA!
FATHER...

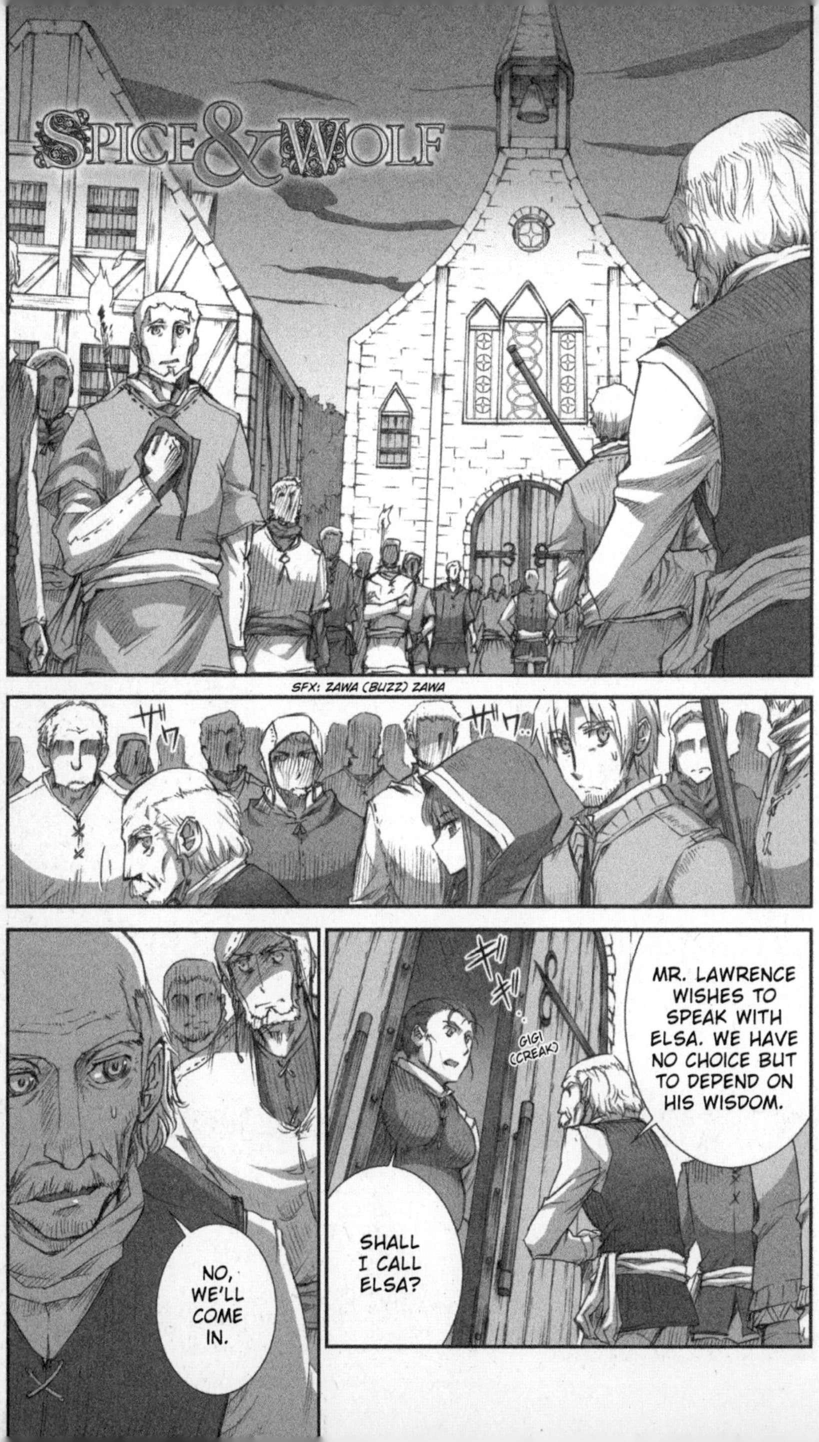
SPICE & WOLF
SFX: ZAWA (BUZZ) ZAWA
MR. LAWRENCE WISHES TO SPEAK WITH ELSA. WE HAVE NO CHOICE BUT TO DEPEND ON HIS WISDOM.
GIGI (CREAK)
SHALL I CALL ELSA?
NO, WE'LL COME IN.

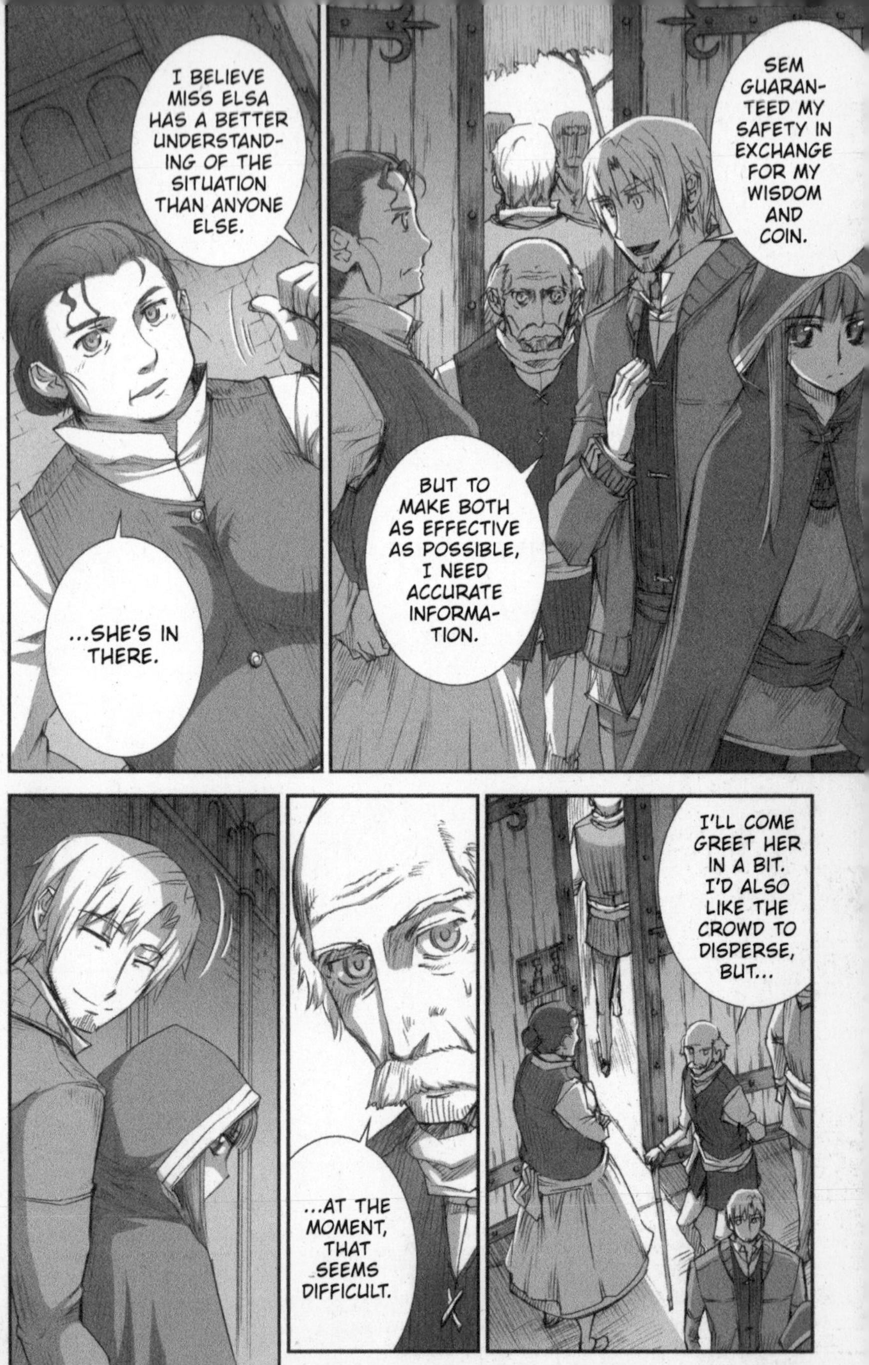
SEM GUARANTEED MY SAFETY IN EXCHANGE FOR MY WISDOM AND COIN.
BUT TO MAKE BOTH AS EFFECTIVE AS POSSIBLE, I NEED ACCURATE INFORMATION.
I BELIEVE MISS ELSA HAS A BETTER UNDERSTANDING OF THE SITUATION THAN ANYONE ELSE.
...SHE'S IN THERE.
I'LL COME GREET HER IN A BIT. I'D ALSO LIKE THE CROWD TO DISPERSE, BUT...
...AT THE MOMENT, THAT SEEMS DIFFICULT.

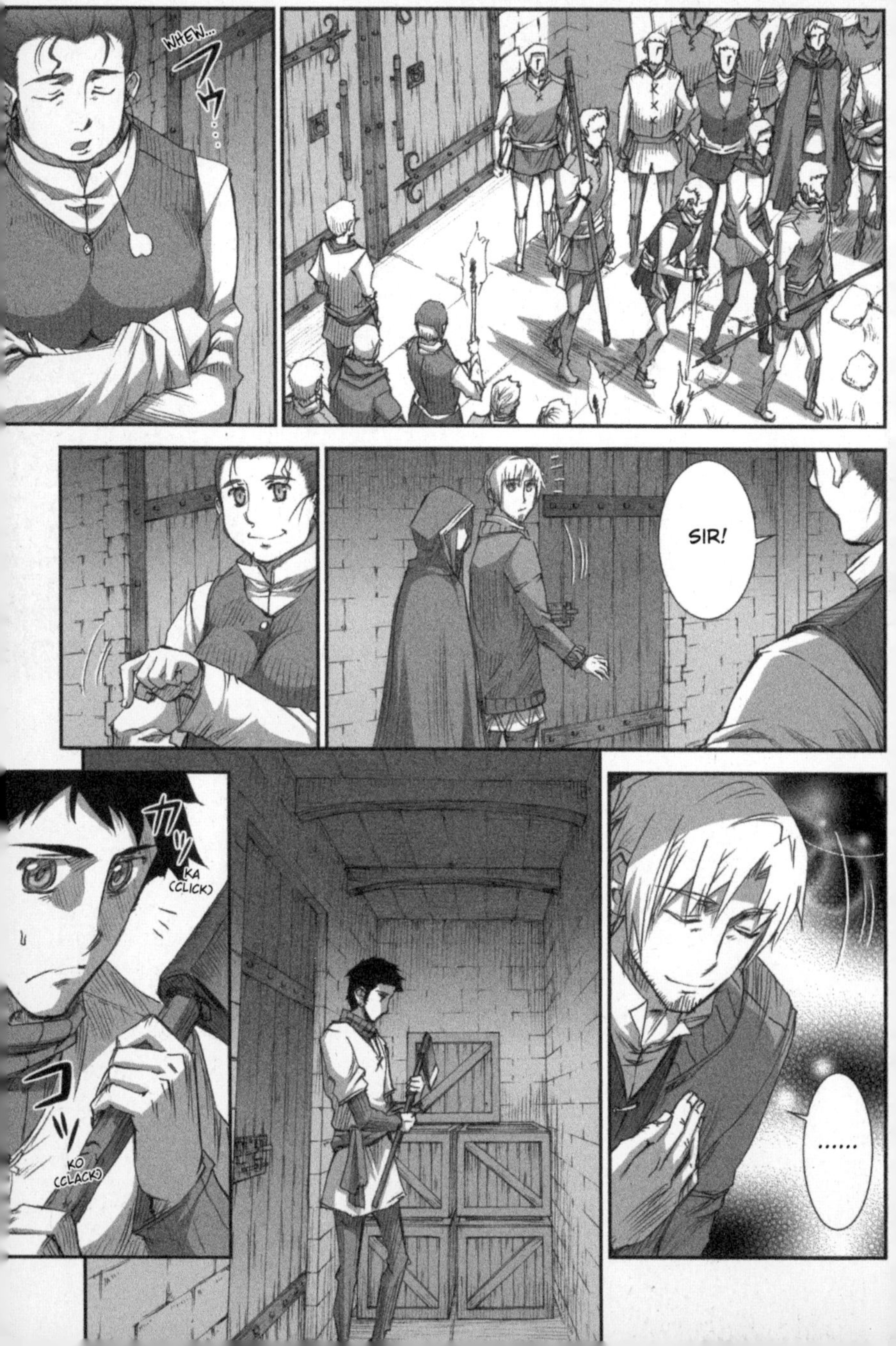

WHEW...
フゥ...
SIR!
......
カッ
KA (CLICK)
KO (CLACK)

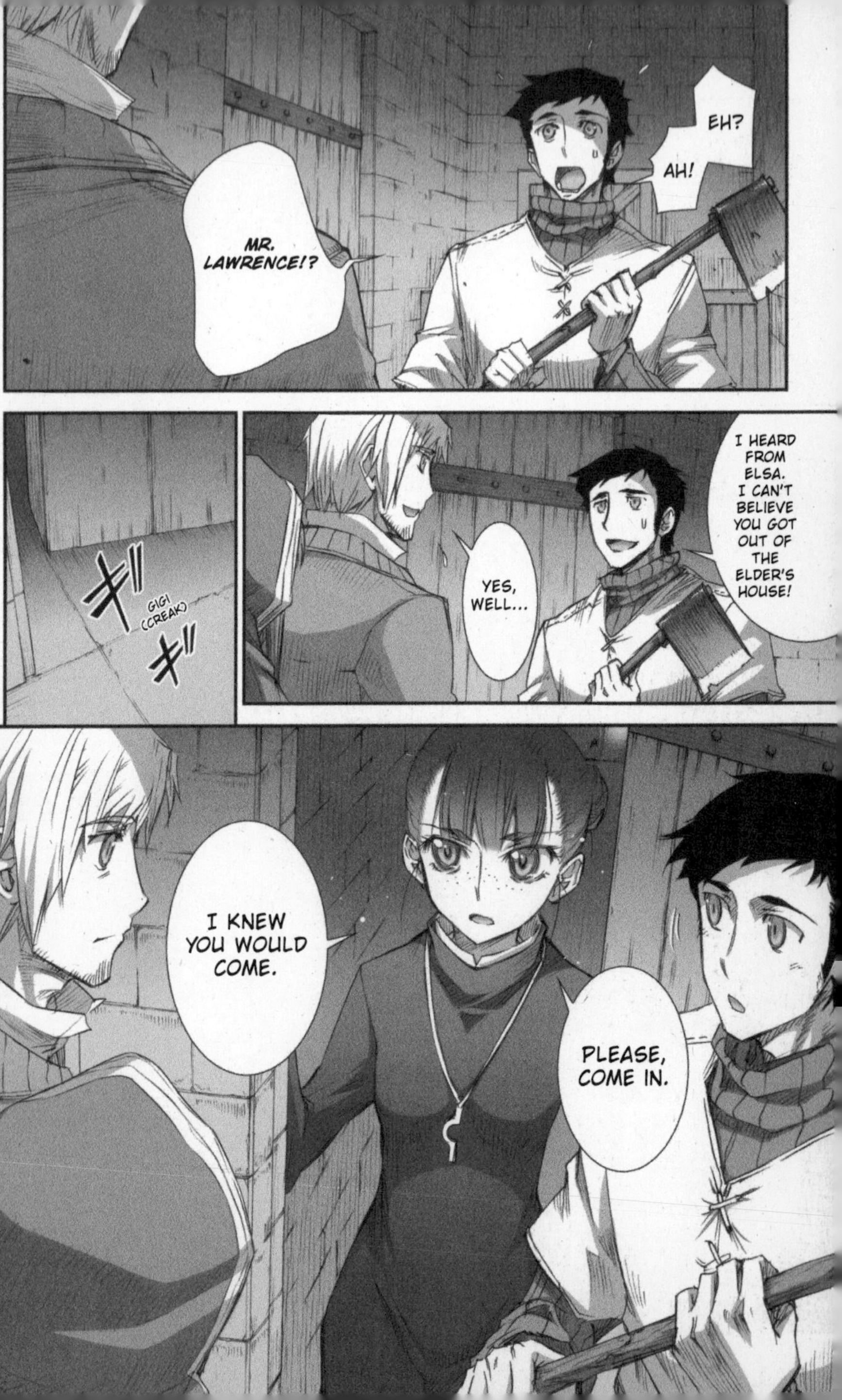
EH?
AH!
MR. LAWRENCE!?
I HEARD FROM ELSA. I CAN'T BELIEVE YOU GOT OUT OF THE ELDER'S HOUSE!
YES, WELL...
GIGI (CREAK)
PLEASE, COME IN.
I KNEW YOU WOULD COME.

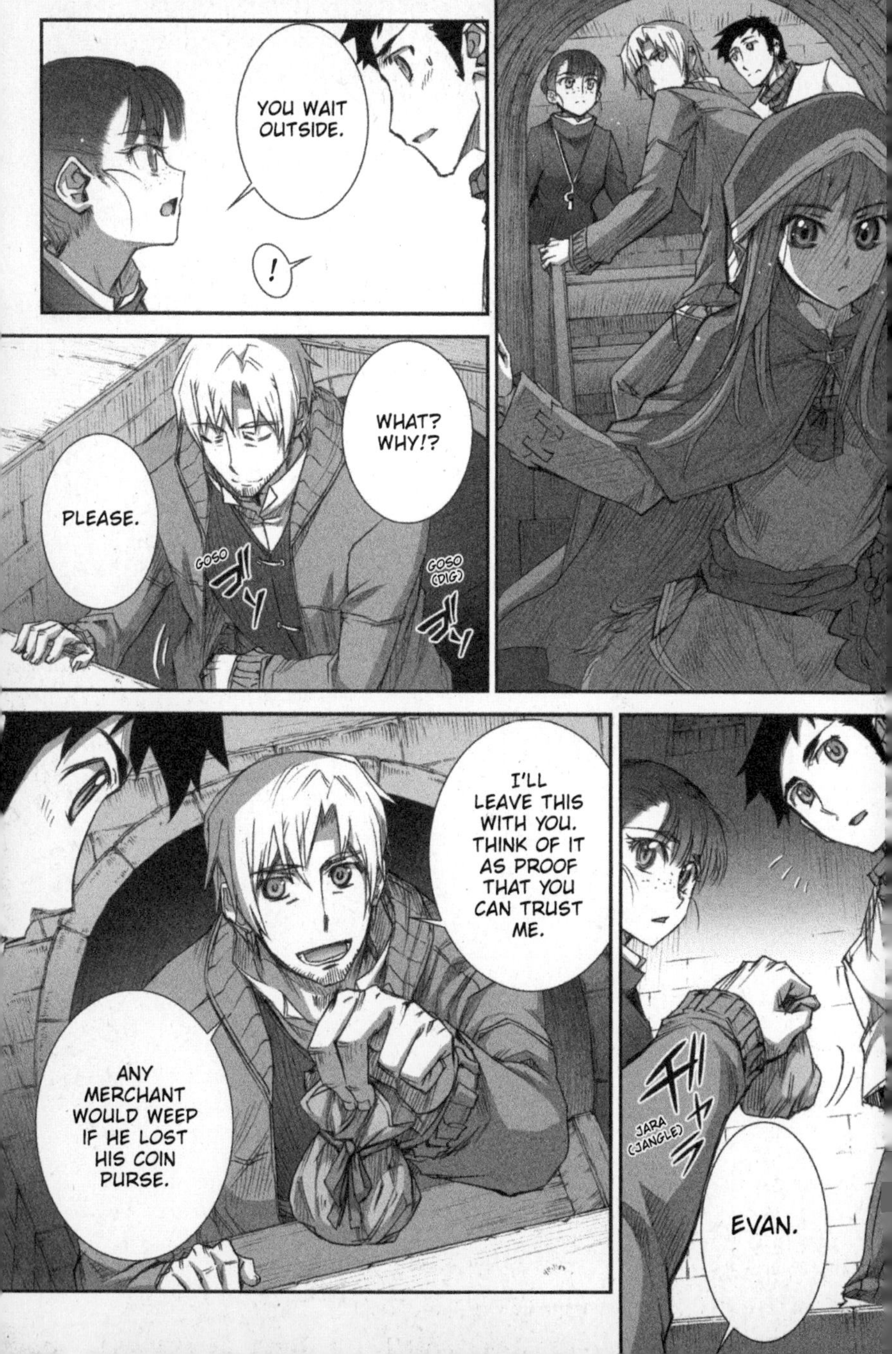
YOU WAIT OUTSIDE.
!
WHAT? WHY!?
PLEASE.
GOSO (DIG)
GOSO
JARA (JANGLE)
EVAN.
I'LL LEAVE THIS WITH YOU. THINK OF IT AS PROOF THAT YOU CAN TRUST ME.
ANY MERCHANT WOULD WEEP IF HE LOST HIS COIN PURSE.

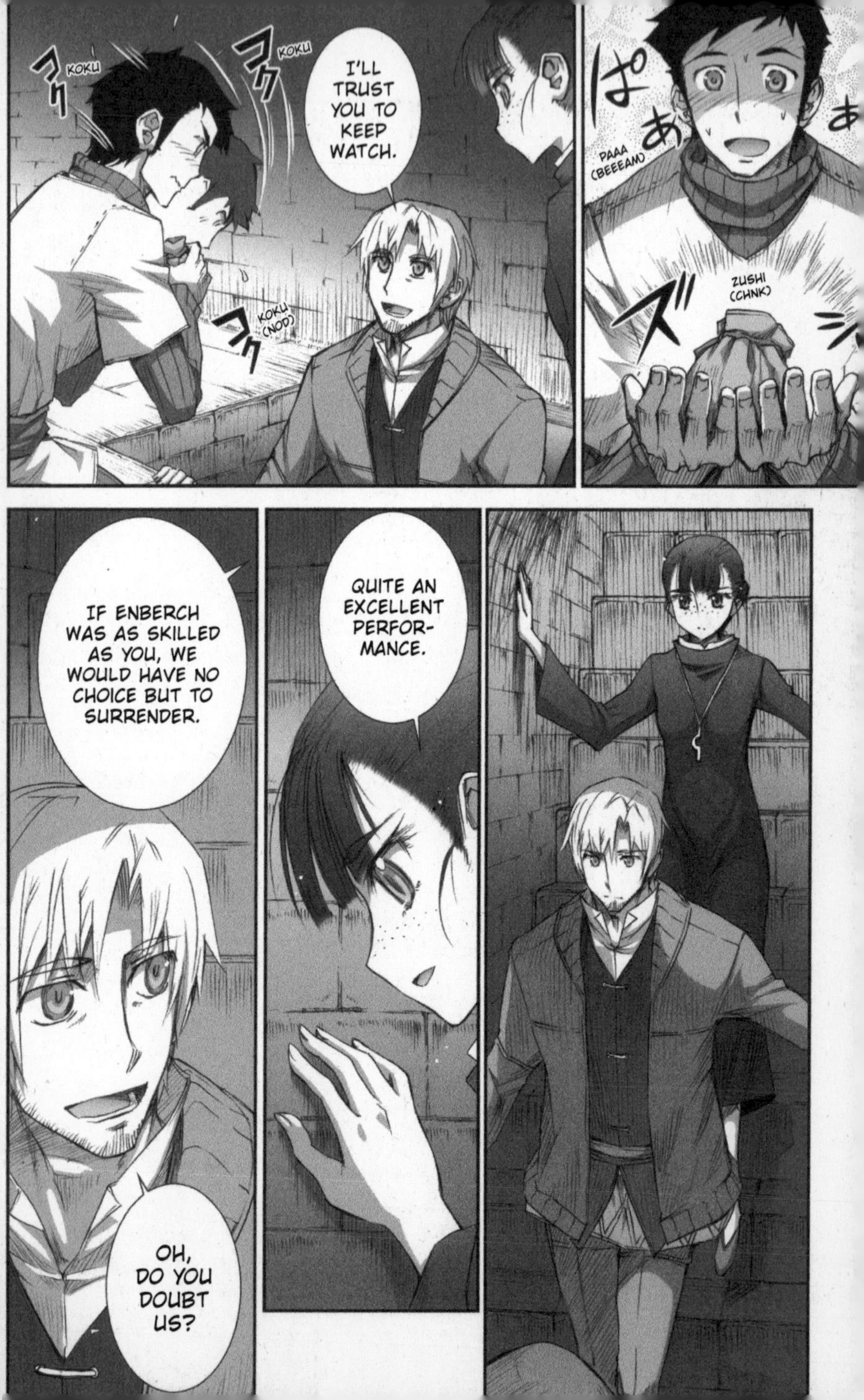
PAAA (BEEEAM)
ZUSHI (CHNK)
KOKU
I'LL TRUST YOU TO KEEP WATCH.
KOKU
KOKU (NOD)
QUITE AN EXCELLENT PERFOR-MANCE.
IF ENBERCH WAS AS SKILLED AS YOU, WE WOULD HAVE NO CHOICE BUT TO SURRENDER.
OH, DO YOU DOUBT US?

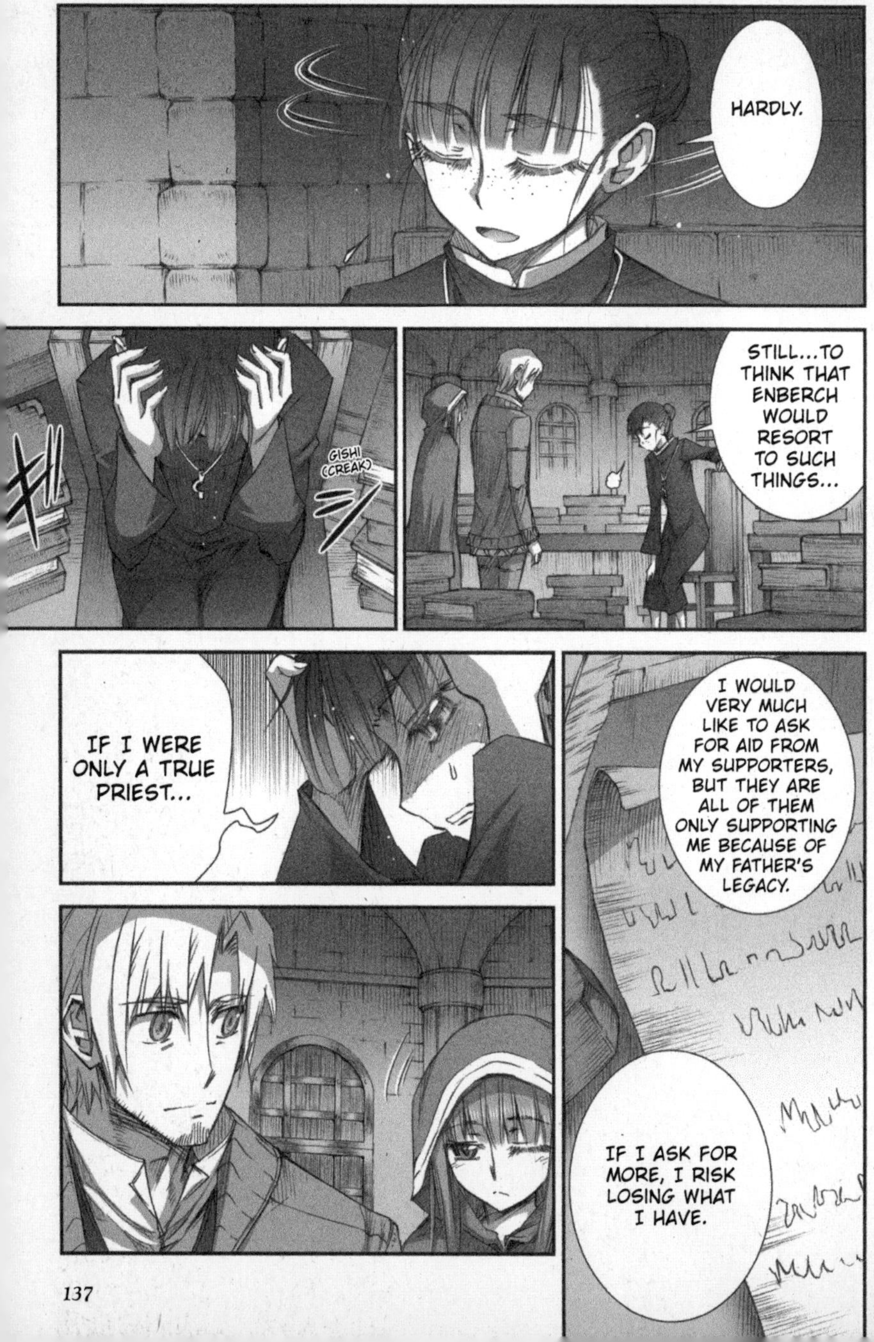
HARDLY.
STILL...TO THINK THAT ENBERCH WOULD RESORT TO SUCH THINGS...
GISHI (CREAK)
I WOULD VERY MUCH LIKE TO ASK FOR AID FROM MY SUPPORTERS, BUT THEY ARE ALL OF THEM ONLY SUPPORTING ME BECAUSE OF MY FATHER'S LEGACY.
IF I ASK FOR MORE, I RISK LOSING WHAT I HAVE.
IF I WERE ONLY A TRUE PRIEST...

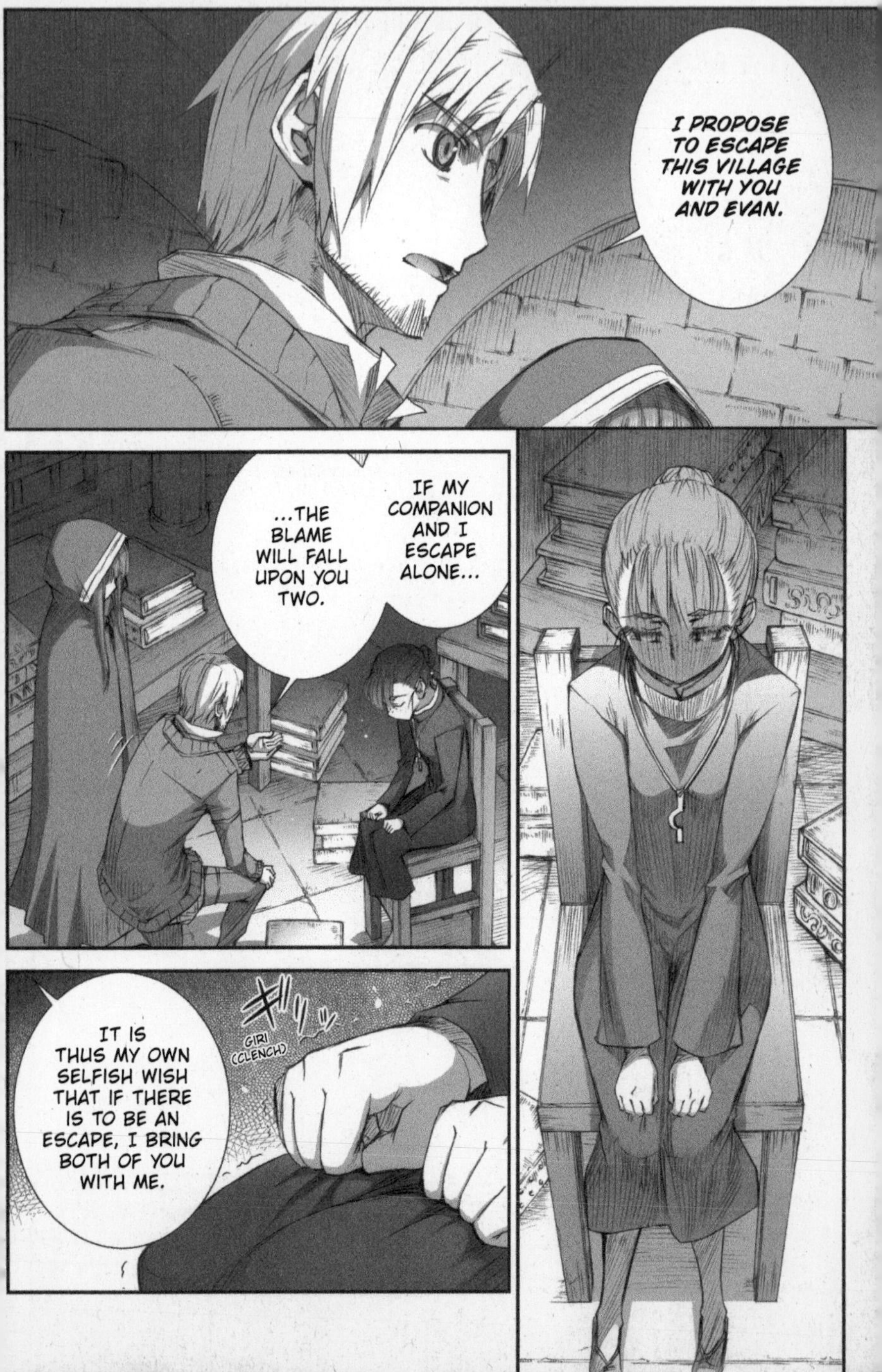
I PROPOSE TO ESCAPE THIS VILLAGE WITH YOU AND EVAN.
IF MY COMPANION AND I ESCAPE ALONE...
...THE BLAME WILL FALL UPON YOU TWO.
GIRI (CLENCH)
IT IS THUS MY OWN SELFISH WISH THAT IF THERE IS TO BE AN ESCAPE, I BRING BOTH OF YOU WITH ME.

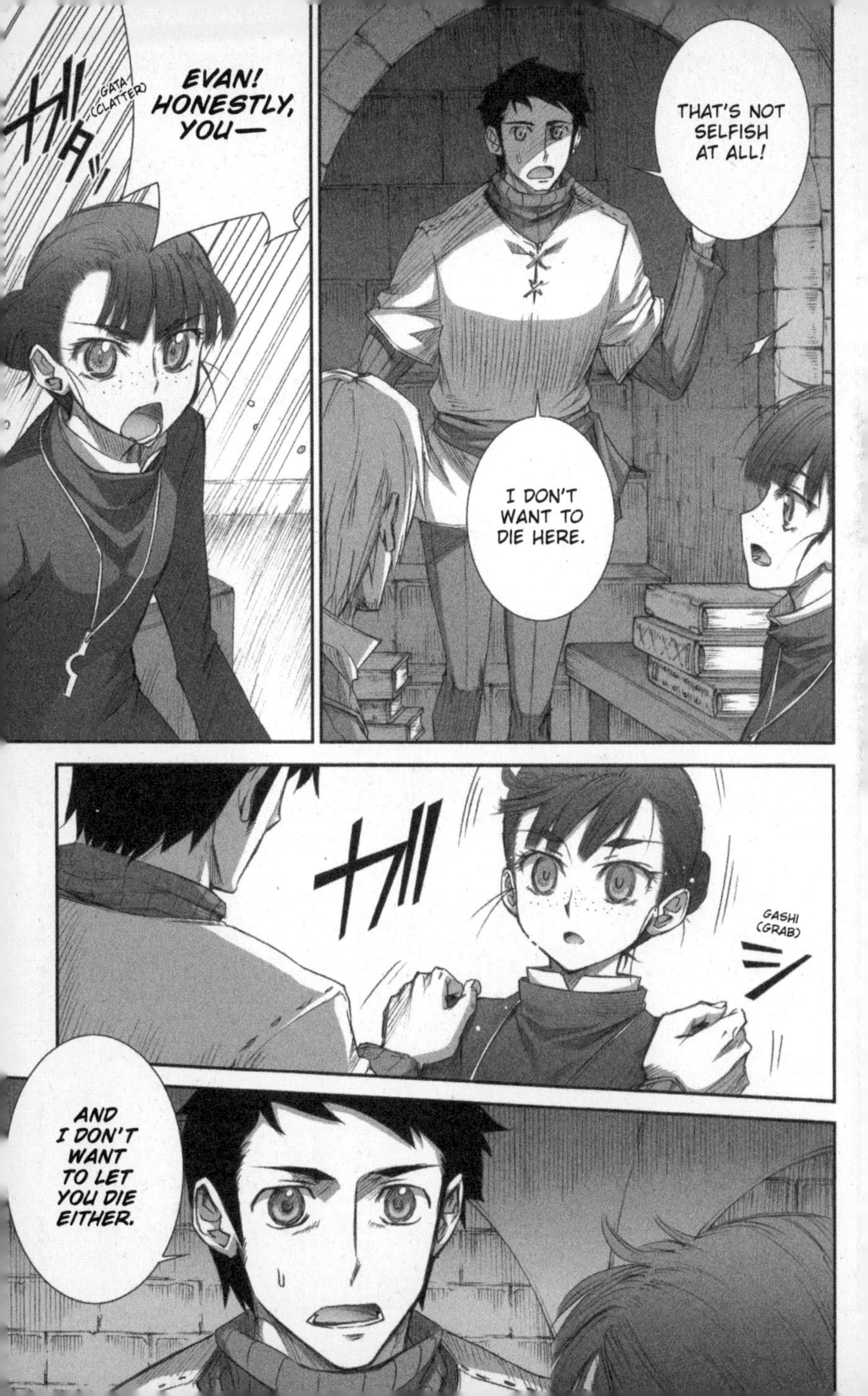
THAT'S NOT SELFISH AT ALL!
I DON'T WANT TO DIE HERE.
GATA (CLATTER)
EVAN! HONESTLY, YOU—
GASHI (GRAB)
AND I DON'T WANT TO LET YOU DIE EITHER.

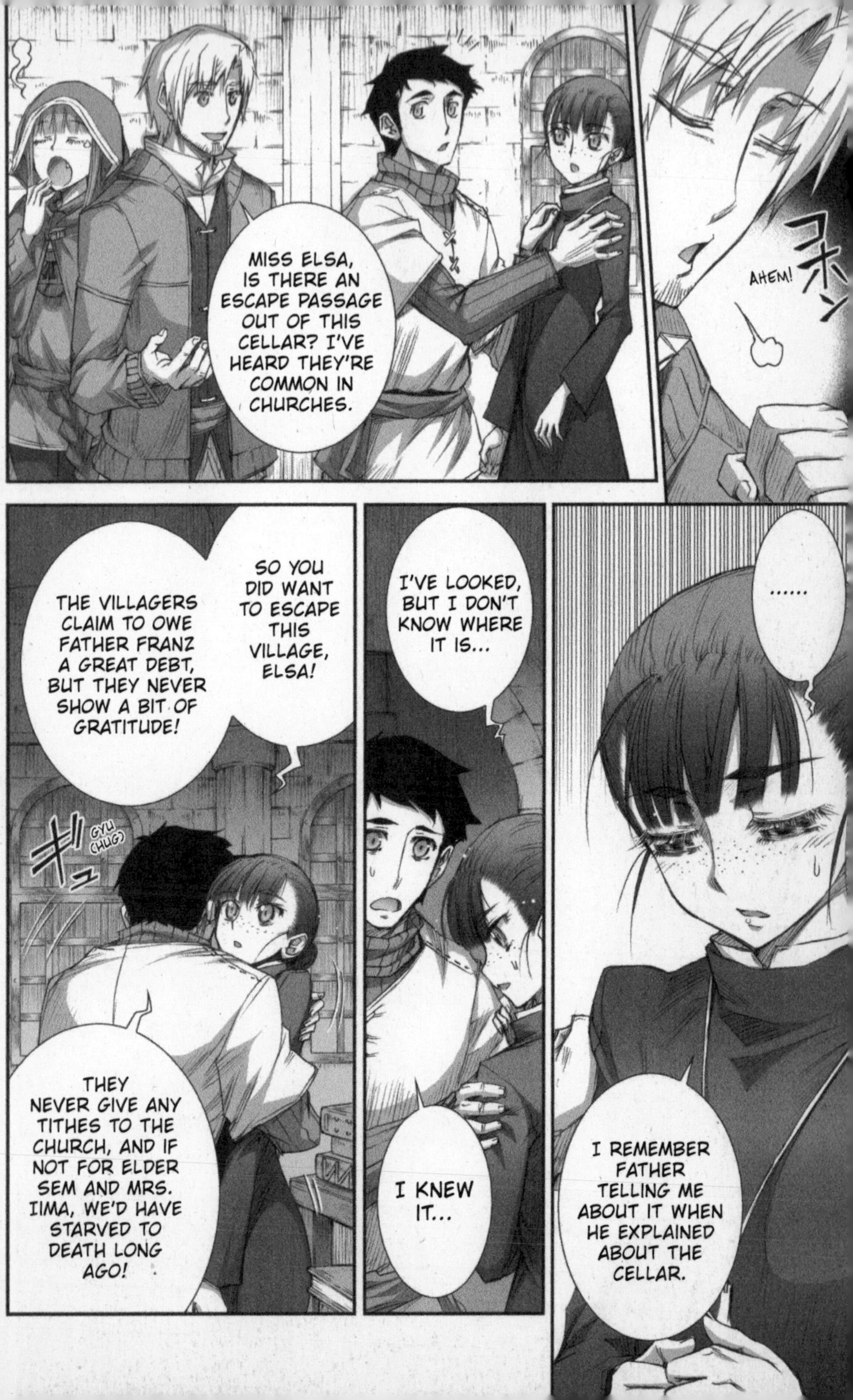
コホン
AHEM!
MISS ELSA, IS THERE AN ESCAPE PASSAGE OUT OF THIS CELLAR? I'VE HEARD THEY'RE COMMON IN CHURCHES.
......
I REMEMBER FATHER TELLING ME ABOUT IT WHEN HE EXPLAINED ABOUT THE CELLAR.
I'VE LOOKED, BUT I DON'T KNOW WHERE IT IS...
I KNEW IT...
SO YOU DID WANT TO ESCAPE THIS VILLAGE, ELSA!
THE VILLAGERS CLAIM TO OWE FATHER FRANZ A GREAT DEBT, BUT THEY NEVER SHOW A BIT OF GRATITUDE!
ギュ
GYU (HUG)
THEY NEVER GIVE ANY TITHES TO THE CHURCH, AND IF NOT FOR ELDER SEM AND MRS. IIMA, WE'D HAVE STARVED TO DEATH LONG AGO!

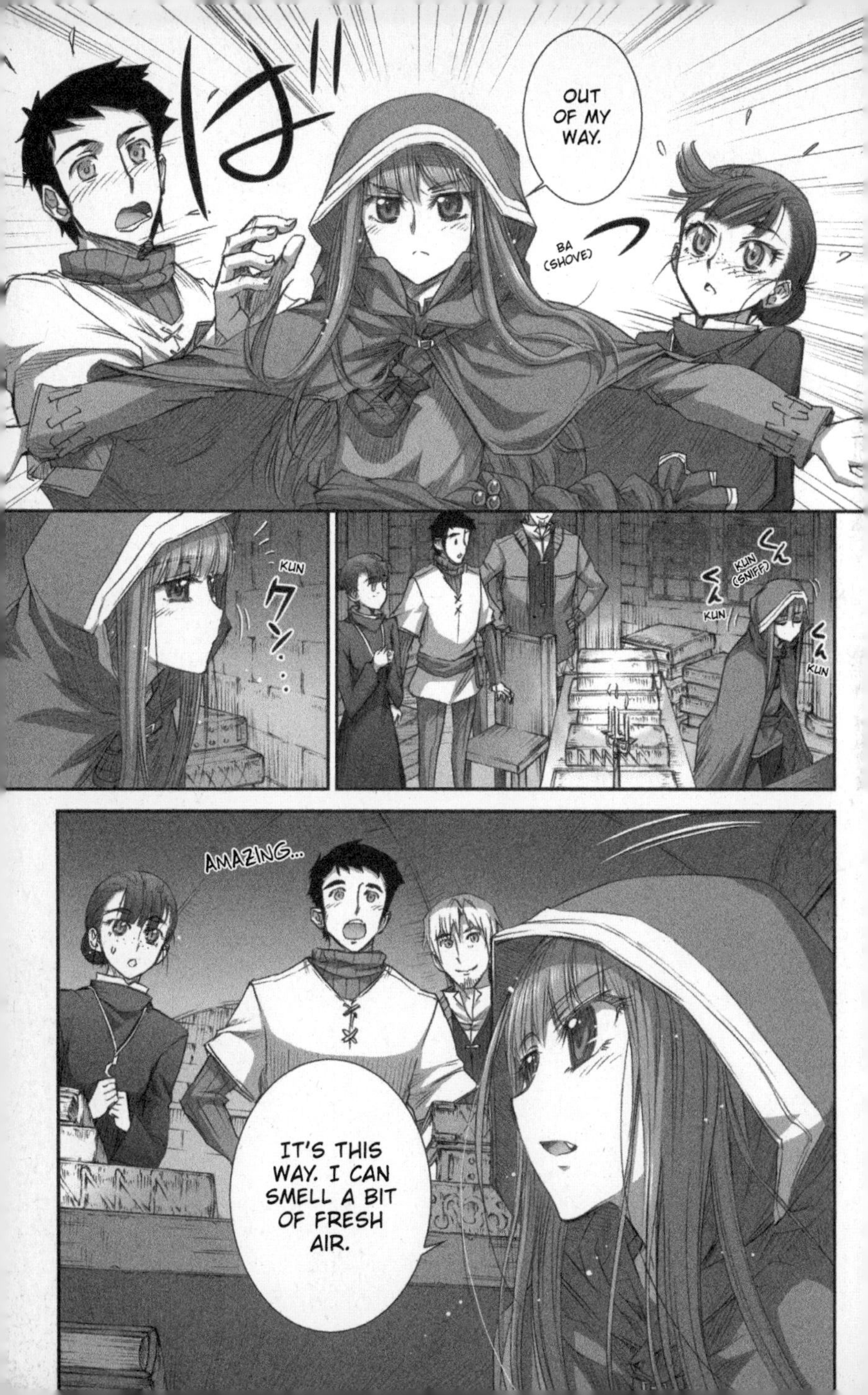
OUT OF MY WAY.
BA (SHOVE)
ばッ
くん
KUN (SNIFF)
くん
KUN
くん
KUN
KUN
クン…
AMAZING...
IT'S THIS WAY. I CAN SMELL A BIT OF FRESH AIR.

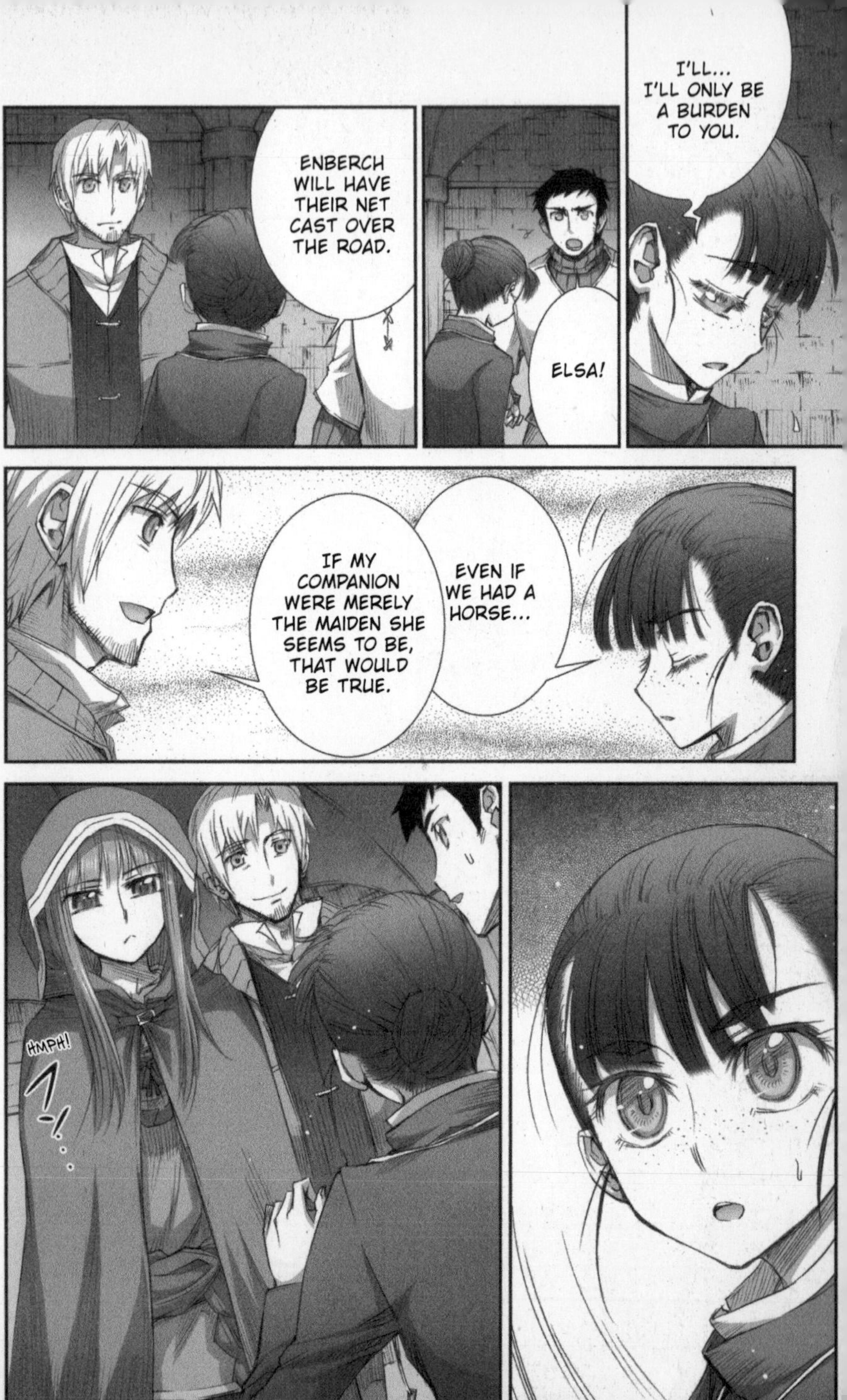
I'LL... I'LL ONLY BE A BURDEN TO YOU.
ELSA!
ENBERCH WILL HAVE THEIR NET CAST OVER THE ROAD.
EVEN IF WE HAD A HORSE...
IF MY COMPANION WERE MERELY THE MAIDEN SHE SEEMS TO BE, THAT WOULD BE TRUE.
HMPH!

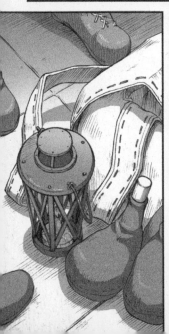

SPEAKING IN TERMS OF OUTCOMES, WE CAN ESCAPE.

WE CAN ESCAPE WHENEVER WE WISH.

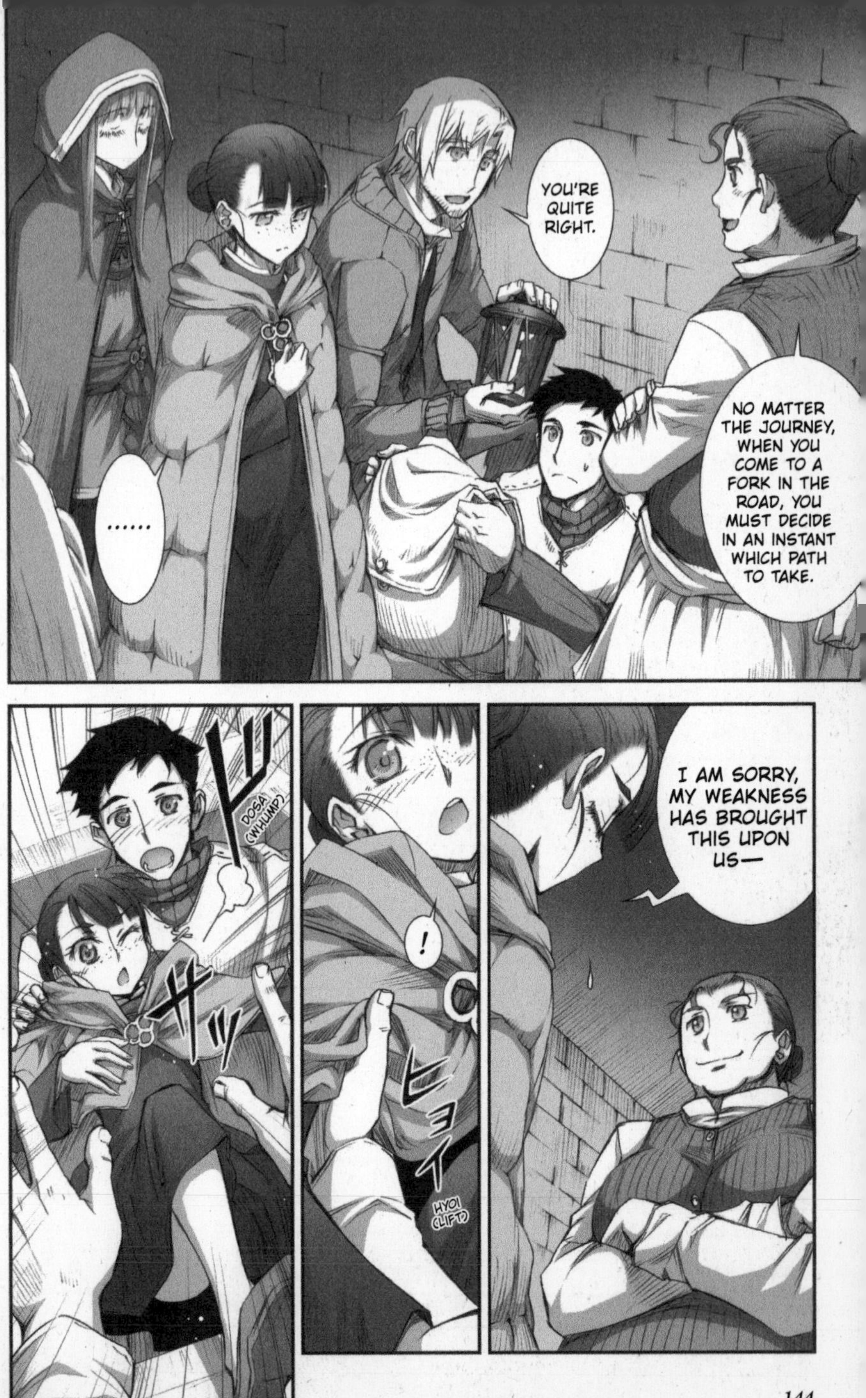

NO MATTER THE JOURNEY, WHEN YOU COME TO A FORK IN THE ROAD, YOU MUST DECIDE IN AN INSTANT WHICH PATH TO TAKE.
YOU'RE QUITE RIGHT.
......
I AM SORRY, MY WEAKNESS HAS BROUGHT THIS UPON US—
!
HYOI (LIFT)
DOSA (WHUMP)

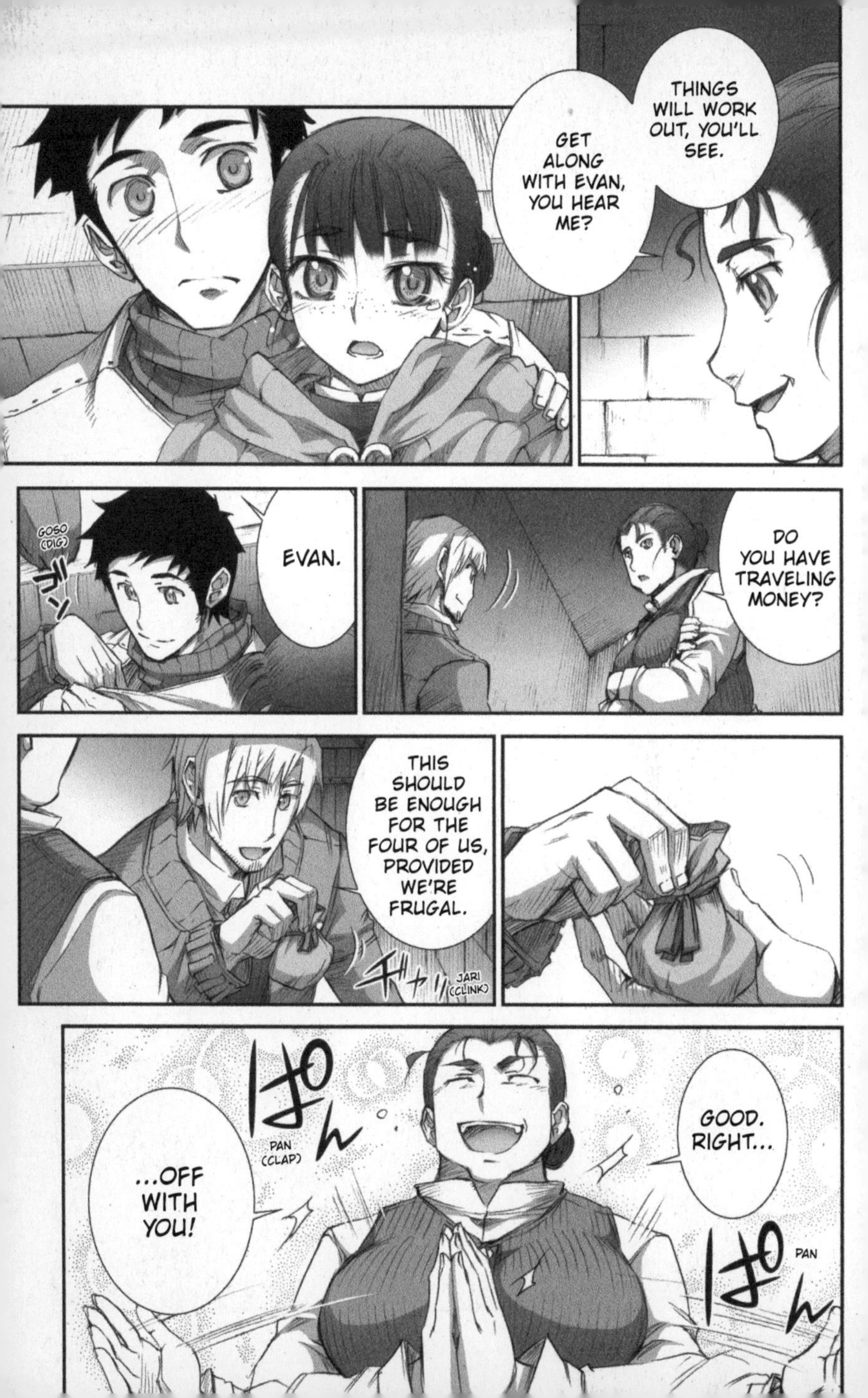
THINGS WILL WORK OUT, YOU'LL SEE.
GET ALONG WITH EVAN, YOU HEAR ME?
DO YOU HAVE TRAVELING MONEY?
EVAN.
GOSO (DIG)
THIS SHOULD BE ENOUGH FOR THE FOUR OF US, PROVIDED WE'RE FRUGAL.
JARI (CLINK)
GOOD. RIGHT...
PAN
PAN (CLAP)
...OFF WITH YOU!

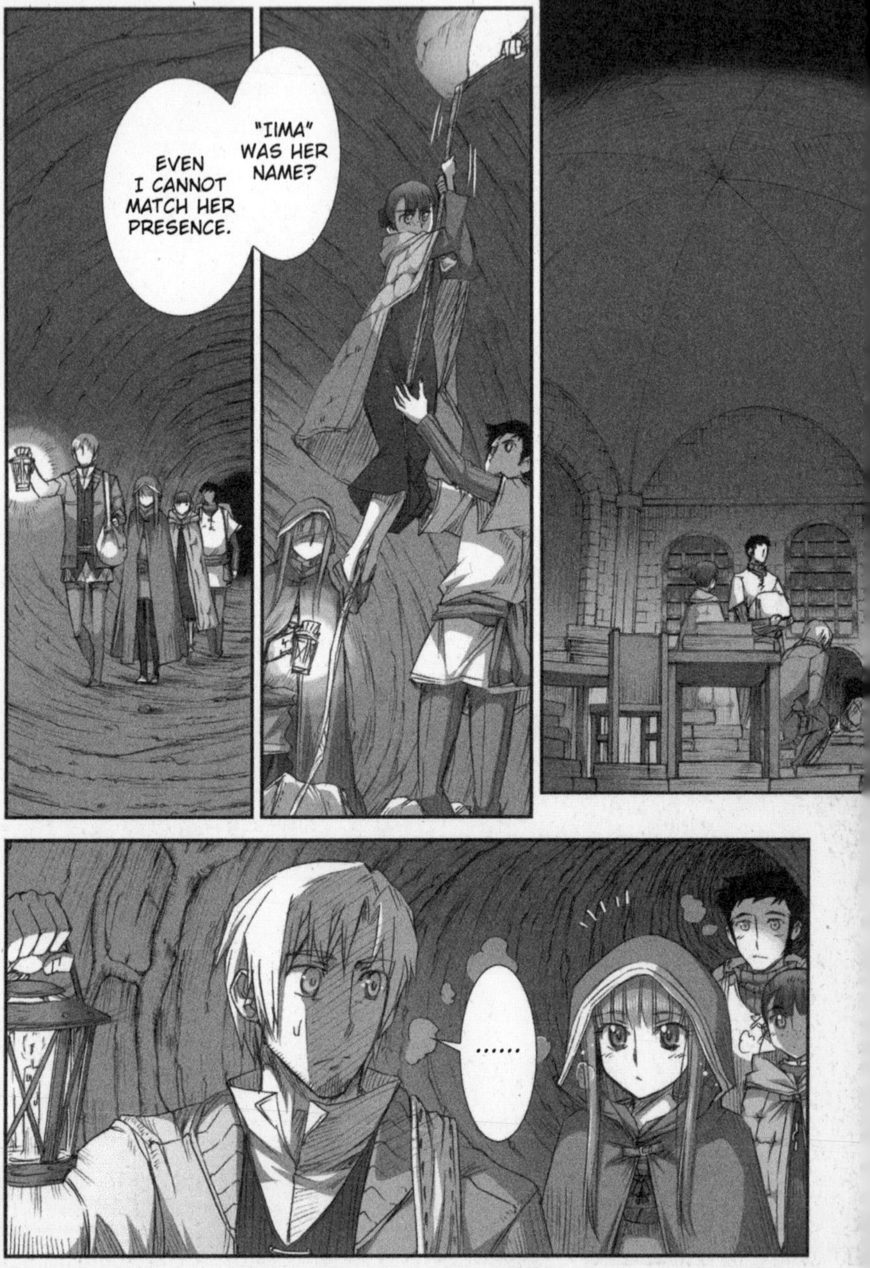
"IIMA" WAS HER NAME?
EVEN I CANNOT MATCH HER PRESENCE.
......

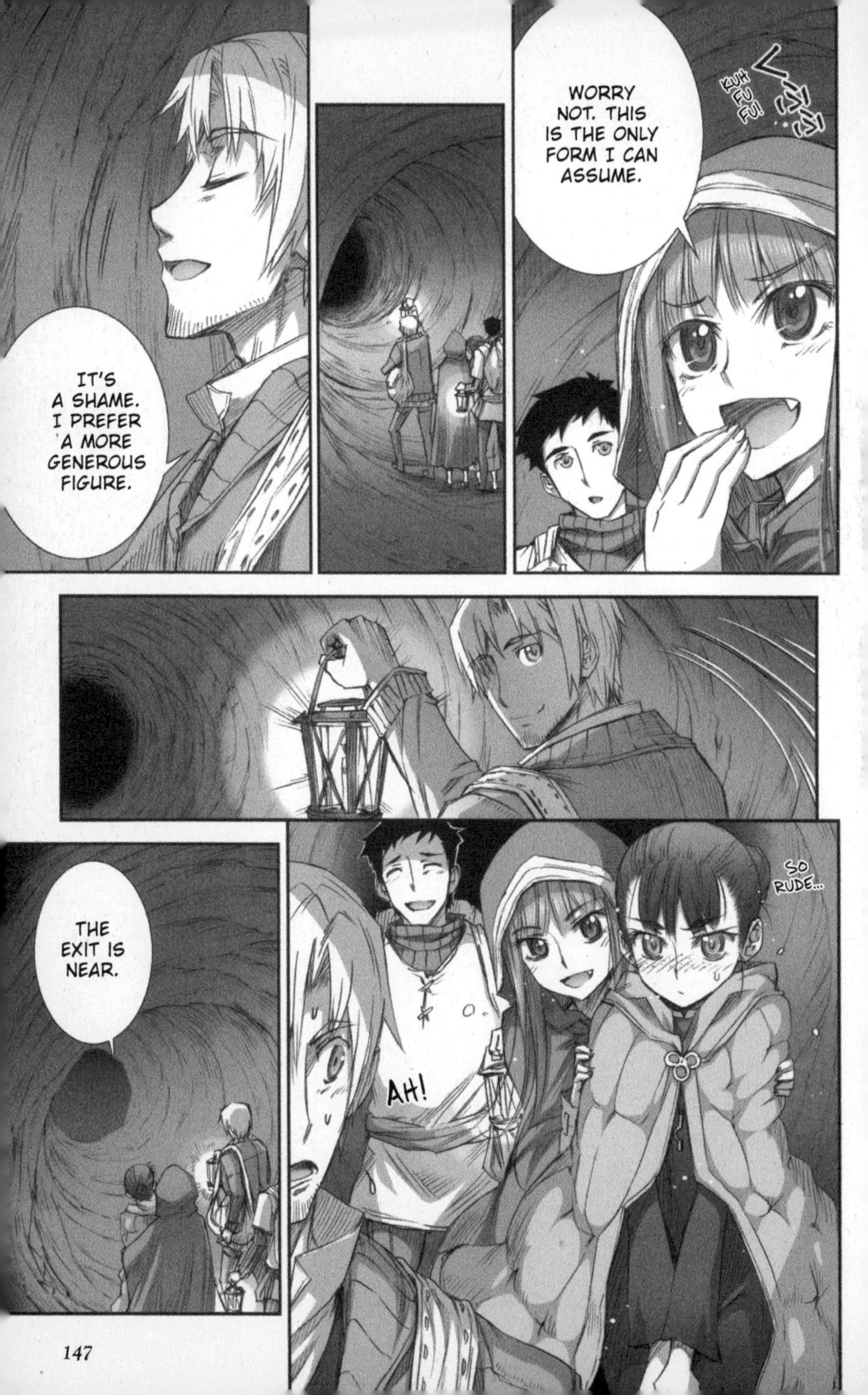
KUH FU FU!
WORRY NOT. THIS IS THE ONLY FORM I CAN ASSUME.
IT'S A SHAME. I PREFER A MORE GENEROUS FIGURE.
SO RUDE...
AH!
THE EXIT IS NEAR.

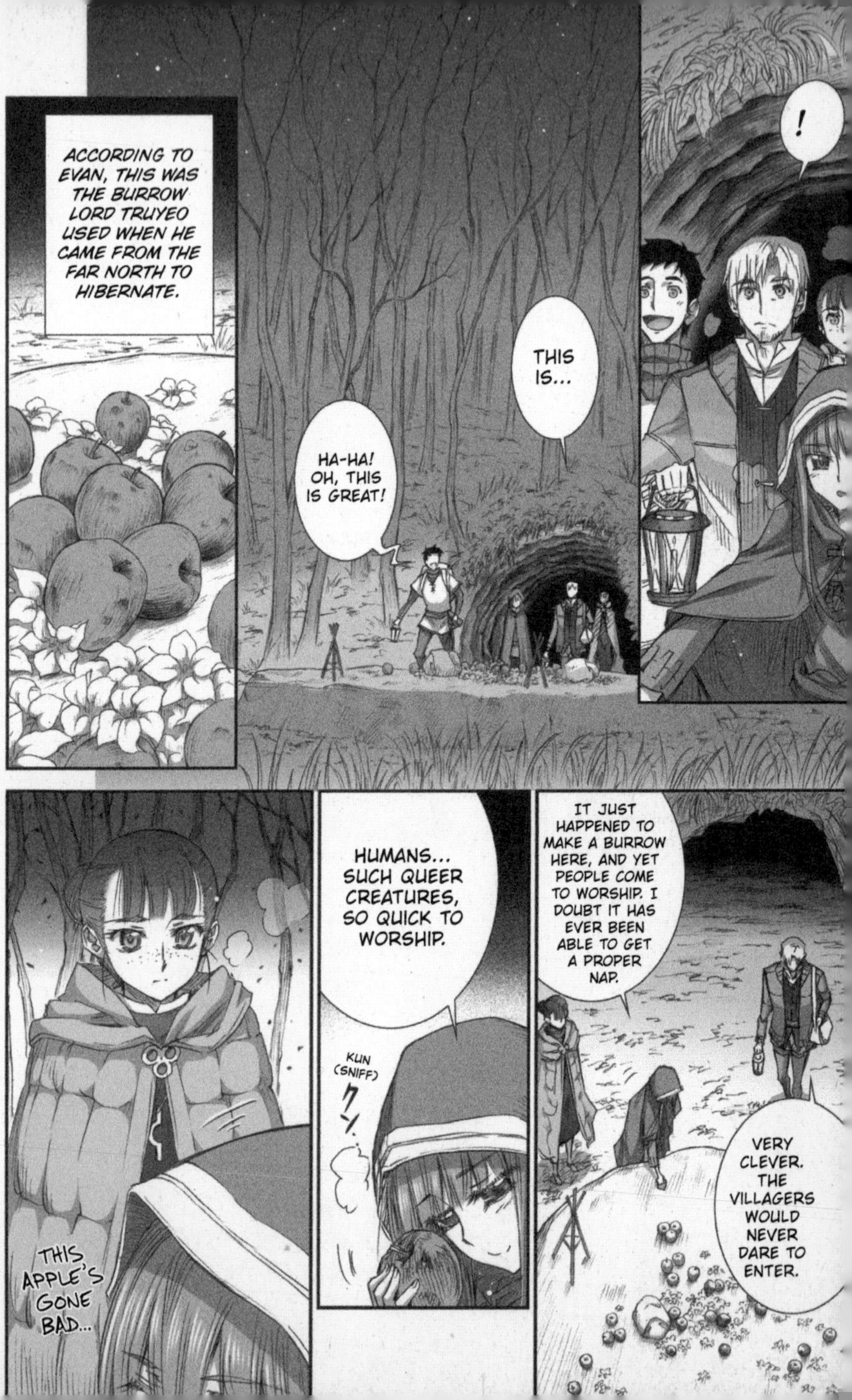
!
THIS IS...
HA-HA! OH, THIS IS GREAT!
ACCORDING TO EVAN, THIS WAS THE BURROW LORD TRUYEO USED WHEN HE CAME FROM THE FAR NORTH TO HIBERNATE.
IT JUST HAPPENED TO MAKE A BURROW HERE, AND YET PEOPLE COME TO WORSHIP. I DOUBT IT HAS EVER BEEN ABLE TO GET A PROPER NAP.
VERY CLEVER. THE VILLAGERS WOULD NEVER DARE TO ENTER.
HUMANS... SUCH QUEER CREATURES, SO QUICK TO WORSHIP.
KUN (SNIFF)
THIS APPLE'S GONE BAD...

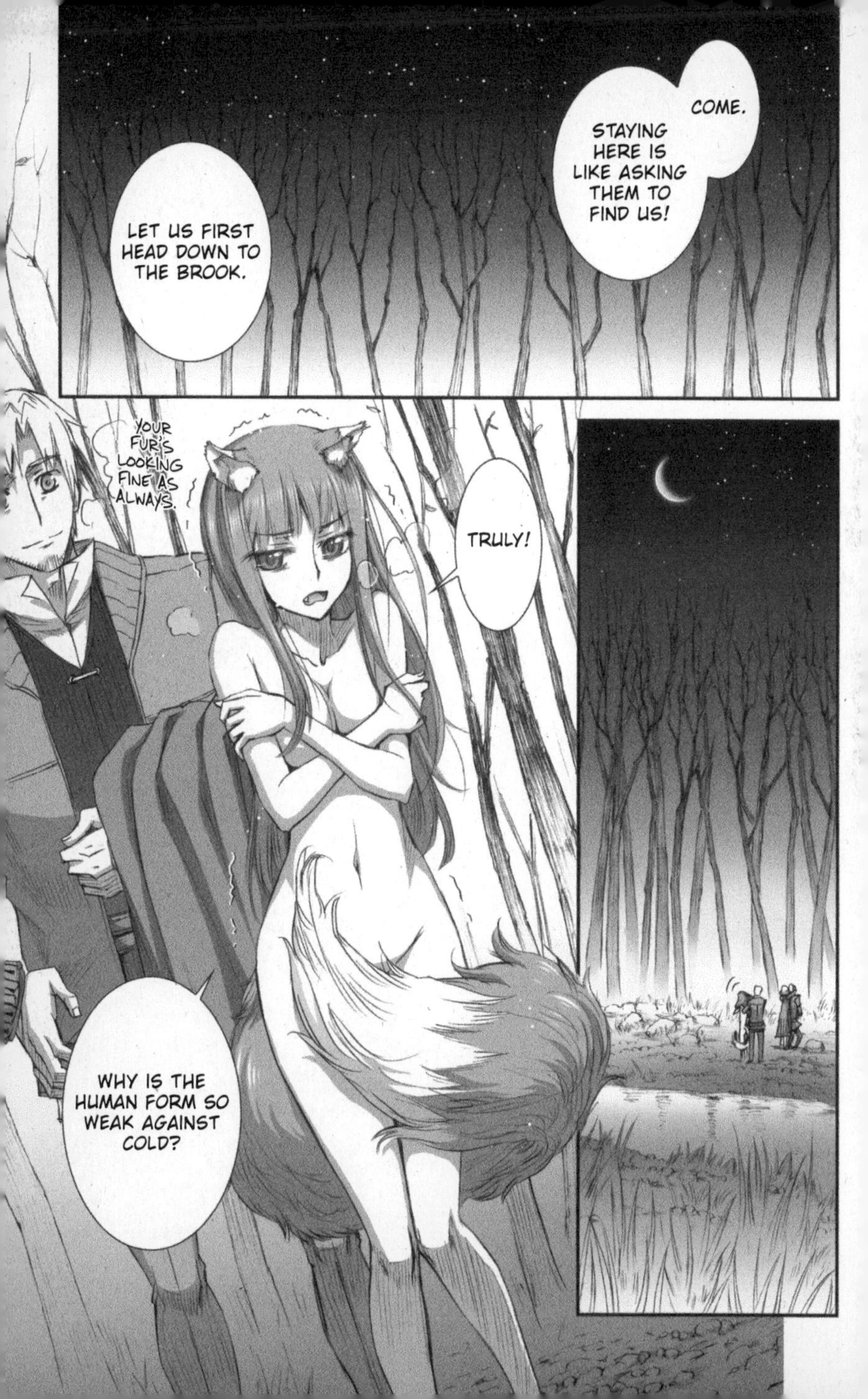
COME. STAYING HERE IS LIKE ASKING THEM TO FIND US!
LET US FIRST HEAD DOWN TO THE BROOK.
TRULY!
YOUR FUR'S LOOKING FINE AS ALWAYS.
WHY IS THE HUMAN FORM SO WEAK AGAINST COLD?

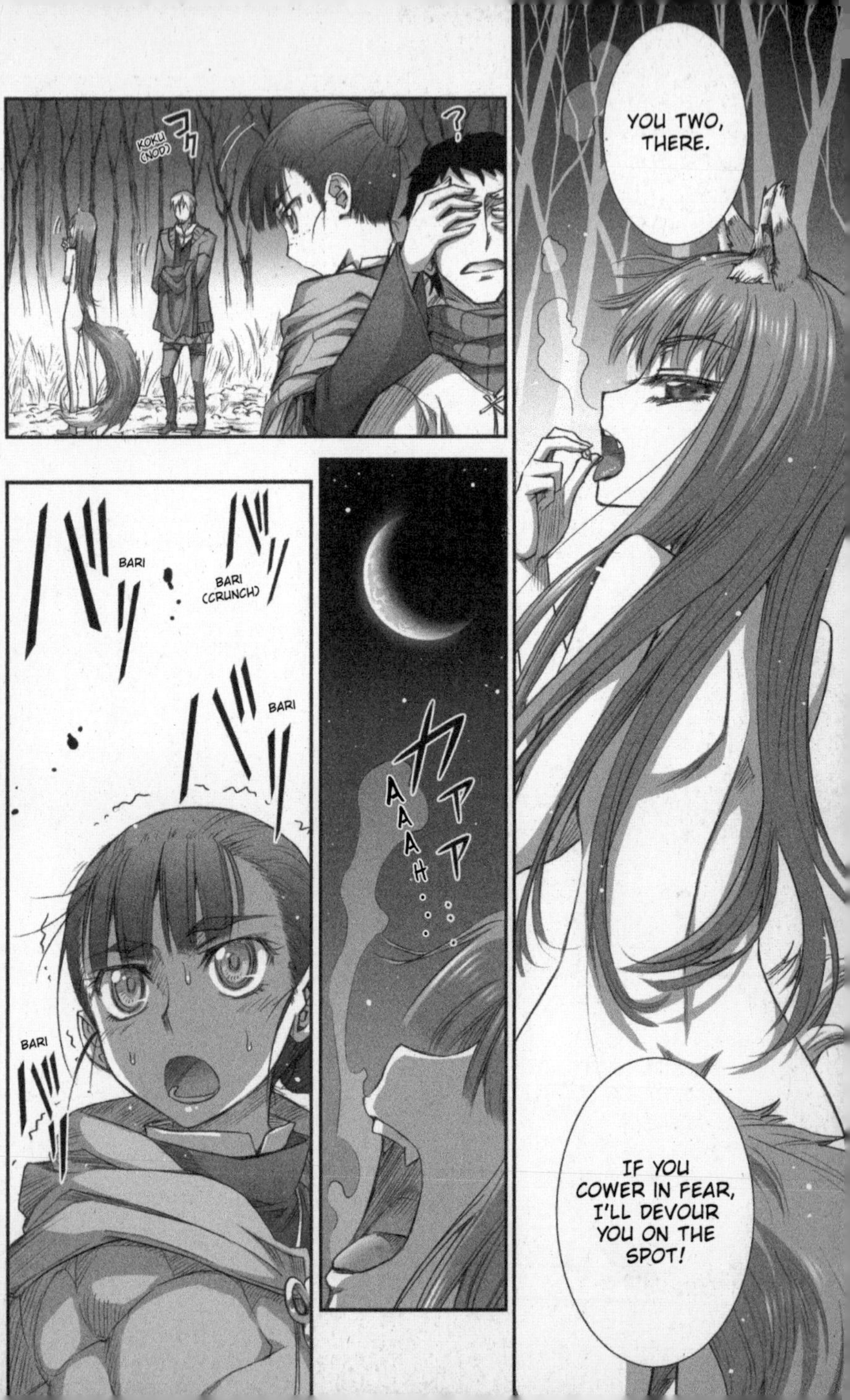
YOU TWO, THERE.
IF YOU COWER IN FEAR, I'LL DEVOUR YOU ON THE SPOT!
?
KOKU (NOD)
AAAH...
BARI
BARI (CRUNCH)
BARI
BARI

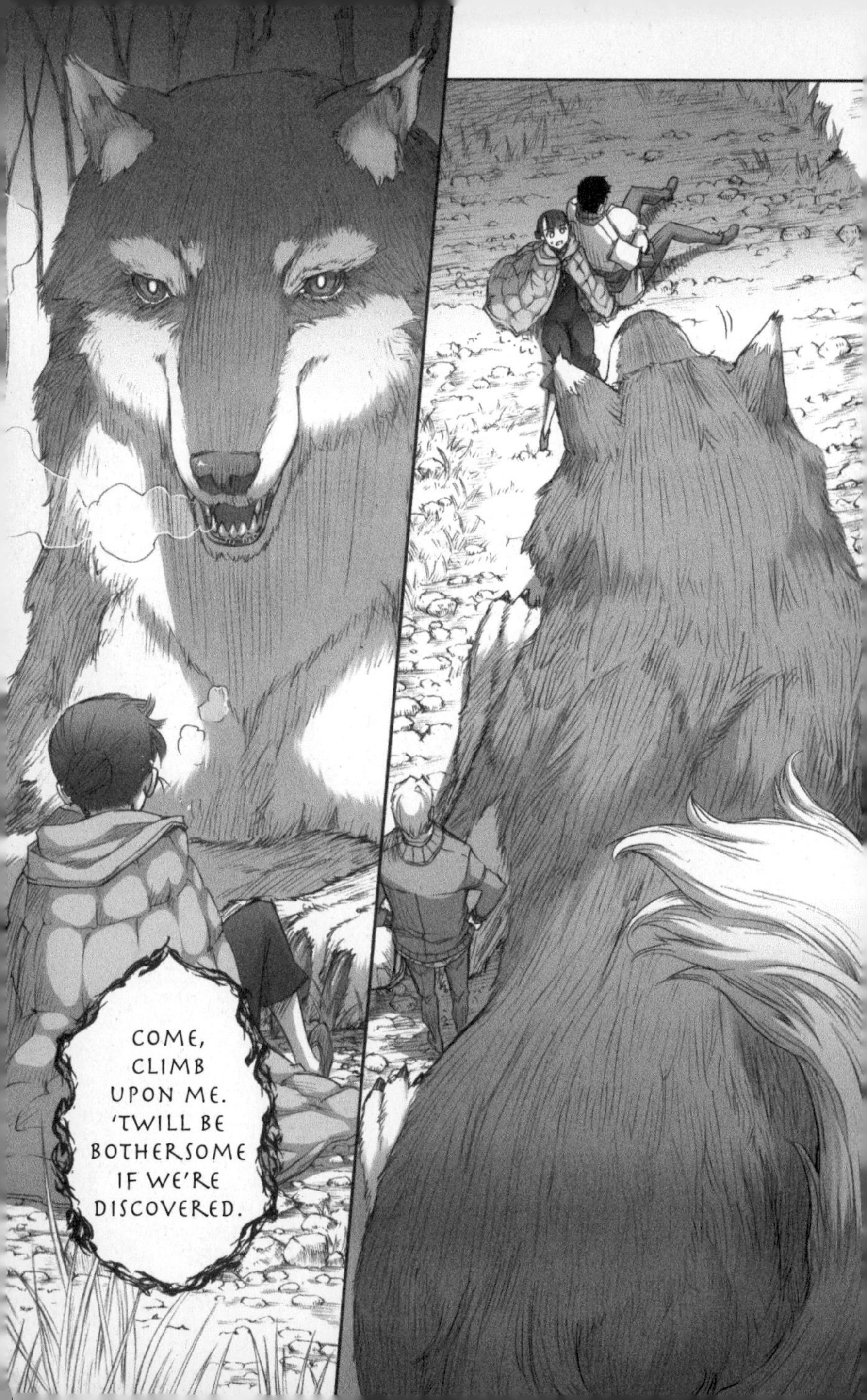
COME, CLIMB UPON ME. 'TWILL BE BOTHERSOME IF WE'RE DISCOVERED.

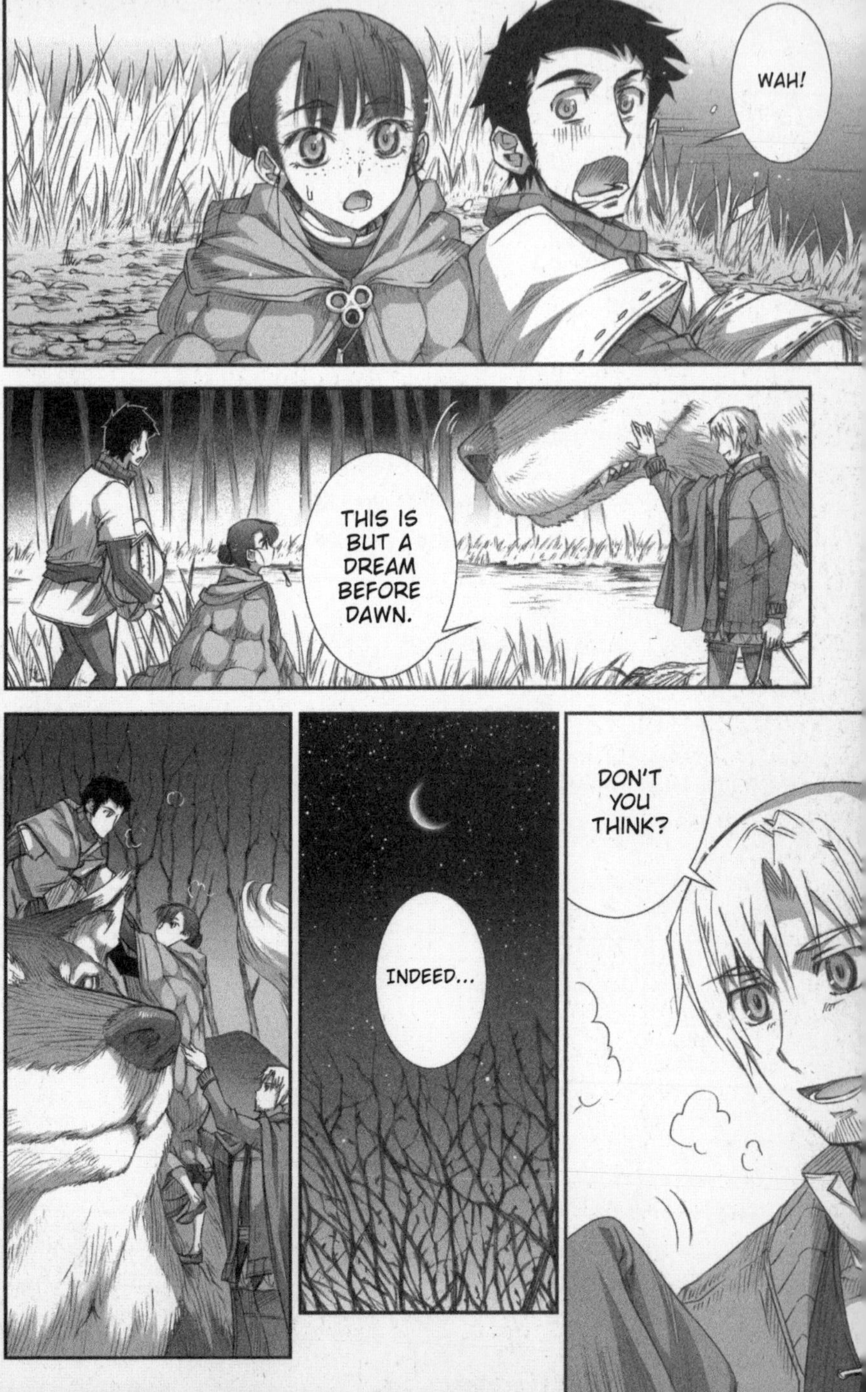
WAH!
THIS IS BUT A DREAM BEFORE DAWN.
DON'T YOU THINK?
INDEED...

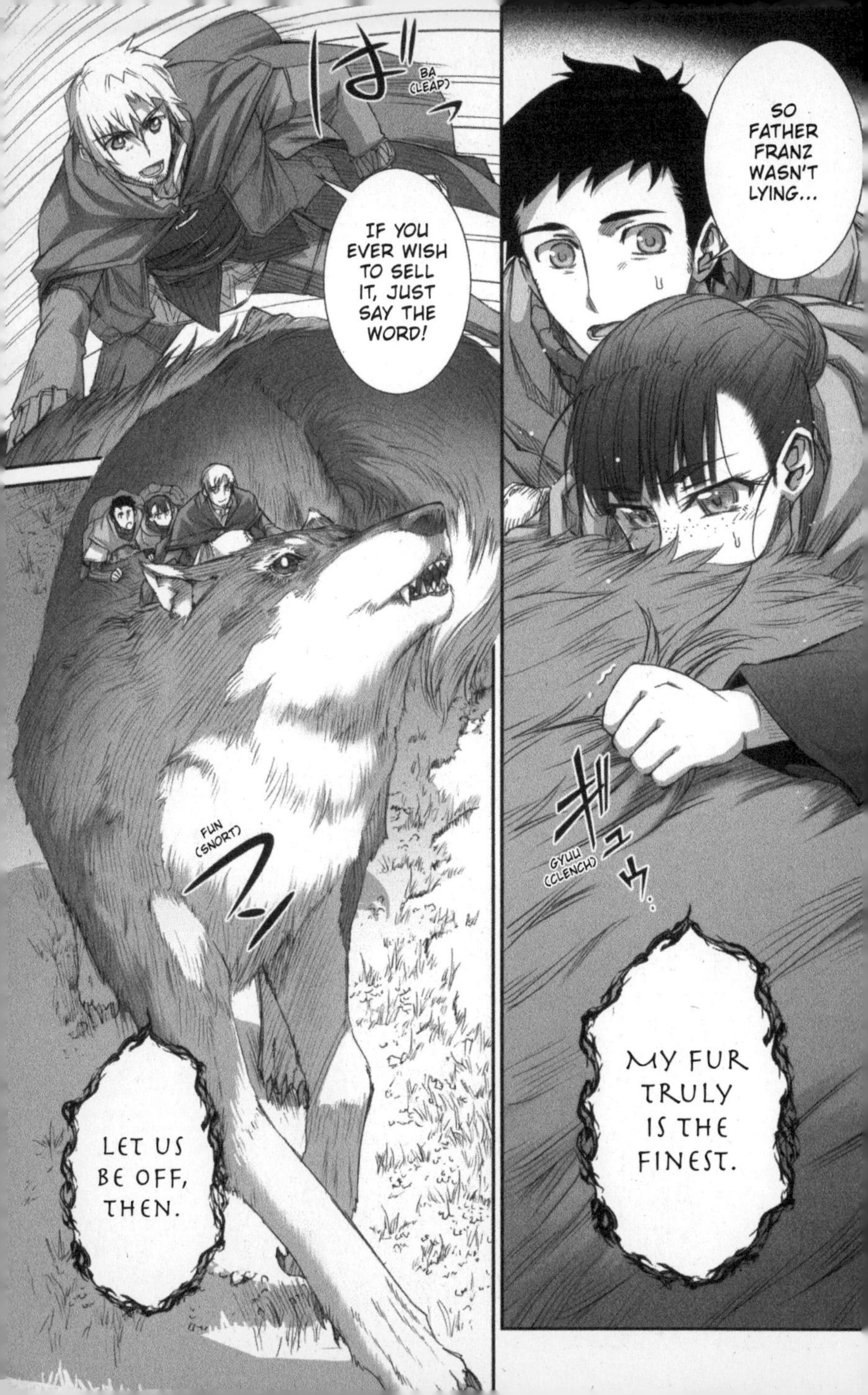
SO FATHER FRANZ WASN'T LYING...
GYUU (CLENCH)
MY FUR TRULY IS THE FINEST.
BA (LEAP)
IF YOU EVER WISH TO SELL IT, JUST SAY THE WORD!
FUN (SNORT)
LET US BE OFF, THEN.

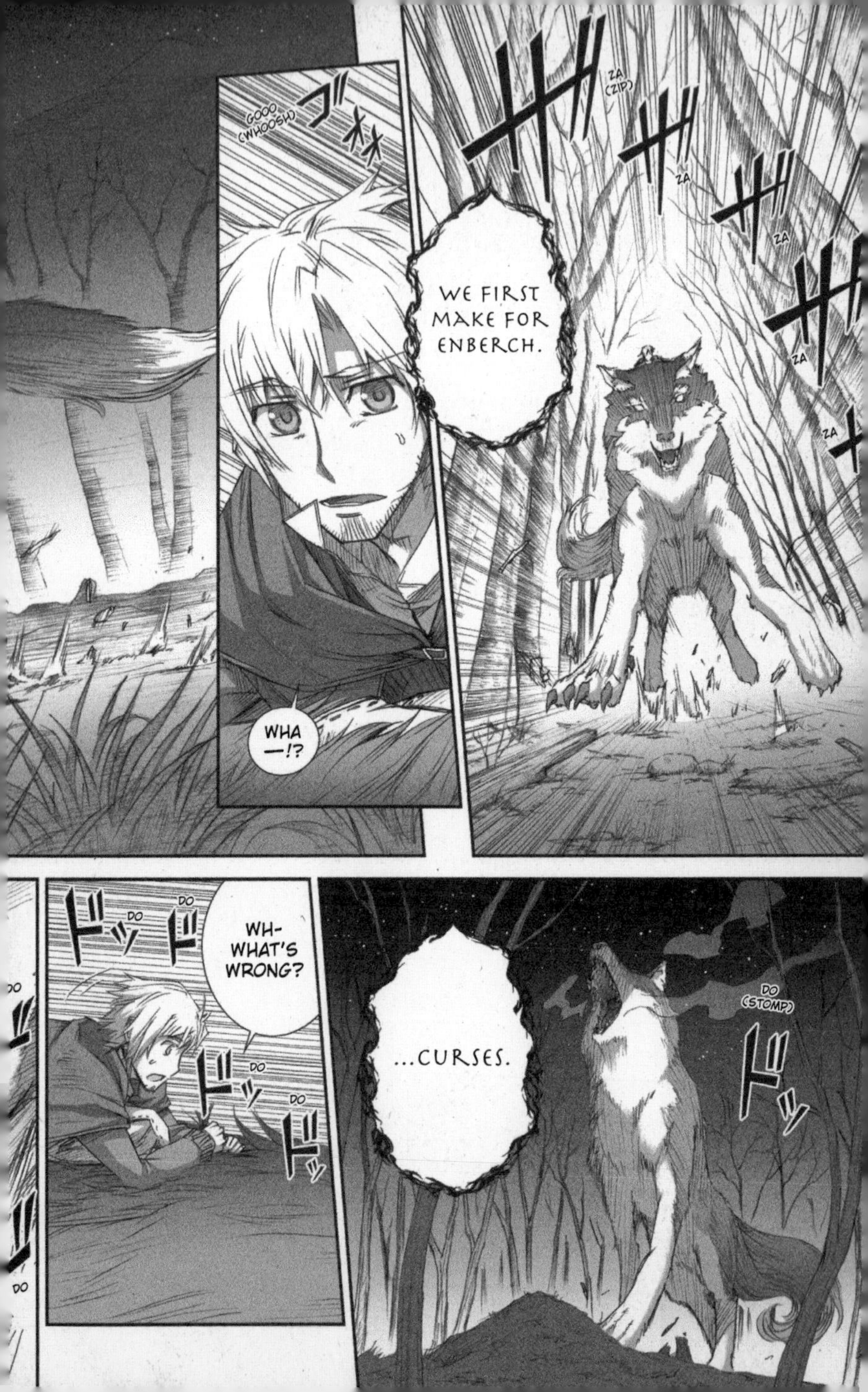
ZA (ZIP)
ZA
ZA
ZA
ZA
WE FIRST MAKE FOR ENBERCH.
GOOO (WHOOSH)
WHA—!?
DO (STOMP)
...CURSES.
DO
DO
WH- WHAT'S WRONG?
DO
DO
DO
DO

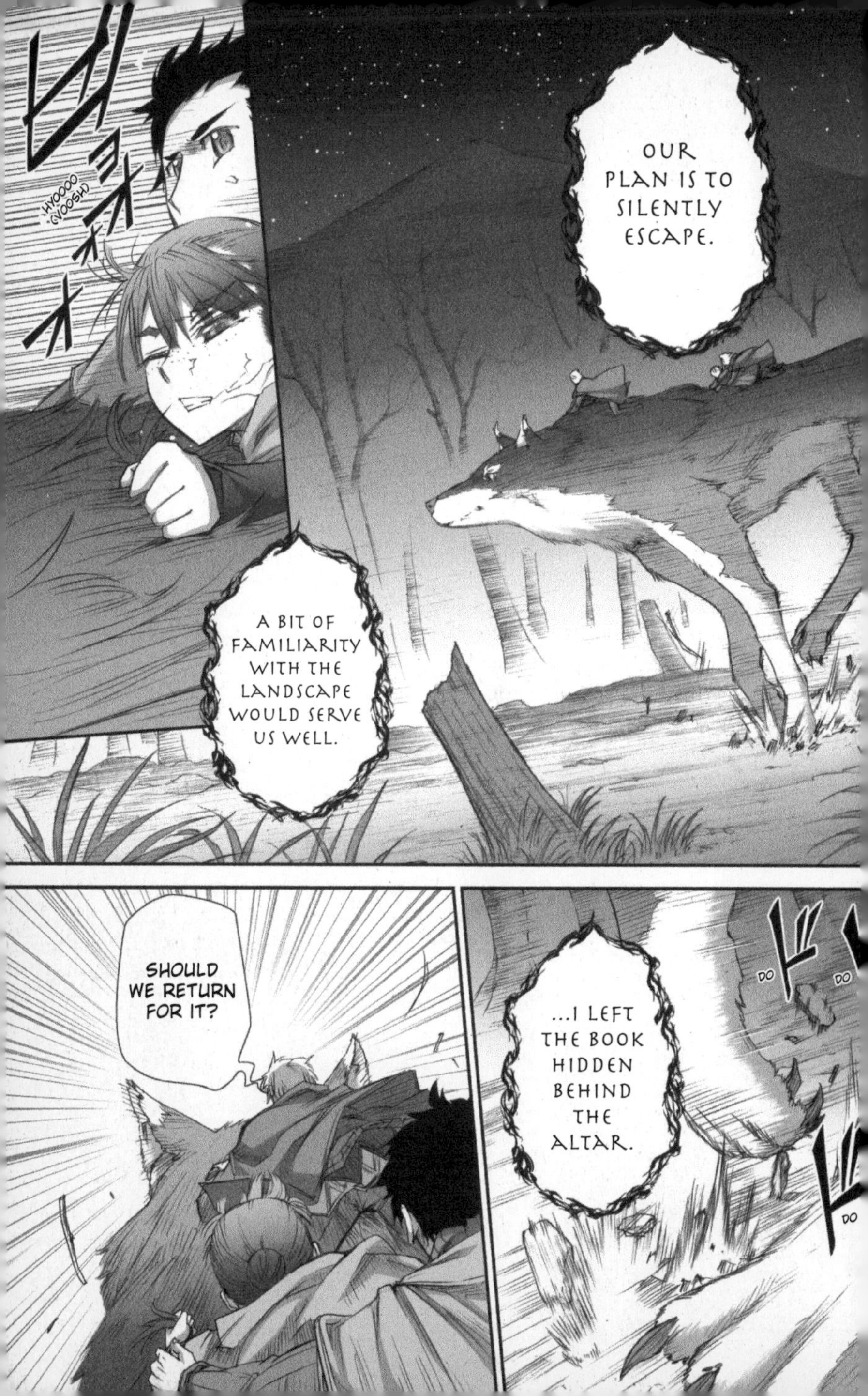
OUR PLAN IS TO SILENTLY ESCAPE.
A BIT OF FAMILIARITY WITH THE LANDSCAPE WOULD SERVE US WELL.
HYOOOO GVOOSH
...I LEFT THE BOOK HIDDEN BEHIND THE ALTAR.
DO DO DO
SHOULD WE RETURN FOR IT?

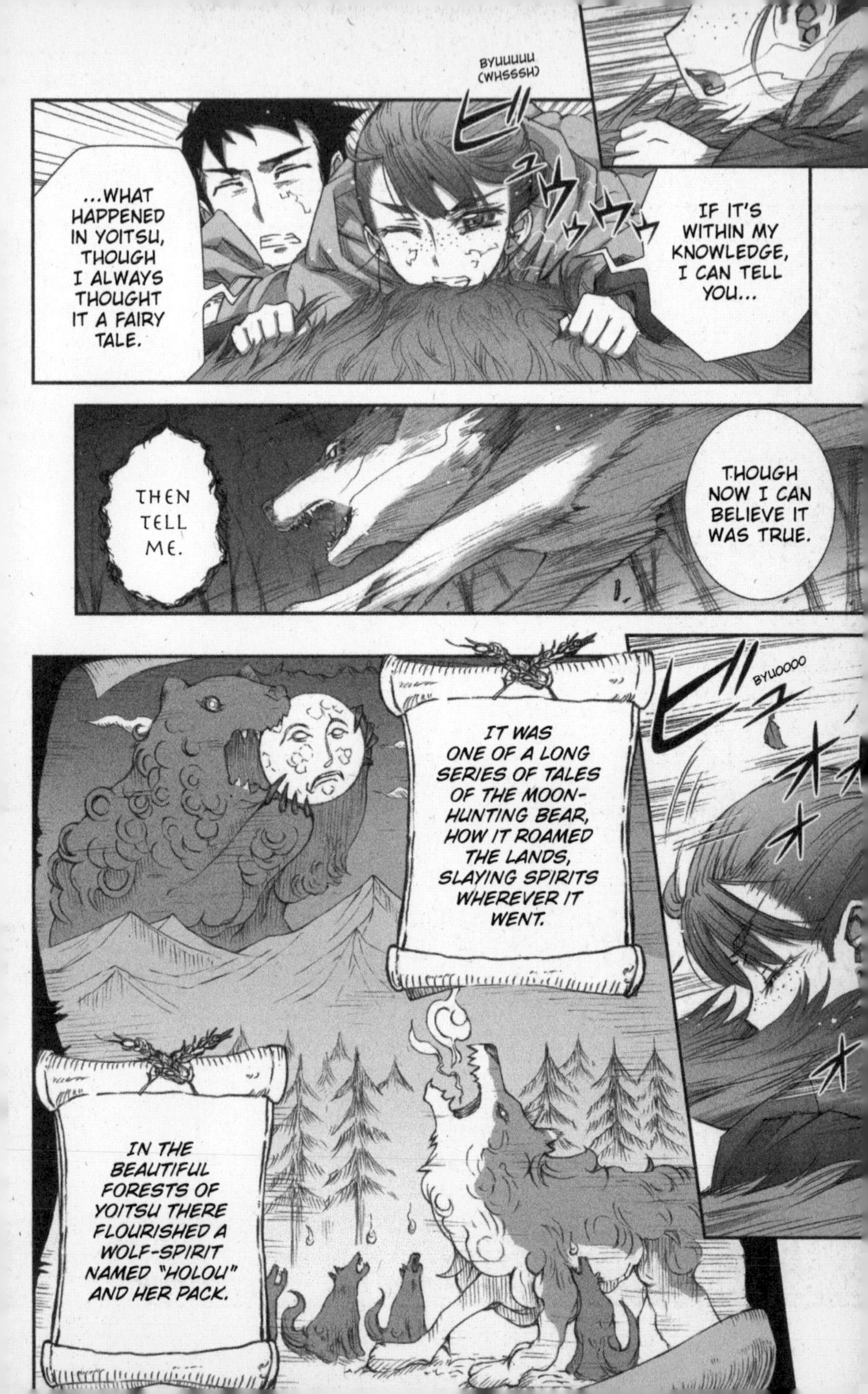
BYUUUUU (WHSSSH)
IF IT'S WITHIN MY KNOWLEDGE, I CAN TELL YOU...
...WHAT HAPPENED IN YOITSU, THOUGH I ALWAYS THOUGHT IT A FAIRY TALE.
THOUGH NOW I CAN BELIEVE IT WAS TRUE.
THEN TELL ME.
BYUOOOO
IT WAS ONE OF A LONG SERIES OF TALES OF THE MOON-HUNTING BEAR, HOW IT ROAMED THE LANDS, SLAYING SPIRITS WHEREVER IT WENT.
IN THE BEAUTIFUL FORESTS OF YOITSU THERE FLOURISHED A WOLF-SPIRIT NAMED "HOLOU" AND HER PACK.

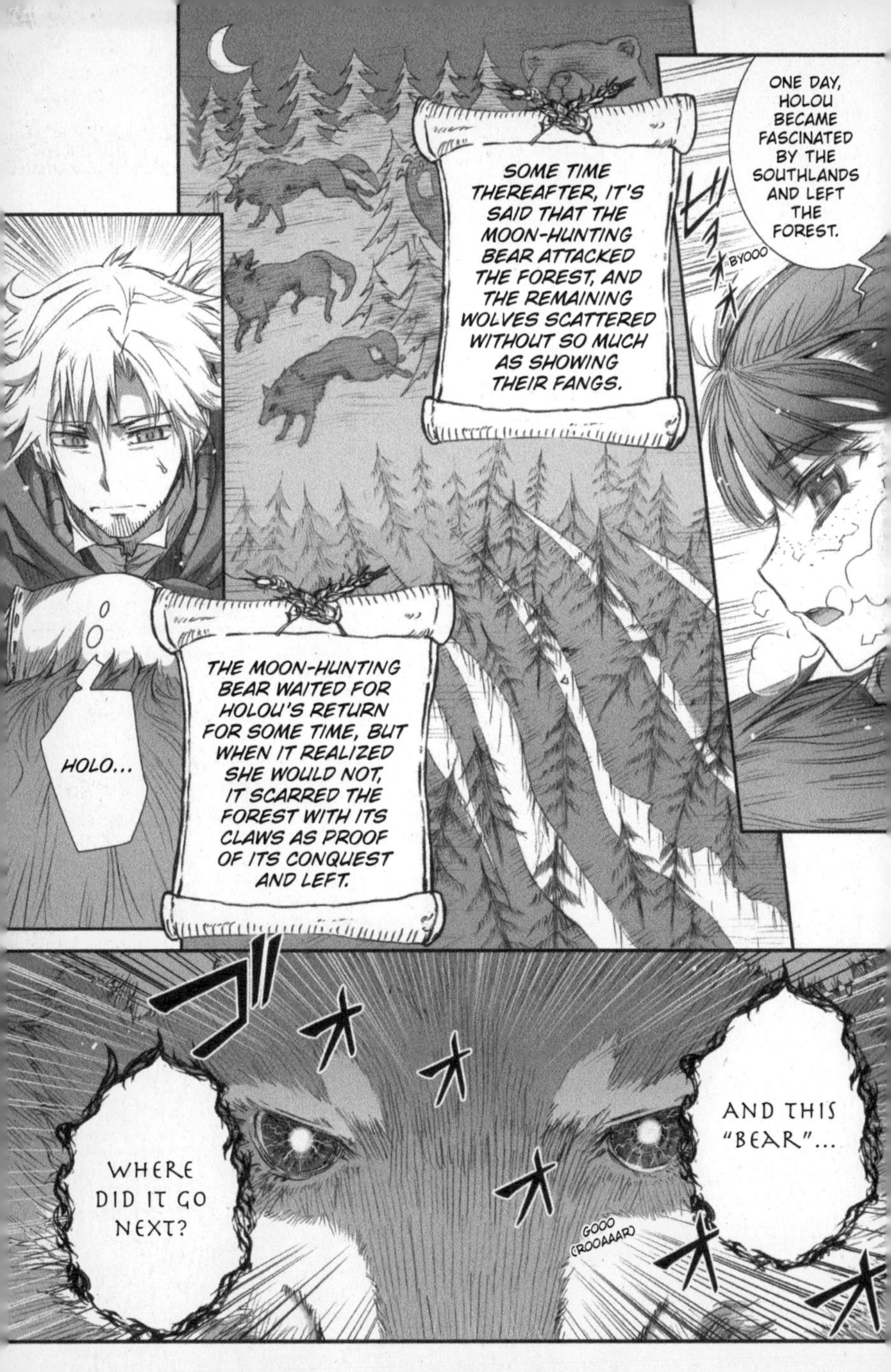
ONE DAY, HOLOU BECAME FASCINATED BY THE SOUTHLANDS AND LEFT THE FOREST.
BYOOO
SOME TIME THEREAFTER, IT'S SAID THAT THE MOON-HUNTING BEAR ATTACKED THE FOREST, AND THE REMAINING WOLVES SCATTERED WITHOUT SO MUCH AS SHOWING THEIR FANGS.
THE MOON-HUNTING BEAR WAITED FOR HOLOU'S RETURN FOR SOME TIME, BUT WHEN IT REALIZED SHE WOULD NOT, IT SCARRED THE FOREST WITH ITS CLAWS AS PROOF OF ITS CONQUEST AND LEFT.
HOLO...
AND THIS "BEAR"...
GOOO (ROOAAAR)
WHERE DID IT GO NEXT?

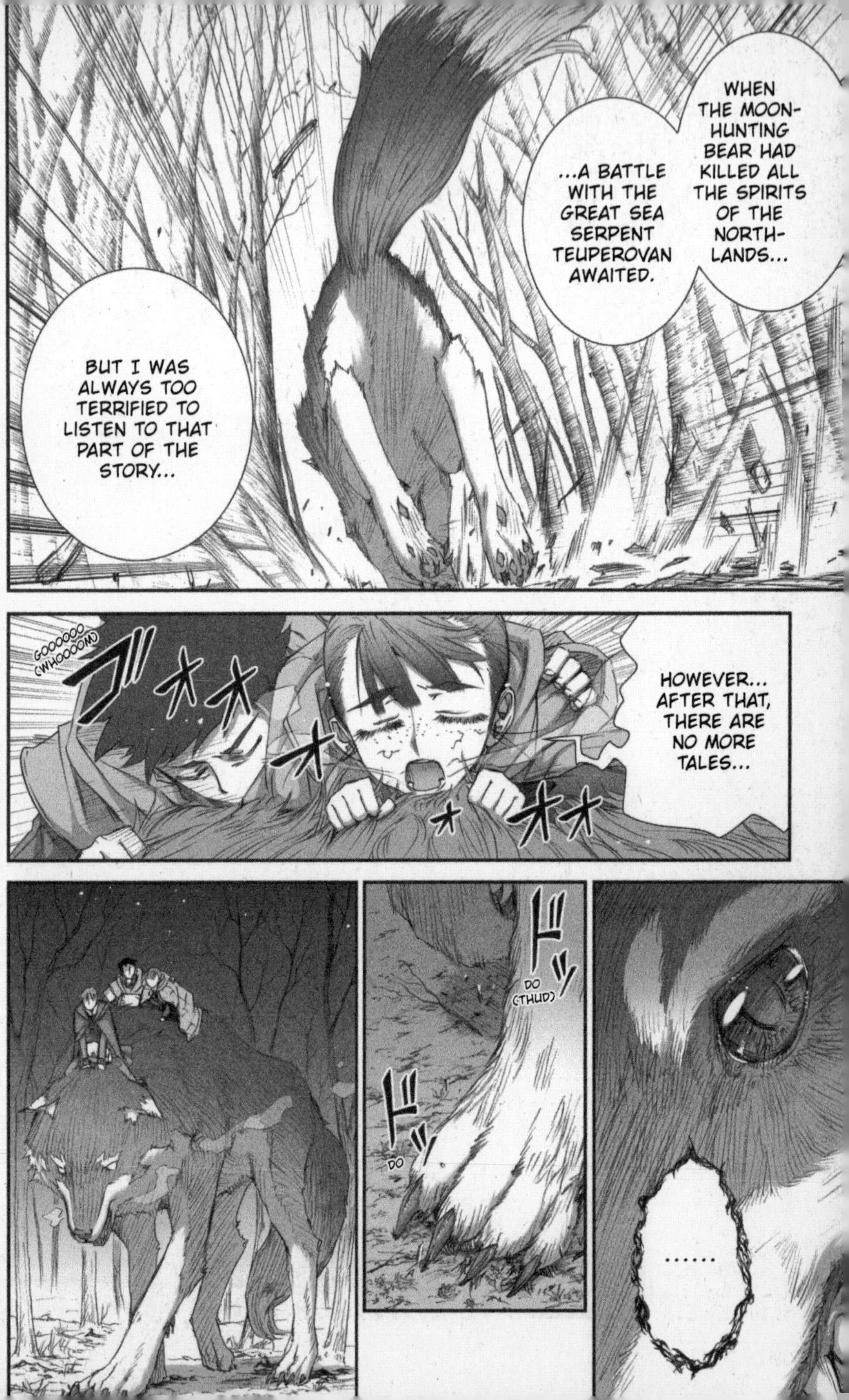
WHEN THE MOON-HUNTING BEAR HAD KILLED ALL THE SPIRITS OF THE NORTH-LANDS...
...A BATTLE WITH THE GREAT SEA SERPENT TEUPEROVAN AWAITED.
BUT I WAS ALWAYS TOO TERRIFIED TO LISTEN TO THAT PART OF THE STORY...
HOWEVER... AFTER THAT, THERE ARE NO MORE TALES...
ゴオオオオオオ
GOOOOOOO (WHOOOOM)
......
ドッ
DO (THUD)
ドッ
DO

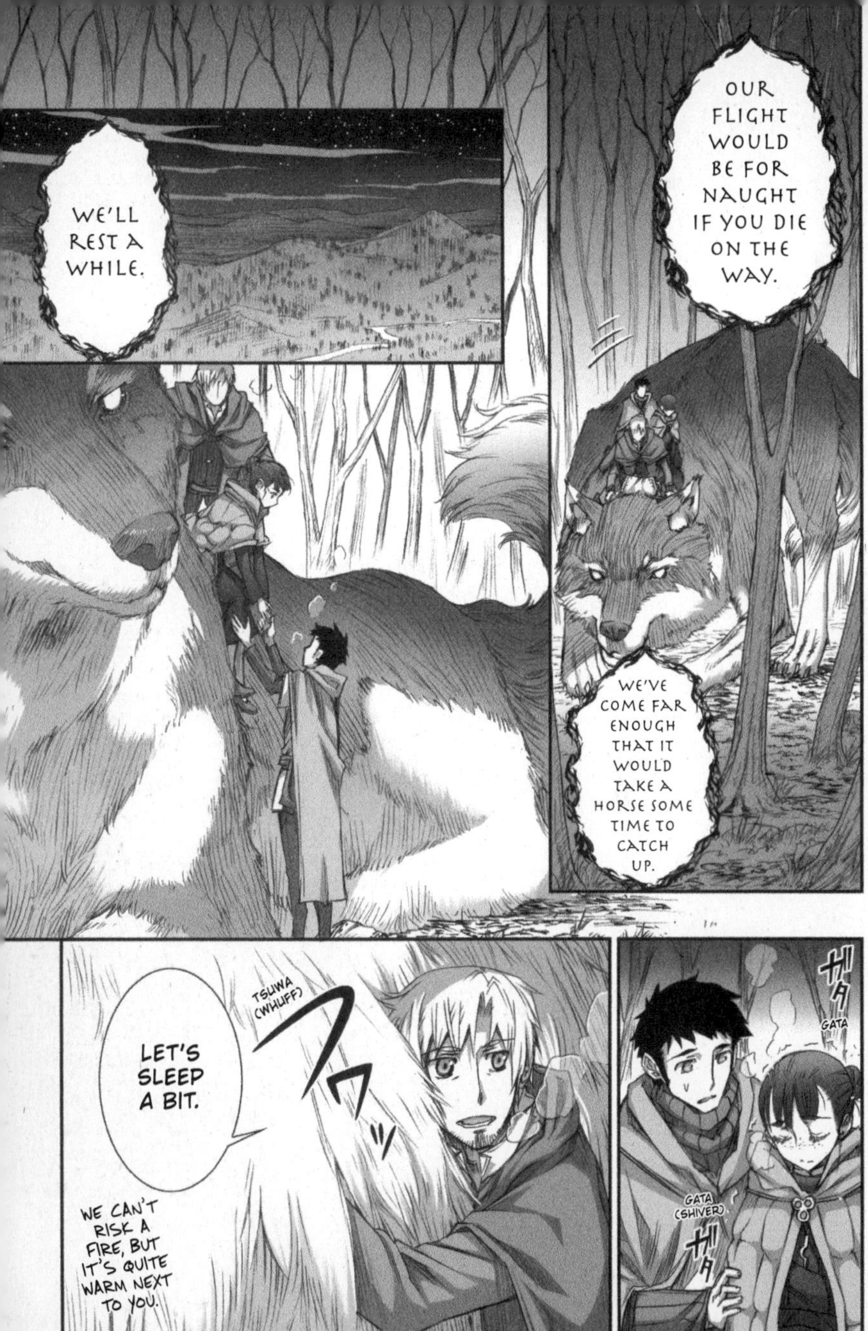

OUR FLIGHT WOULD BE FOR NAUGHT IF YOU DIE ON THE WAY.
WE'VE COME FAR ENOUGH THAT IT WOULD TAKE A HORSE SOME TIME TO CATCH UP.
WE'LL REST A WHILE.
ガタ
GATA
GATA (SHIVER)
ガタ
TSUWA (WHUFF)
フワッ
LET'S SLEEP A BIT.
WE CAN'T RISK A FIRE, BUT IT'S QUITE WARM NEXT TO YOU.

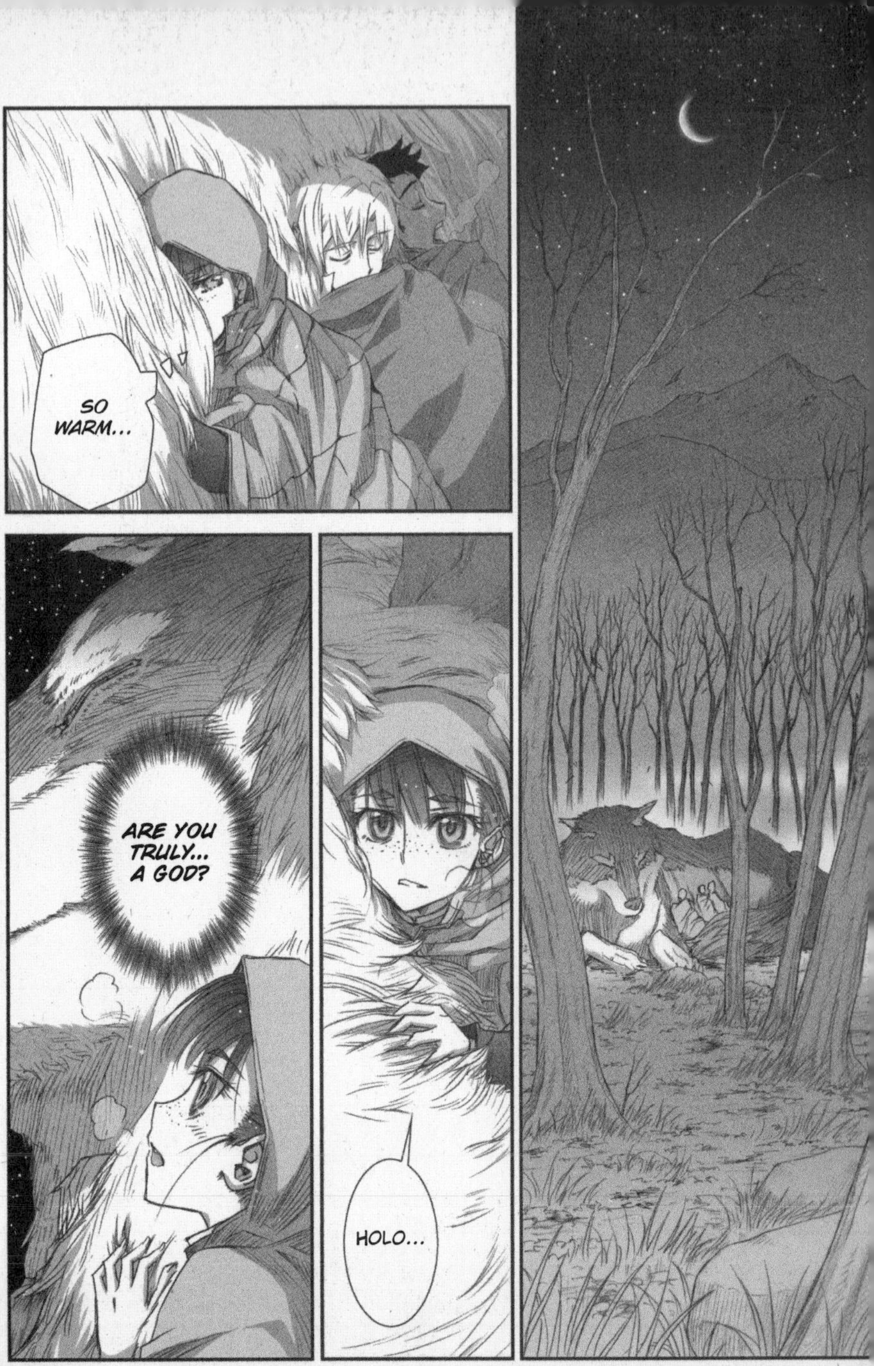
SO WARM...
HOLO...
ARE YOU TRULY... A GOD?

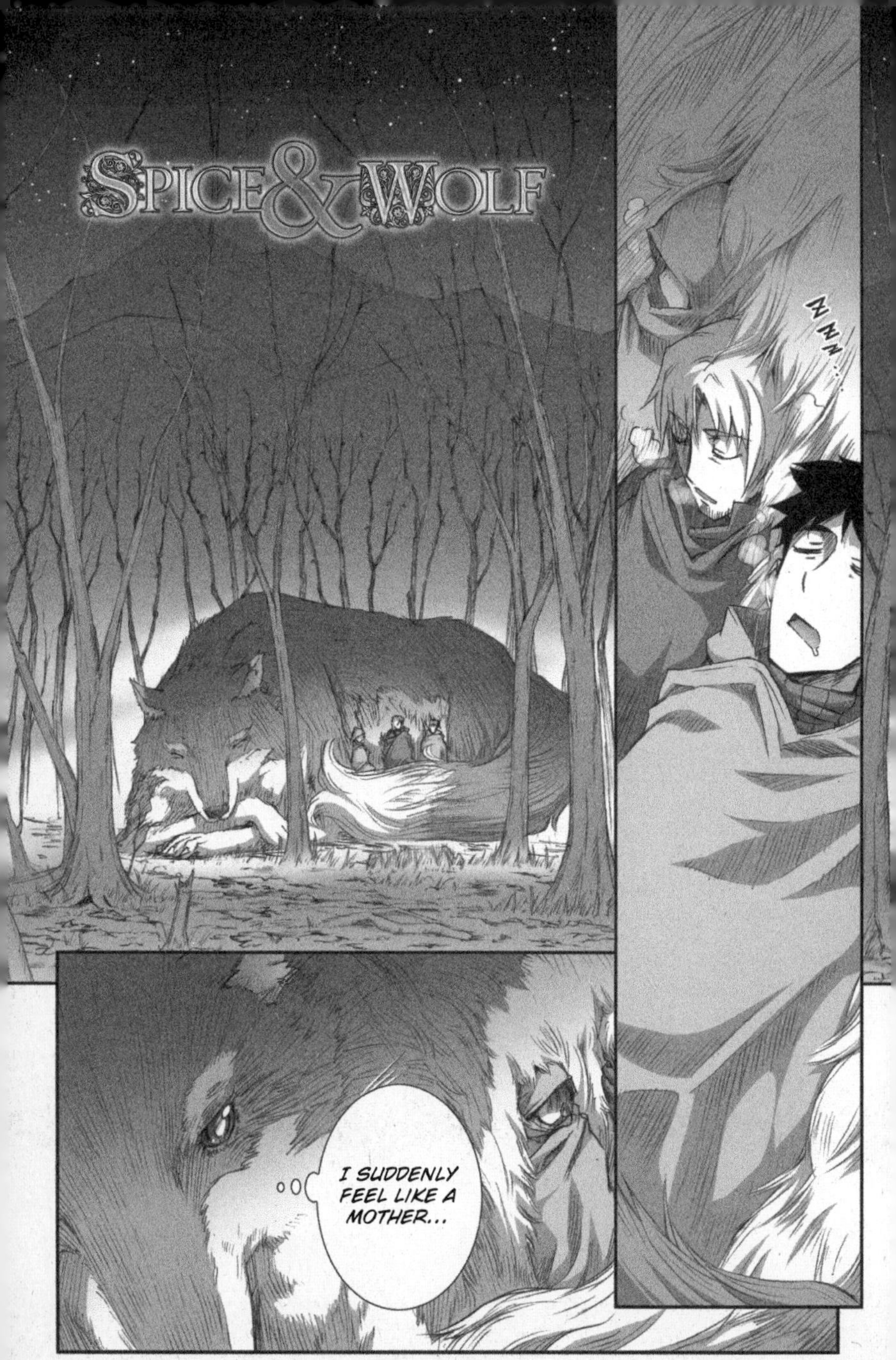
SPICE & WOLF
Z Z Z ...
I SUDDENLY FEEL LIKE A MOTHER...

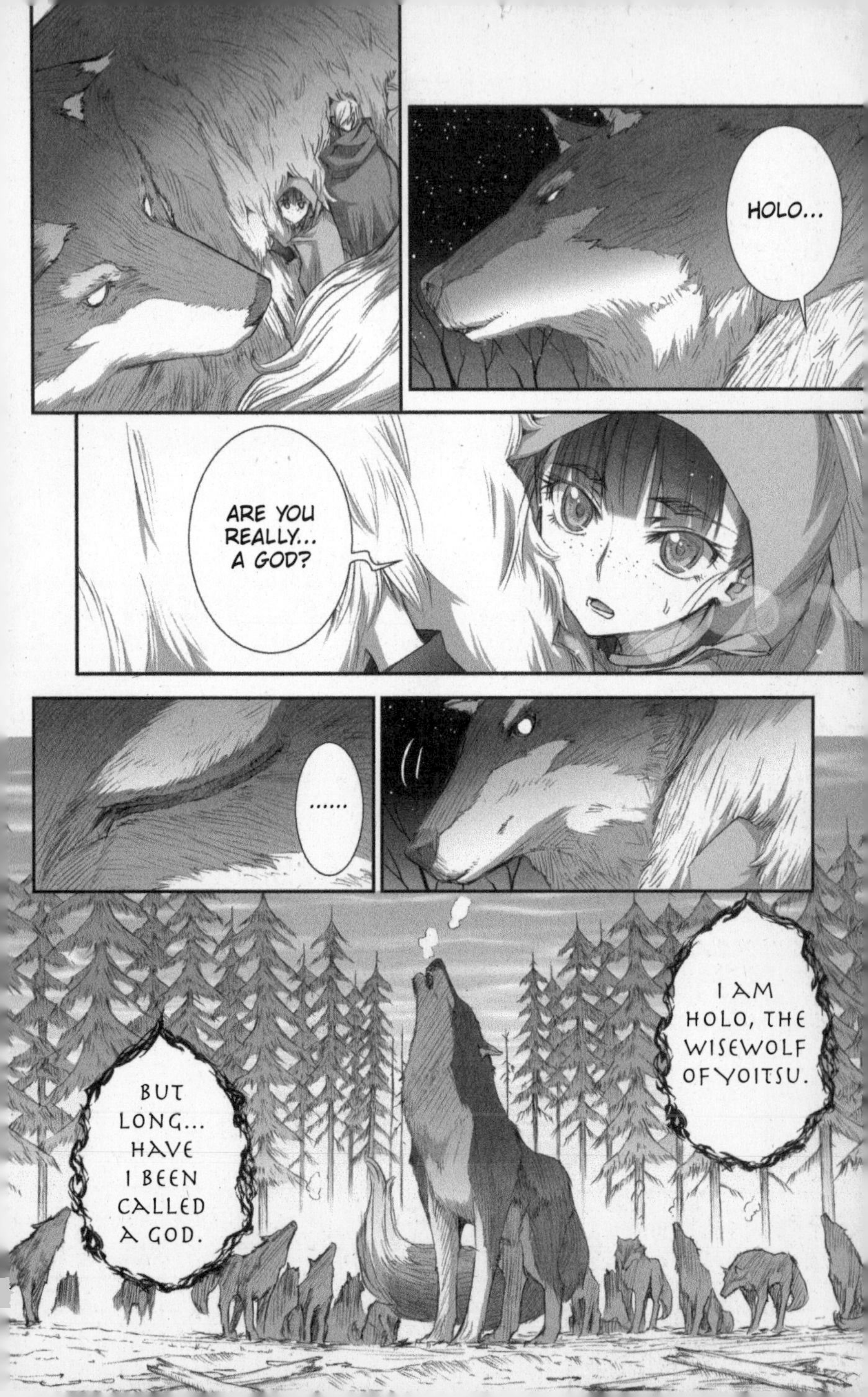
HOLO...
ARE YOU REALLY... A GOD?
......
I AM HOLO, THE WISEWOLF OF YOITSU.
BUT LONG... HAVE I BEEN CALLED A GOD.

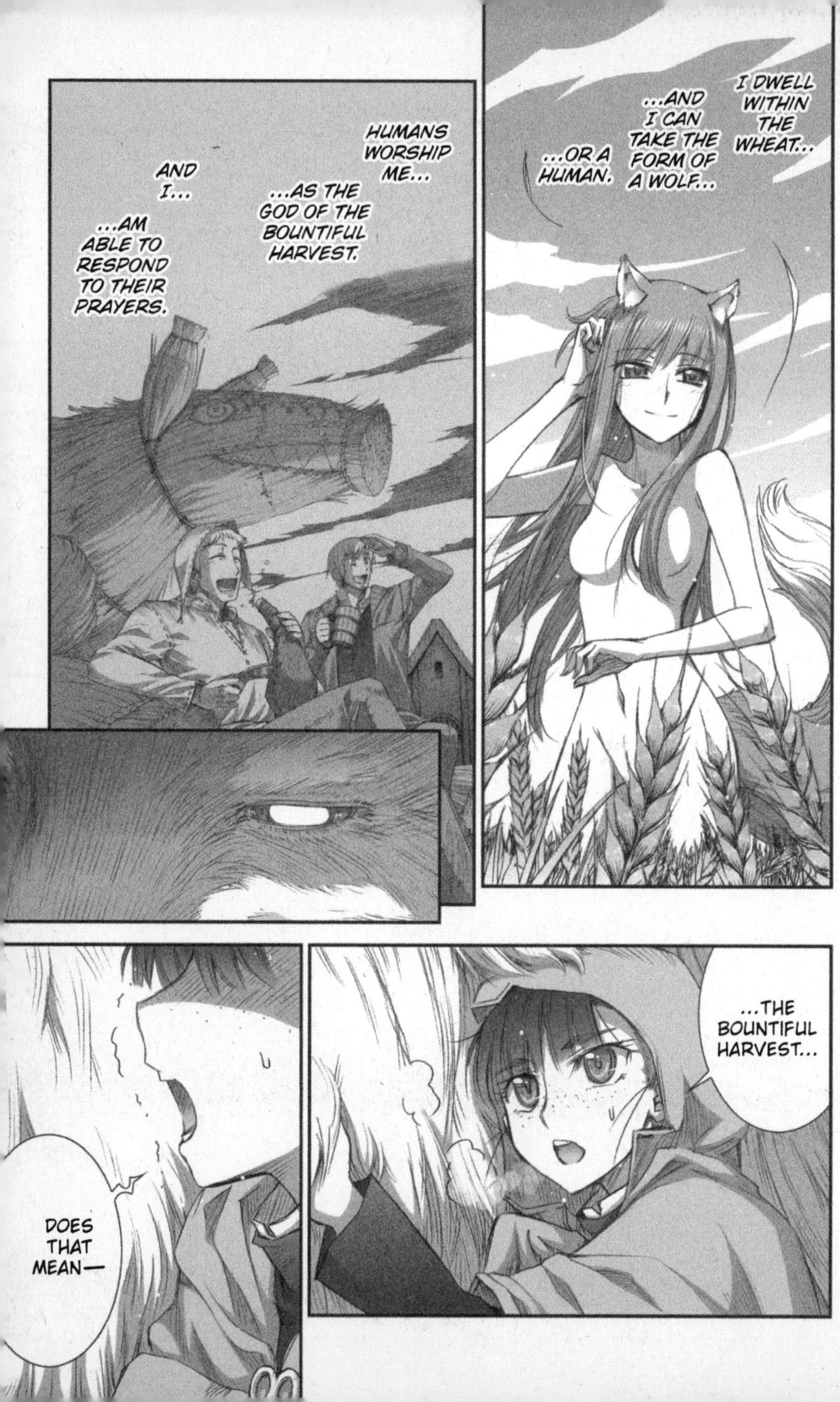
I DWELL WITHIN THE WHEAT...
...AND I CAN TAKE THE FORM OF A WOLF...
...OR A HUMAN.
HUMANS WORSHIP ME...
...AS THE GOD OF THE BOUNTIFUL HARVEST.
AND I...
...AM ABLE TO RESPOND TO THEIR PRAYERS.
...THE BOUNTIFUL HARVEST...
DOES THAT MEAN—

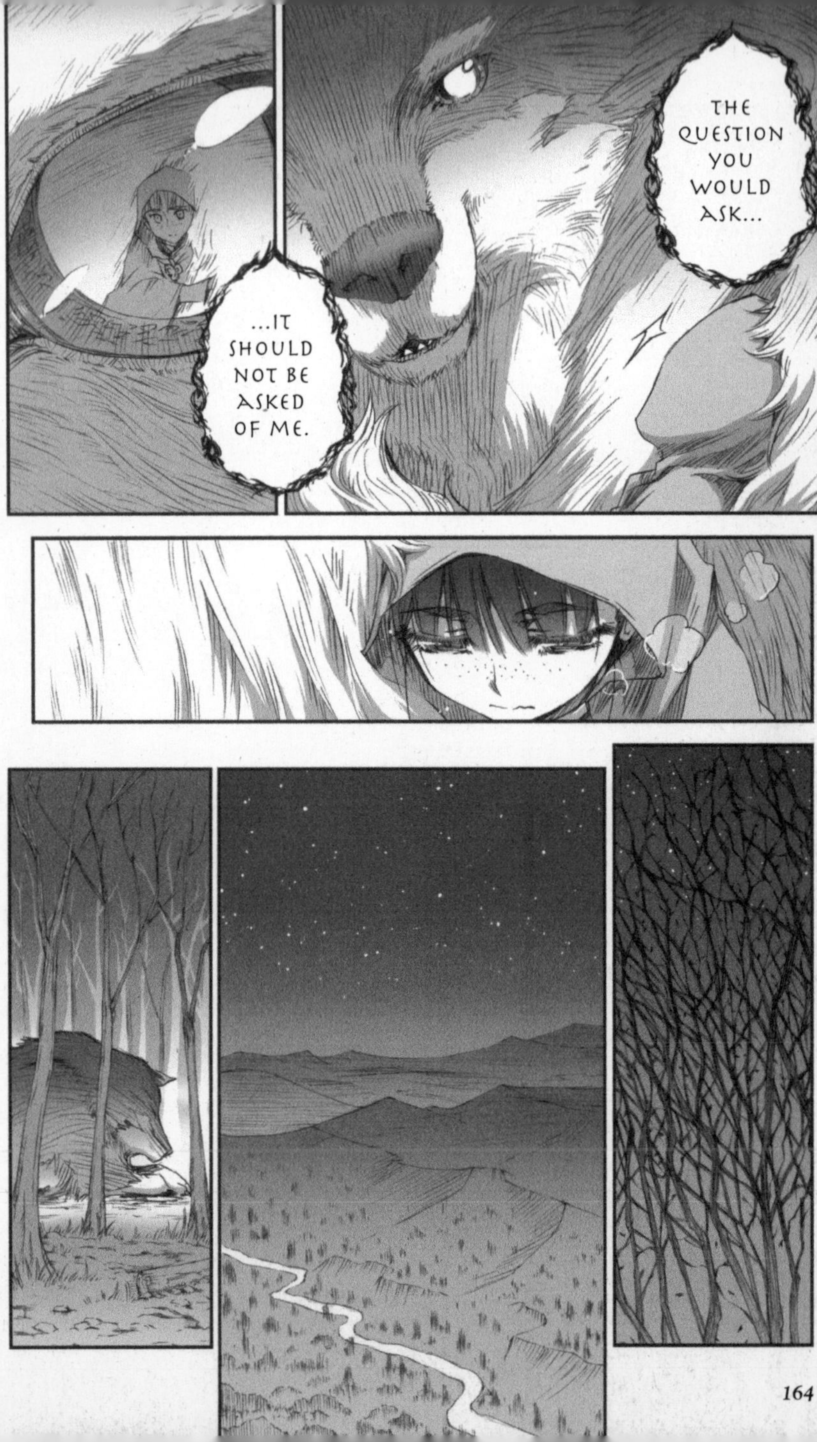
THE QUESTION YOU WOULD ASK...
...IT SHOULD NOT BE ASKED OF ME.

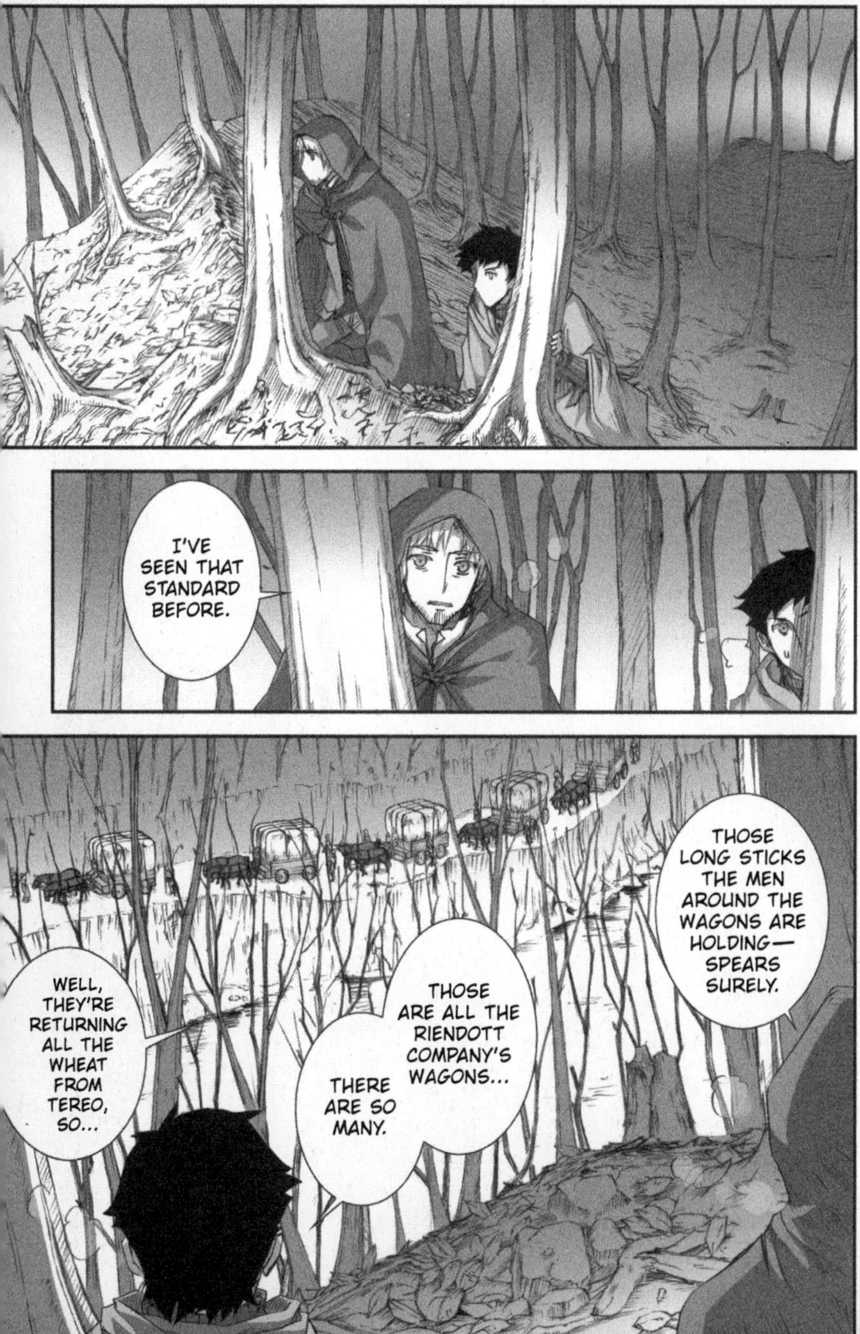
I'VE SEEN THAT STANDARD BEFORE.
THOSE LONG STICKS THE MEN AROUND THE WAGONS ARE HOLDING— SPEARS SURELY.
THOSE ARE ALL THE RIENDOTT COMPANY'S WAGONS...
THERE ARE SO MANY.
WELL, THEY'RE RETURNING ALL THE WHEAT FROM TEREO, SO...

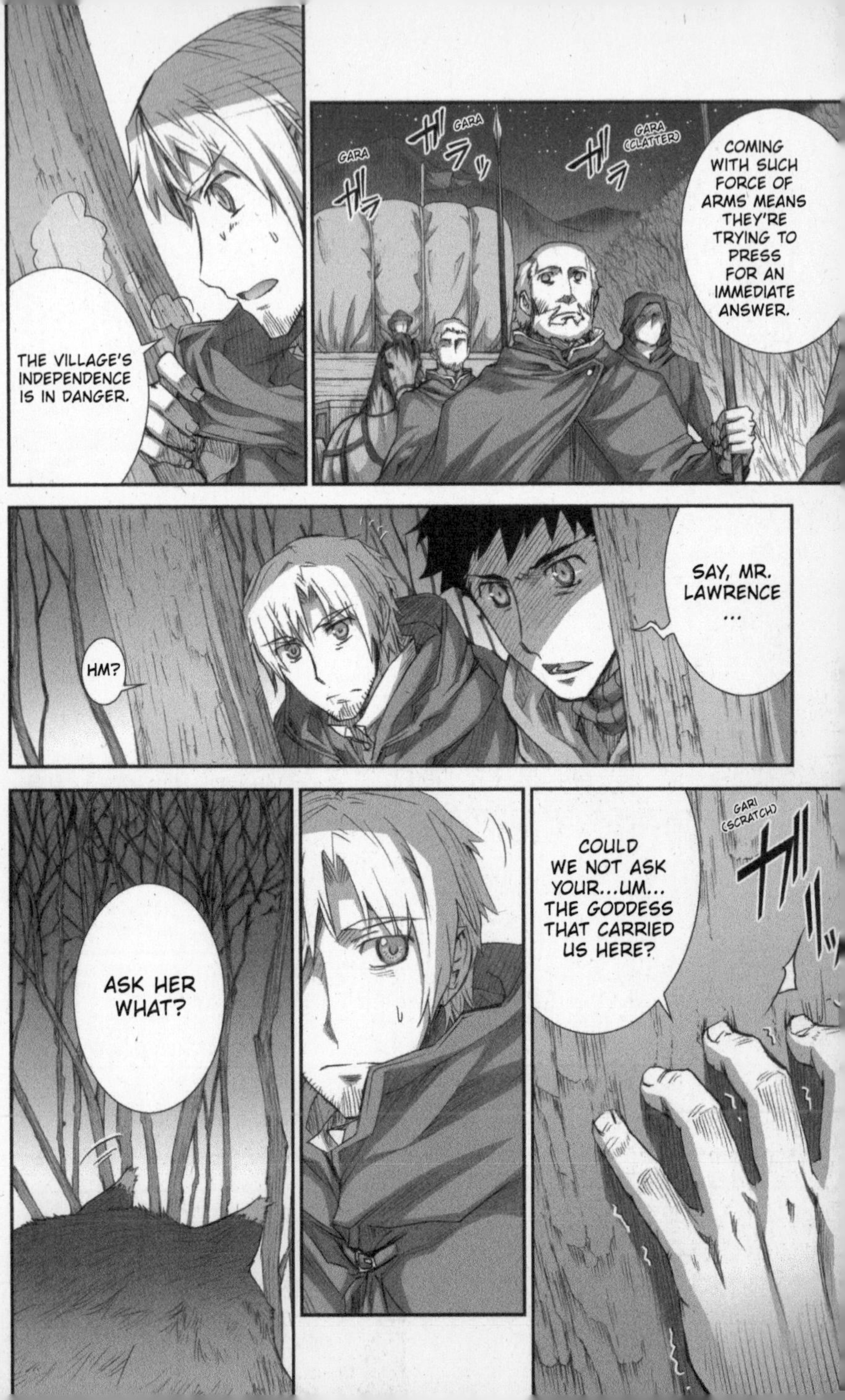
COMING WITH SUCH FORCE OF ARMS MEANS THEY'RE TRYING TO PRESS FOR AN IMMEDIATE ANSWER.
GARA (CLATTER)
GARA
GARA
THE VILLAGE'S INDEPENDENCE IS IN DANGER.
SAY, MR. LAWRENCE ...
HM?
GARI (SCRATCH)
COULD WE NOT ASK YOUR...UM... THE GODDESS THAT CARRIED US HERE?
ASK HER WHAT?

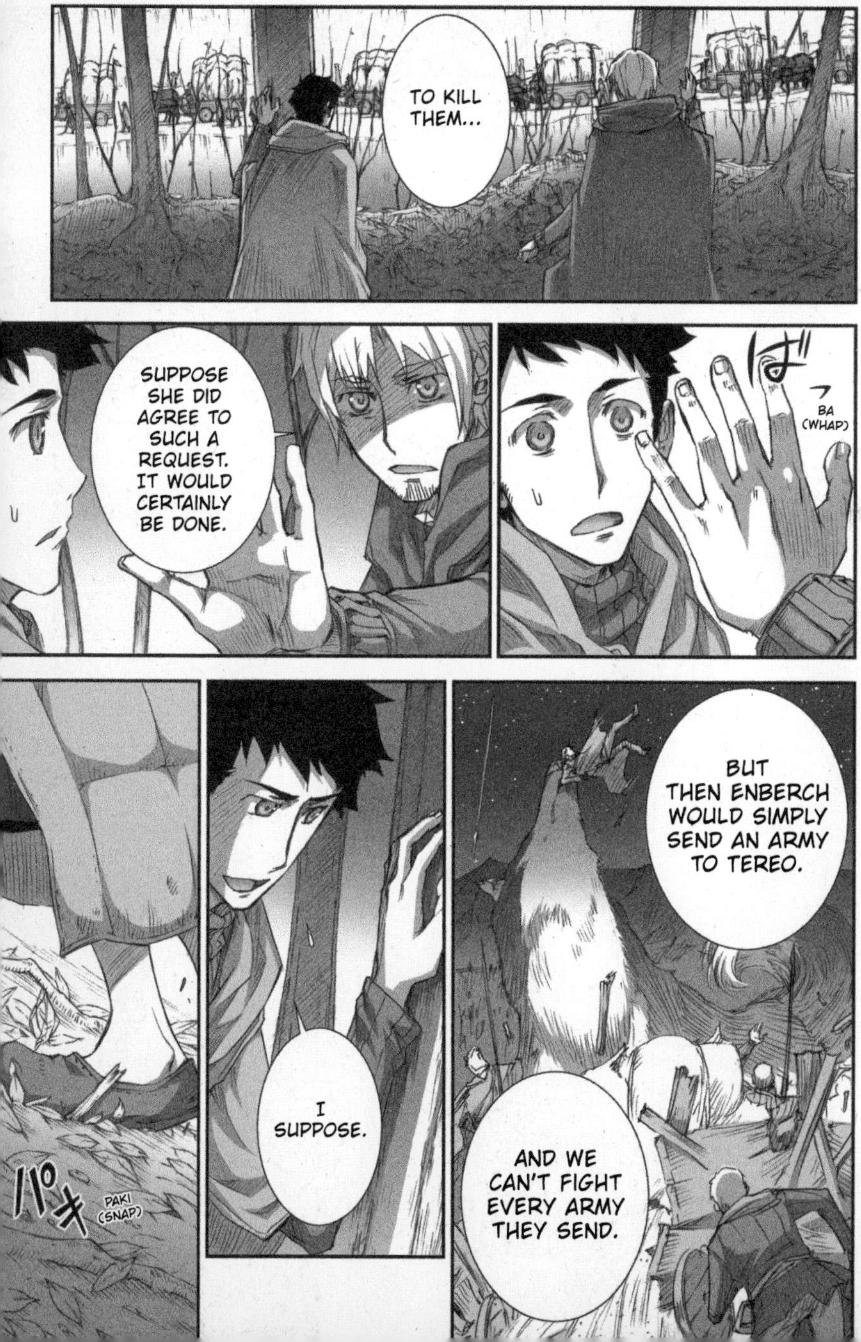
TO KILL THEM...
ぱっ
BA (WHAP)
SUPPOSE SHE DID AGREE TO SUCH A REQUEST. IT WOULD CERTAINLY BE DONE.
BUT THEN ENBERCH WOULD SIMPLY SEND AN ARMY TO TEREO.
AND WE CAN'T FIGHT EVERY ARMY THEY SEND.
I SUPPOSE.
パキ
PAKI (SNAP)

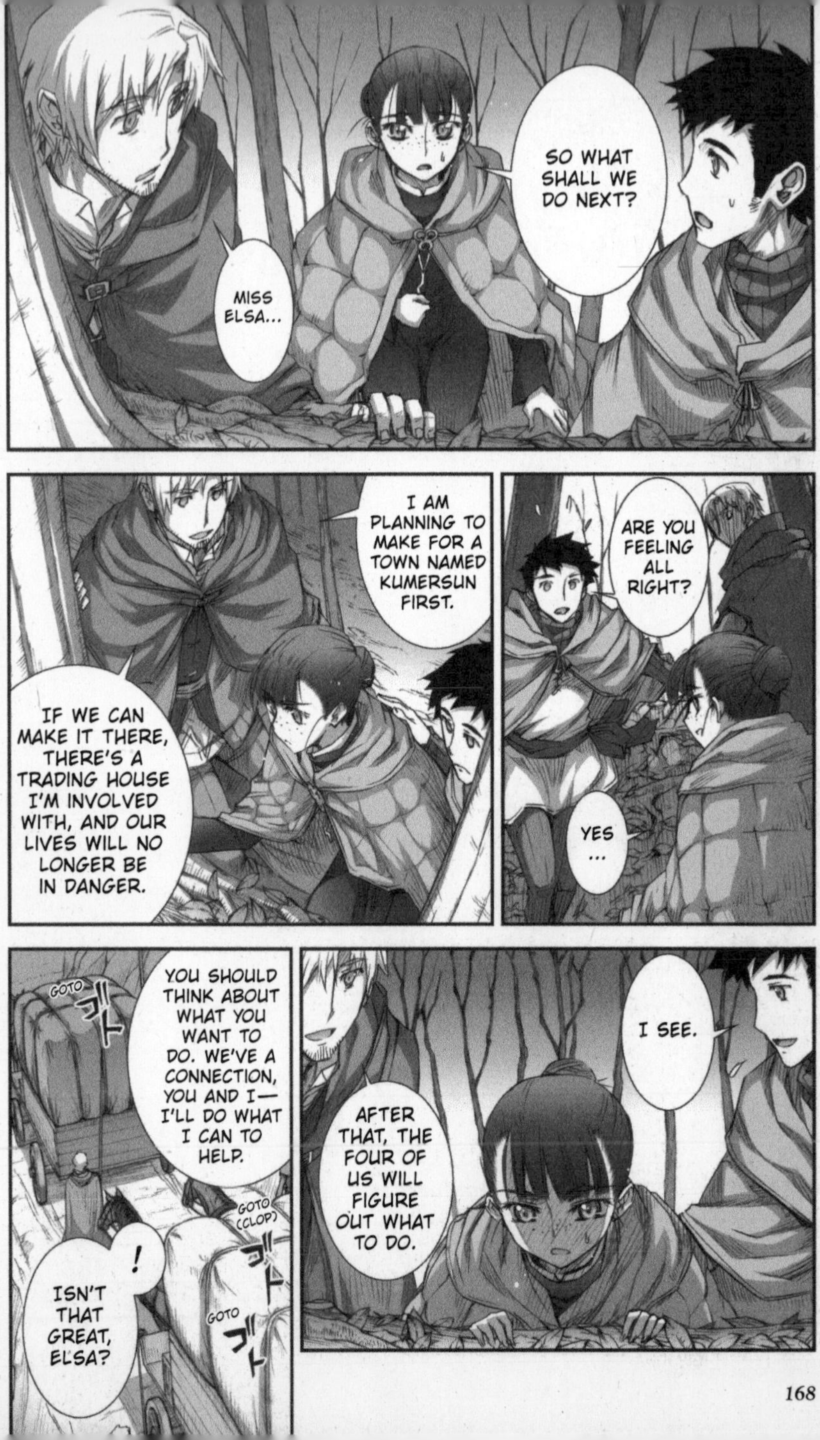
SO WHAT SHALL WE DO NEXT?
MISS ELSA...
ARE YOU FEELING ALL RIGHT?
YES ...
I AM PLANNING TO MAKE FOR A TOWN NAMED KUMERSUN FIRST.
IF WE CAN MAKE IT THERE, THERE'S A TRADING HOUSE I'M INVOLVED WITH, AND OUR LIVES WILL NO LONGER BE IN DANGER.
I SEE.
AFTER THAT, THE FOUR OF US WILL FIGURE OUT WHAT TO DO.
YOU SHOULD THINK ABOUT WHAT YOU WANT TO DO. WE'VE A CONNECTION, YOU AND I— I'LL DO WHAT I CAN TO HELP.
GOTO ゴト
GOTO (CLOP) ゴト
!
ISN'T THAT GREAT, ELSA?
GOTO ゴト

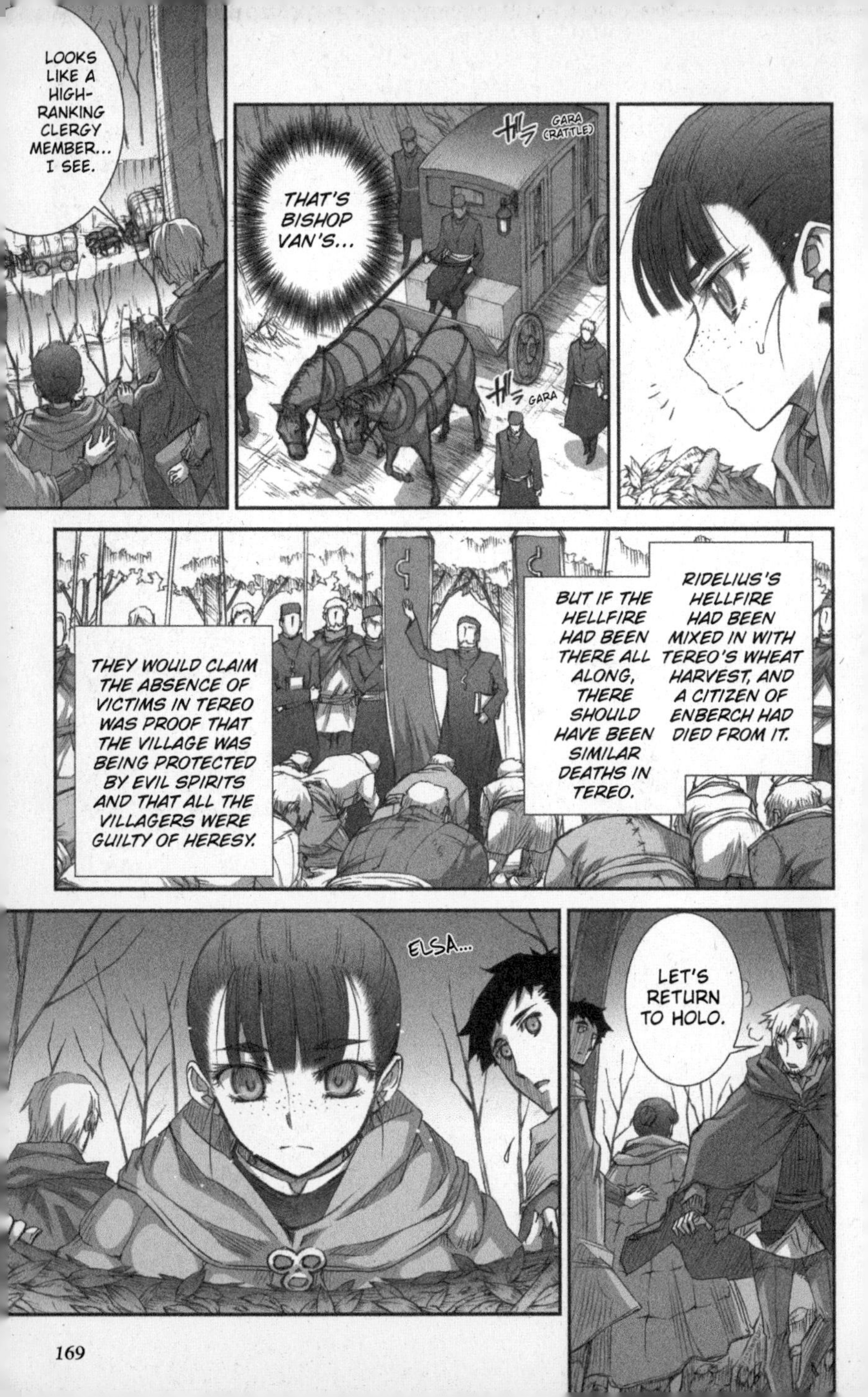

GARA (RATTLE)
THAT'S BISHOP VAN'S...
GARA
LOOKS LIKE A HIGH-RANKING CLERGY MEMBER... I SEE.
RIDELIUS'S HELLFIRE HAD BEEN MIXED IN WITH TEREO'S WHEAT HARVEST, AND A CITIZEN OF ENBERCH HAD DIED FROM IT.
BUT IF THE HELLFIRE HAD BEEN THERE ALL ALONG, THERE SHOULD HAVE BEEN SIMILAR DEATHS IN TEREO.
THEY WOULD CLAIM THE ABSENCE OF VICTIMS IN TEREO WAS PROOF THAT THE VILLAGE WAS BEING PROTECTED BY EVIL SPIRITS AND THAT ALL THE VILLAGERS WERE GUILTY OF HERESY.
LET'S RETURN TO HOLO.
ELSA...

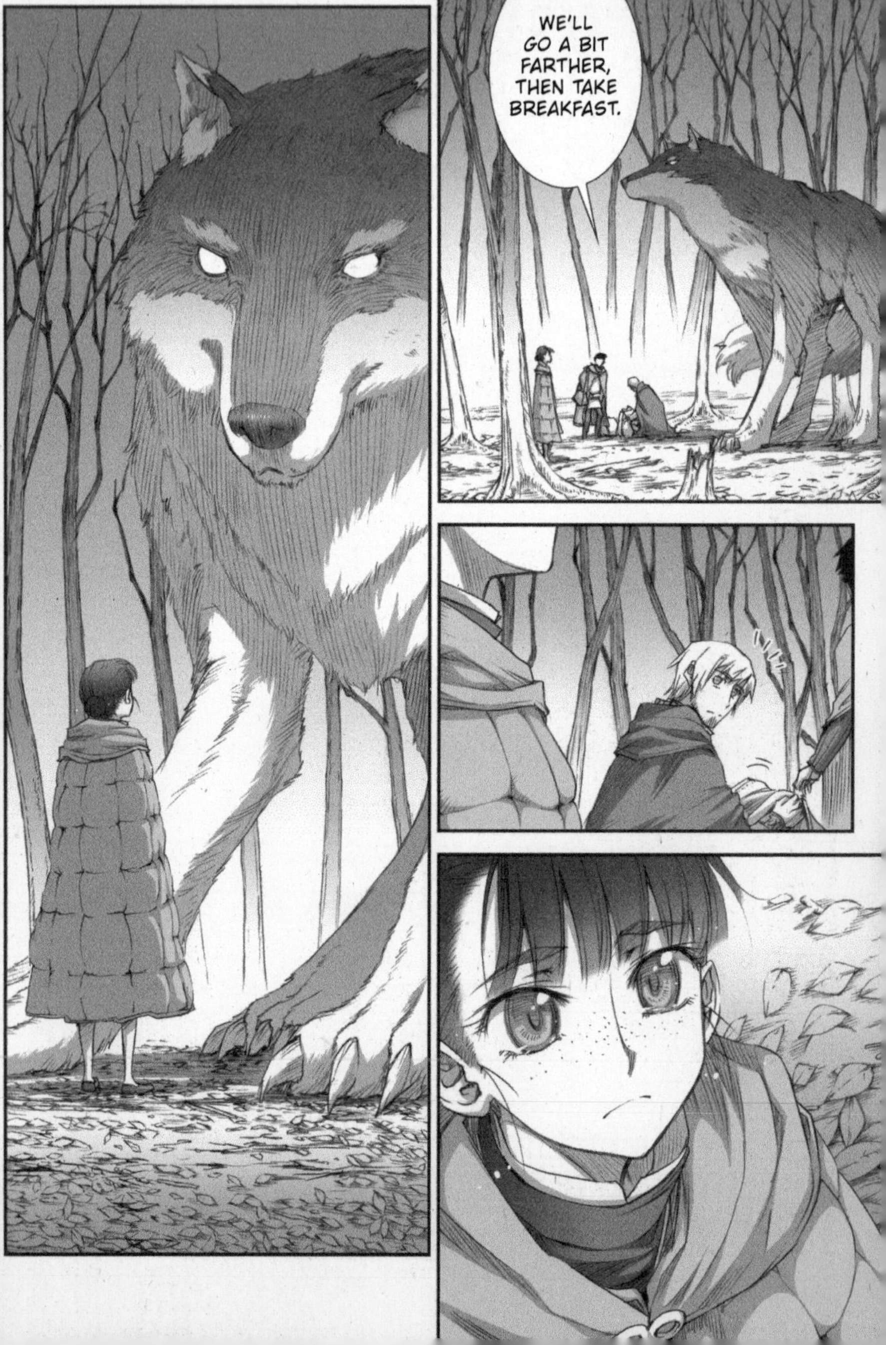
WE'LL GO A BIT FARTHER, THEN TAKE BREAKFAST.

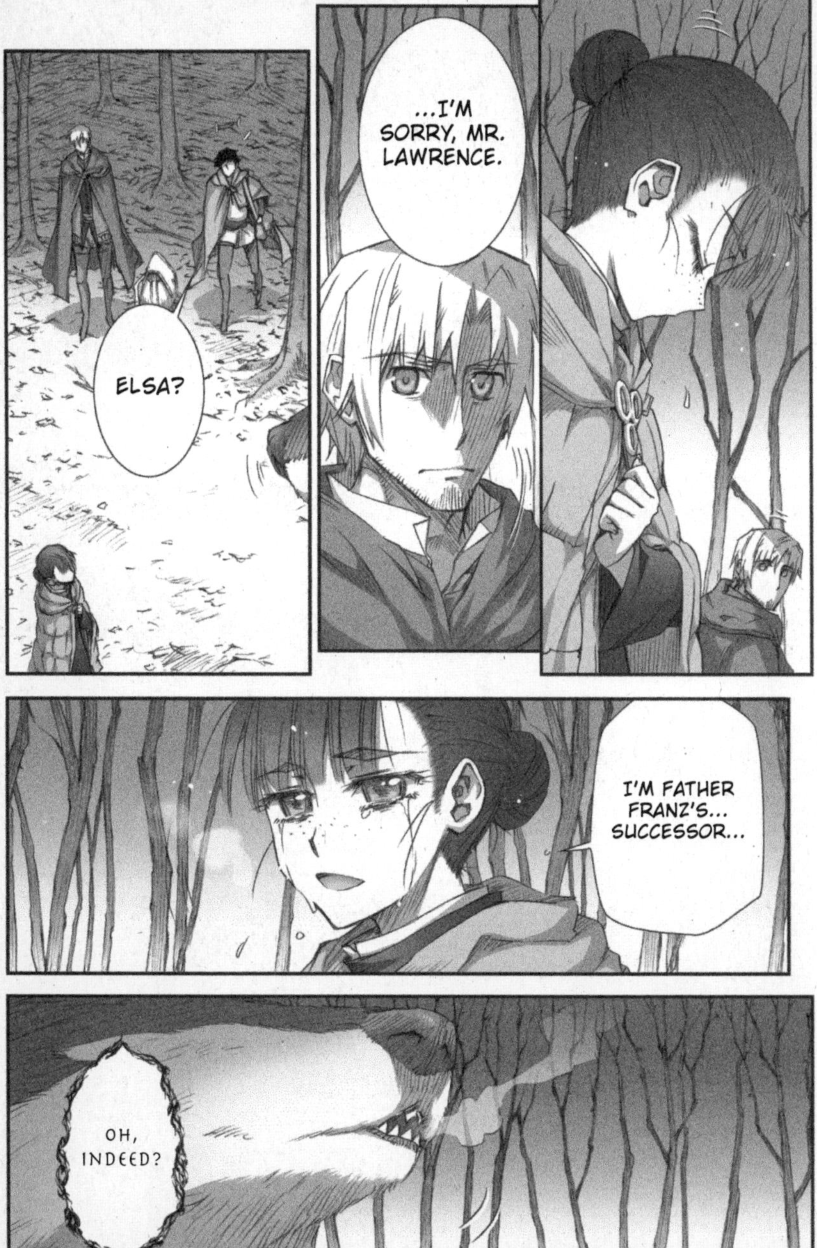
...I'M SORRY, MR. LAWRENCE.
ELSA?
I'M FATHER FRANZ'S... SUCCESSOR...
OH, INDEED?

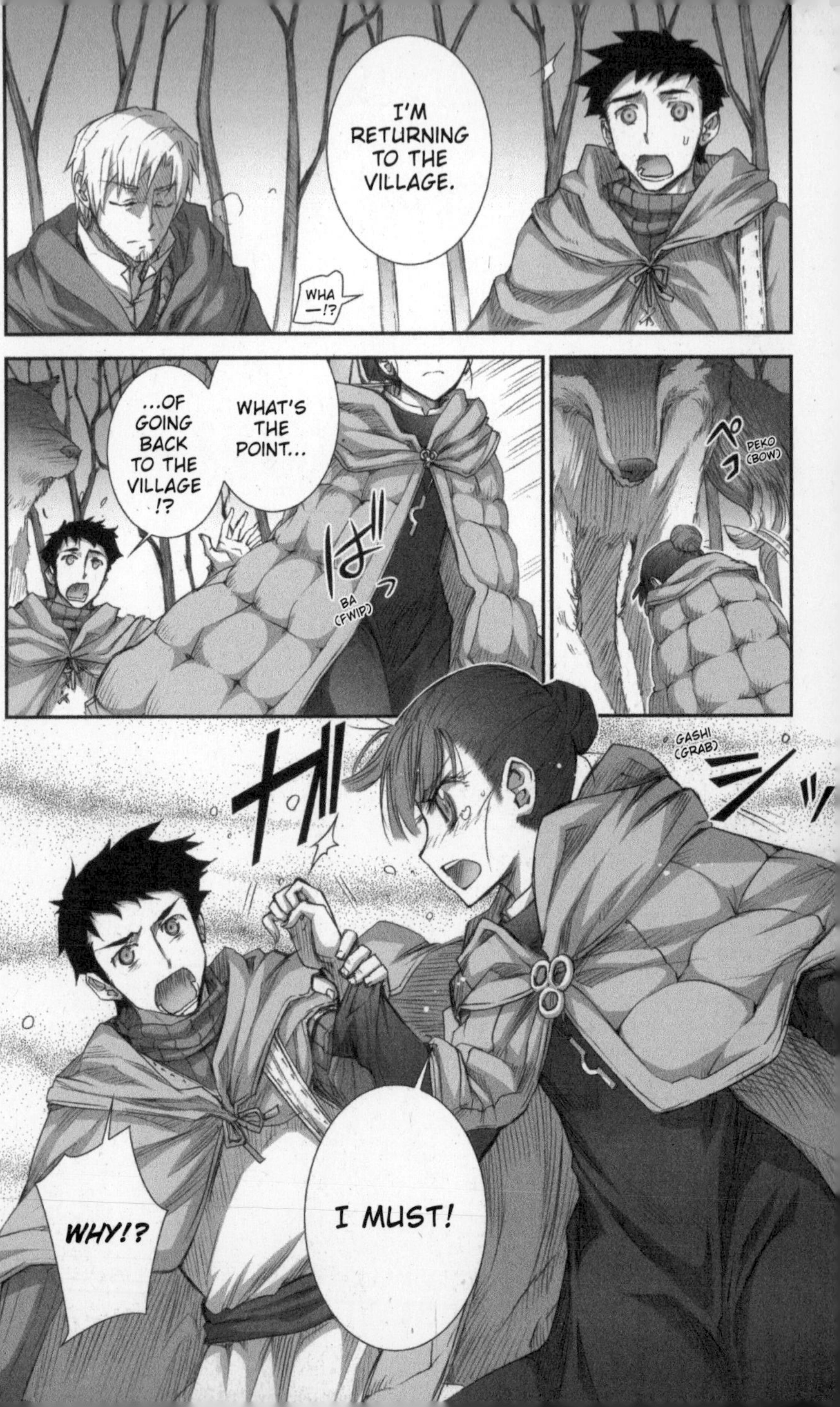
I'M RETURNING TO THE VILLAGE.
WHA—!?
PEKO (BOW)
WHAT'S THE POINT...
...OF GOING BACK TO THE VILLAGE!?
BA (FWIP)
GASHI (GRAB)
I MUST!
WHY!?

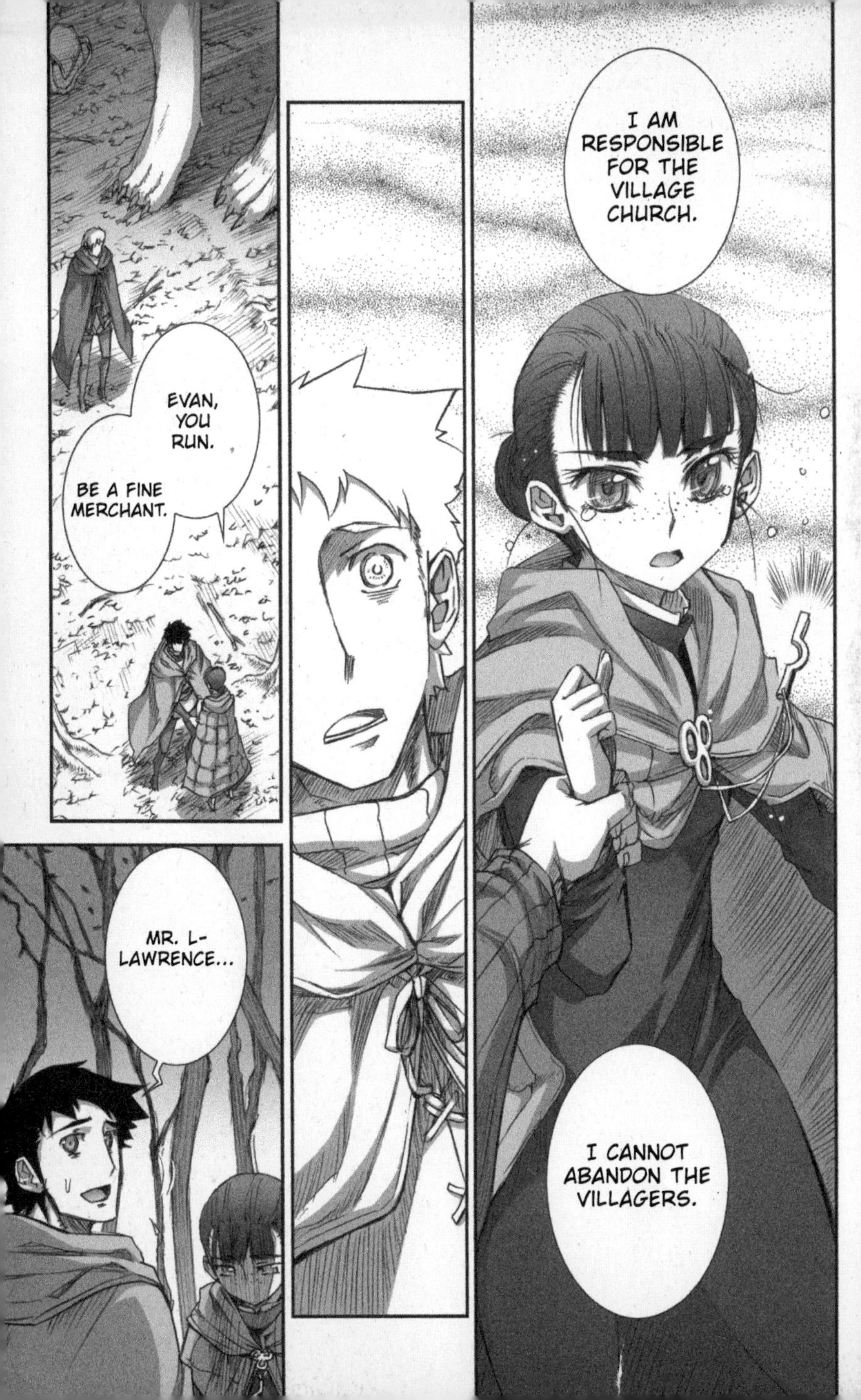
I AM RESPONSIBLE FOR THE VILLAGE CHURCH.
I CANNOT ABANDON THE VILLAGERS.
EVAN, YOU RUN.
BE A FINE MERCHANT.
MR. L-LAWRENCE...

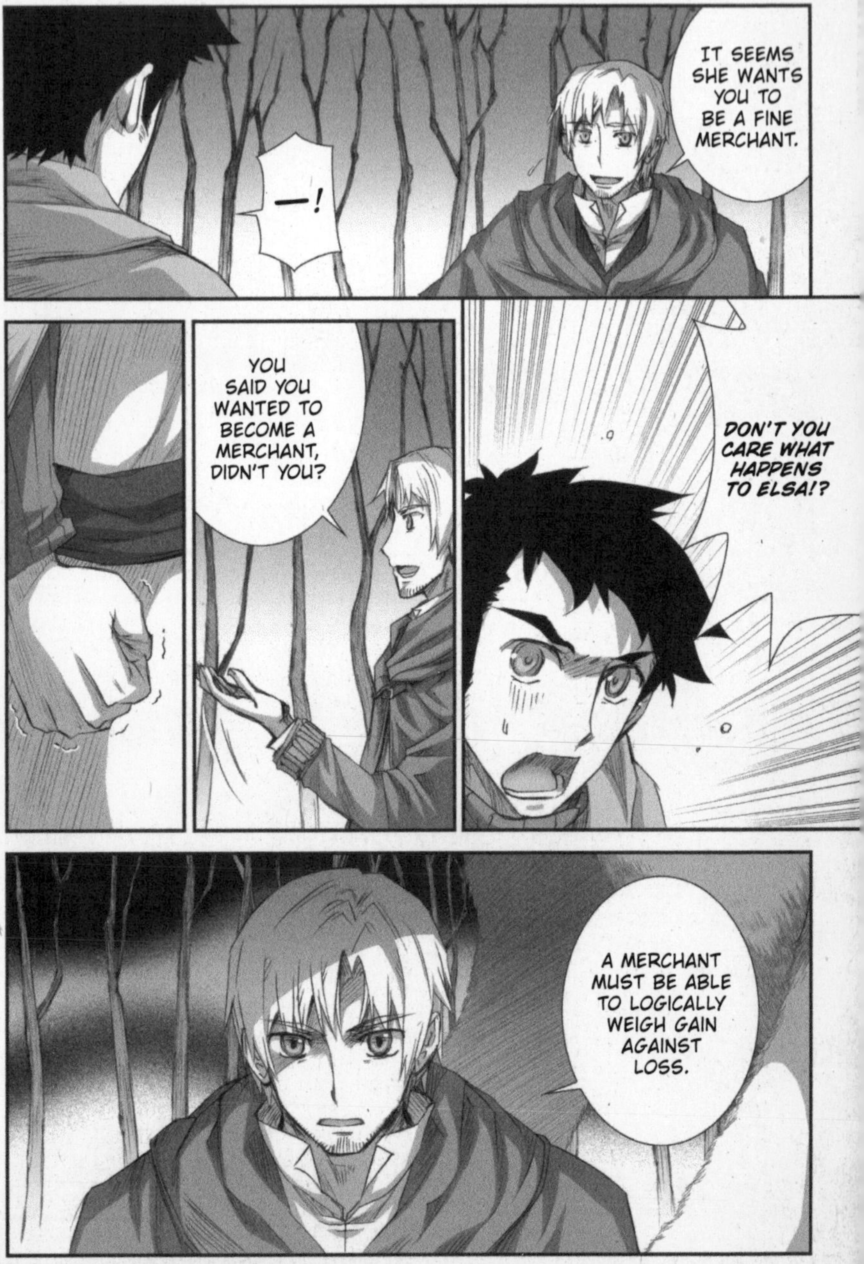
IT SEEMS SHE WANTS YOU TO BE A FINE MERCHANT.
—!
DON'T YOU CARE WHAT HAPPENS TO ELSA!?
YOU SAID YOU WANTED TO BECOME A MERCHANT, DIDN'T YOU?
A MERCHANT MUST BE ABLE TO LOGICALLY WEIGH GAIN AGAINST LOSS.

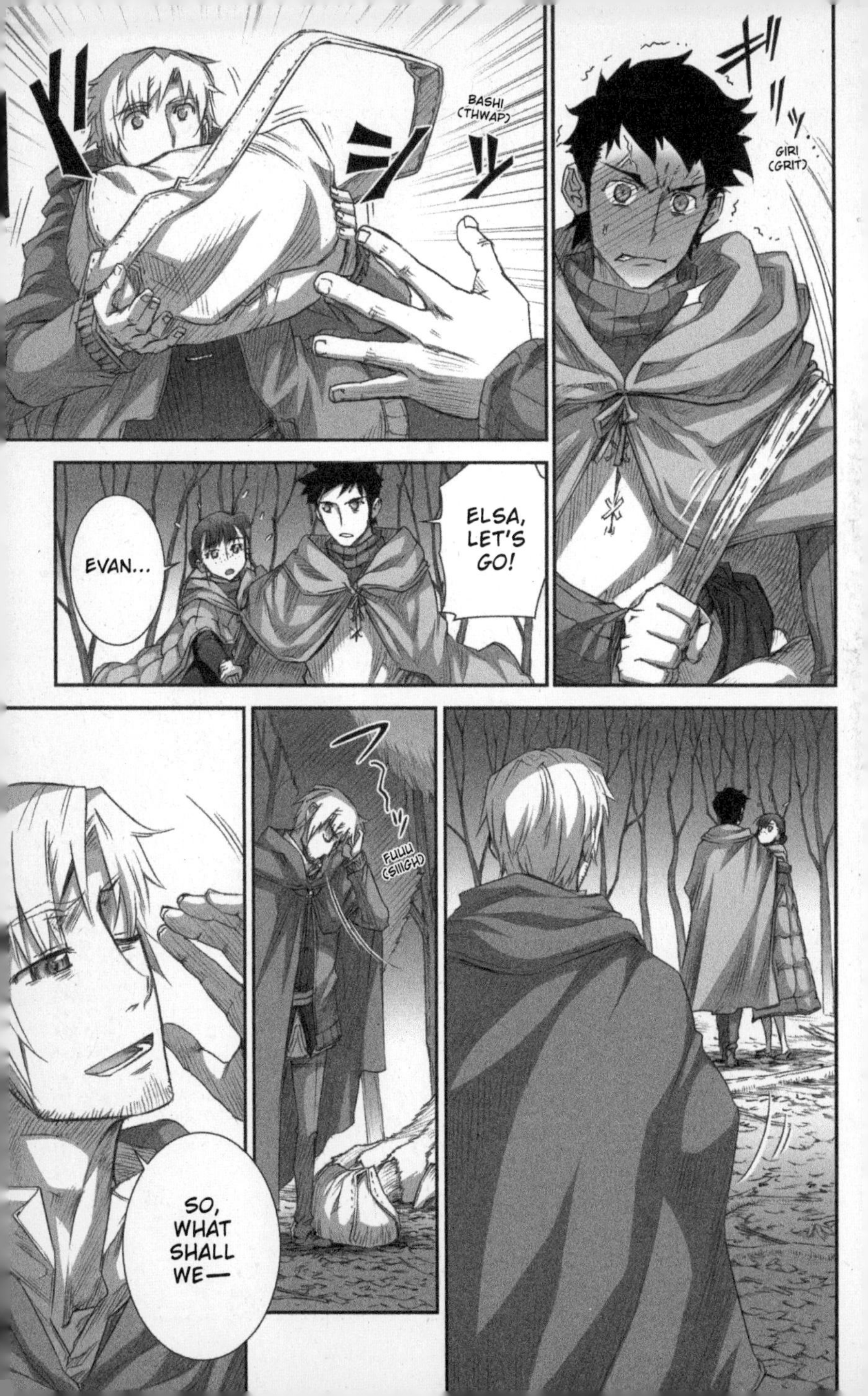
GIRI
(GRIT)
BASHI
(THWAP)
ELSA, LET'S GO!
EVAN...
FUUU
(SIIIGH)
SO, WHAT SHALL WE—

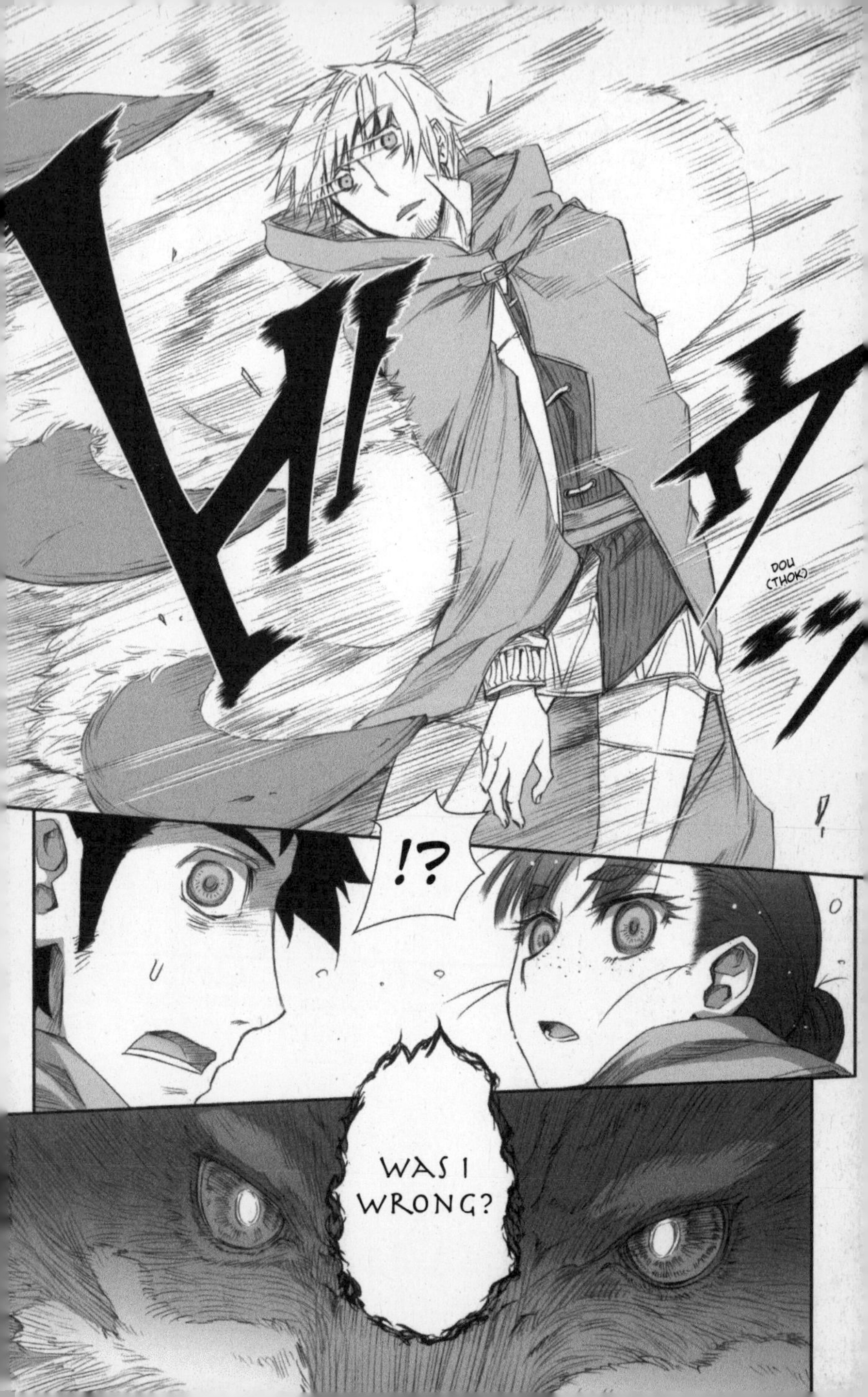
DOU
(THOK)
!?
WAS I
WRONG?

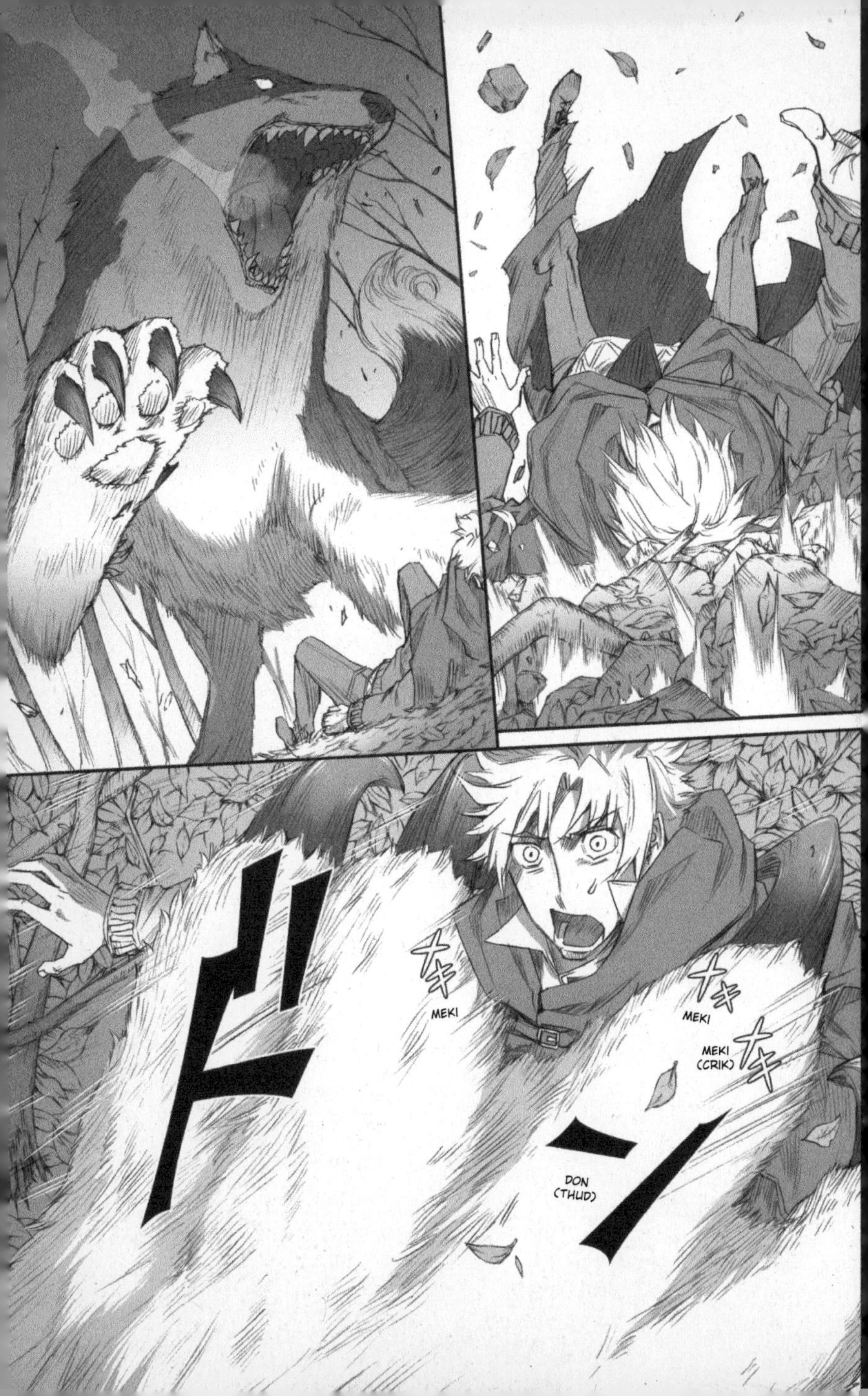
MEKI
MEKI (CRIK)
MEKI
DON (THUD)

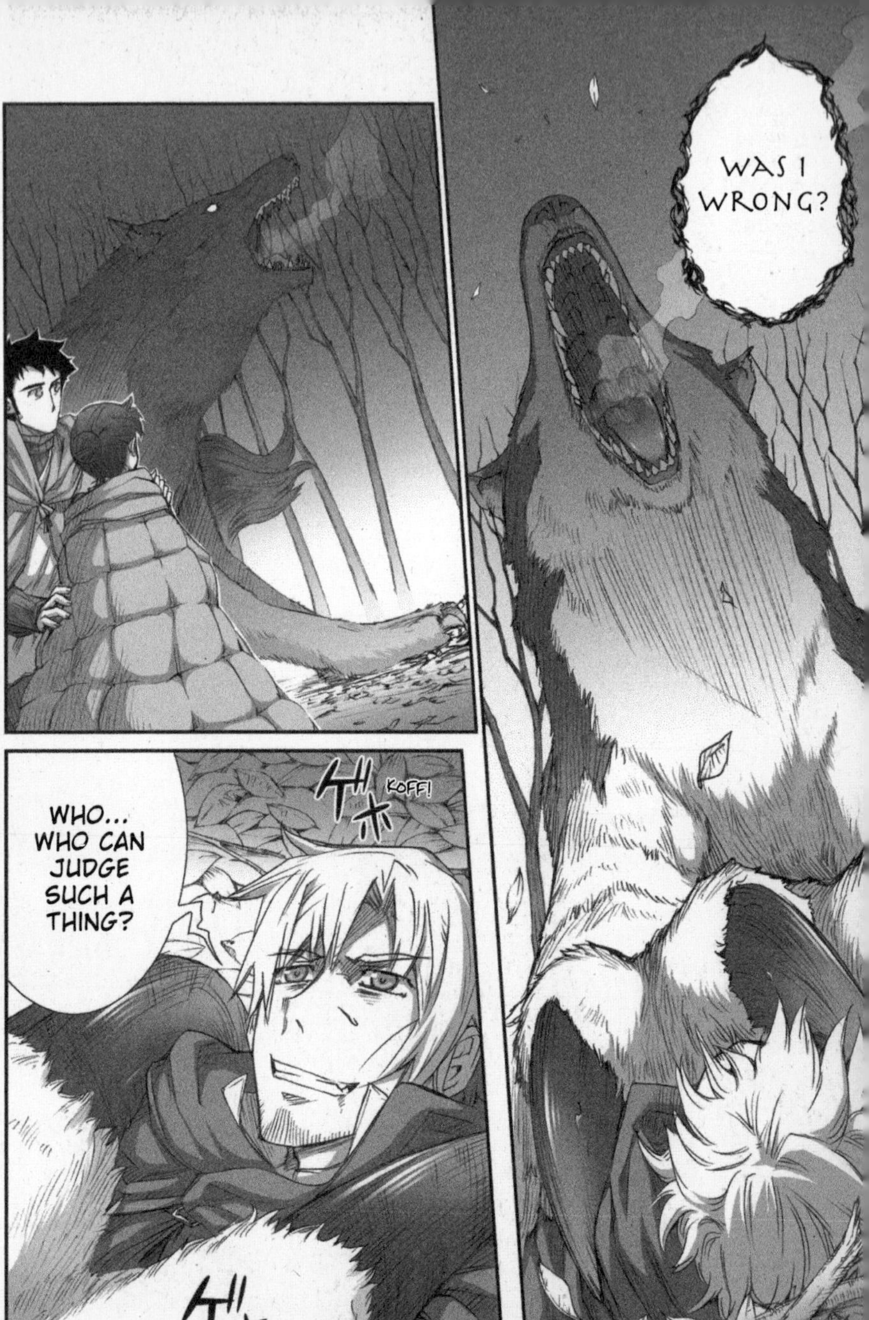
WAS I WRONG?
ゲホ
KOFF!
WHO... WHO CAN JUDGE SUCH A THING?
ゲホ
KOFF!

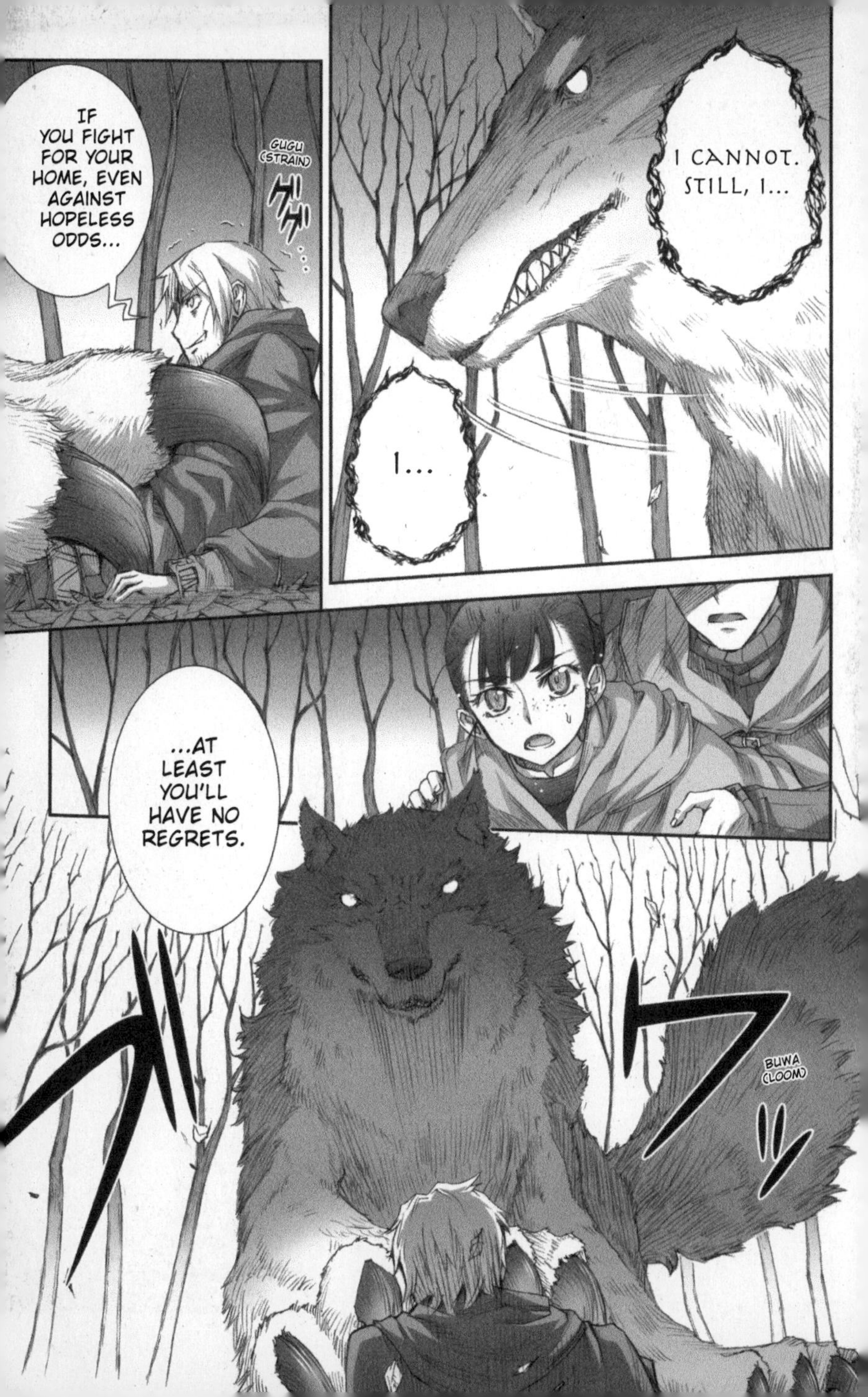
I CANNOT. STILL, I...
I...
IF YOU FIGHT FOR YOUR HOME, EVEN AGAINST HOPELESS ODDS...
GUGU (STRAIN)
...AT LEAST YOU'LL HAVE NO REGRETS.
BUWA (LOOM)

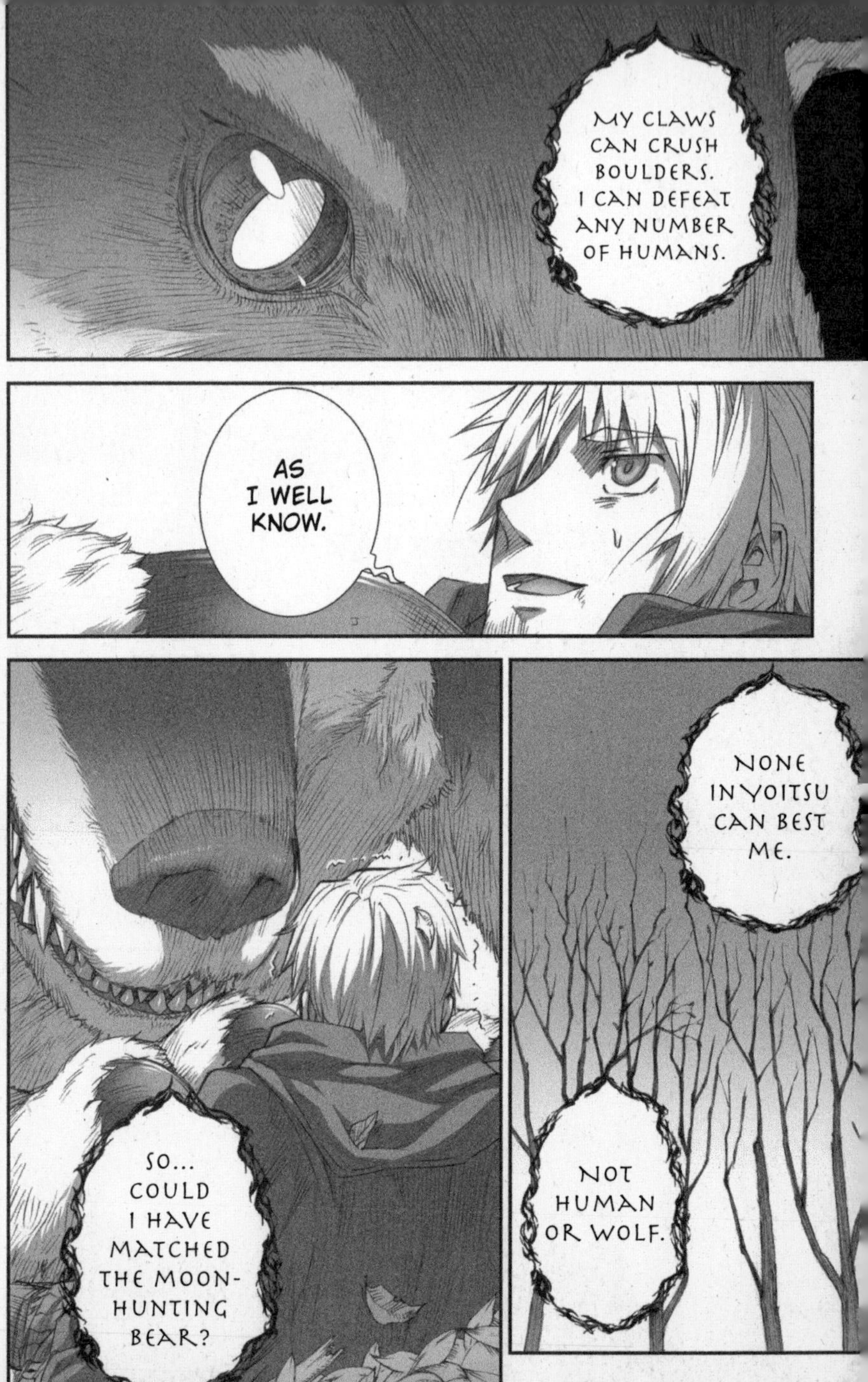
MY CLAWS CAN CRUSH BOULDERS. I CAN DEFEAT ANY NUMBER OF HUMANS.
AS I WELL KNOW.
NONE IN YOITSU CAN BEST ME.
NOT HUMAN OR WOLF.
SO... COULD I HAVE MATCHED THE MOON-HUNTING BEAR?

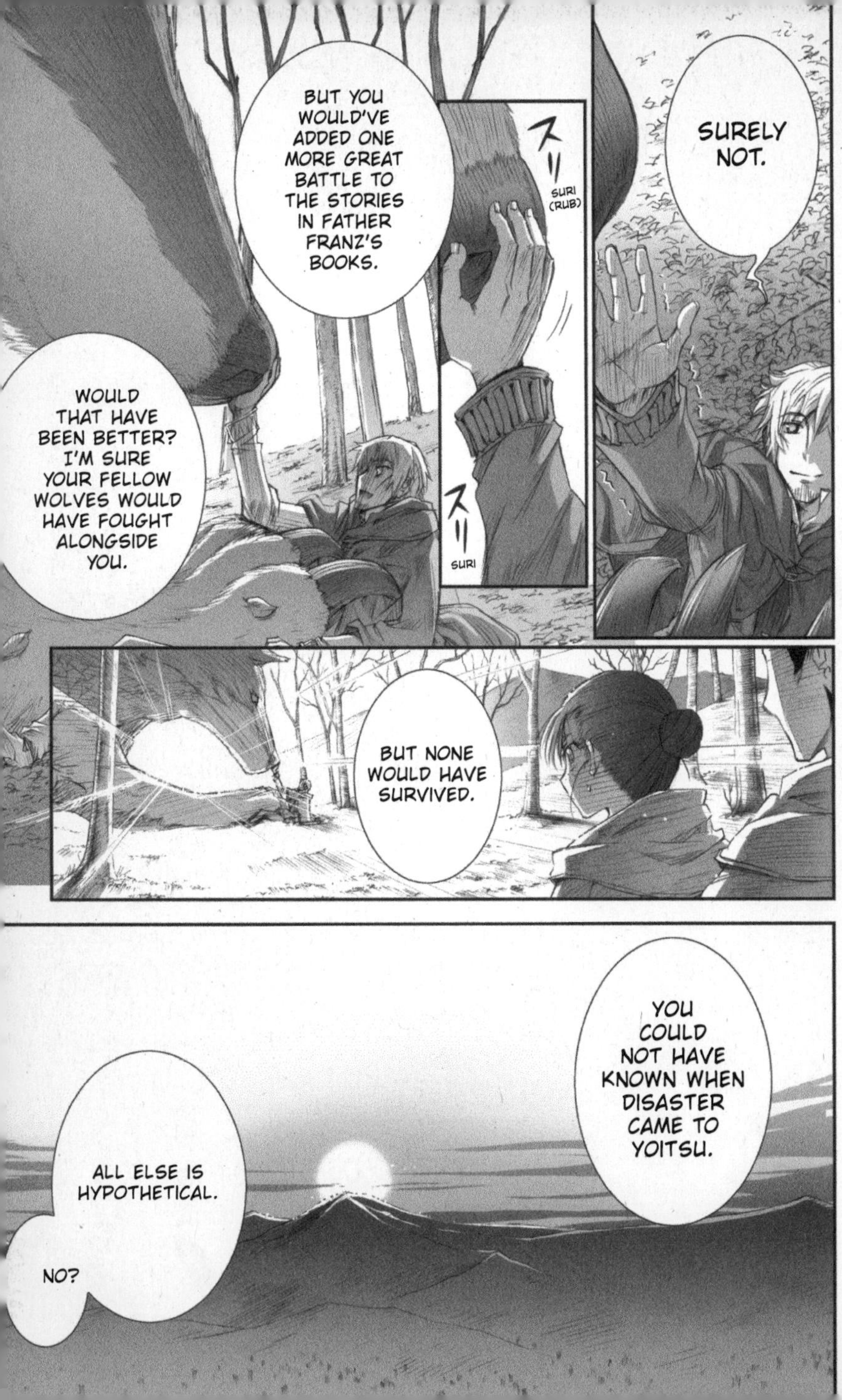
SURELY NOT.
スリ
SURI (RUB)
スリ
SURI
BUT YOU WOULD'VE ADDED ONE MORE GREAT BATTLE TO THE STORIES IN FATHER FRANZ'S BOOKS.
WOULD THAT HAVE BEEN BETTER? I'M SURE YOUR FELLOW WOLVES WOULD HAVE FOUGHT ALONGSIDE YOU.
BUT NONE WOULD HAVE SURVIVED.
YOU COULD NOT HAVE KNOWN WHEN DISASTER CAME TO YOITSU.
ALL ELSE IS HYPOTHETICAL.
NO?

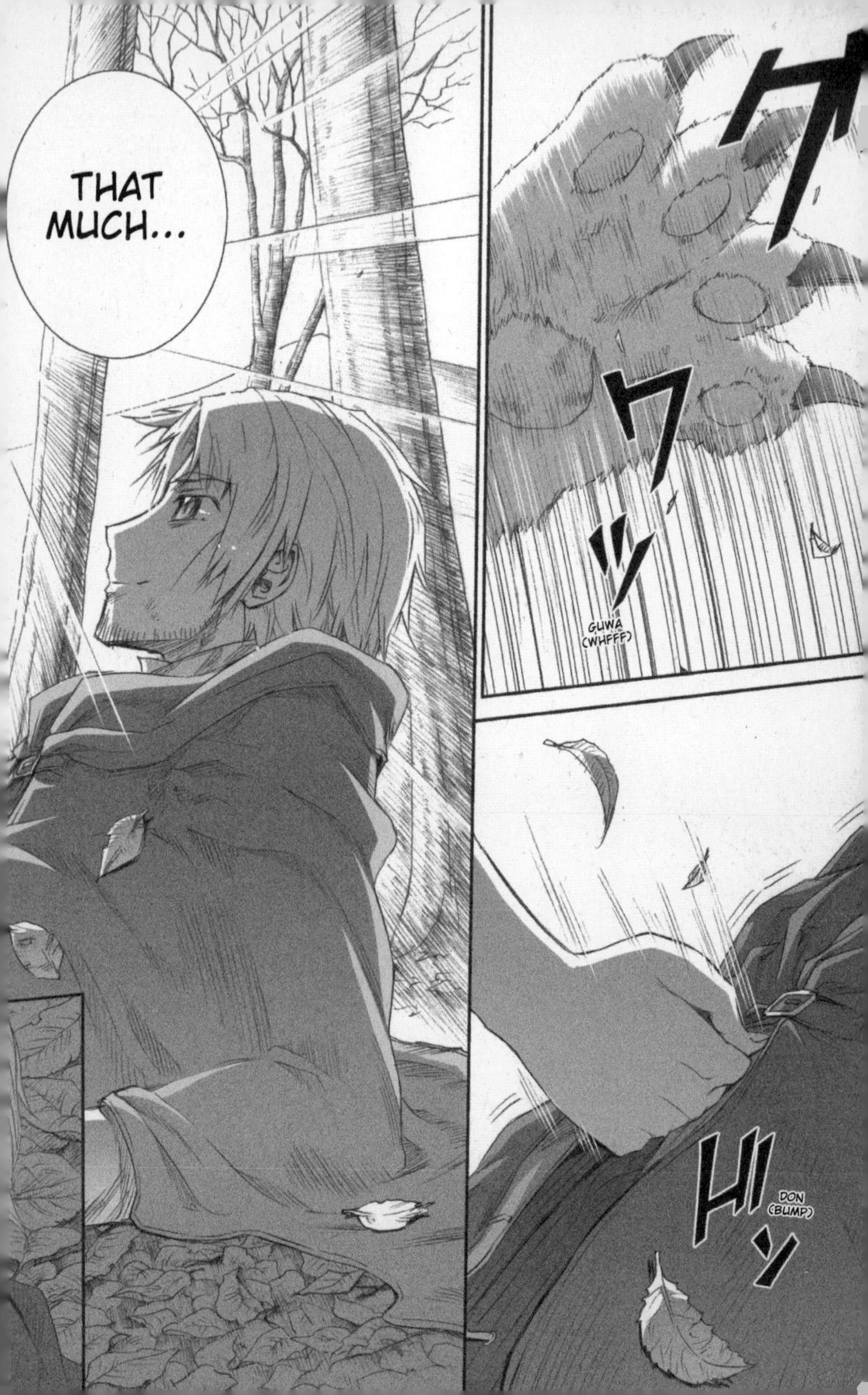
GUWA (WHFFF)
DON (BUMP)
THAT MUCH...

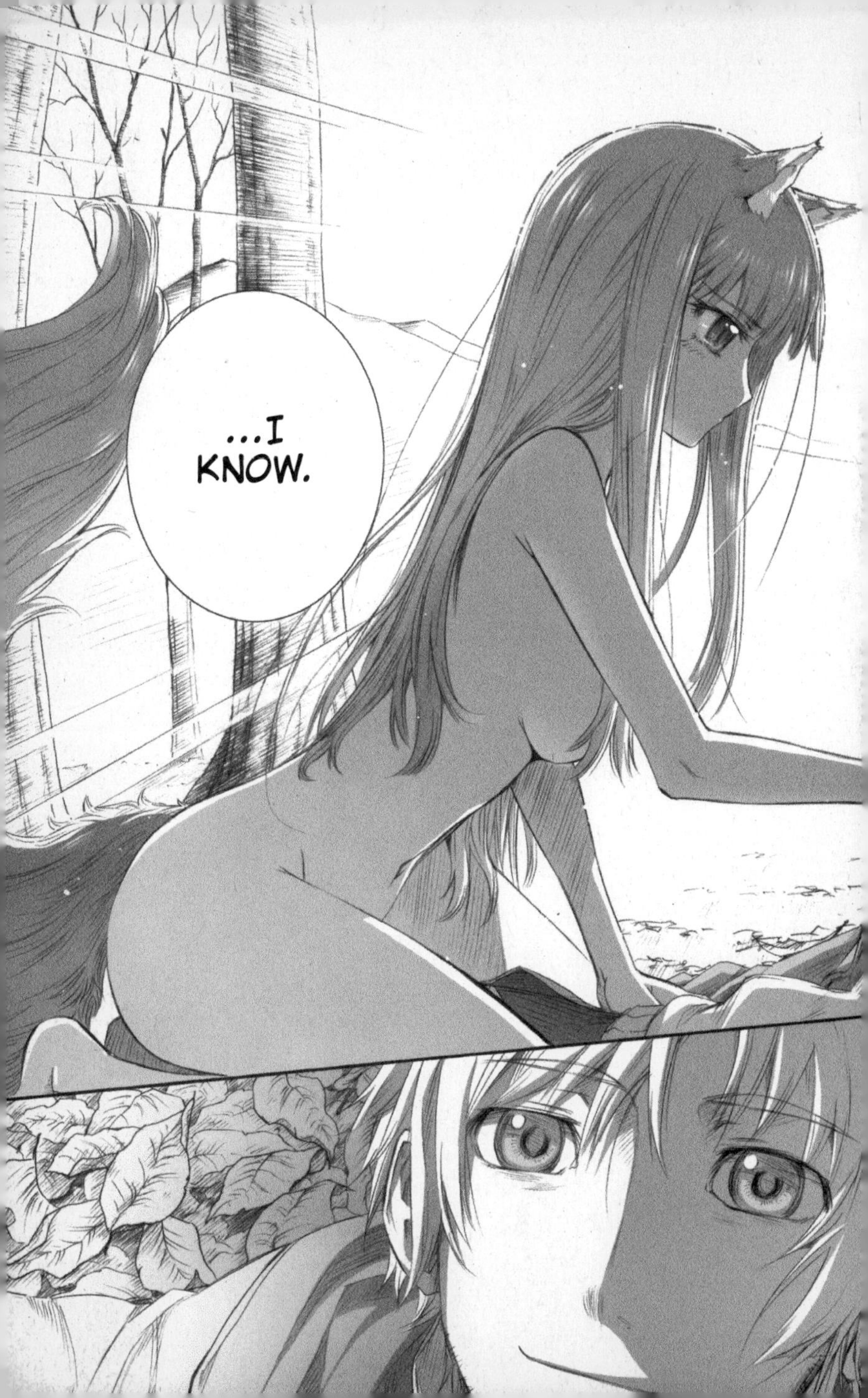
...I KNOW.

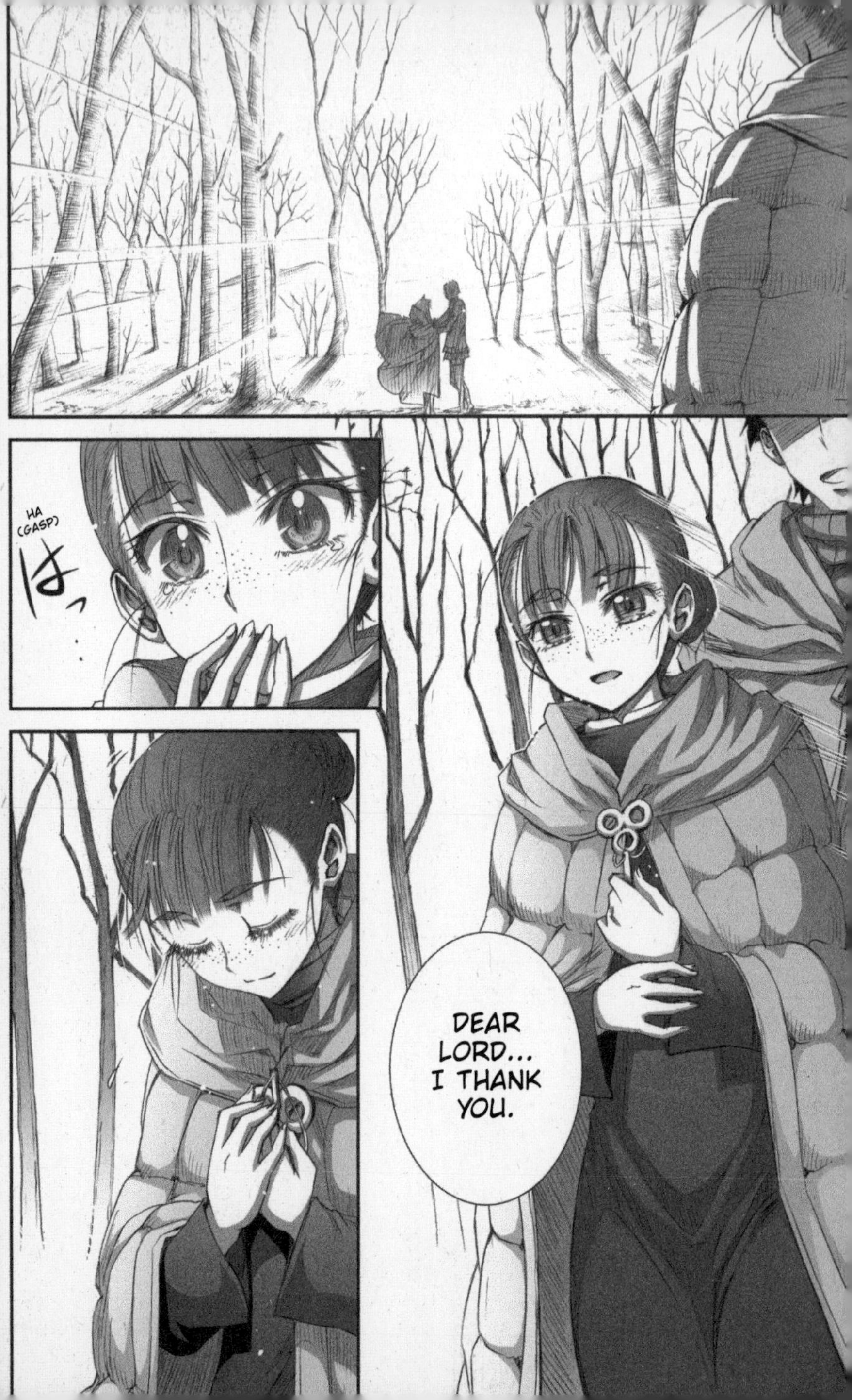
HA (GASP)
はっ
DEAR LORD... I THANK YOU.

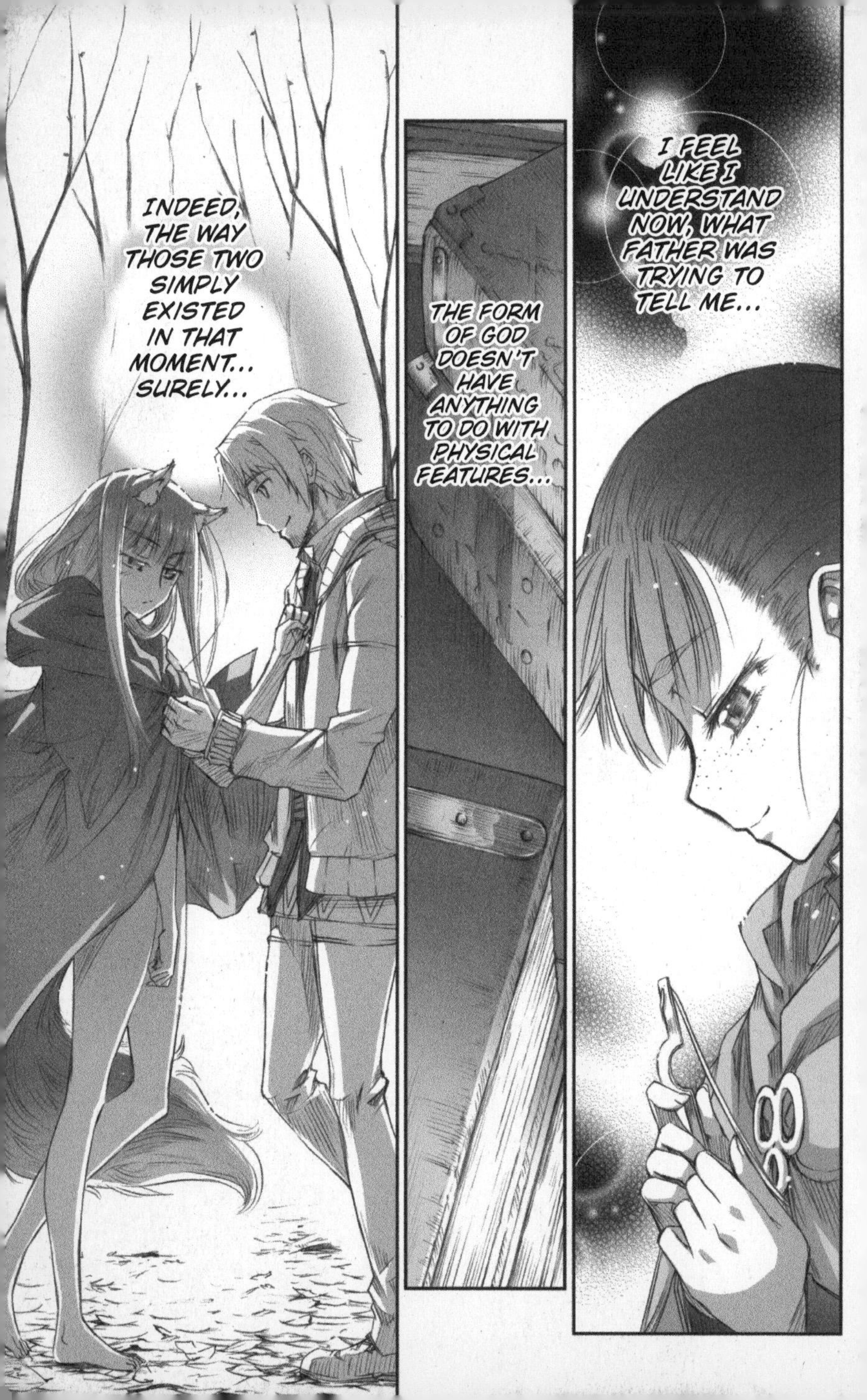
I FEEL LIKE I UNDERSTAND NOW, WHAT FATHER WAS TRYING TO TELL ME...
THE FORM OF GOD DOESN'T HAVE ANYTHING TO DO WITH PHYSICAL FEATURES...
INDEED, THE WAY THOSE TWO SIMPLY EXISTED IN THAT MOMENT... SURELY...

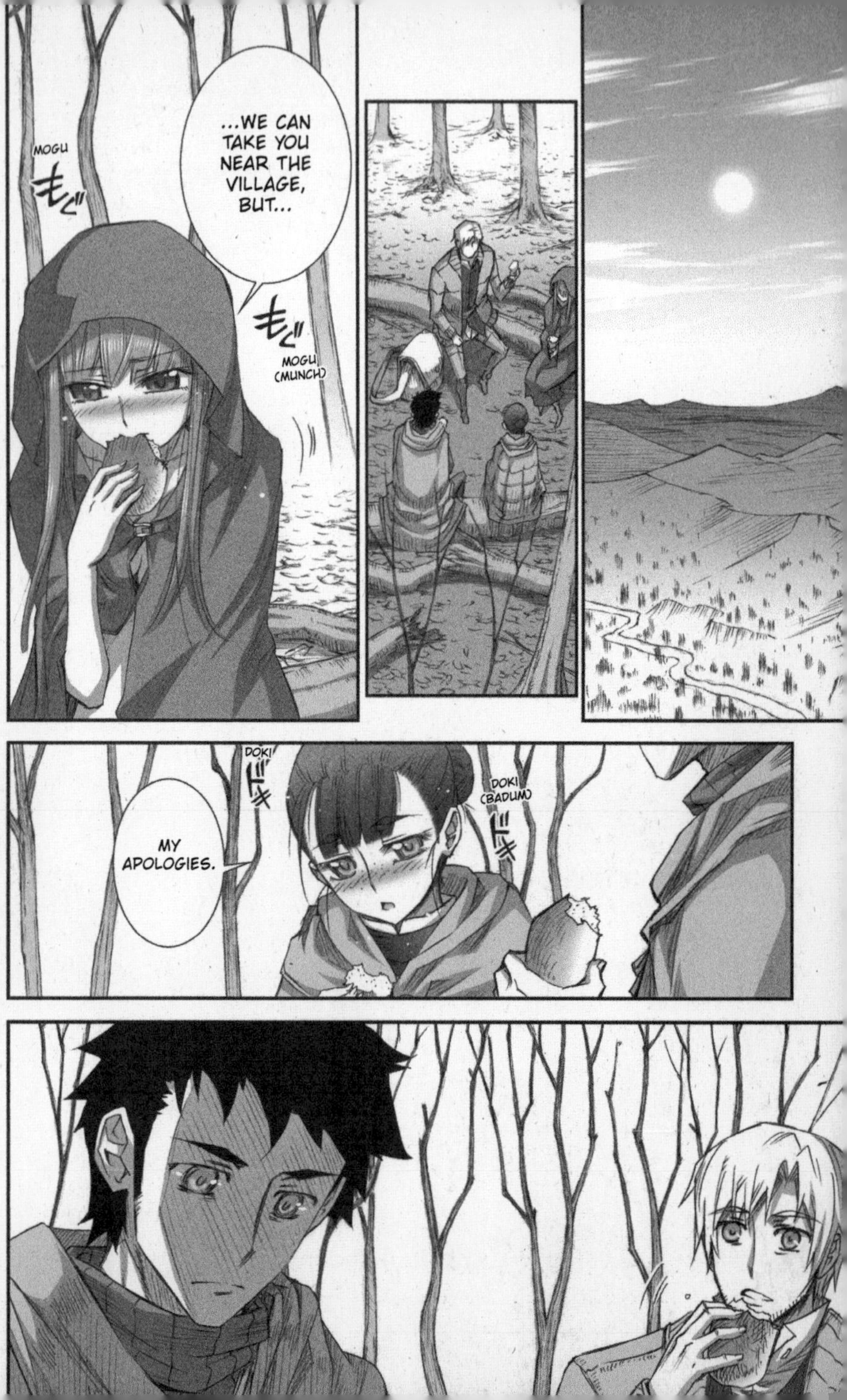
...WE CAN TAKE YOU NEAR THE VILLAGE, BUT...
もぐ
MOGU (MUNCH)
もぐ
MOGU
ドキ
DOKI (BADUM)
ドキ
DOKI
MY APOLOGIES.

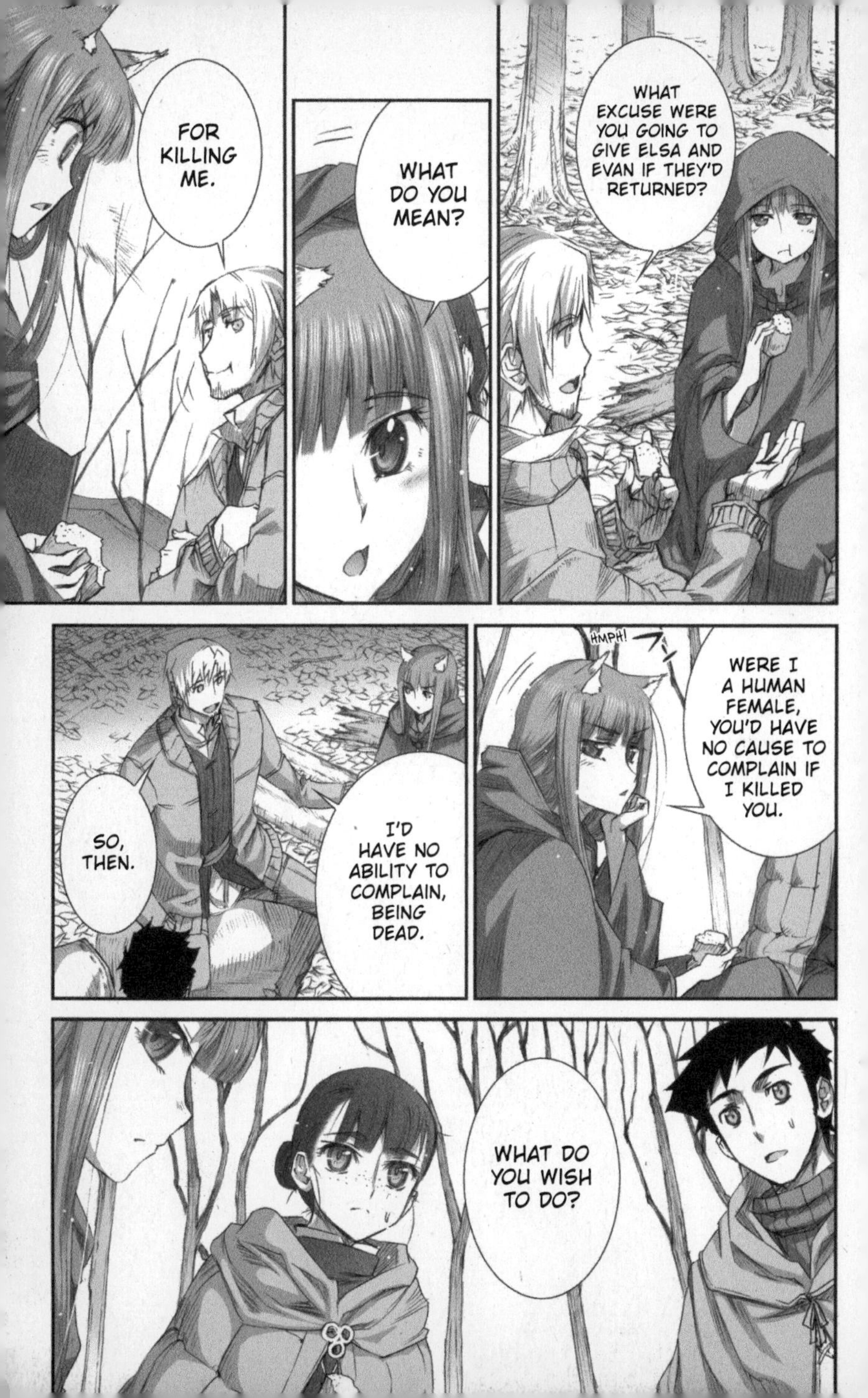
WHAT EXCUSE WERE YOU GOING TO GIVE ELSA AND EVAN IF THEY'D RETURNED?
WHAT DO YOU MEAN?
FOR KILLING ME.
HMPH!
WERE I A HUMAN FEMALE, YOU'D HAVE NO CAUSE TO COMPLAIN IF I KILLED YOU.
I'D HAVE NO ABILITY TO COMPLAIN, BEING DEAD.
SO, THEN.
WHAT DO YOU WISH TO DO?

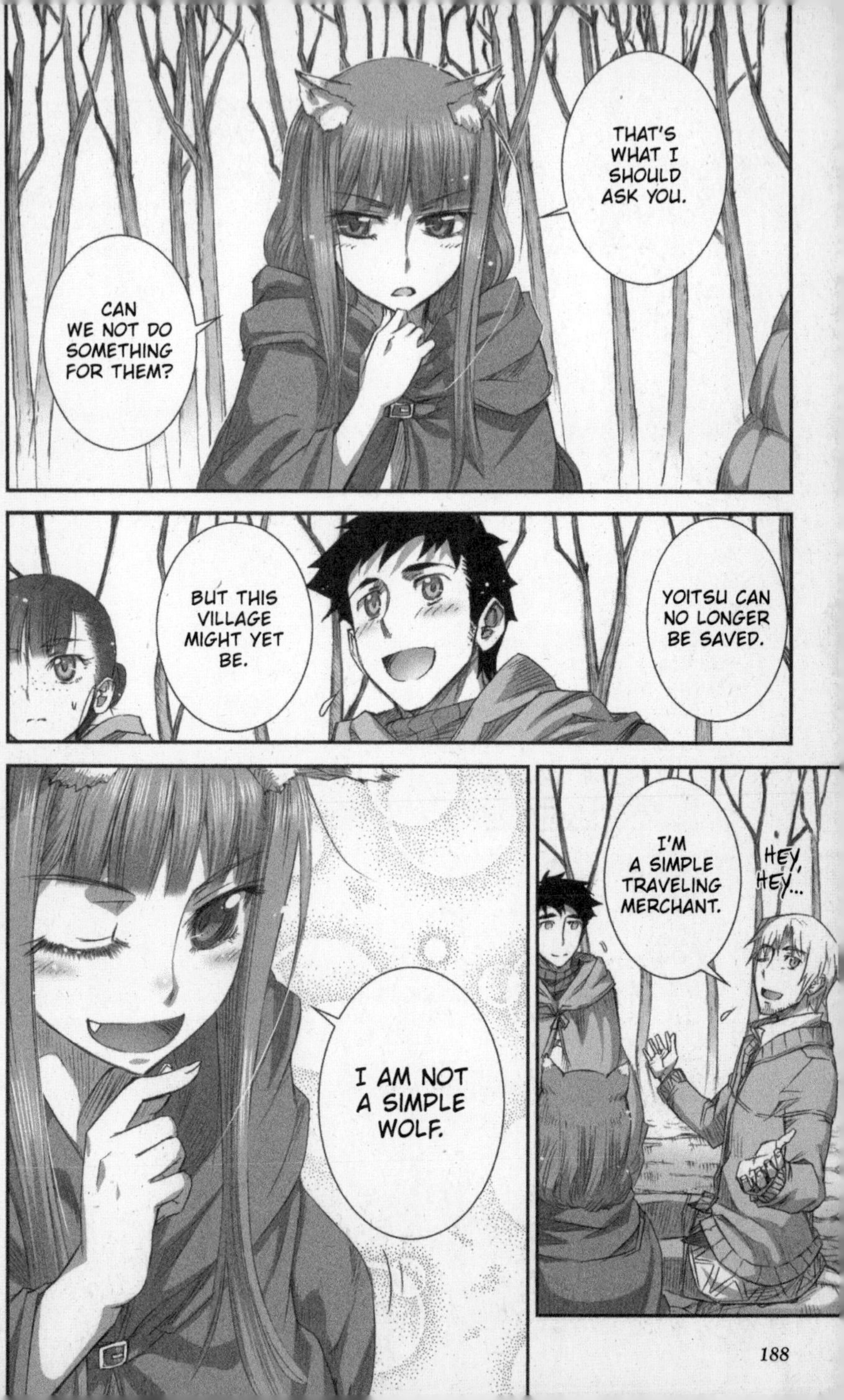
THAT'S WHAT I SHOULD ASK YOU.
CAN WE NOT DO SOMETHING FOR THEM?
YOITSU CAN NO LONGER BE SAVED.
BUT THIS VILLAGE MIGHT YET BE.
HEY, HEY...
I'M A SIMPLE TRAVELING MERCHANT.
I AM NOT A SIMPLE WOLF.

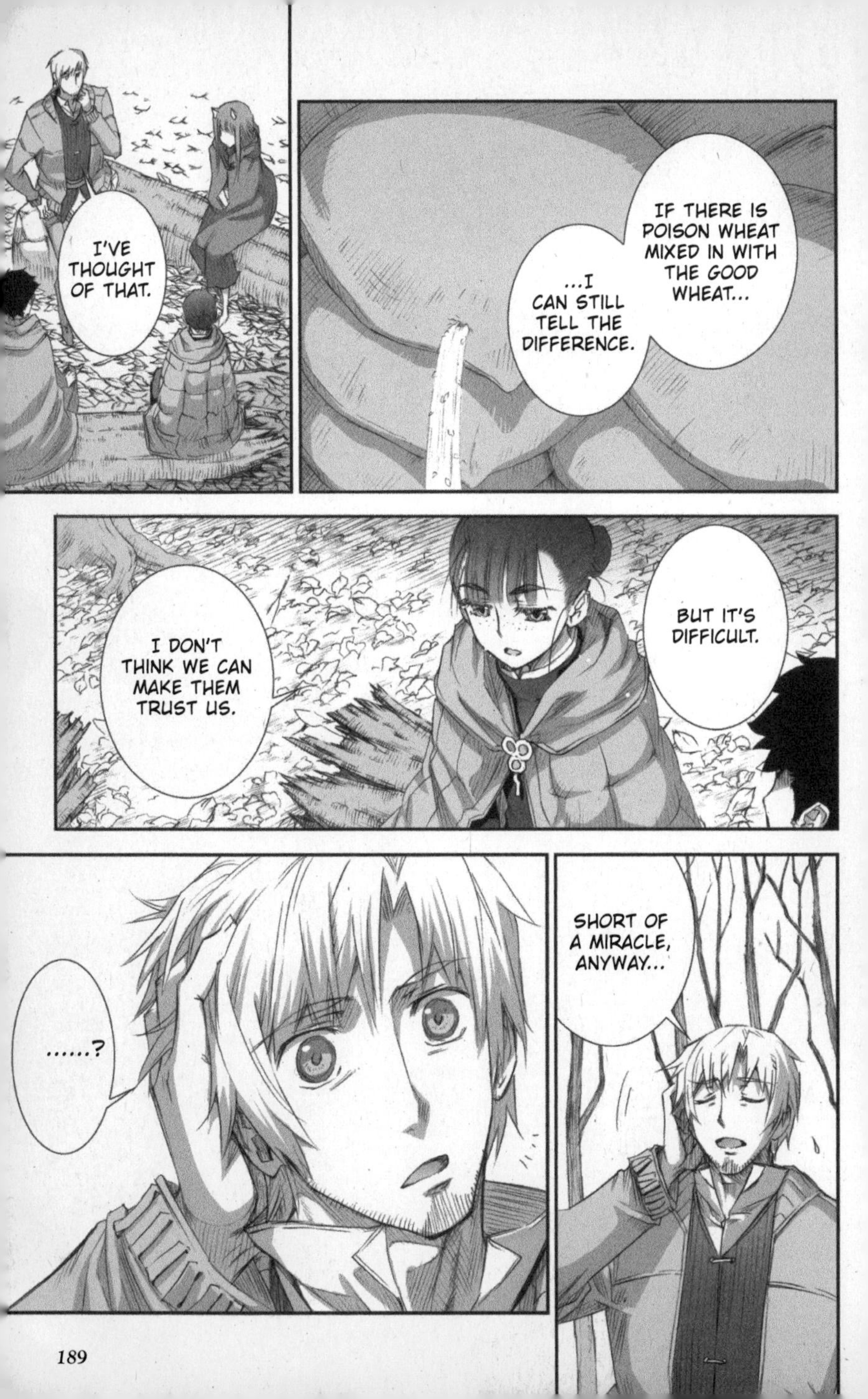
IF THERE IS POISON WHEAT MIXED IN WITH THE GOOD WHEAT...
...I CAN STILL TELL THE DIFFERENCE.
I'VE THOUGHT OF THAT.
BUT IT'S DIFFICULT.
I DON'T THINK WE CAN MAKE THEM TRUST US.
SHORT OF A MIRACLE, ANYWAY...
......?

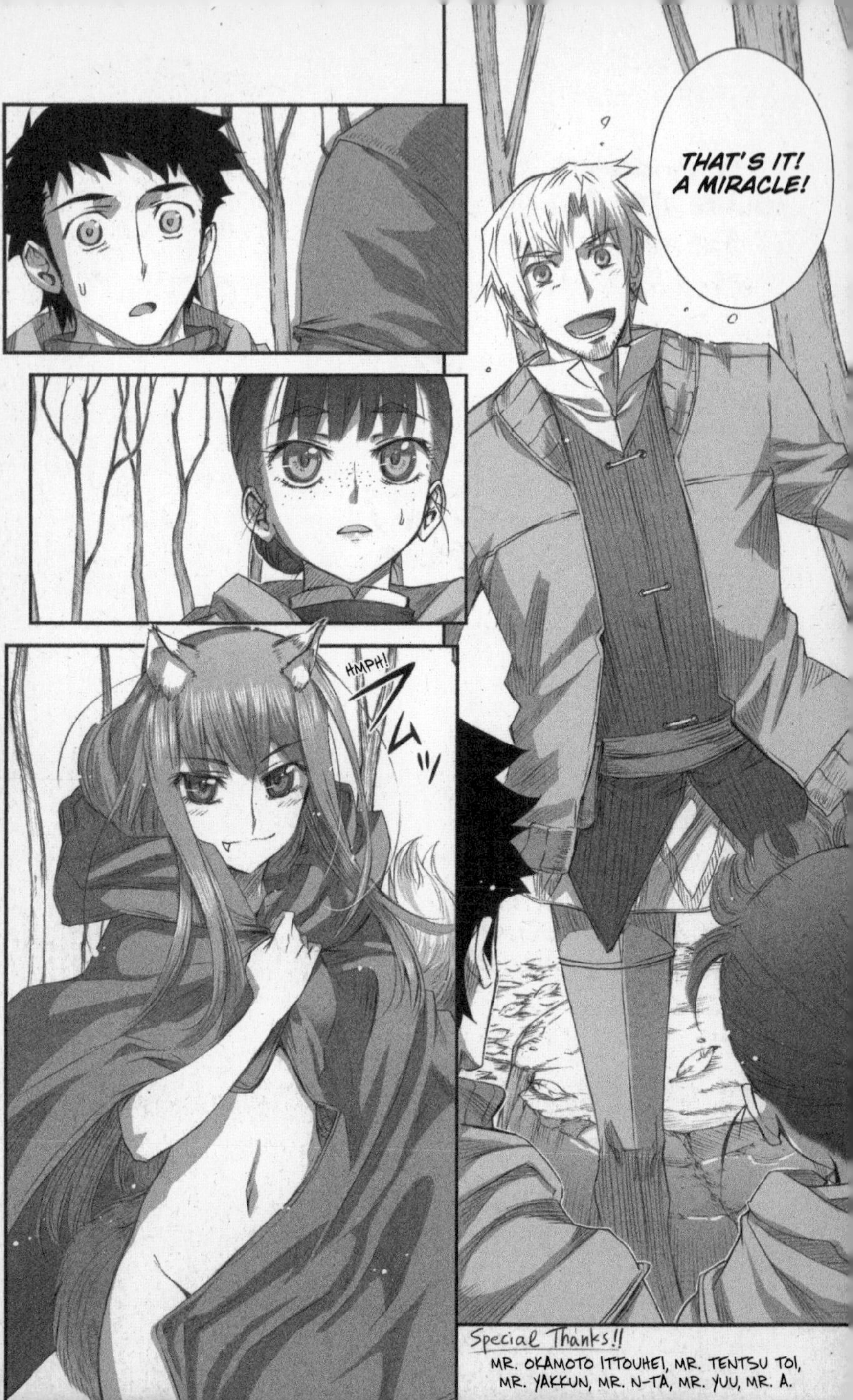
THAT'S IT! A MIRACLE!
HMPH!

Special Thanks!!
MR. OKAMOTO ITTOUHEI, MR. TENTSU TOI, MR. YAKKUN, MR. N-TA, MR. YUU, MR. A.